Writer
JOE BRUSHA

Artwork
MARC ROSETE

Colors
WALTER PEREYRA

Letters
FABIO AMELIA

Editor
DAVE FRANCHINI

Art Direction & Design
CHRISTOPHER COTE

Cover Art
MARC ROSETE
GROSTIETA

Executive Editor
RALPH TEDESCO

Grimm Universe created by
JOE BRUSHA
RALPH TEDESCO

This volume reprints Death Force #1-6 and Grimm Fairy Tales Genesis: Heroes Reborn "Death Force: Totems" short story published by Zenescope Entertainment. First Edition, February 2017 • ISBN: 978-1942275480

zenescope
WWW.ZENESCOPE.COM

Joe Brusha President & Chief Creative Officer
Christopher Cote Art Director
Dave Franchini Assistant Editor
Jessica Rossana Assistant Editor
Joi Dariel Production Manager

Jennifer Bermel Director of Business Development
Jason Condeelis Direct Market Sales & Customer Service
Adam Kelly Marketing and Social Media Manager
Stu Kropnick Operations Manager
Ralph Tedesco VP Film & Television

DEATH FORCE

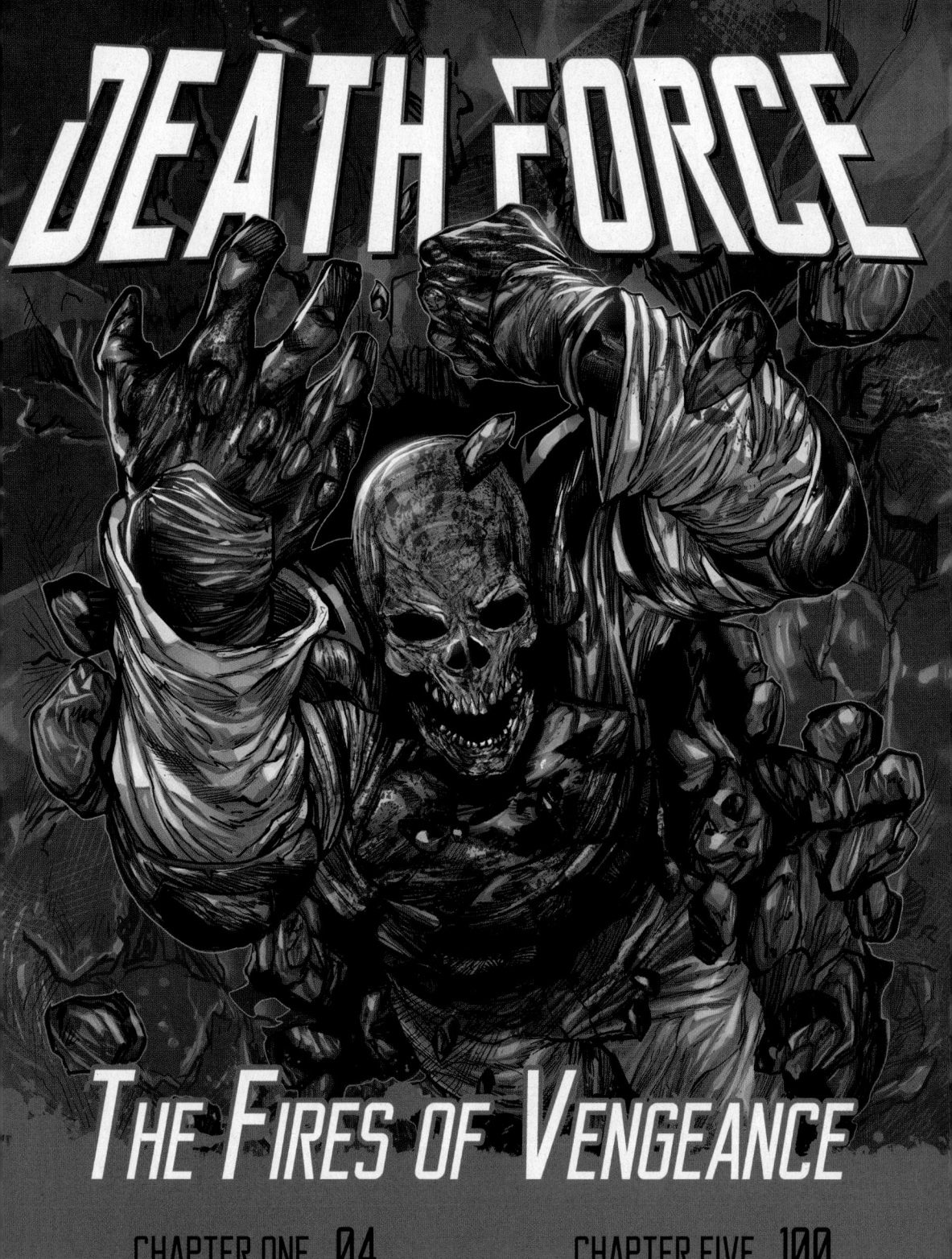

THE FIRES OF VENGEANCE

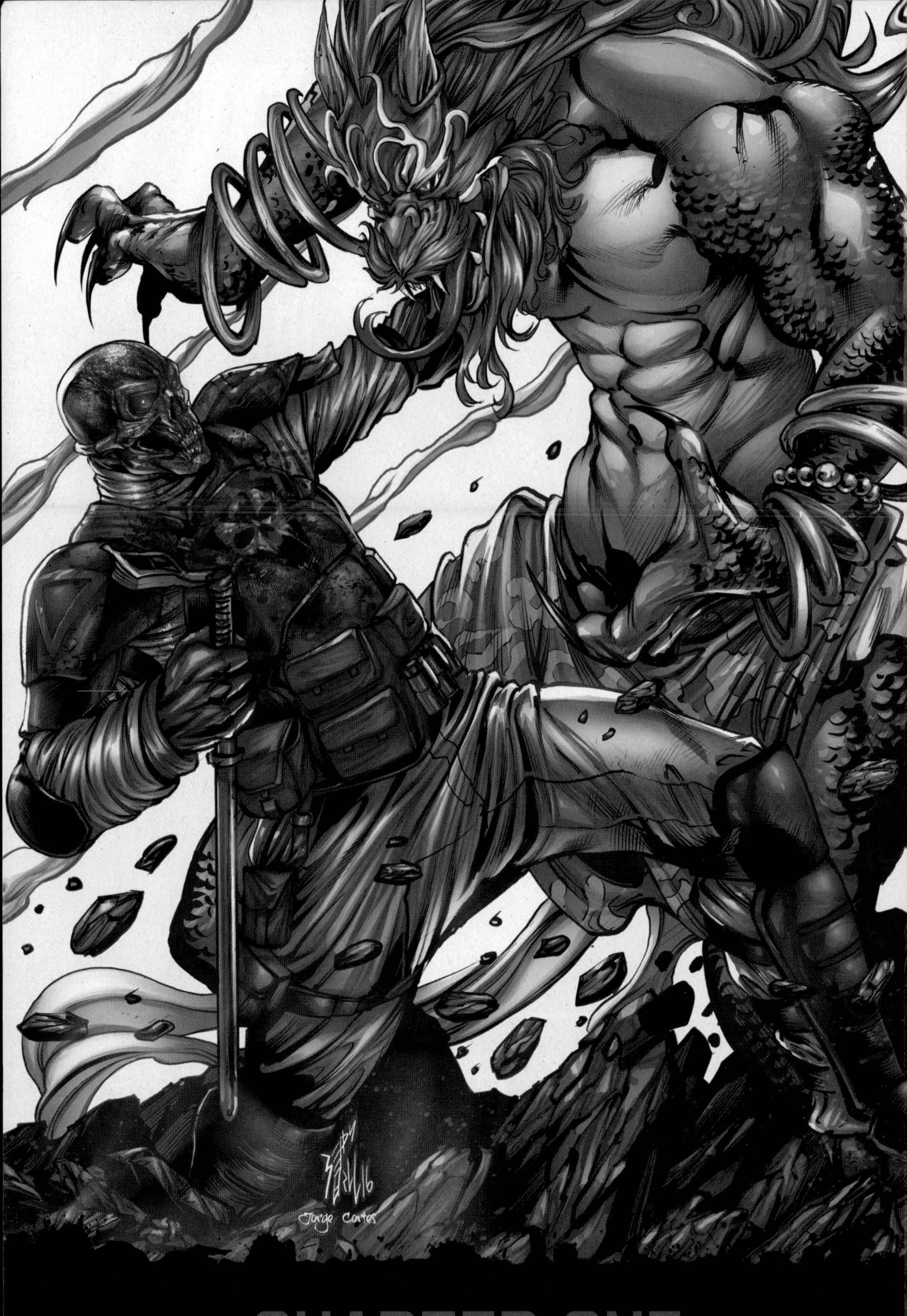
Jorge Cortes

CHAPTER ONE

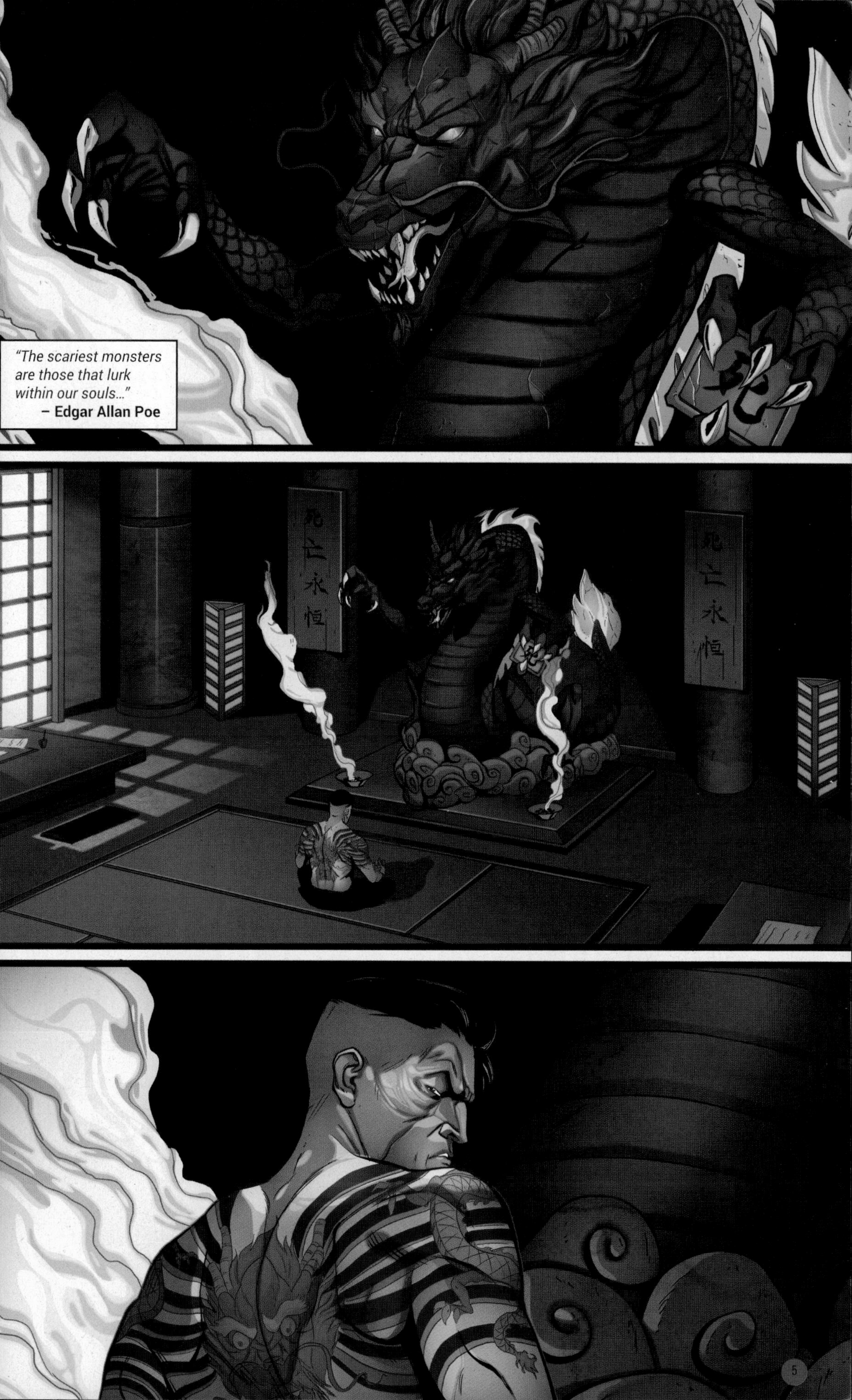
"The scariest monsters are those that lurk within our souls..."
– Edgar Allan Poe
死亡永恒
死亡永恒

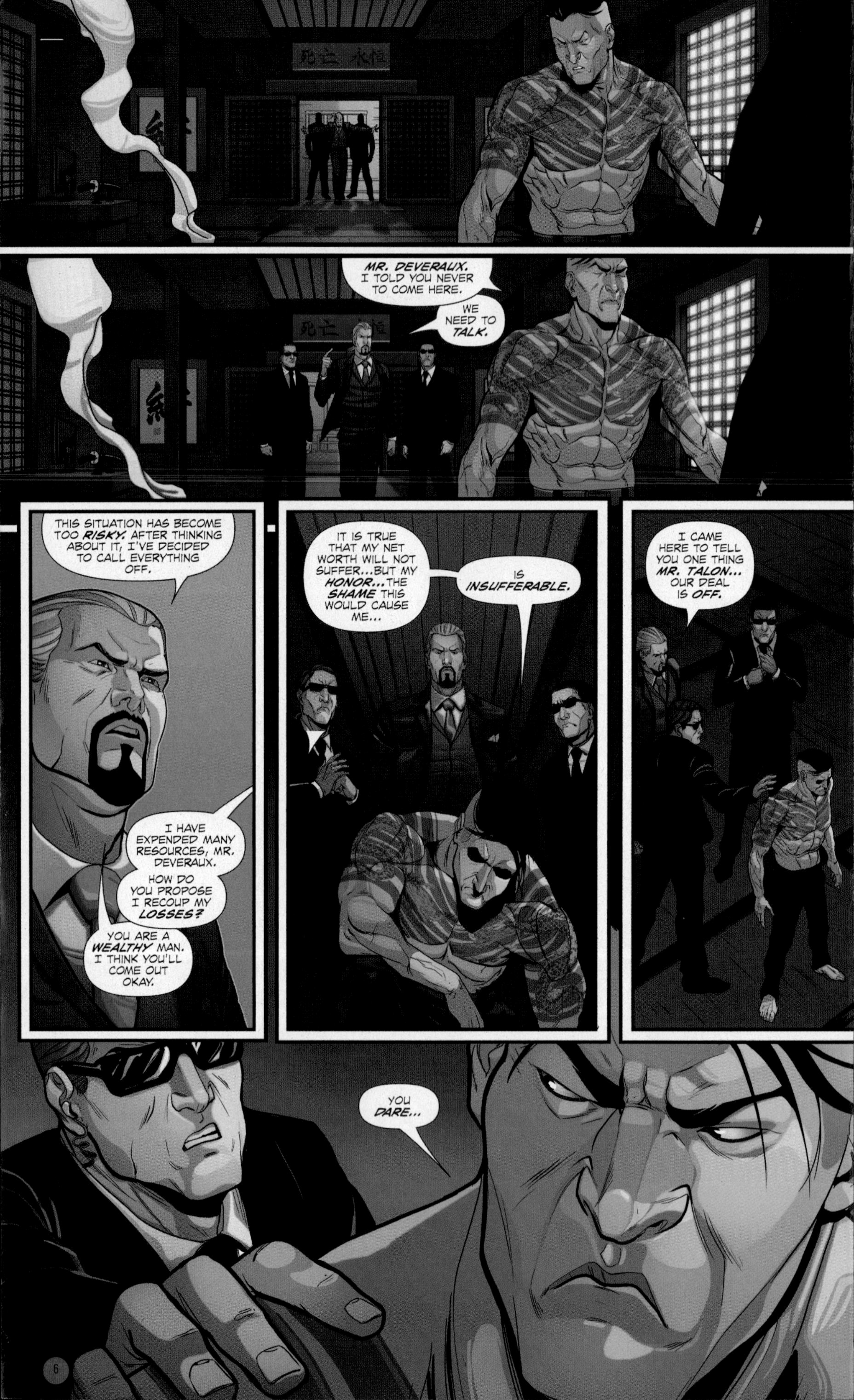
死亡 永恒
MR. DEVERAUX. I TOLD YOU NEVER TO COME HERE.
WE NEED TO TALK.
THIS SITUATION HAS BECOME TOO RISKY. AFTER THINKING ABOUT IT, I'VE DECIDED TO CALL EVERYTHING OFF.
I HAVE EXPENDED MANY RESOURCES, MR. DEVERAUX.
HOW DO YOU PROPOSE I RECOUP MY LOSSES?
YOU ARE A WEALTHY MAN. I THINK YOU'LL COME OUT OKAY.
IT IS TRUE THAT MY NET WORTH WILL NOT SUFFER...BUT MY HONOR...THE SHAME THIS WOULD CAUSE ME...
IS INSUFFERABLE.
I CAME HERE TO TELL YOU ONE THING MR. TALON... OUR DEAL IS OFF.
YOU DARE...

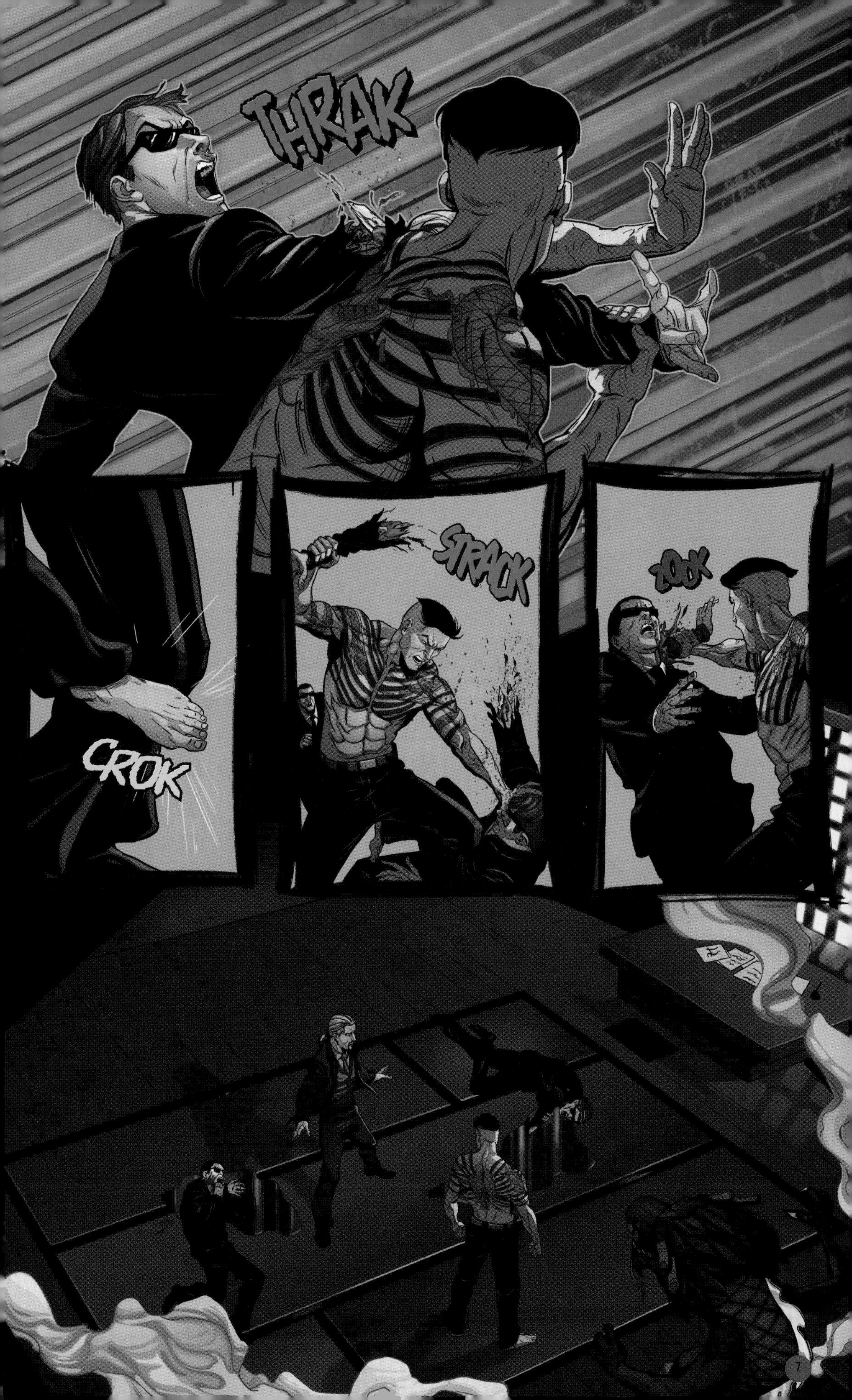
THRAK
CROK
STRACK
ZOOK

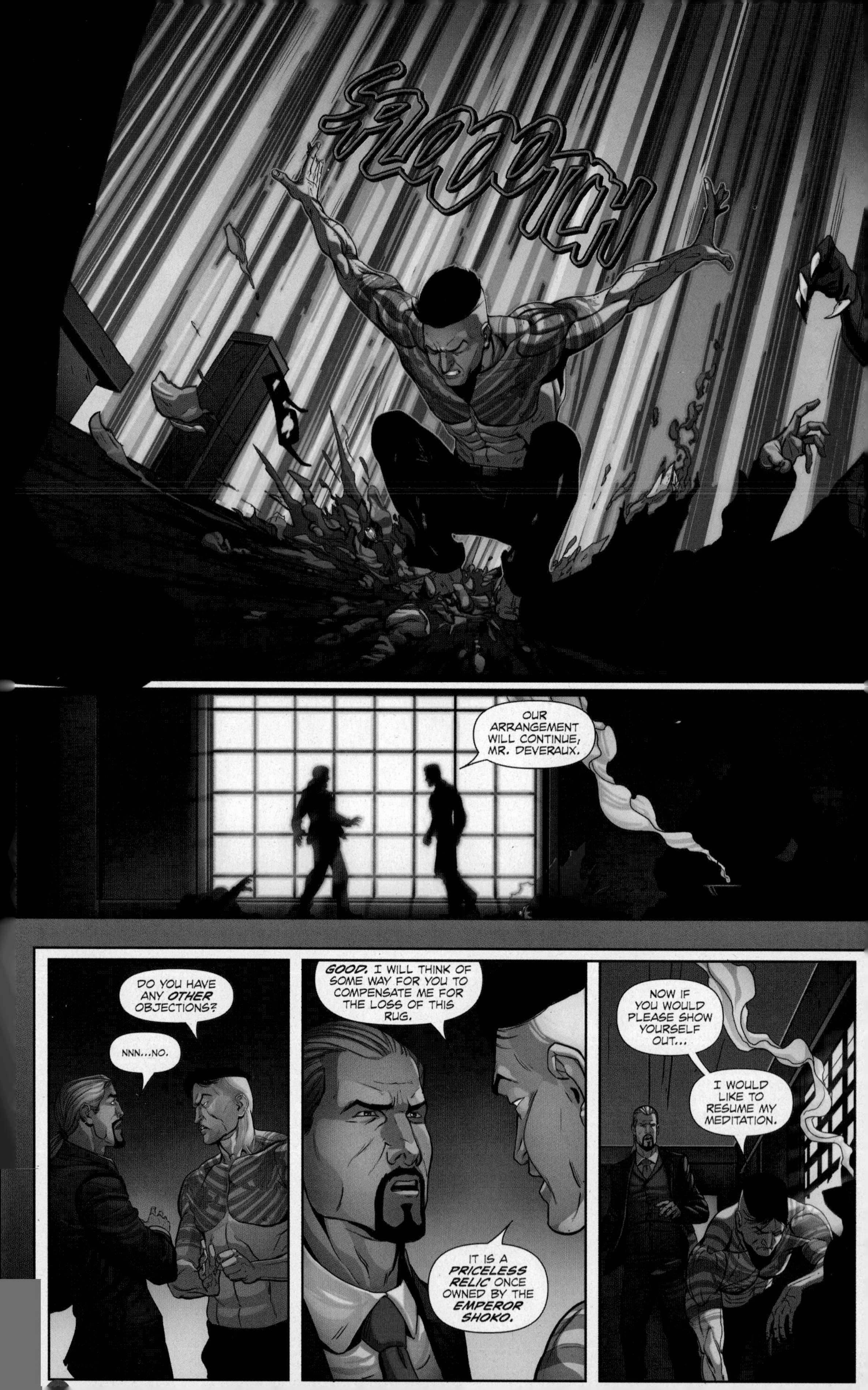
SPLOOOTCH
OUR ARRANGEMENT WILL CONTINUE, MR. DEVERAUX.
DO YOU HAVE ANY *OTHER* OBJECTIONS?
NNN...NO.
GOOD. I WILL THINK OF SOME WAY FOR YOU TO COMPENSATE ME FOR THE LOSS OF THIS RUG.
IT IS A *PRICELESS RELIC* ONCE OWNED BY THE *EMPEROR SHOKO.*
NOW IF YOU WOULD PLEASE SHOW YOURSELF OUT...
I WOULD LIKE TO RESUME MY MEDITATION.

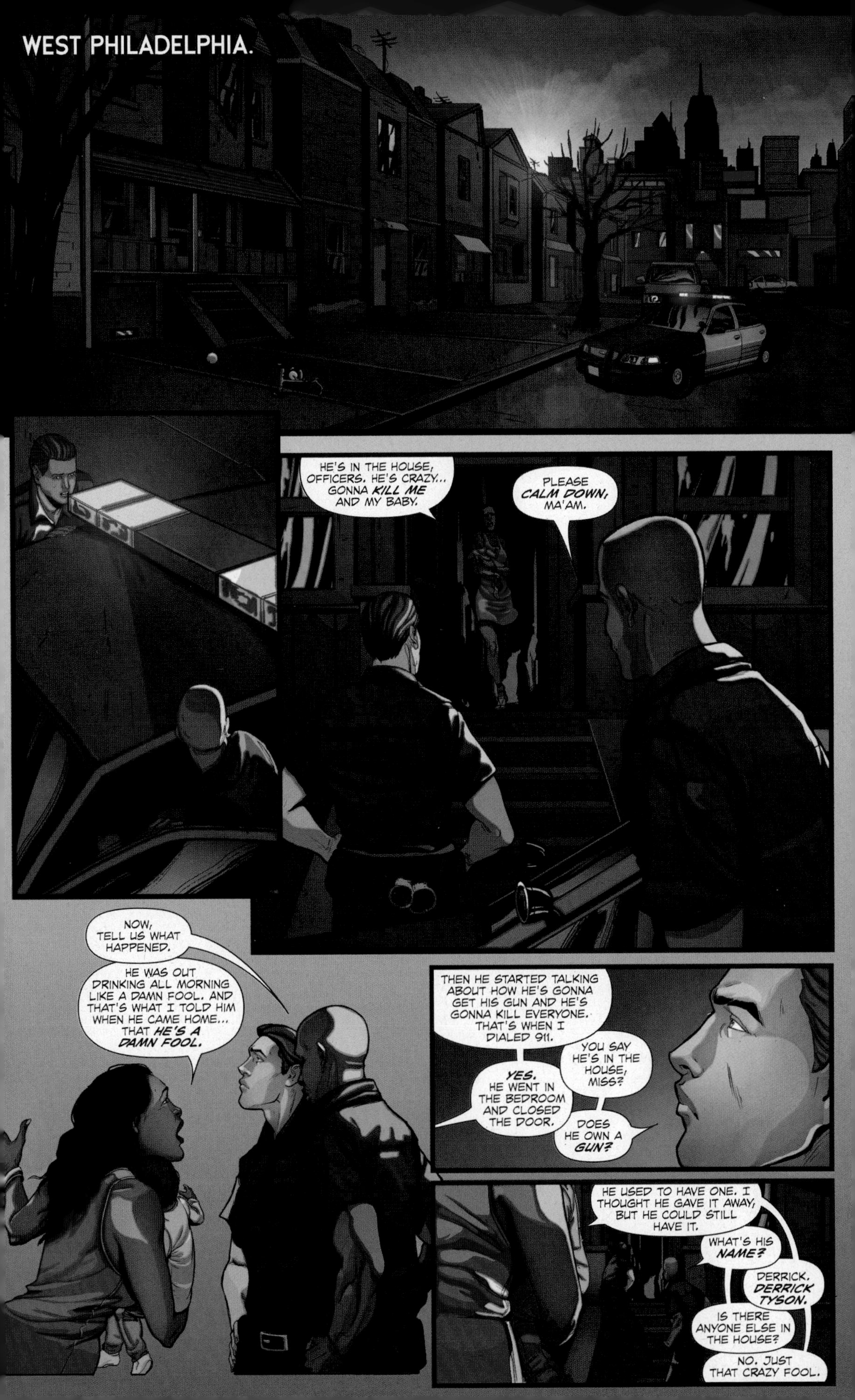
WEST PHILADELPHIA.
HE'S IN THE HOUSE, OFFICERS. HE'S CRAZY... GONNA KILL ME AND MY BABY.
PLEASE CALM DOWN, MA'AM.
NOW, TELL US WHAT HAPPENED.
HE WAS OUT DRINKING ALL MORNING LIKE A DAMN FOOL. AND THAT'S WHAT I TOLD HIM WHEN HE CAME HOME... THAT HE'S A DAMN FOOL.
THEN HE STARTED TALKING ABOUT HOW HE'S GONNA GET HIS GUN AND HE'S GONNA KILL EVERYONE. THAT'S WHEN I DIALED 911.
YOU SAY HE'S IN THE HOUSE, MISS?
YES. HE WENT IN THE BEDROOM AND CLOSED THE DOOR.
DOES HE OWN A GUN?
HE USED TO HAVE ONE. I THOUGHT HE GAVE IT AWAY, BUT HE COULD STILL HAVE IT.
WHAT'S HIS NAME?
DERRICK. DERRICK TYSON.
IS THERE ANYONE ELSE IN THE HOUSE?
NO. JUST THAT CRAZY FOOL.

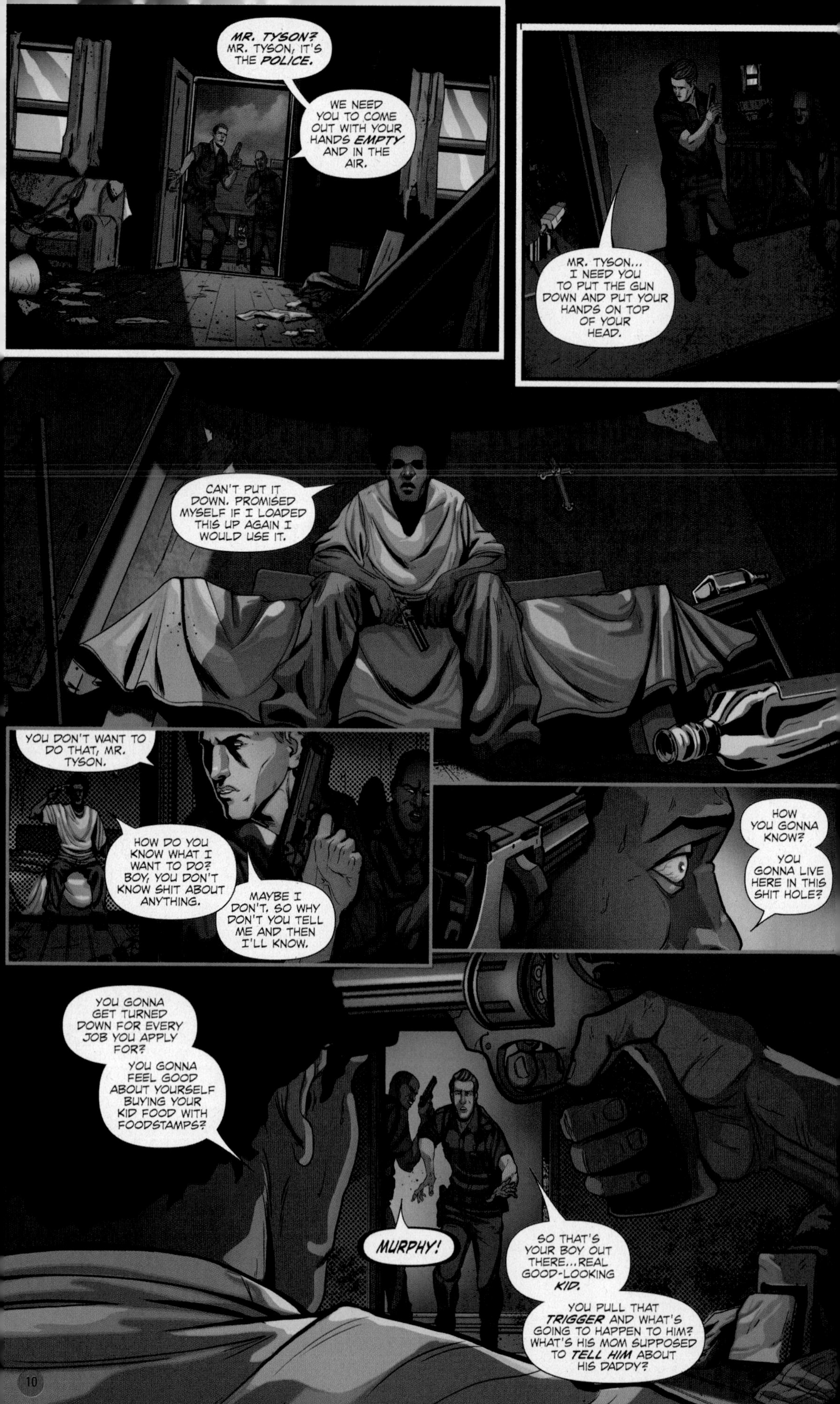

MR. TYSON? MR. TYSON, IT'S THE POLICE.
WE NEED YOU TO COME OUT WITH YOUR HANDS EMPTY AND IN THE AIR.
MR. TYSON... I NEED YOU TO PUT THE GUN DOWN AND PUT YOUR HANDS ON TOP OF YOUR HEAD.
CAN'T PUT IT DOWN. PROMISED MYSELF IF I LOADED THIS UP AGAIN I WOULD USE IT.
YOU DON'T WANT TO DO THAT, MR. TYSON.
HOW DO YOU KNOW WHAT I WANT TO DO? BOY, YOU DON'T KNOW SHIT ABOUT ANYTHING.
MAYBE I DON'T. SO WHY DON'T YOU TELL ME AND THEN I'LL KNOW.
HOW YOU GONNA KNOW?
YOU GONNA LIVE HERE IN THIS SHIT HOLE?
YOU GONNA GET TURNED DOWN FOR EVERY JOB YOU APPLY FOR?
YOU GONNA FEEL GOOD ABOUT YOURSELF BUYING YOUR KID FOOD WITH FOODSTAMPS?
MURPHY!
SO THAT'S YOUR BOY OUT THERE...REAL GOOD-LOOKING KID.
YOU PULL THAT TRIGGER AND WHAT'S GOING TO HAPPEN TO HIM? WHAT'S HIS MOM SUPPOSED TO TELL HIM ABOUT HIS DADDY?

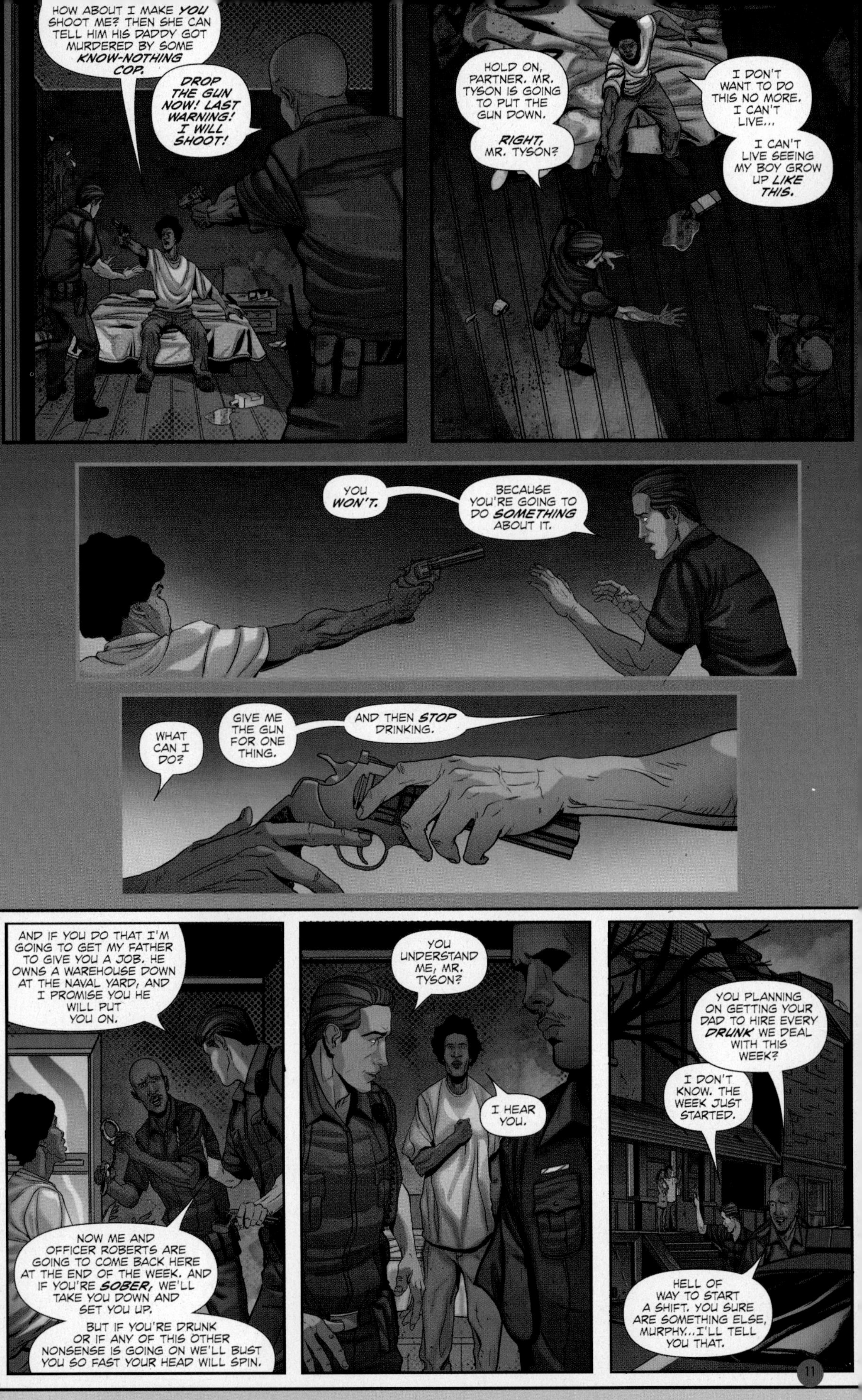
HOW ABOUT I MAKE YOU SHOOT ME? THEN SHE CAN TELL HIM HIS DADDY GOT MURDERED BY SOME KNOW-NOTHING COP.
DROP THE GUN NOW! LAST WARNING! I WILL SHOOT!
HOLD ON, PARTNER. MR. TYSON IS GOING TO PUT THE GUN DOWN.
RIGHT, MR. TYSON?
I DON'T WANT TO DO THIS NO MORE. I CAN'T LIVE...
I CAN'T LIVE SEEING MY BOY GROW UP LIKE THIS.
YOU WON'T.
BECAUSE YOU'RE GOING TO DO SOMETHING ABOUT IT.
WHAT CAN I DO?
GIVE ME THE GUN FOR ONE THING.
AND THEN STOP DRINKING.
AND IF YOU DO THAT I'M GOING TO GET MY FATHER TO GIVE YOU A JOB. HE OWNS A WAREHOUSE DOWN AT THE NAVAL YARD, AND I PROMISE YOU HE WILL PUT YOU ON.
NOW ME AND OFFICER ROBERTS ARE GOING TO COME BACK HERE AT THE END OF THE WEEK. AND IF YOU'RE SOBER, WE'LL TAKE YOU DOWN AND SET YOU UP.
BUT IF YOU'RE DRUNK OR IF ANY OF THIS OTHER NONSENSE IS GOING ON WE'LL BUST YOU SO FAST YOUR HEAD WILL SPIN.
YOU UNDERSTAND ME, MR. TYSON?
I HEAR YOU.
YOU PLANNING ON GETTING YOUR DAD TO HIRE EVERY DRUNK WE DEAL WITH THIS WEEK?
I DON'T KNOW. THE WEEK JUST STARTED.
HELL OF WAY TO START A SHIFT. YOU SURE ARE SOMETHING ELSE, MURPHY...I'LL TELL YOU THAT.

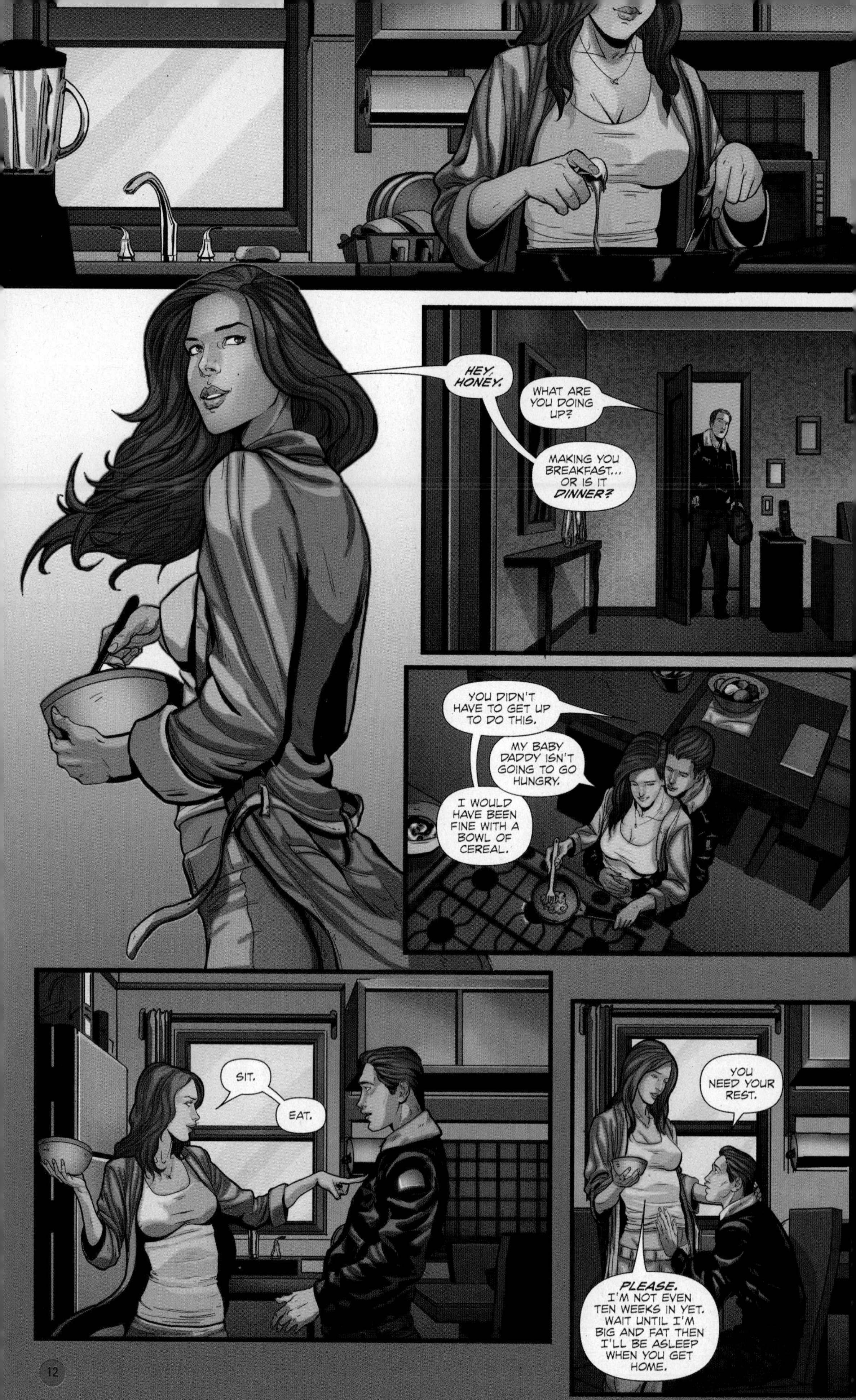
HEY, HONEY.
WHAT ARE YOU DOING UP?
MAKING YOU BREAKFAST... OR IS IT DINNER?
YOU DIDN'T HAVE TO GET UP TO DO THIS.
MY BABY DADDY ISN'T GOING TO GO HUNGRY.
I WOULD HAVE BEEN FINE WITH A BOWL OF CEREAL.
SIT.
EAT.
YOU NEED YOUR REST.
PLEASE. I'M NOT EVEN TEN WEEKS IN YET. WAIT UNTIL I'M BIG AND FAT THEN I'LL BE ASLEEP WHEN YOU GET HOME.

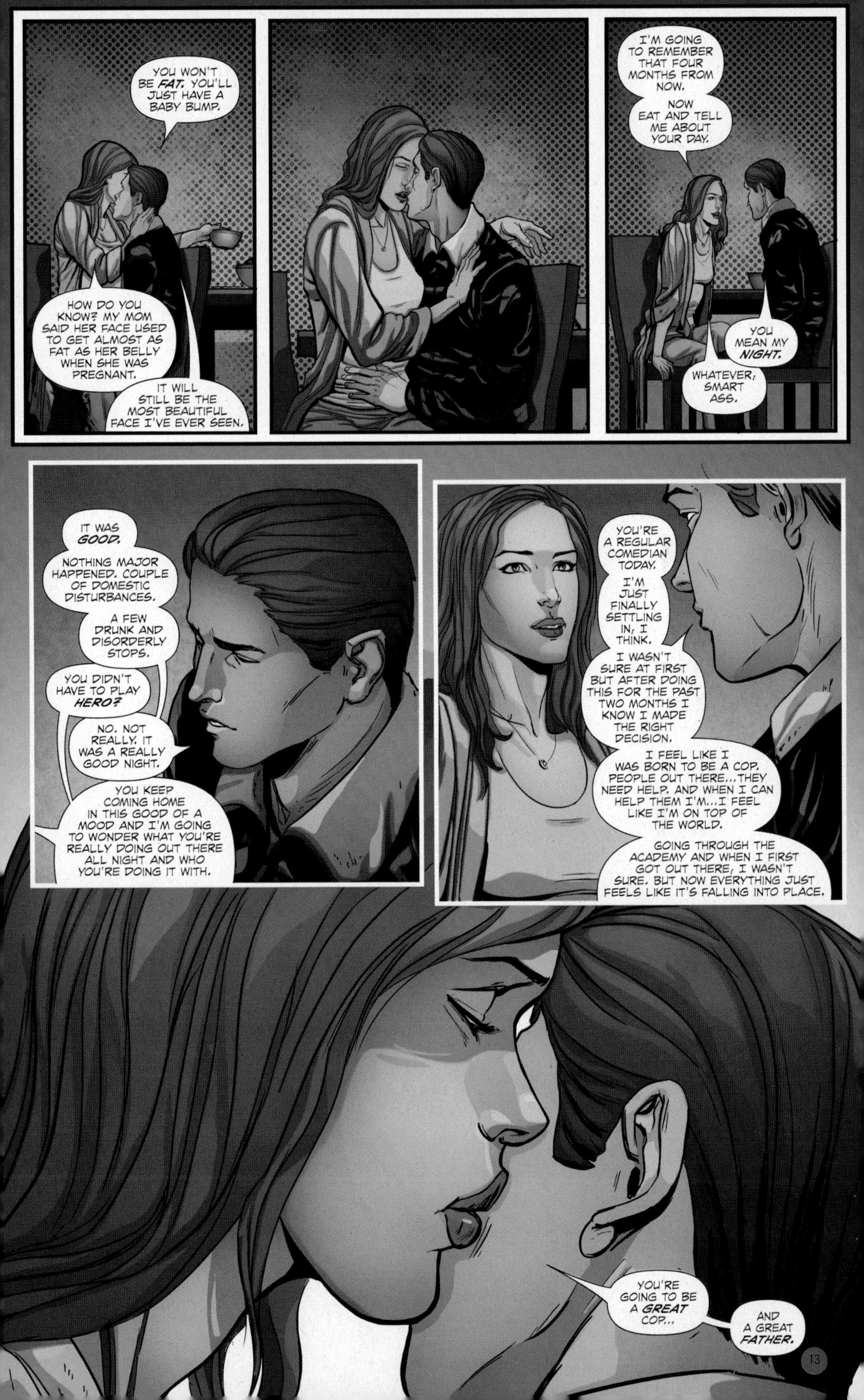

YOU WON'T BE FAT. YOU'LL JUST HAVE A BABY BUMP.
HOW DO YOU KNOW? MY MOM SAID HER FACE USED TO GET ALMOST AS FAT AS HER BELLY WHEN SHE WAS PREGNANT.
IT WILL STILL BE THE MOST BEAUTIFUL FACE I'VE EVER SEEN.
I'M GOING TO REMEMBER THAT FOUR MONTHS FROM NOW.
NOW EAT AND TELL ME ABOUT YOUR DAY.
YOU MEAN MY NIGHT.
WHATEVER, SMART ASS.
IT WAS GOOD.
NOTHING MAJOR HAPPENED. COUPLE OF DOMESTIC DISTURBANCES.
A FEW DRUNK AND DISORDERLY STOPS.
YOU DIDN'T HAVE TO PLAY HERO?
NO. NOT REALLY. IT WAS A REALLY GOOD NIGHT.
YOU KEEP COMING HOME IN THIS GOOD OF A MOOD AND I'M GOING TO WONDER WHAT YOU'RE REALLY DOING OUT THERE ALL NIGHT AND WHO YOU'RE DOING IT WITH.
YOU'RE A REGULAR COMEDIAN TODAY.
I'M JUST FINALLY SETTLING IN, I THINK.
I WASN'T SURE AT FIRST BUT AFTER DOING THIS FOR THE PAST TWO MONTHS I KNOW I MADE THE RIGHT DECISION.
I FEEL LIKE I WAS BORN TO BE A COP. PEOPLE OUT THERE...THEY NEED HELP. AND WHEN I CAN HELP THEM I'M...I FEEL LIKE I'M ON TOP OF THE WORLD.
GOING THROUGH THE ACADEMY AND WHEN I FIRST GOT OUT THERE, I WASN'T SURE. BUT NOW EVERYTHING JUST FEELS LIKE IT'S FALLING INTO PLACE.
YOU'RE GOING TO BE A GREAT COP...
AND A GREAT FATHER.

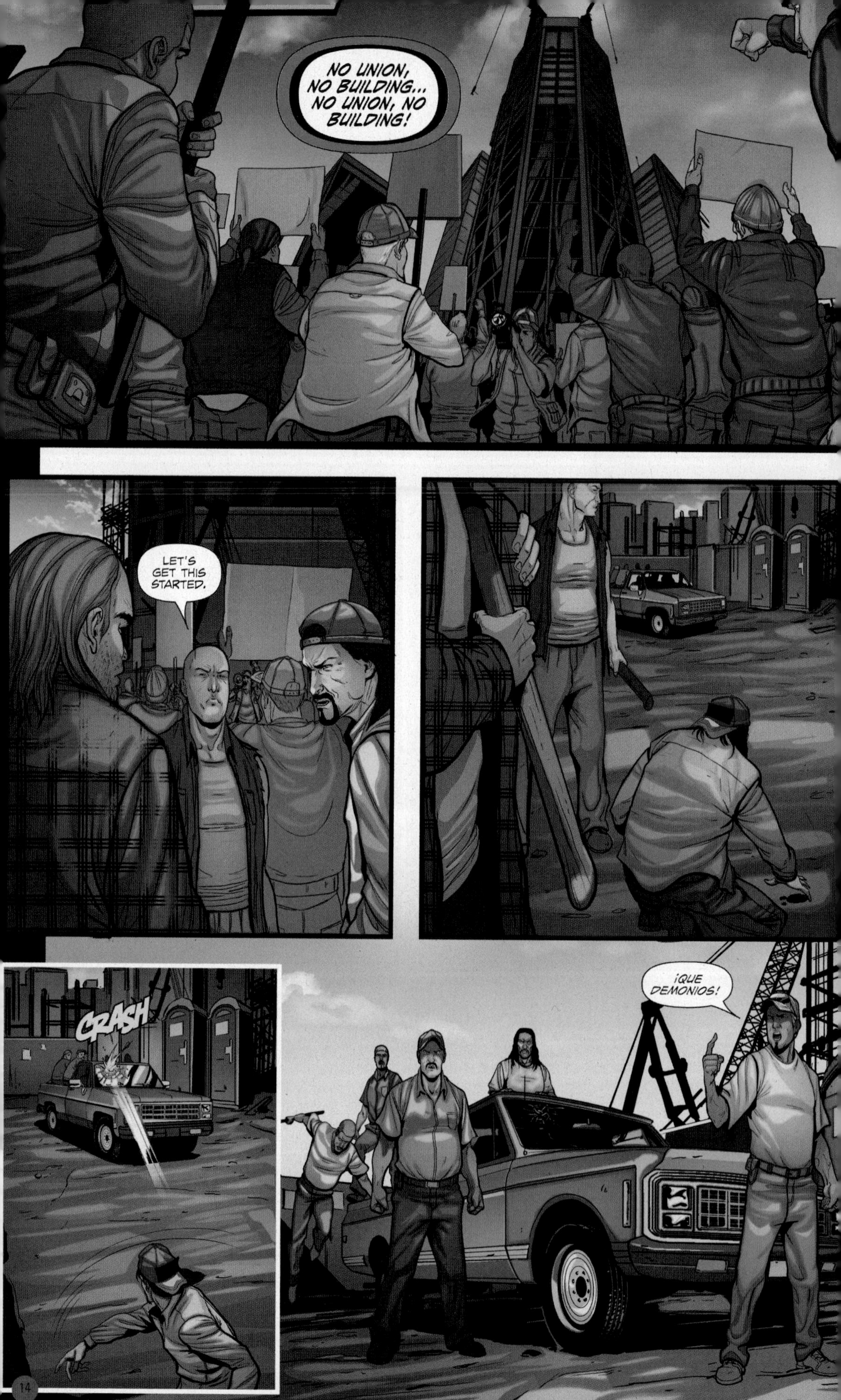
NO UNION, NO BUILDING... NO UNION, NO BUILDING!
LET'S GET THIS STARTED.
CRASH
¡QUE DEMONIOS!

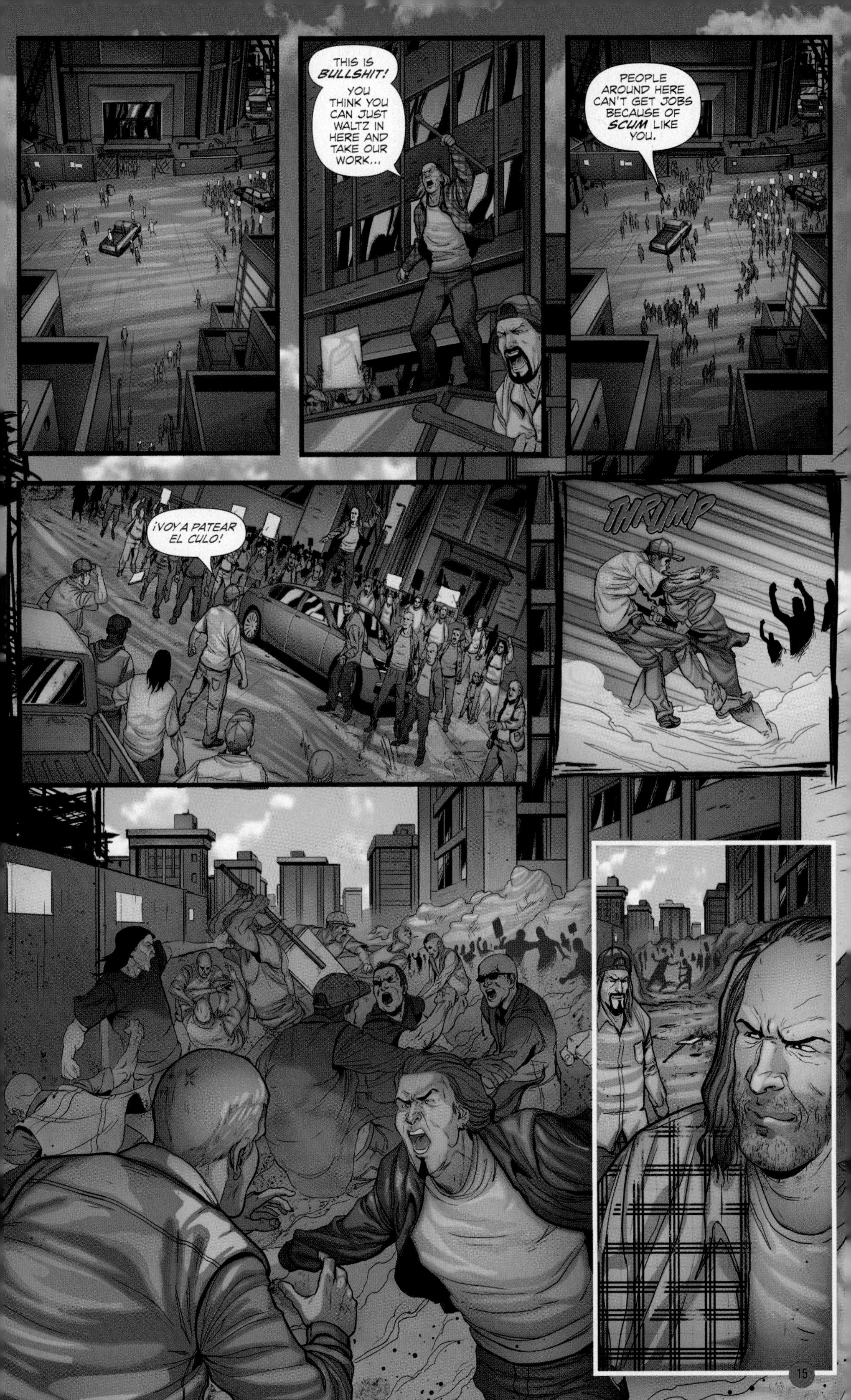
THIS IS BULLSHIT! YOU THINK YOU CAN JUST WALTZ IN HERE AND TAKE OUR WORK...
PEOPLE AROUND HERE CAN'T GET JOBS BECAUSE OF SCUM LIKE YOU.
¡VOY A PATEAR EL CULO!
THRUMP

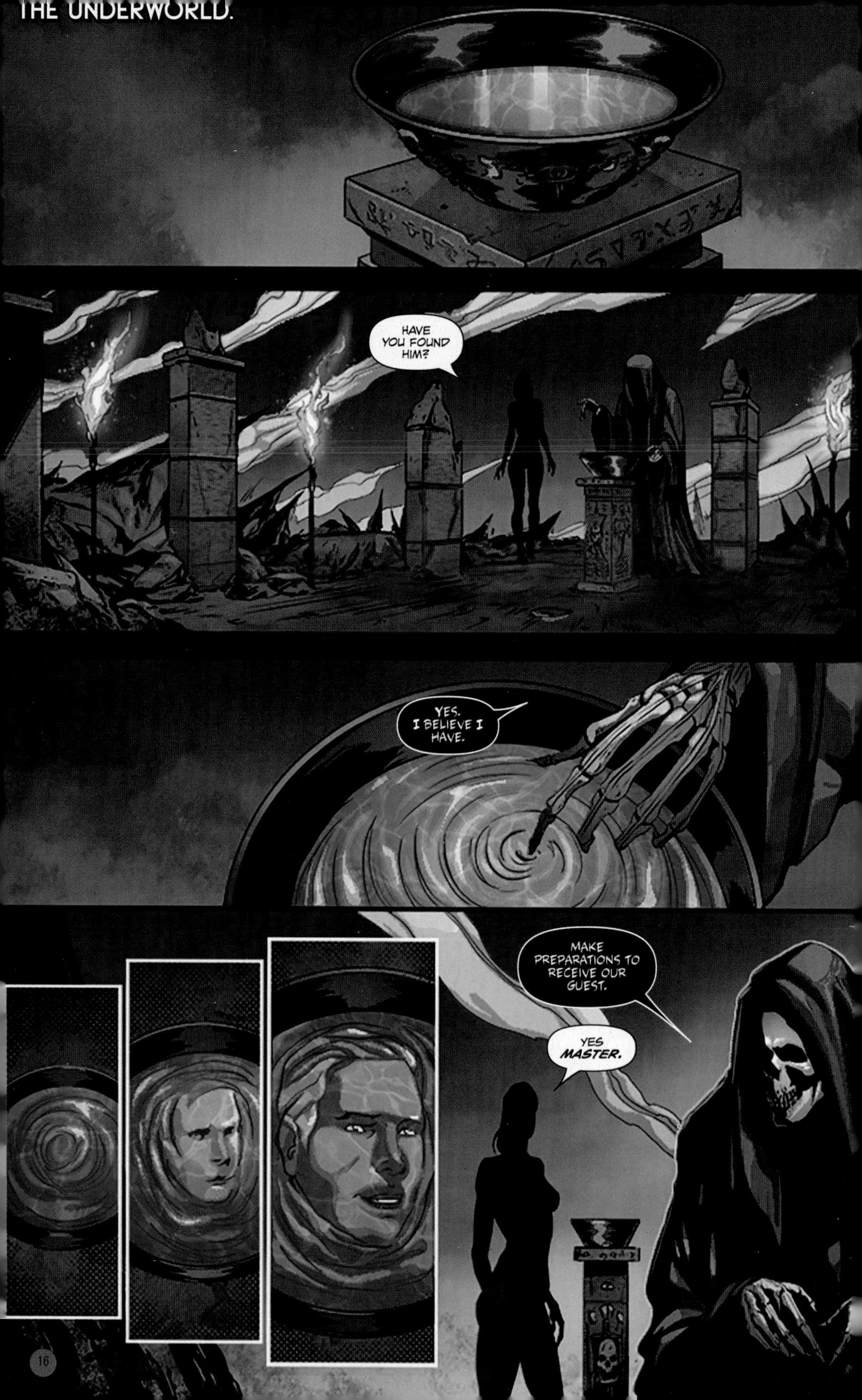

THE UNDERWORLD.
HAVE YOU FOUND HIM?
YES. I BELIEVE I HAVE.
MAKE PREPARATIONS TO RECEIVE OUR GUEST.
YES MASTER.

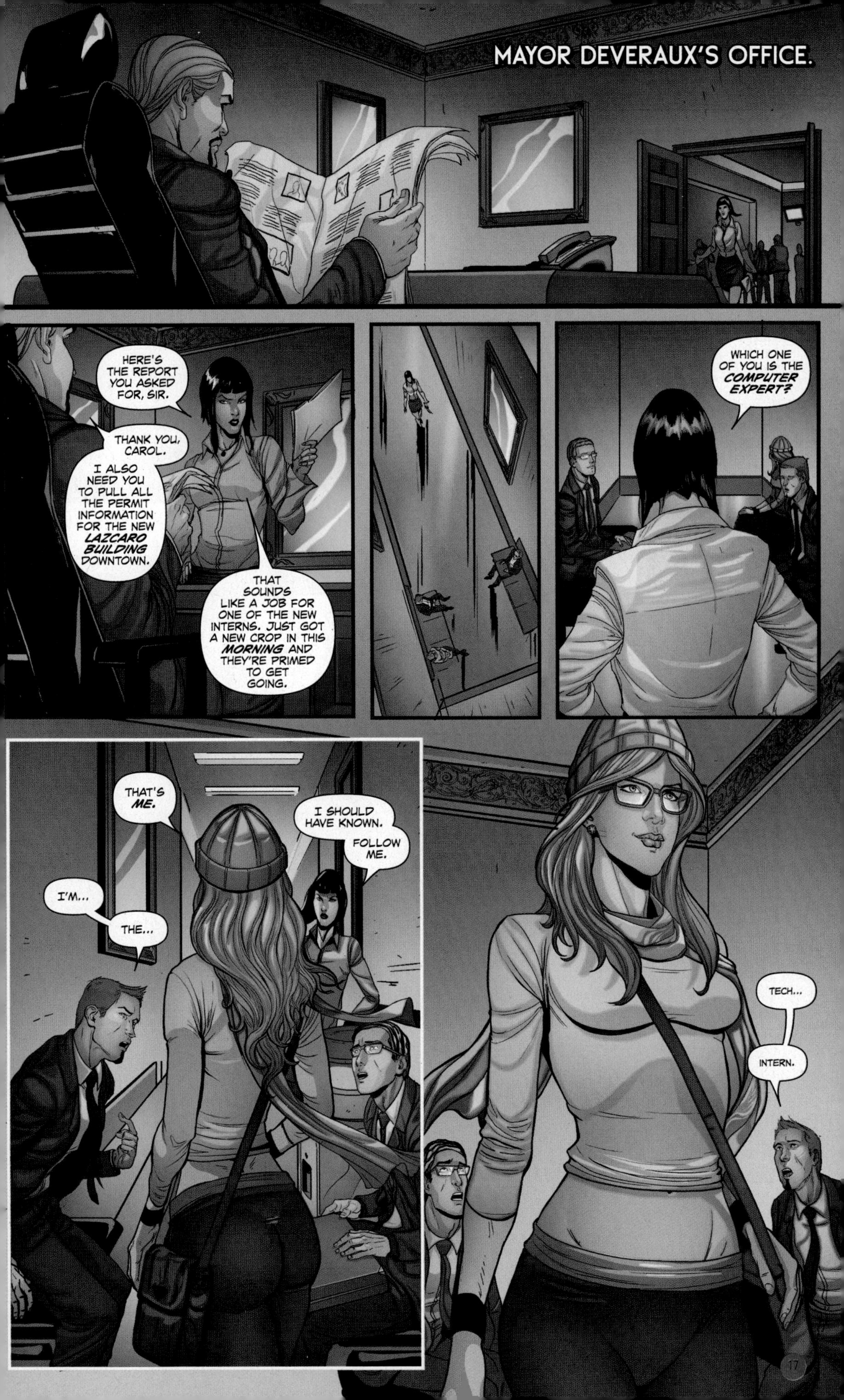
MAYOR DEVERAUX'S OFFICE.
HERE'S THE REPORT YOU ASKED FOR, SIR.
THANK YOU, CAROL.
I ALSO NEED YOU TO PULL ALL THE PERMIT INFORMATION FOR THE NEW LAZCARO BUILDING DOWNTOWN.
THAT SOUNDS LIKE A JOB FOR ONE OF THE NEW INTERNS. JUST GOT A NEW CROP IN THIS MORNING AND THEY'RE PRIMED TO GET GOING.
WHICH ONE OF YOU IS THE COMPUTER EXPERT?
THAT'S ME.
I SHOULD HAVE KNOWN.
FOLLOW ME.
I'M...
THE...
TECH...
INTERN.

I NEED YOU TO LOOK UP AND PRINT ALL THE PERMITS FOR THIS BUILDING.

AND STAY OFF THE FACEBOOK AND OTHER CRAP.

IF YOU DON'T, I'LL KNOW, AND THAT WILL BE THE END OF THIS INTERNSHIP.

YOU'RE HERE TO WORK, NOT MESS AROUND. *GOT IT?*

YES MA'AM.

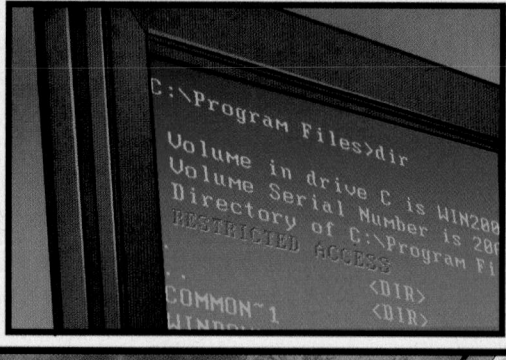

LADY, I COULD REDESIGN YOUR BAD MATCH.COM PROFILE PAGE SO WELL EVEN YOU COULD GET A DATE.

BUT I'VE GOT MUCH MORE IMPORTANT THINGS TO DO THAN THAT OR RUN YOUR STUPID REPORT.

AS IF YOU HAD A *CHANCE* OF KEEPING ME OUT.

```
C:\Program Files>dir
Volume in drive C is WIN200
Volume Serial Number is 200
Directory of C:\Program Fi
RESTRICTED ACCESS
                    <DIR>
COMMON~1            <DIR>
WINDO
```

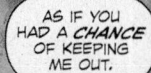

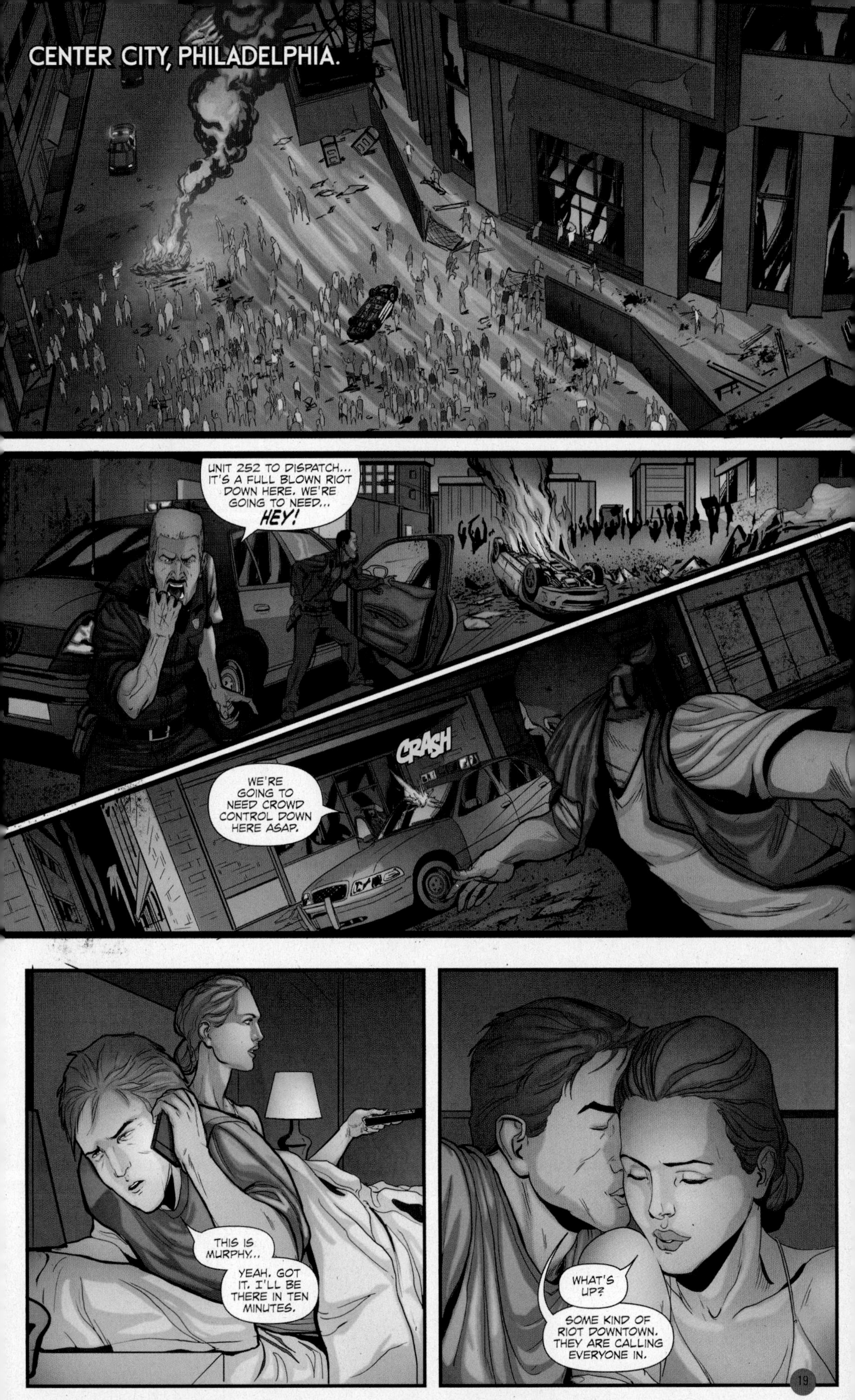
CENTER CITY, PHILADELPHIA.
UNIT 252 TO DISPATCH... IT'S A FULL BLOWN RIOT DOWN HERE. WE'RE GOING TO NEED... HEY!
CRASH
WE'RE GOING TO NEED CROWD CONTROL DOWN HERE ASAP.
THIS IS MURPHY...
YEAH. GOT IT. I'LL BE THERE IN TEN MINUTES.
WHAT'S UP?
SOME KIND OF RIOT DOWNTOWN. THEY ARE CALLING EVERYONE IN.

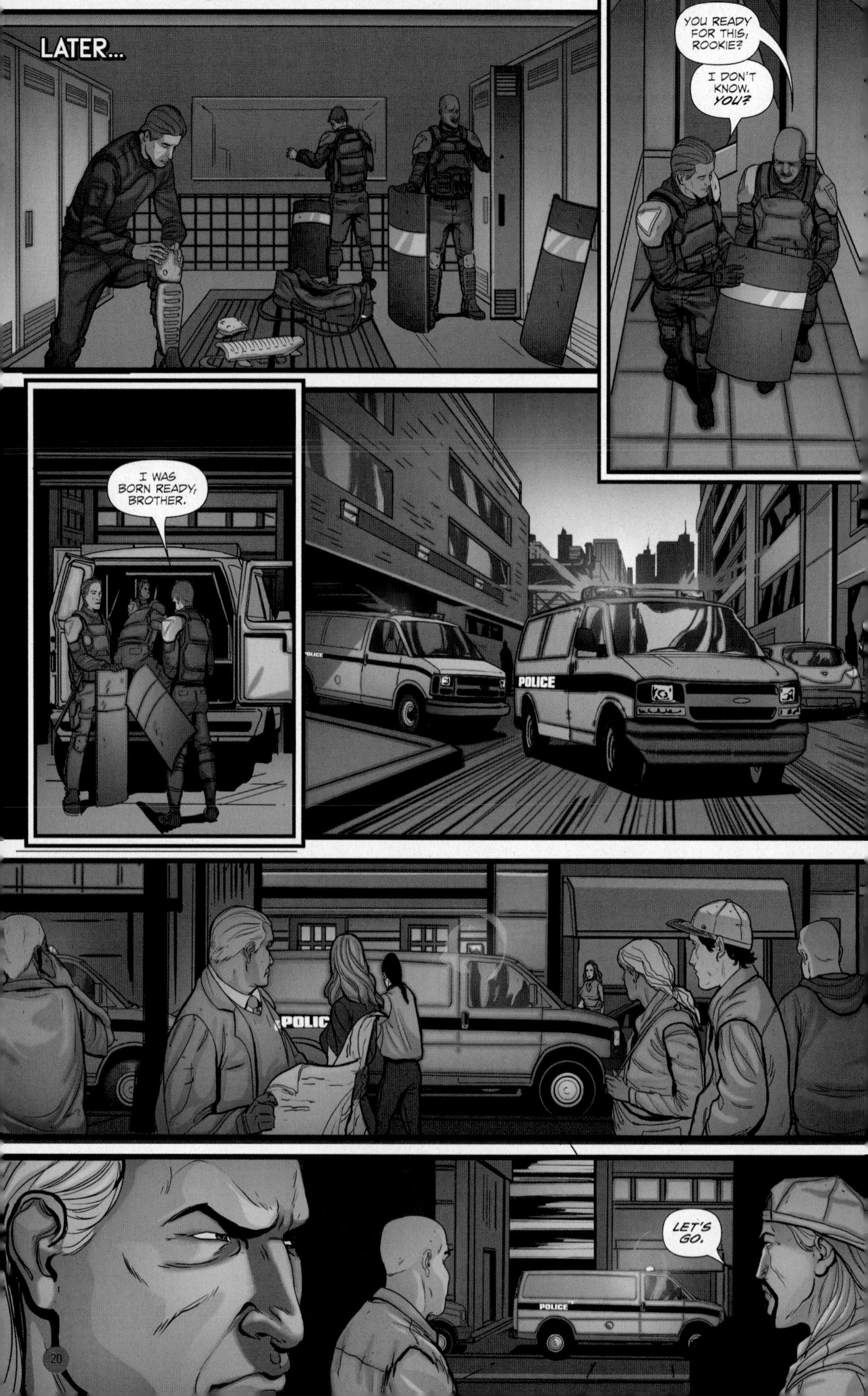
LATER...
YOU READY FOR THIS, ROOKIE?
I DON'T KNOW. YOU?
I WAS BORN READY, BROTHER.
POLICE
POLICE
POLIC
LET'S GO.
POLICE

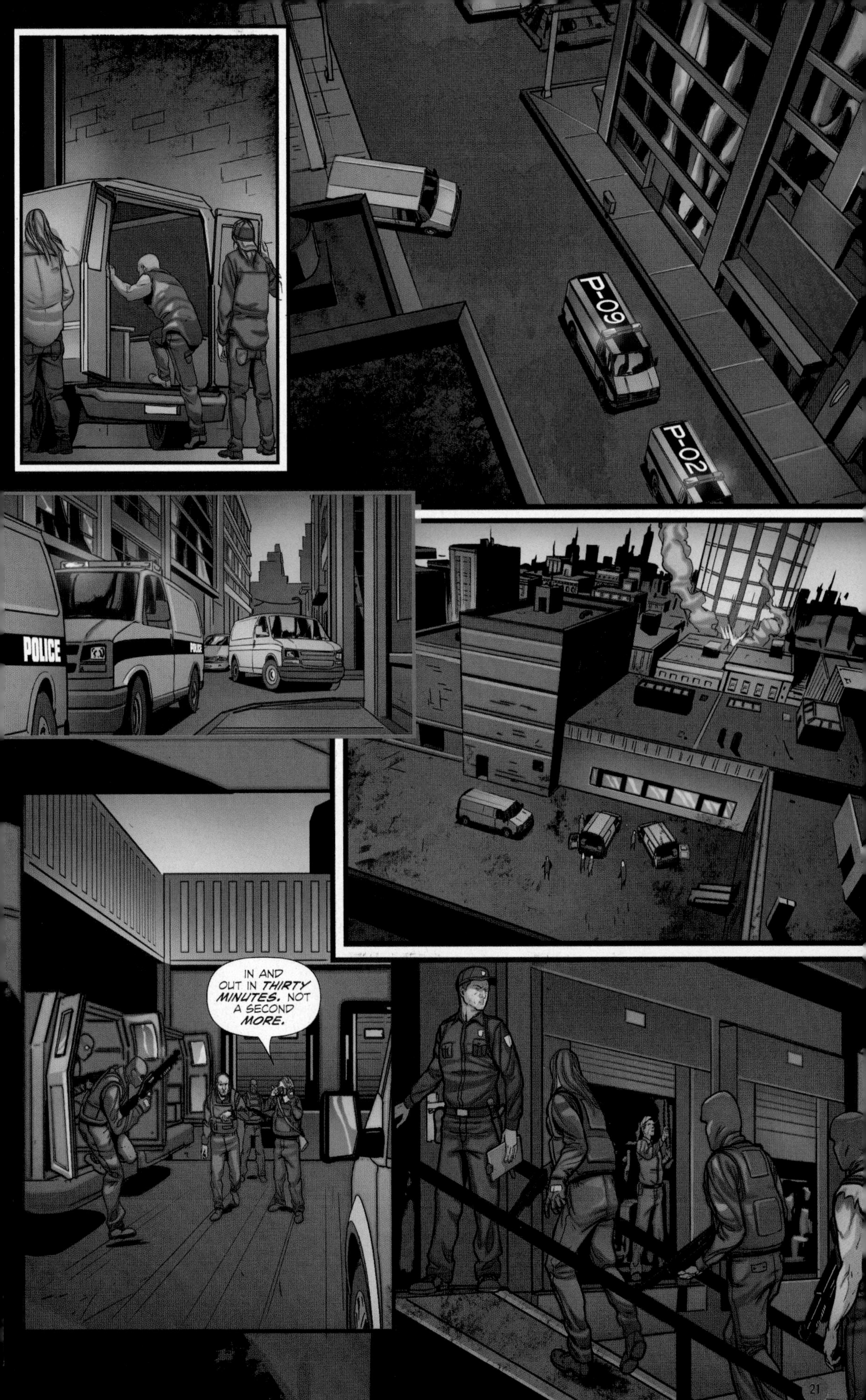
P-09
P-02
POLICE
POLICE
IN AND OUT IN THIRTY MINUTES. NOT A SECOND MORE.

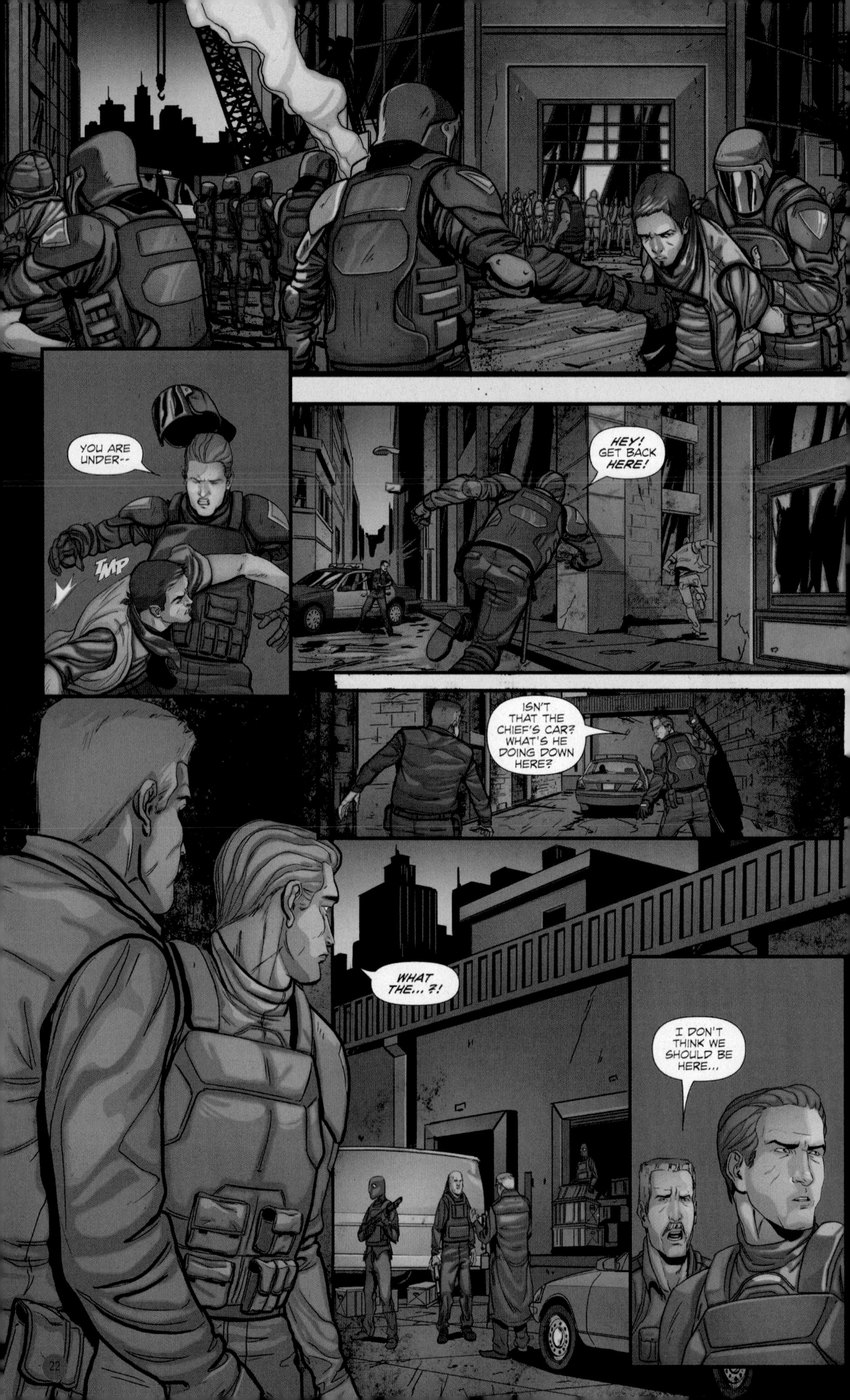
YOU ARE UNDER--
TMP
HEY! GET BACK HERE!
ISN'T THAT THE CHIEF'S CAR? WHAT'S HE DOING DOWN HERE?
WHAT THE... ?!
I DON'T THINK WE SHOULD BE HERE...

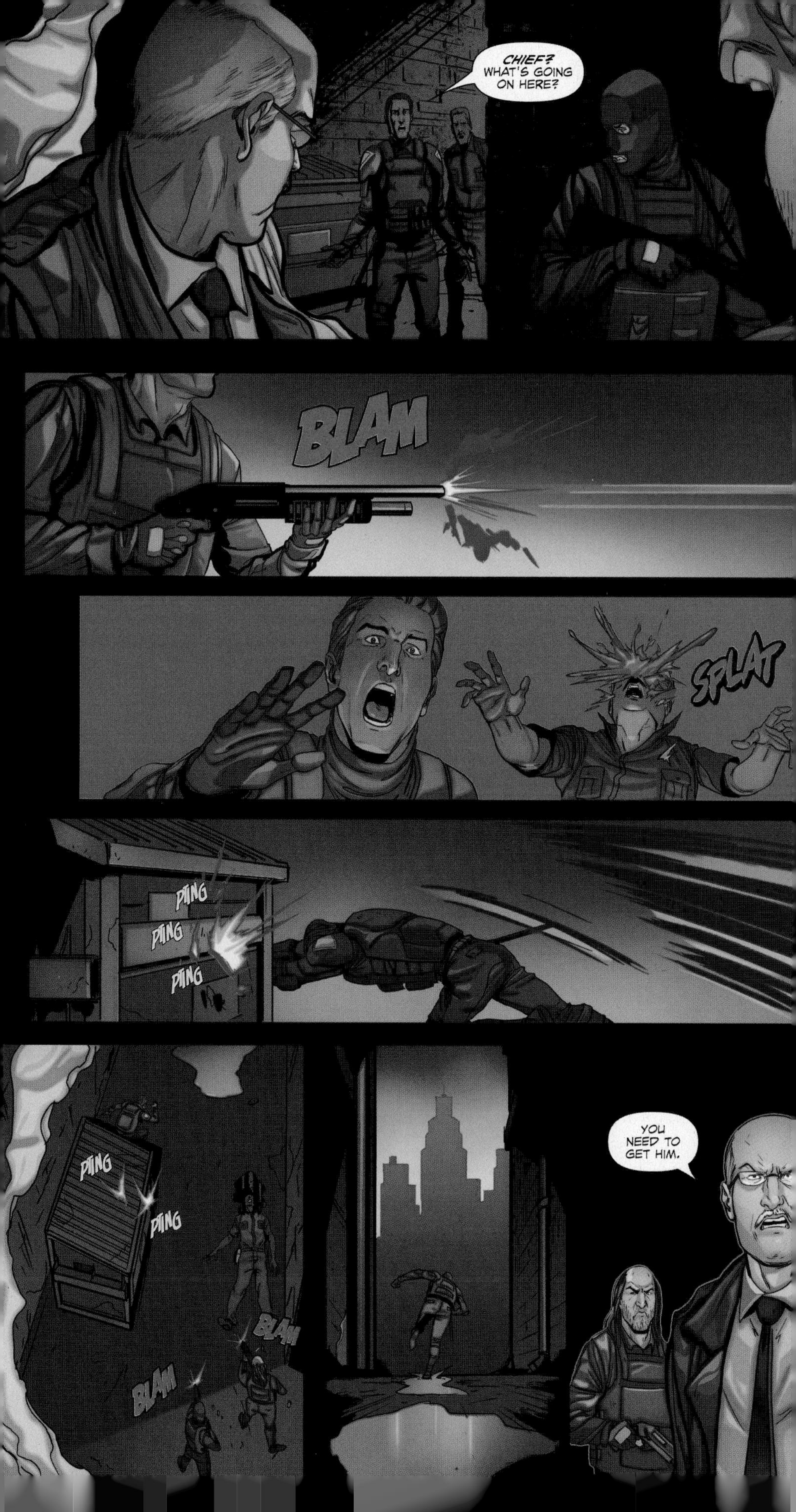
CHIEF? WHAT'S GOING ON HERE?
BLAM
SPLAT
PTING
PTING
PTING
PTING
PTING
BLAM
BLAM
YOU NEED TO GET HIM.

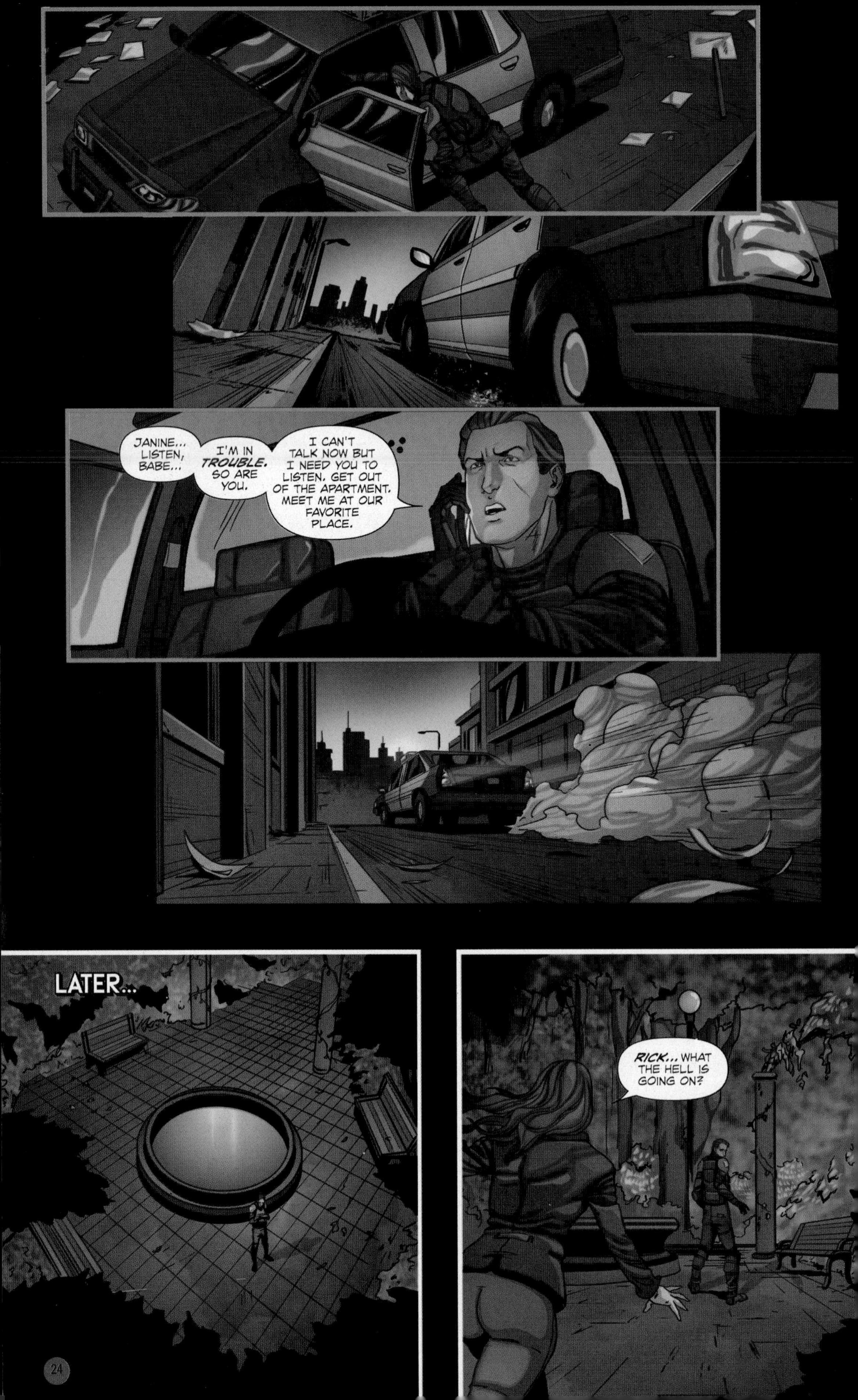
JANINE... LISTEN, BABE...
I'M IN TROUBLE. SO ARE YOU.
I CAN'T TALK NOW BUT I NEED YOU TO LISTEN. GET OUT OF THE APARTMENT. MEET ME AT OUR FAVORITE PLACE.
LATER...
RICK... WHAT THE HELL IS GOING ON?

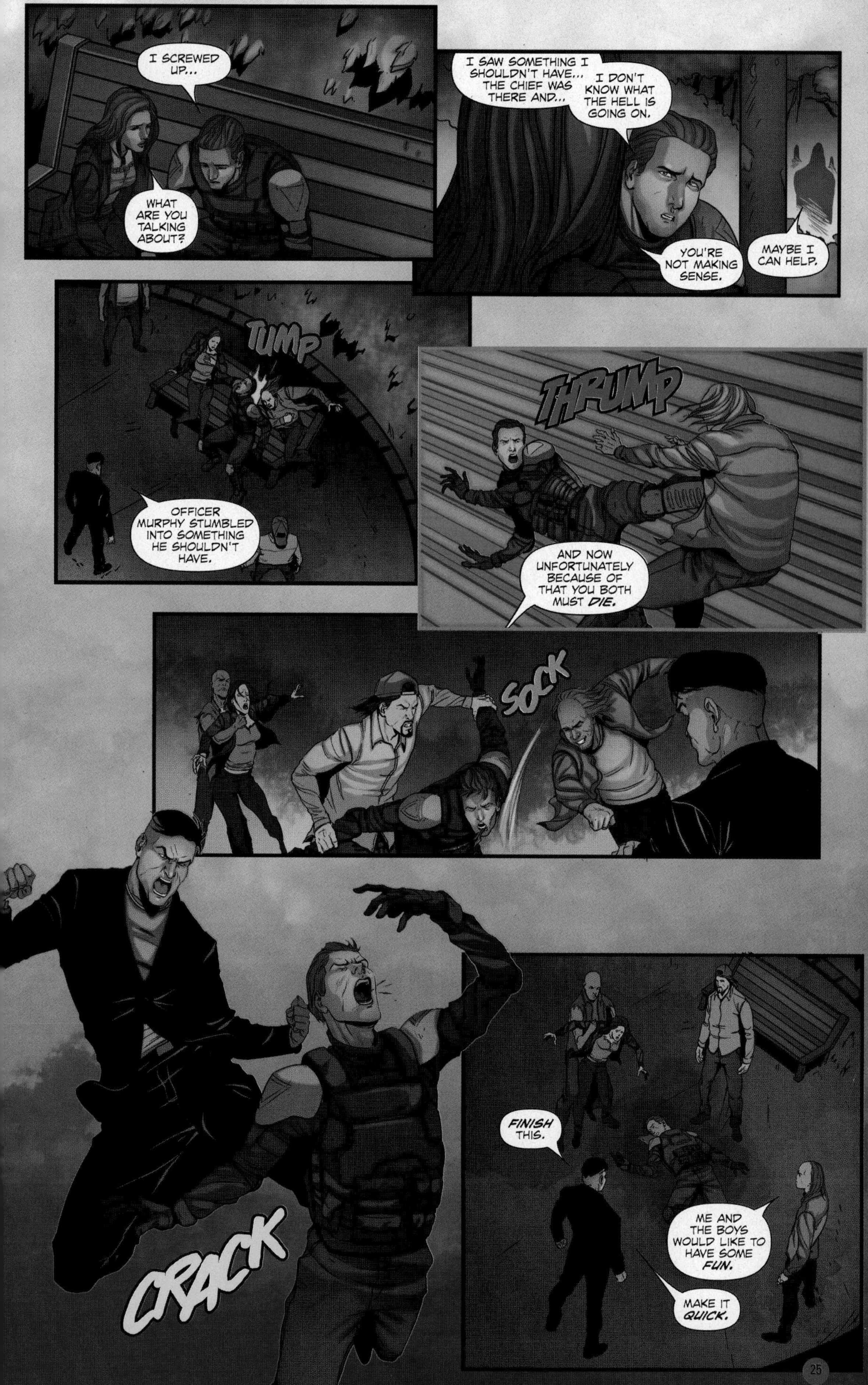
I SCREWED UP...
WHAT ARE YOU TALKING ABOUT?
I SAW SOMETHING I SHOULDN'T HAVE... THE CHIEF WAS THERE AND...
I DON'T KNOW WHAT THE HELL IS GOING ON.
YOU'RE NOT MAKING SENSE.
MAYBE I CAN HELP.
TUMP
OFFICER MURPHY STUMBLED INTO SOMETHING HE SHOULDN'T HAVE.
THRUMP
AND NOW UNFORTUNATELY BECAUSE OF THAT YOU BOTH MUST *DIE*.
SOCK
CRACK
FINISH THIS.
ME AND THE BOYS WOULD LIKE TO HAVE SOME *FUN*.
MAKE IT *QUICK*.

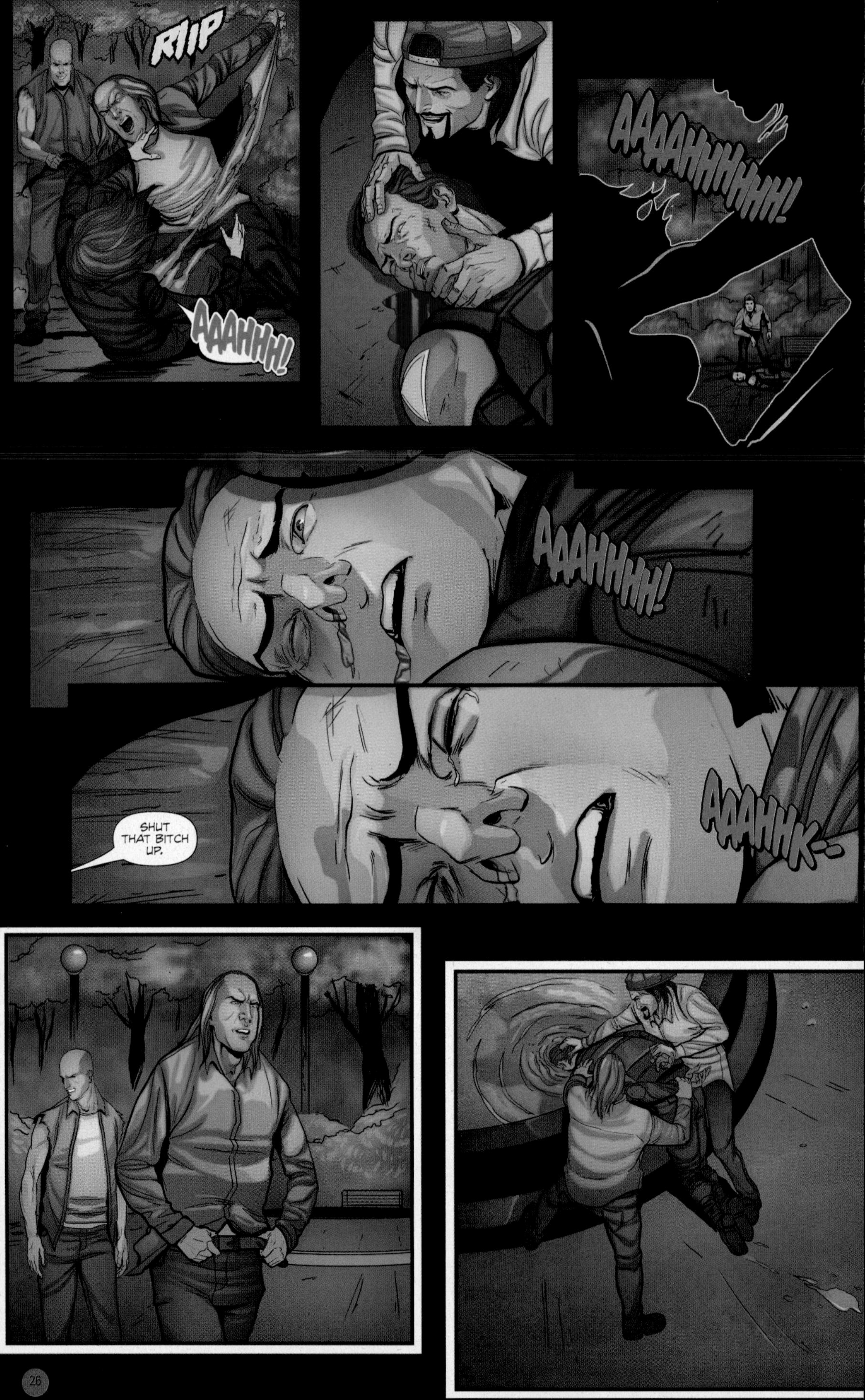

RIIP
AAAHHH!
AAAAHHHHHH!
AAAHHHH!
SHUT THAT BITCH UP.
AAAHHK-

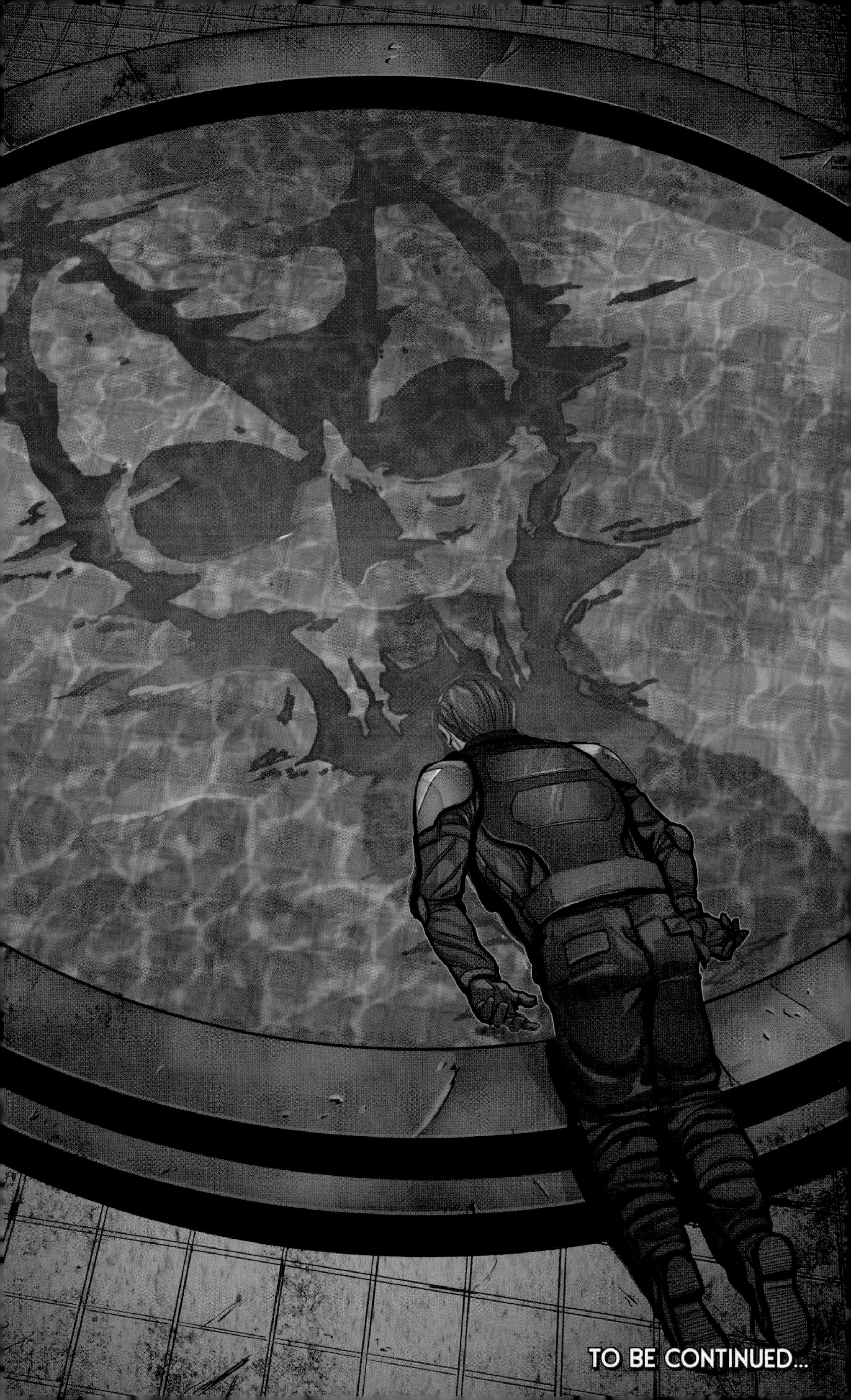
TO BE CONTINUED...

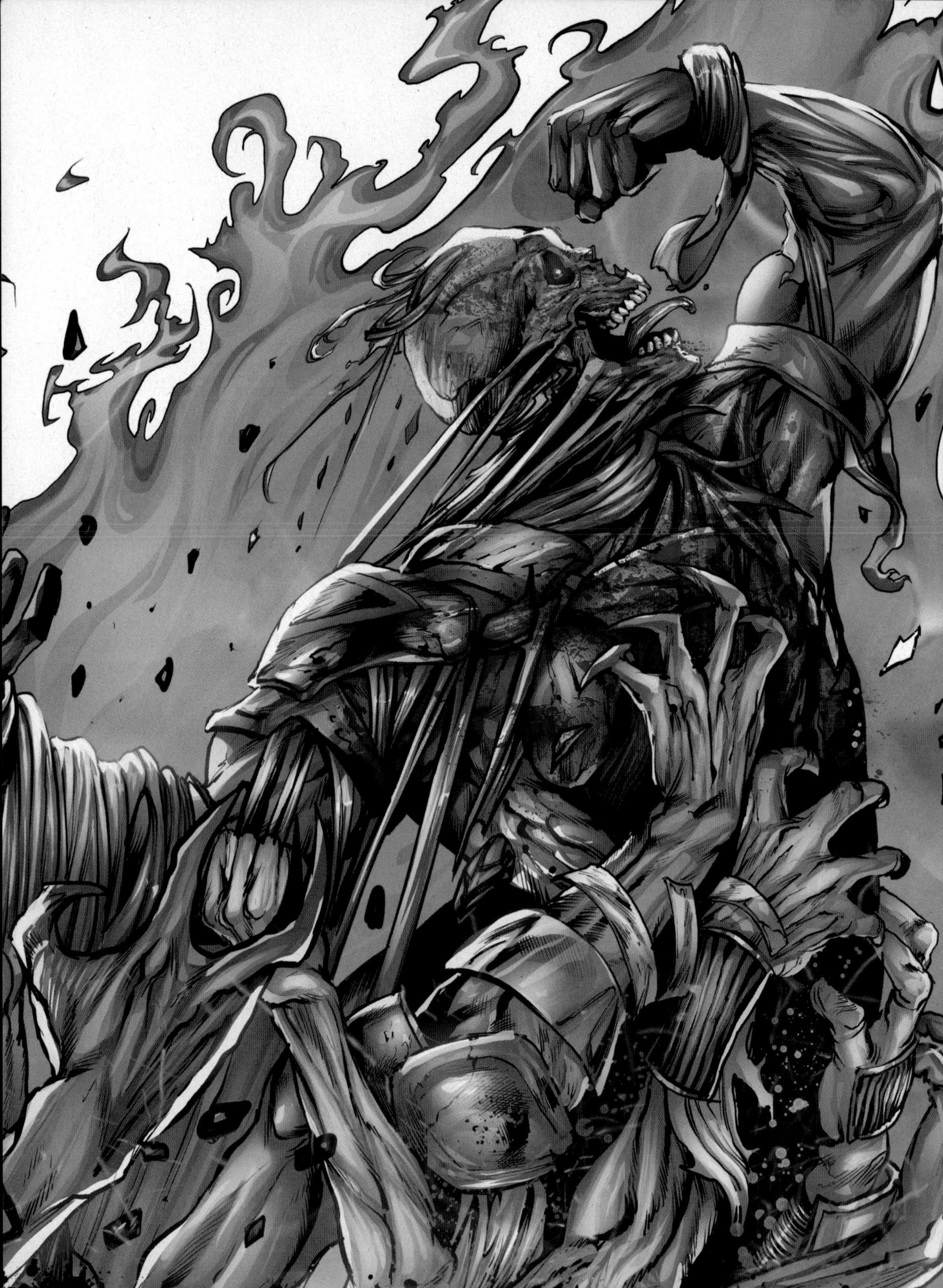

CHAPTER TWO

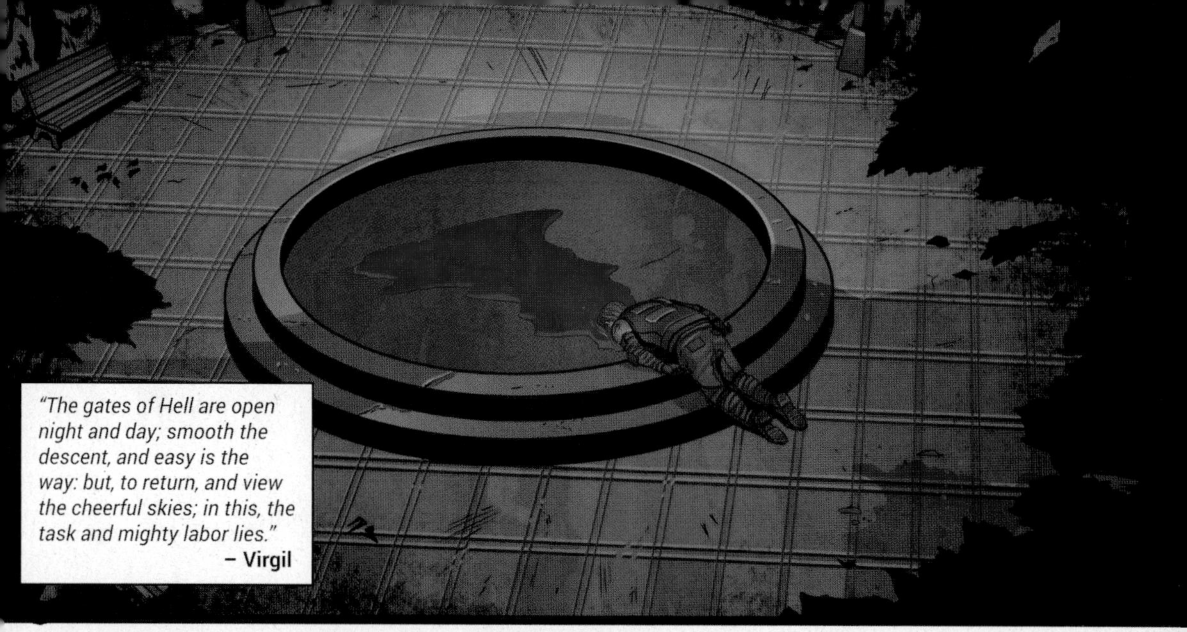
"The gates of Hell are open night and day; smooth the descent, and easy is the way: but, to return, and view the cheerful skies; in this, the task and mighty labor lies."
– Virgil

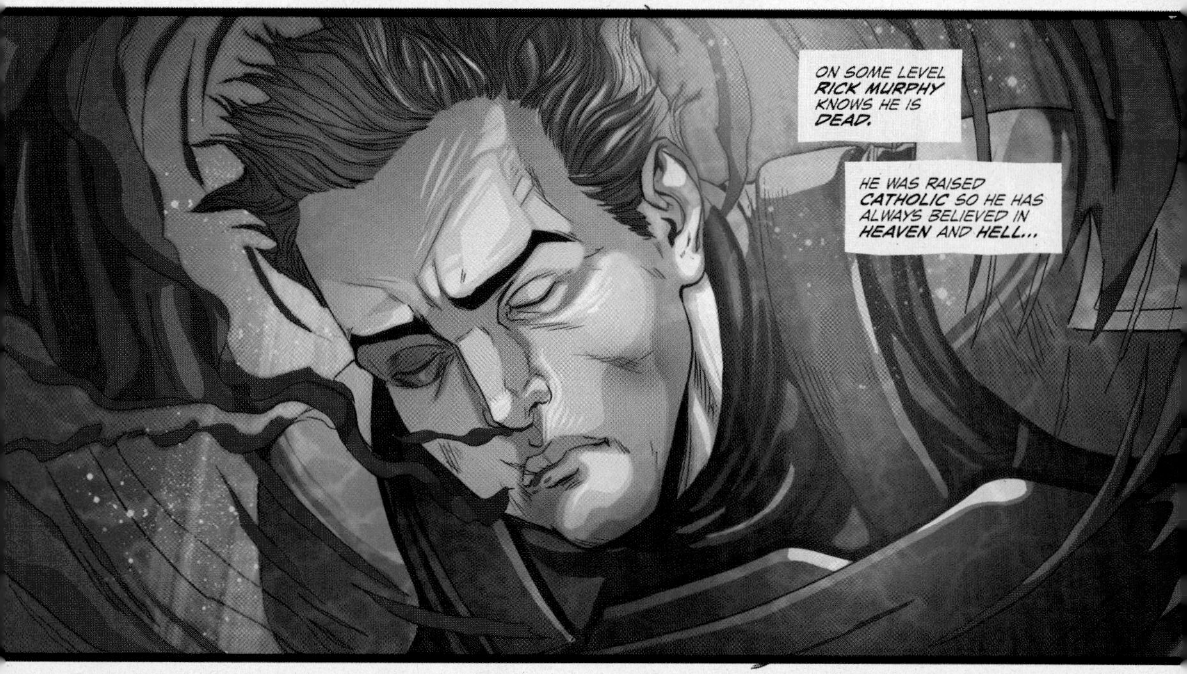
ON SOME LEVEL RICK MURPHY KNOWS HE IS DEAD.
HE WAS RAISED CATHOLIC SO HE HAS ALWAYS BELIEVED IN HEAVEN AND HELL...

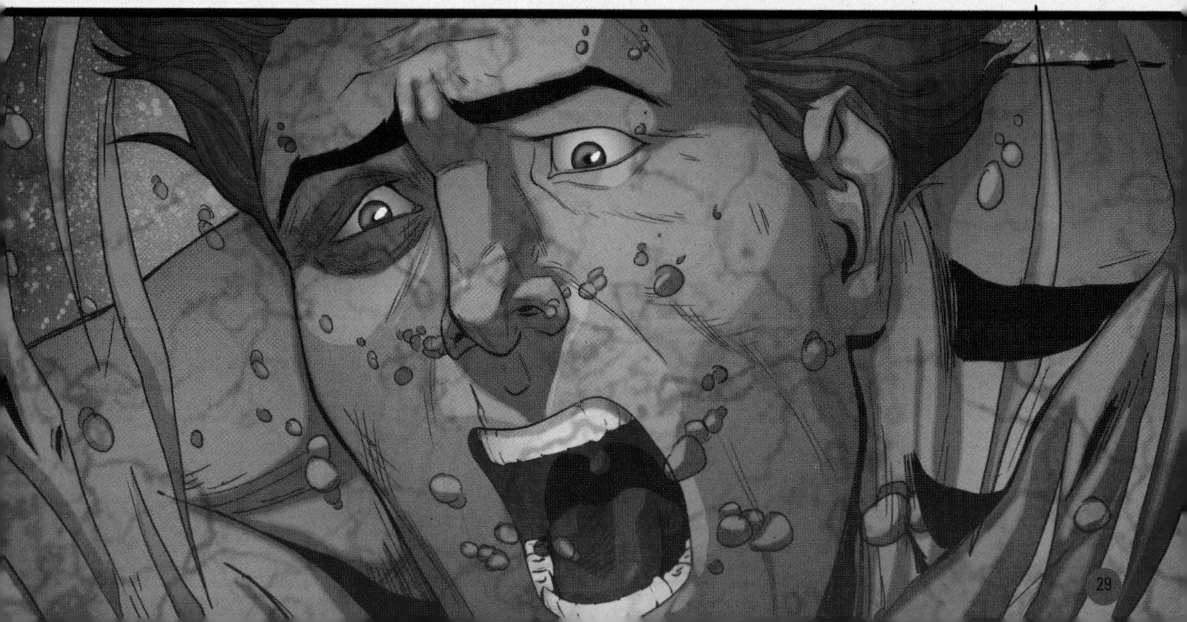

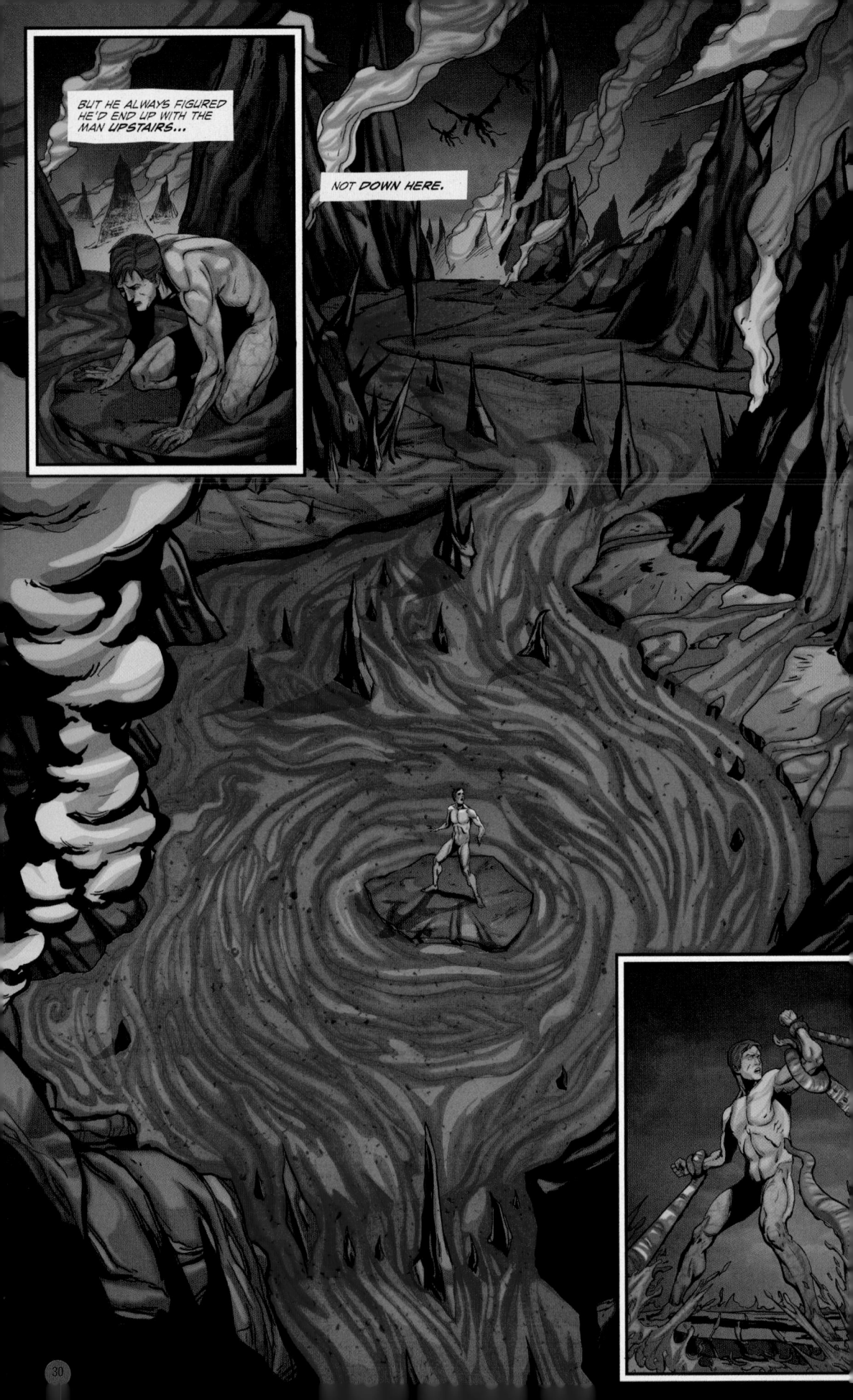

BUT HE ALWAYS FIGURED HE'D END UP WITH THE MAN *UPSTAIRS*...

NOT *DOWN HERE.*

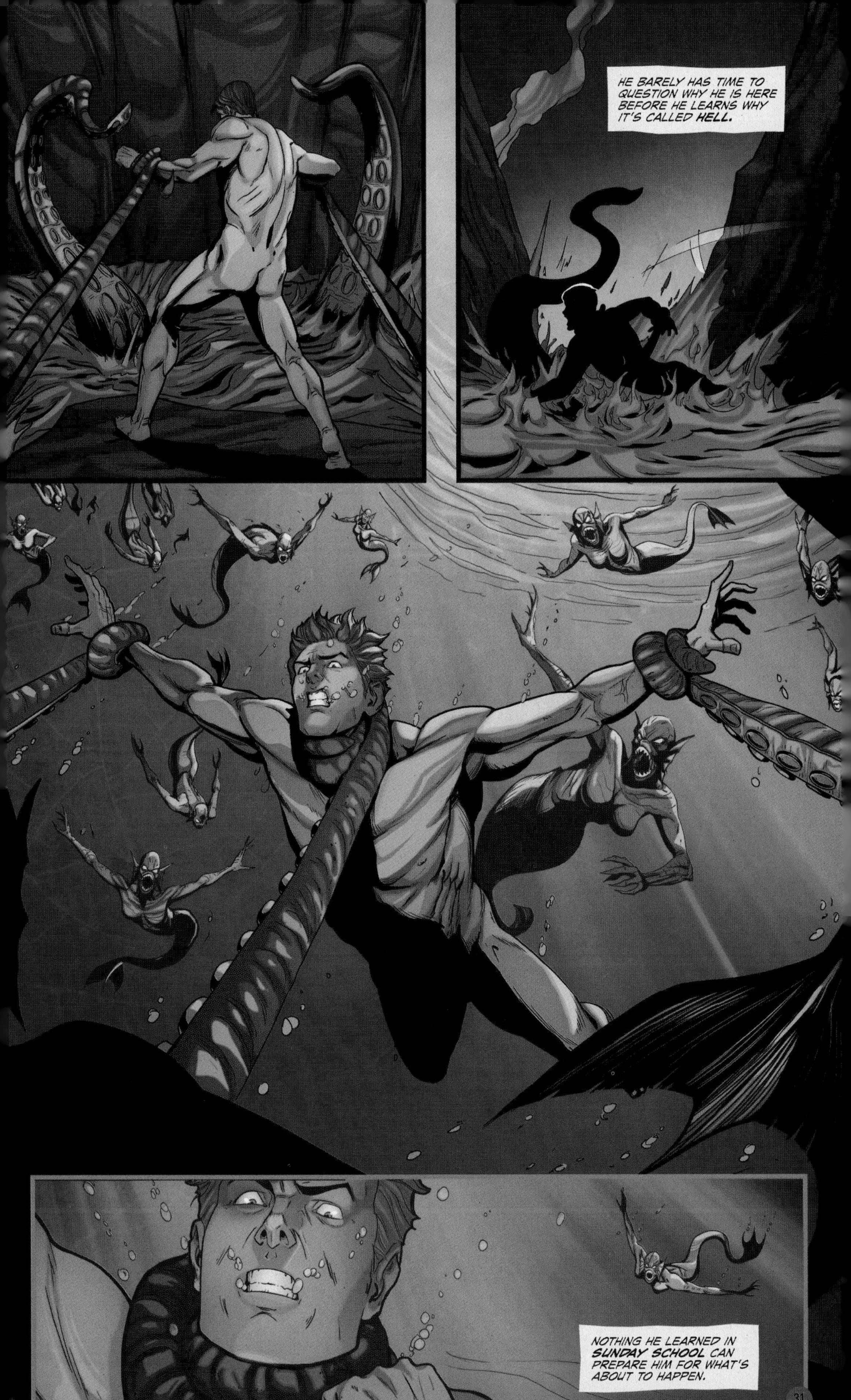
HE BARELY HAS TIME TO QUESTION WHY HE IS HERE BEFORE HE LEARNS WHY IT'S CALLED HELL.
NOTHING HE LEARNED IN SUNDAY SCHOOL CAN PREPARE HIM FOR WHAT'S ABOUT TO HAPPEN.

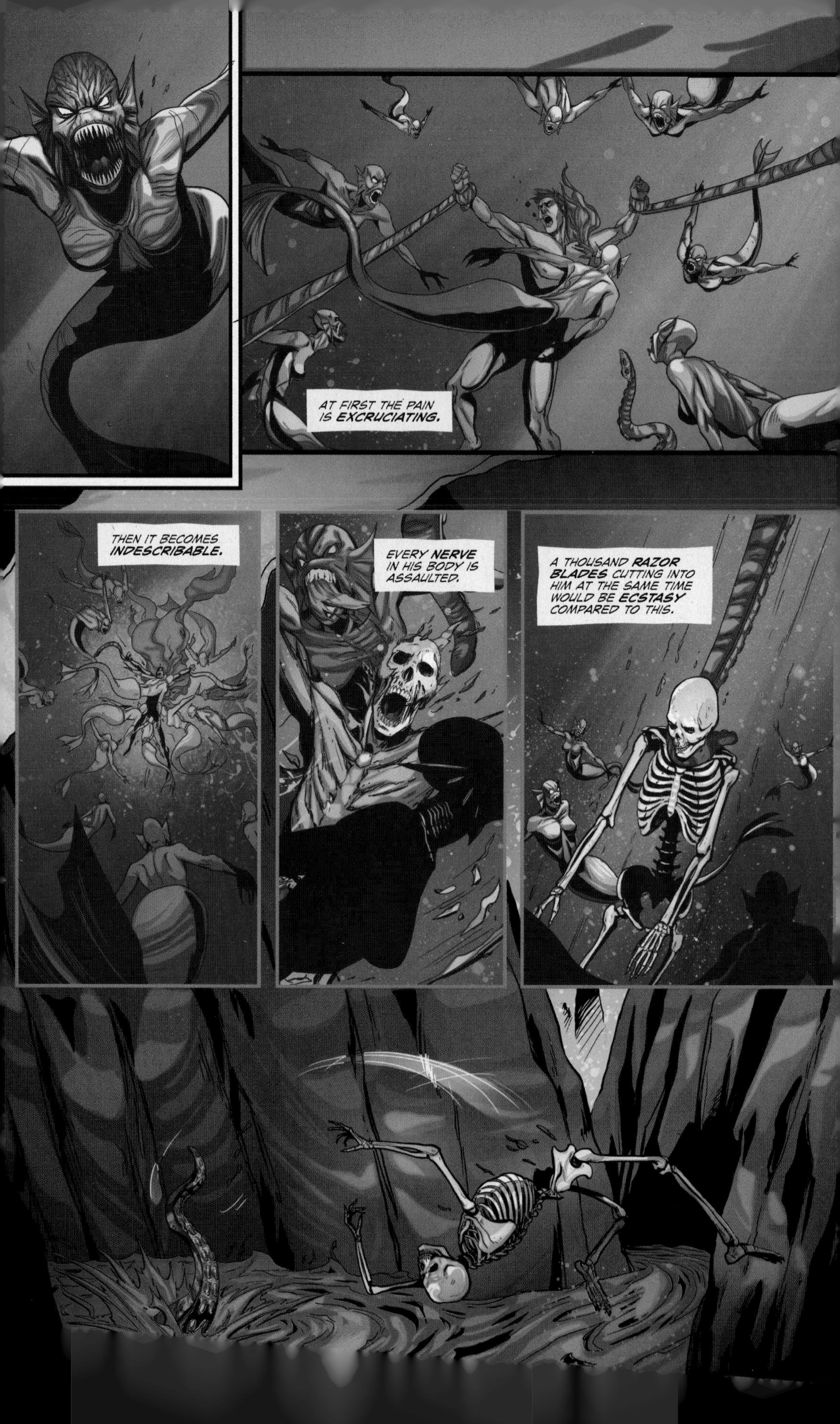
AT FIRST THE PAIN IS EXCRUCIATING.
THEN IT BECOMES INDESCRIBABLE.
EVERY NERVE IN HIS BODY IS ASSAULTED.
A THOUSAND RAZOR BLADES CUTTING INTO HIM AT THE SAME TIME WOULD BE ECSTASY COMPARED TO THIS.

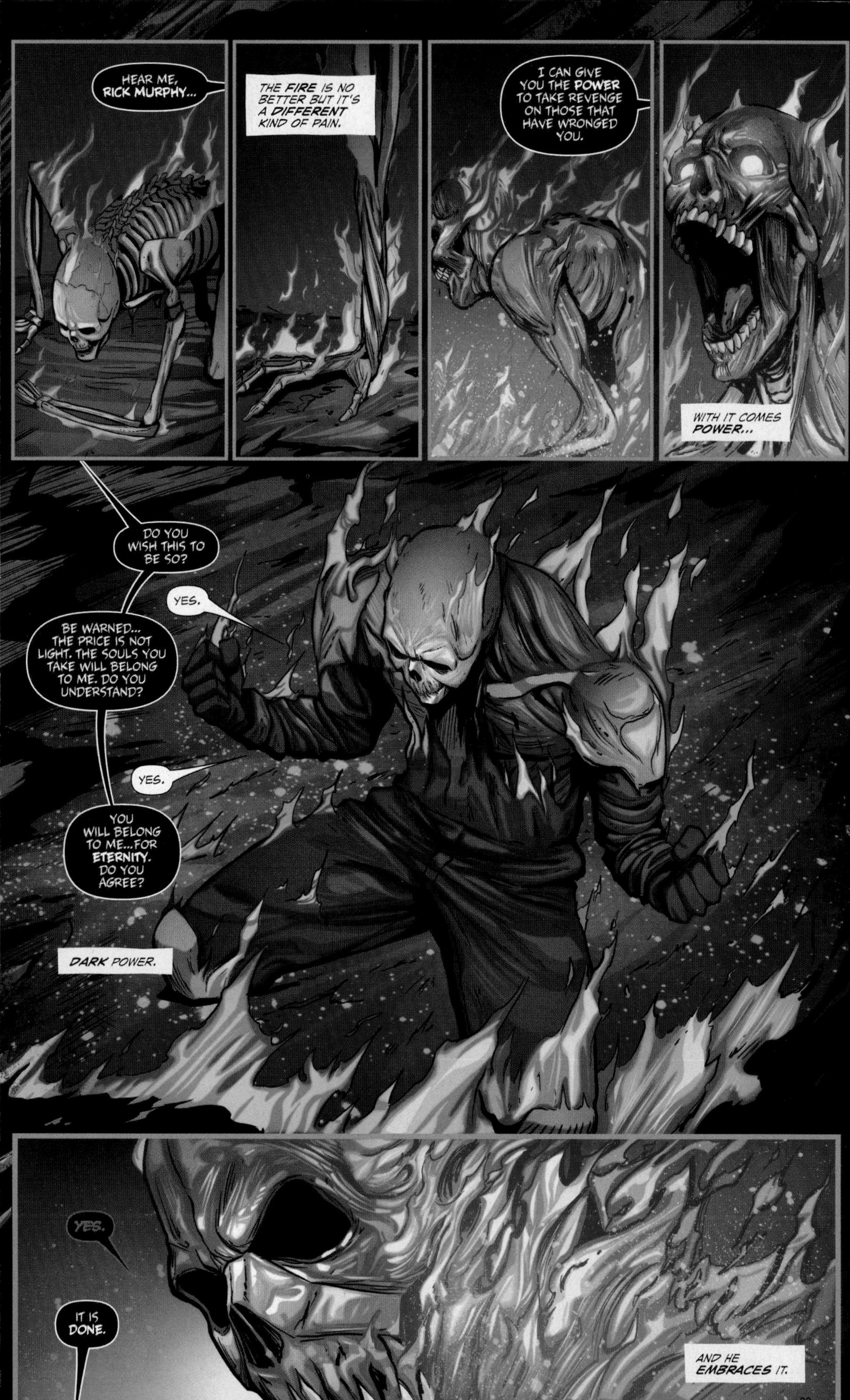

HEAR ME, RICK MURPHY...
THE FIRE IS NO BETTER BUT IT'S A DIFFERENT KIND OF PAIN.
I CAN GIVE YOU THE POWER TO TAKE REVENGE ON THOSE THAT HAVE WRONGED YOU.
WITH IT COMES POWER...
DO YOU WISH THIS TO BE SO?
YES.
BE WARNED... THE PRICE IS NOT LIGHT. THE SOULS YOU TAKE WILL BELONG TO ME. DO YOU UNDERSTAND?
YES.
YOU WILL BELONG TO ME...FOR ETERNITY. DO YOU AGREE?
DARK POWER.
YES.
IT IS DONE.
AND HE EMBRACES IT.

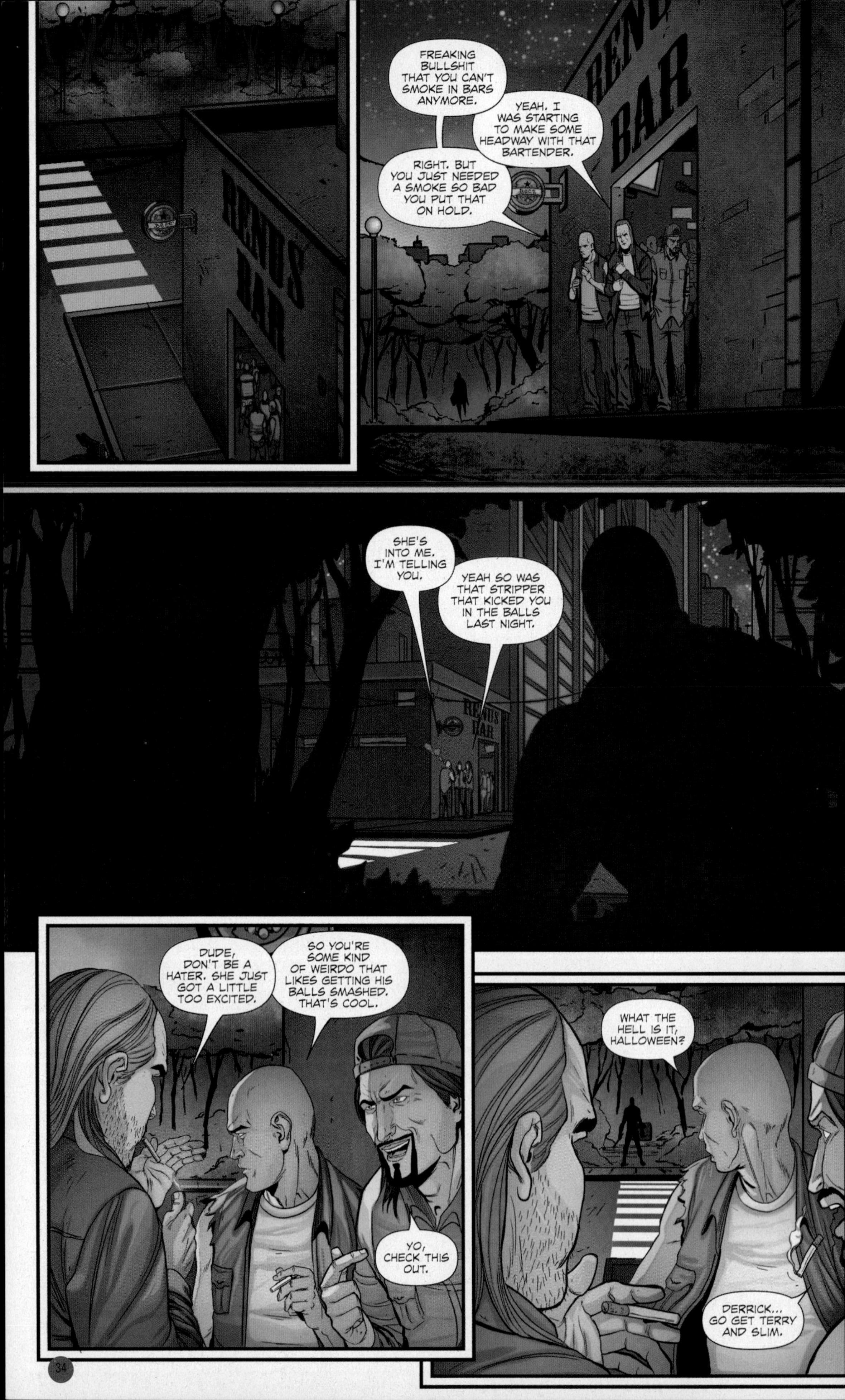
FREAKING BULLSHIT THAT YOU CAN'T SMOKE IN BARS ANYMORE.
YEAH. I WAS STARTING TO MAKE SOME HEADWAY WITH THAT BARTENDER.
RIGHT. BUT YOU JUST NEEDED A SMOKE SO BAD YOU PUT THAT ON HOLD.
SHE'S INTO ME. I'M TELLING YOU.
YEAH SO WAS THAT STRIPPER THAT KICKED YOU IN THE BALLS LAST NIGHT.
DUDE, DON'T BE A HATER. SHE JUST GOT A LITTLE TOO EXCITED.
SO YOU'RE SOME KIND OF WEIRDO THAT LIKES GETTING HIS BALLS SMASHED. THAT'S COOL.
YO, CHECK THIS OUT.
WHAT THE HELL IS IT, HALLOWEEN?
DERRICK... GO GET TERRY AND SLIM.

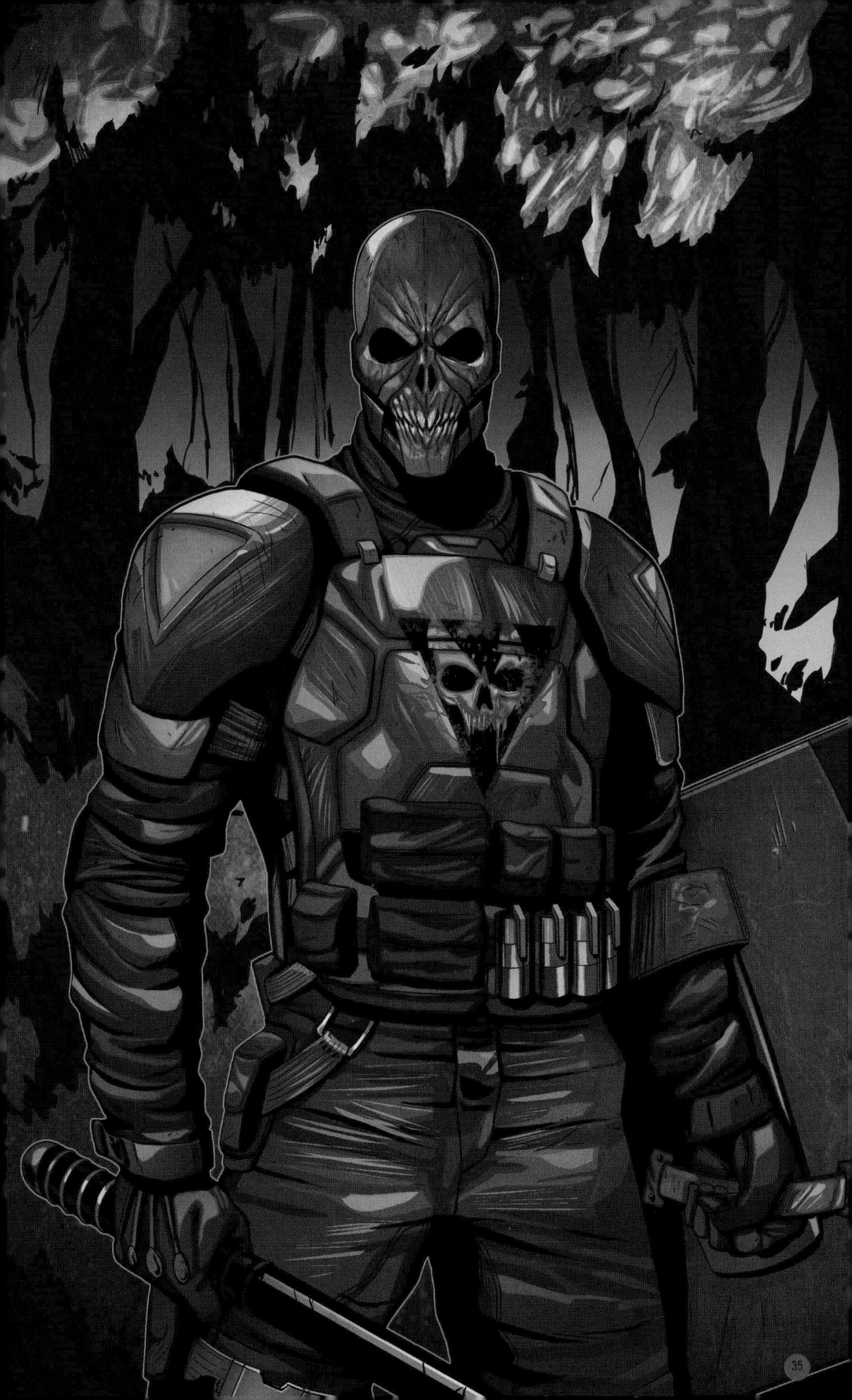

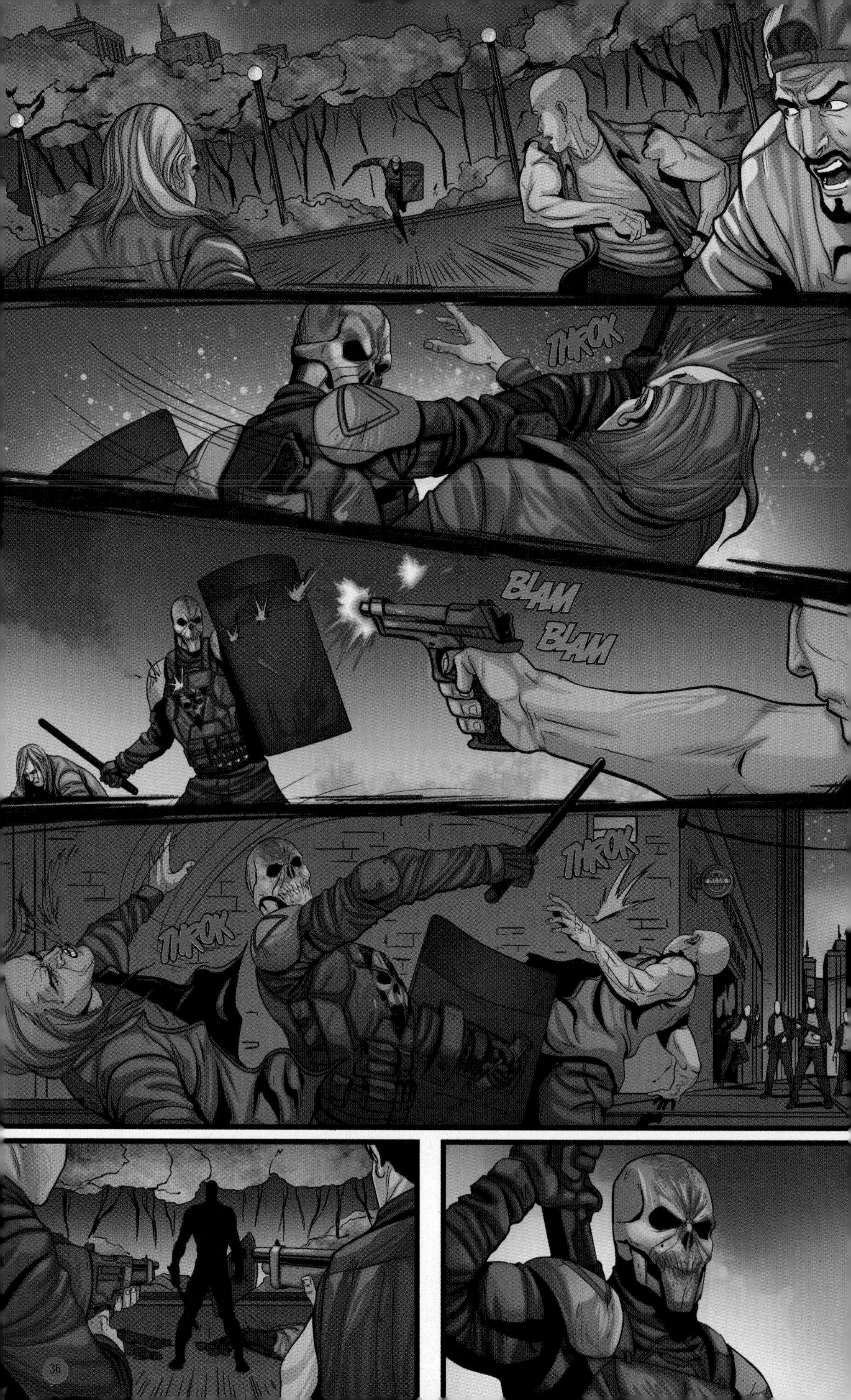
THROK
BLAM
BLAM
THROK
THROK

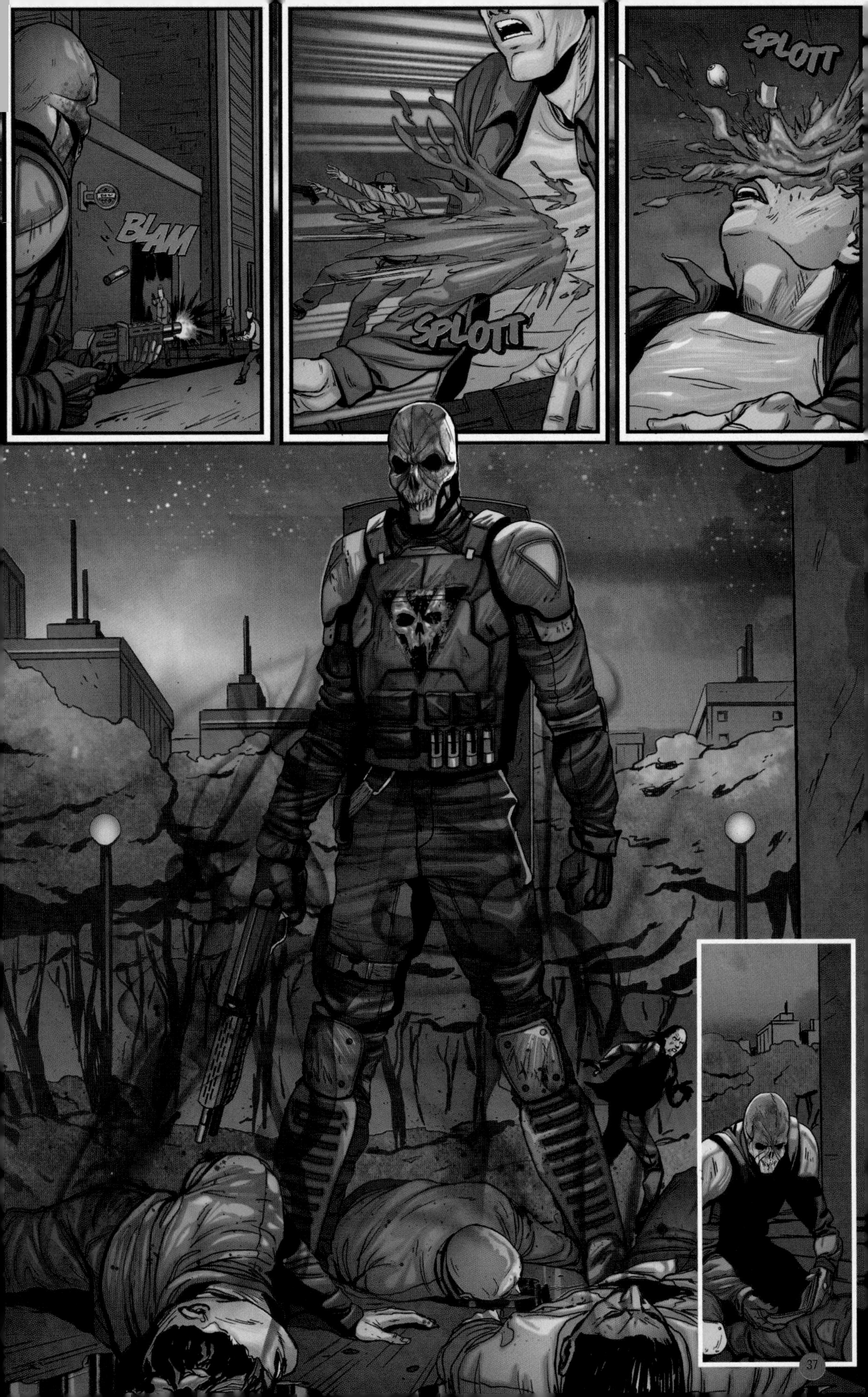
BLAM
SPLOTT
SPLOTT

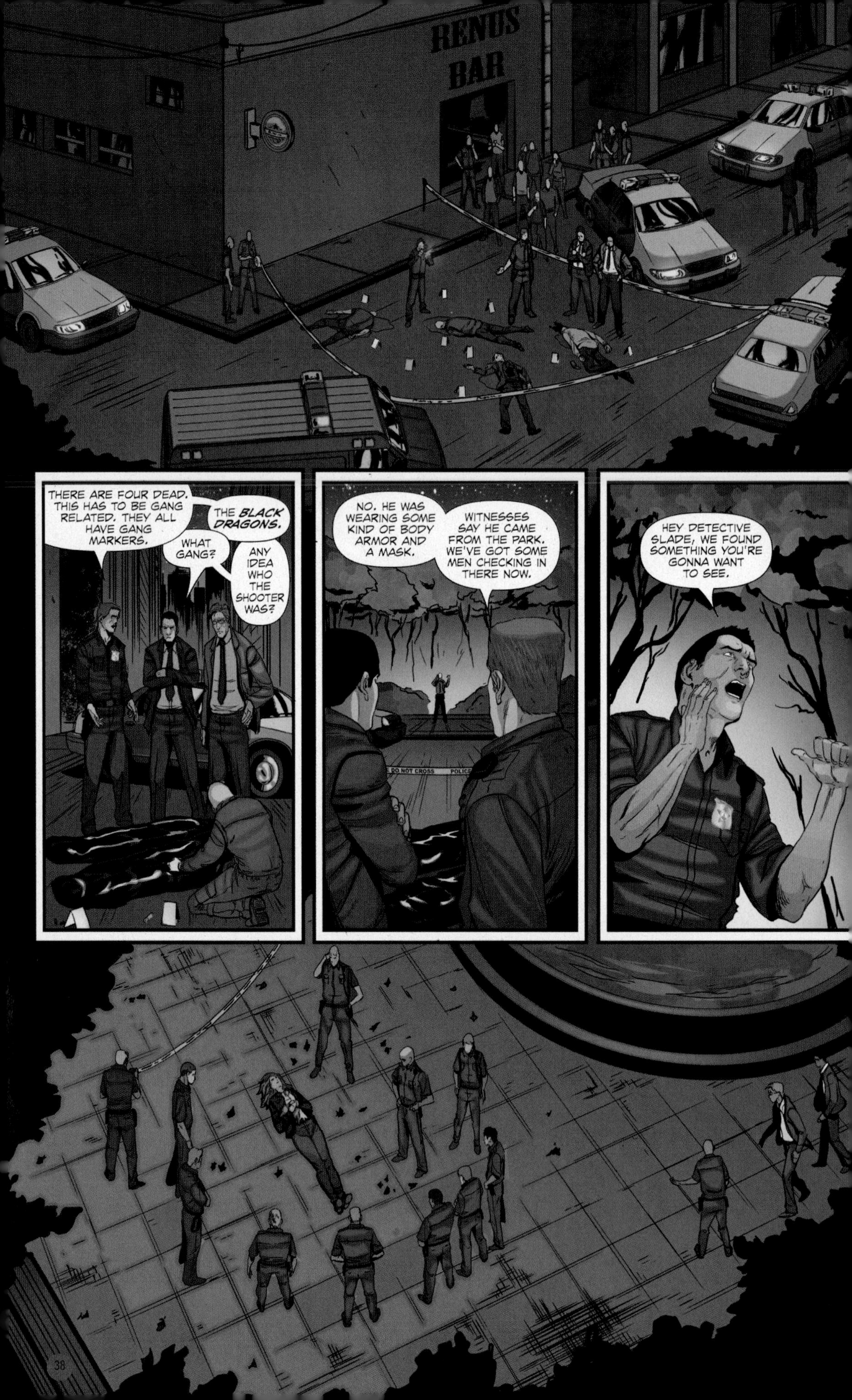
RENUS BAR
THERE ARE FOUR DEAD. THIS HAS TO BE GANG RELATED. THEY ALL HAVE GANG MARKERS.
WHAT GANG?
THE *BLACK DRAGONS.*
ANY IDEA WHO THE SHOOTER WAS?
NO. HE WAS WEARING SOME KIND OF BODY ARMOR AND A MASK.
WITNESSES SAY HE CAME FROM THE PARK. WE'VE GOT SOME MEN CHECKING IN THERE NOW.
DO NOT CROSS
POLICE
HEY DETECTIVE SLADE, WE FOUND SOMETHING YOU'RE GONNA WANT TO SEE.

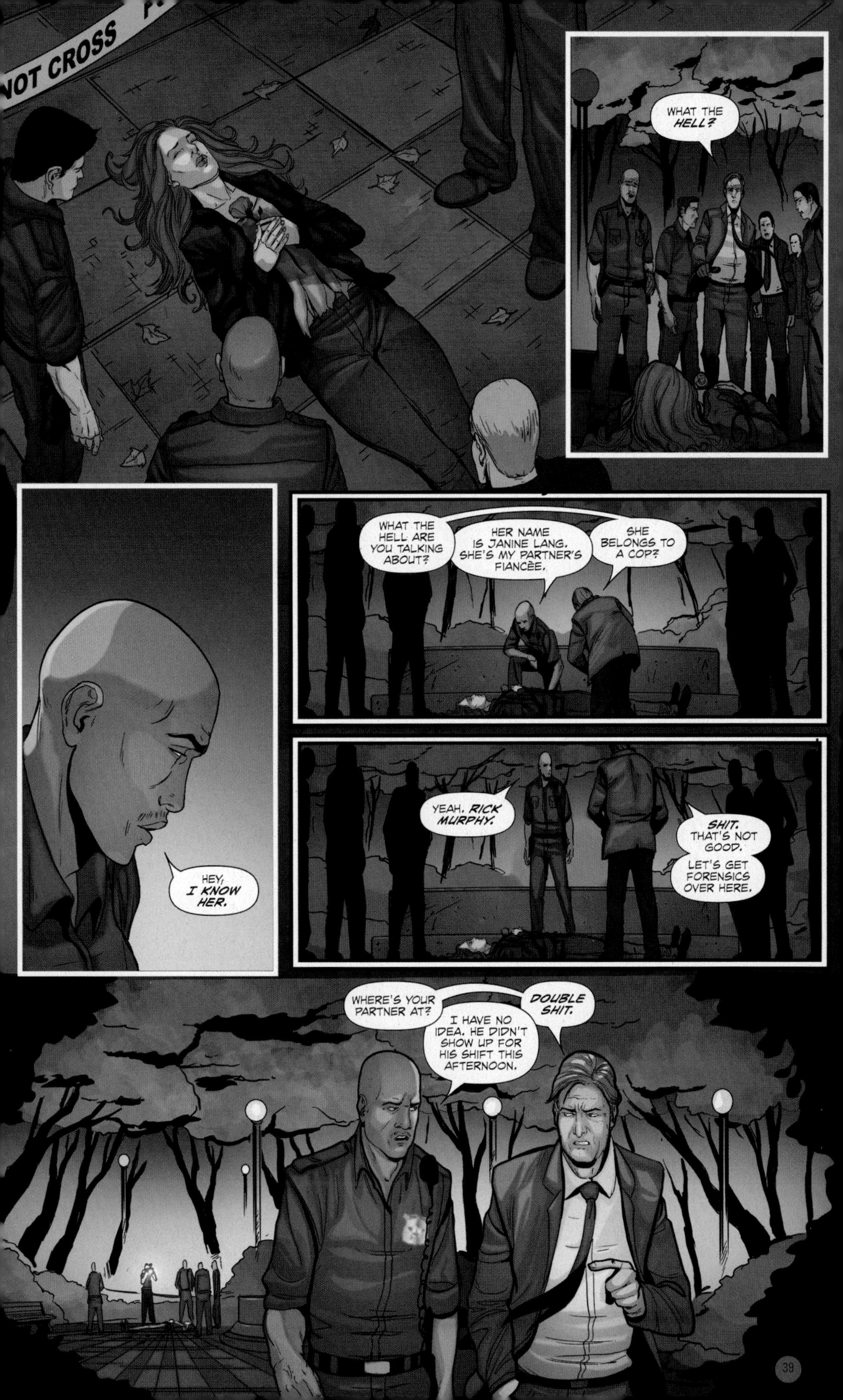
NOT CROSS
WHAT THE HELL?
HEY, I KNOW HER.
WHAT THE HELL ARE YOU TALKING ABOUT?
HER NAME IS JANINE LANG. SHE'S MY PARTNER'S FIANCÉE.
SHE BELONGS TO A COP?
YEAH. RICK MURPHY.
SHIT. THAT'S NOT GOOD.
LET'S GET FORENSICS OVER HERE.
WHERE'S YOUR PARTNER AT?
I HAVE NO IDEA. HE DIDN'T SHOW UP FOR HIS SHIFT THIS AFTERNOON.
DOUBLE SHIT.

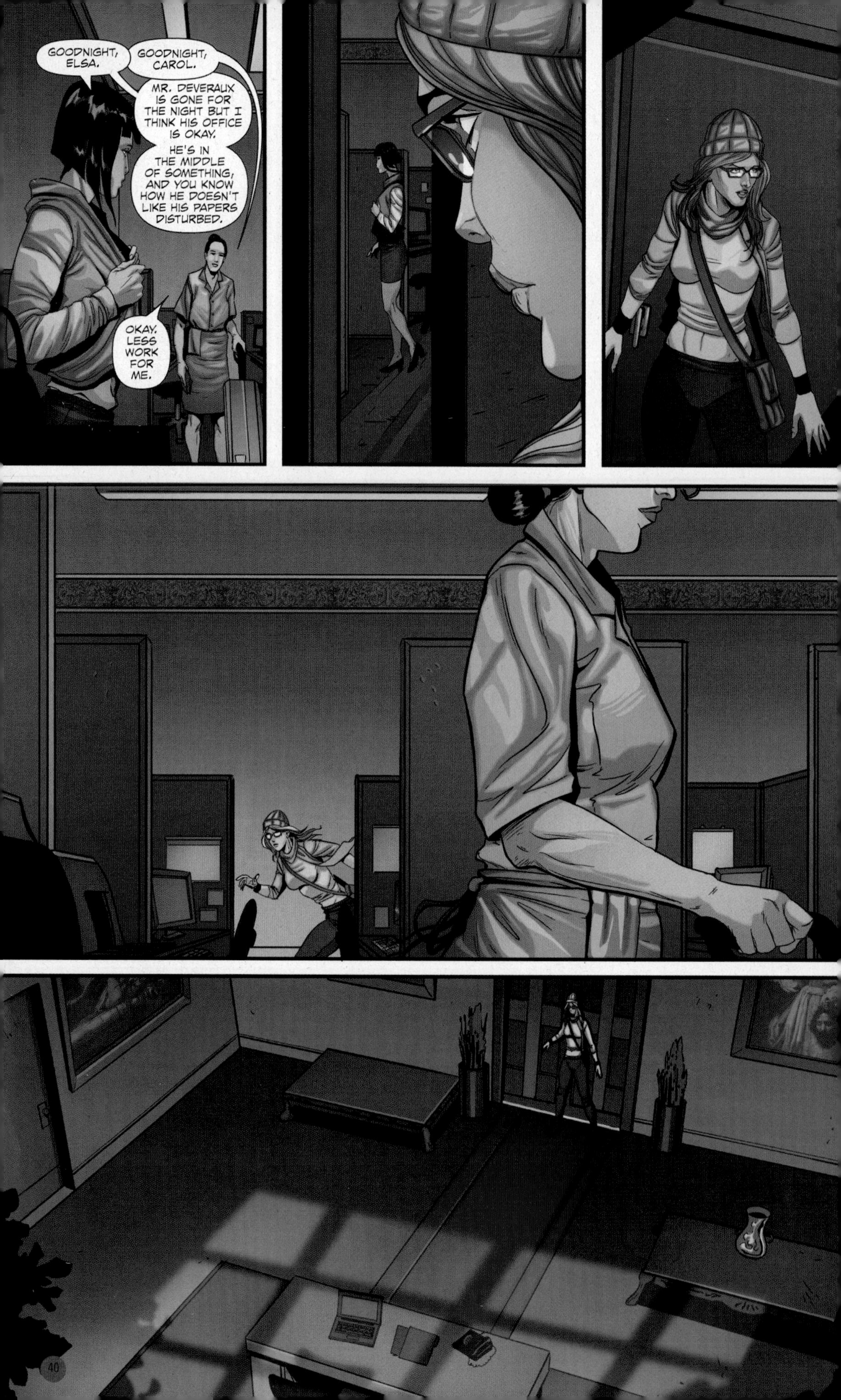
GOODNIGHT, ELSA.
GOODNIGHT, CAROL.
MR. DEVERAUX IS GONE FOR THE NIGHT BUT I THINK HIS OFFICE IS OKAY.
HE'S IN THE MIDDLE OF SOMETHING, AND YOU KNOW HOW HE DOESN'T LIKE HIS PAPERS DISTURBED.
OKAY. LESS WORK FOR ME.

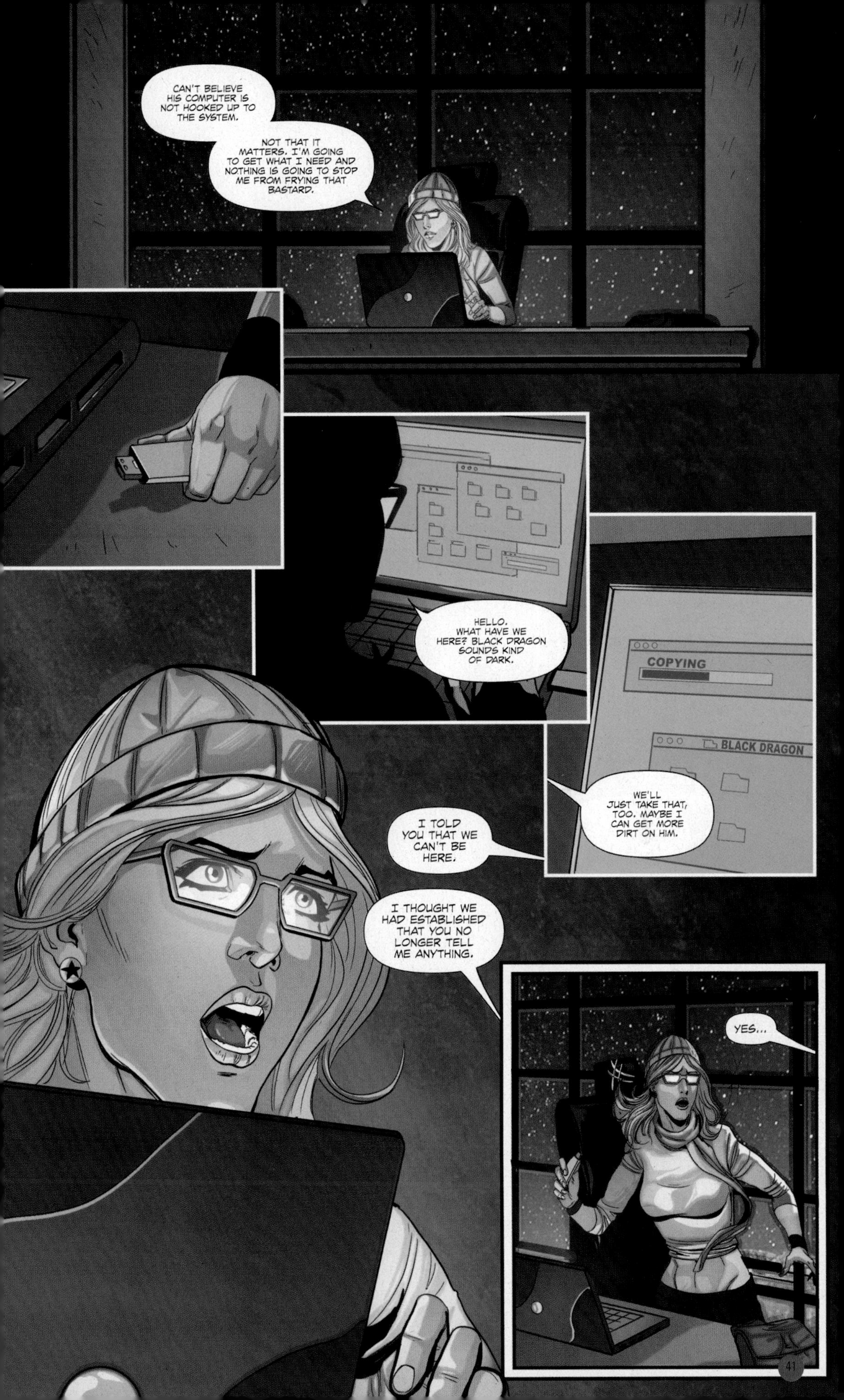
CAN'T BELIEVE HIS COMPUTER IS NOT HOOKED UP TO THE SYSTEM.
NOT THAT IT MATTERS. I'M GOING TO GET WHAT I NEED AND NOTHING IS GOING TO STOP ME FROM FRYING THAT BASTARD.
HELLO. WHAT HAVE WE HERE? BLACK DRAGON SOUNDS KIND OF DARK.
COPYING
BLACK DRAGON
WE'LL JUST TAKE THAT, TOO. MAYBE I CAN GET MORE DIRT ON HIM.
I TOLD YOU THAT WE CAN'T BE HERE.
I THOUGHT WE HAD ESTABLISHED THAT YOU NO LONGER TELL ME ANYTHING.
YES...

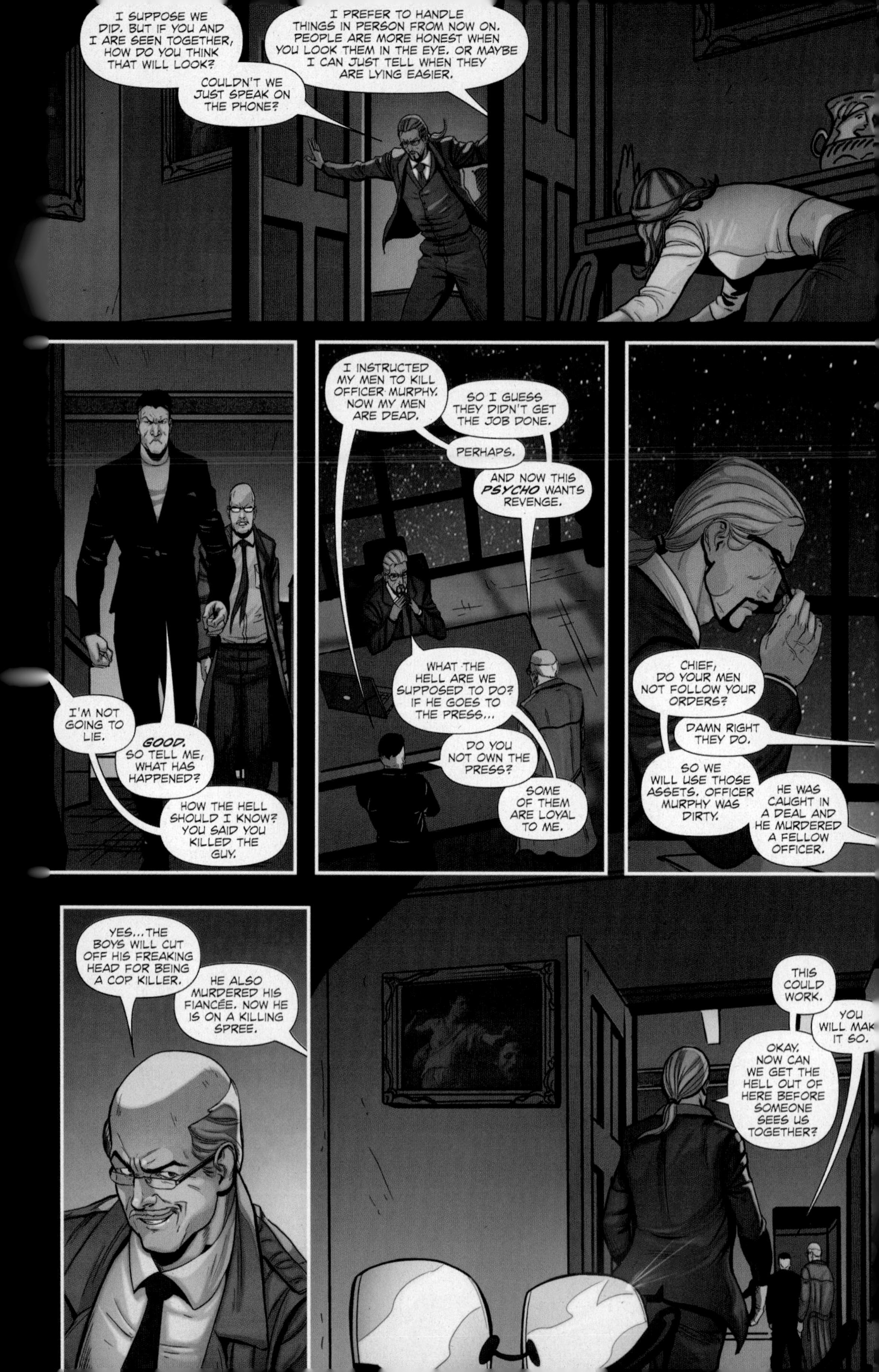
I SUPPOSE WE DID. BUT IF YOU AND I ARE SEEN TOGETHER, HOW DO YOU THINK THAT WILL LOOK?
COULDN'T WE JUST SPEAK ON THE PHONE?
I PREFER TO HANDLE THINGS IN PERSON FROM NOW ON. PEOPLE ARE MORE HONEST WHEN YOU LOOK THEM IN THE EYE. OR MAYBE I CAN JUST TELL WHEN THEY ARE LYING EASIER.
I'M NOT GOING TO LIE.
GOOD. SO TELL ME, WHAT HAS HAPPENED?
HOW THE HELL SHOULD I KNOW? YOU SAID YOU KILLED THE GUY.
I INSTRUCTED MY MEN TO KILL OFFICER MURPHY. NOW MY MEN ARE DEAD.
SO I GUESS THEY DIDN'T GET THE JOB DONE.
PERHAPS.
AND NOW THIS PSYCHO WANTS REVENGE.
WHAT THE HELL ARE WE SUPPOSED TO DO? IF HE GOES TO THE PRESS...
DO YOU NOT OWN THE PRESS?
SOME OF THEM ARE LOYAL TO ME.
CHIEF, DO YOUR MEN NOT FOLLOW YOUR ORDERS?
DAMN RIGHT THEY DO.
SO WE WILL USE THOSE ASSETS. OFFICER MURPHY WAS DIRTY.
HE WAS CAUGHT IN A DEAL AND HE MURDERED A FELLOW OFFICER.
YES...THE BOYS WILL CUT OFF HIS FREAKING HEAD FOR BEING A COP KILLER.
HE ALSO MURDERED HIS FIANCÉE. NOW HE IS ON A KILLING SPREE.
THIS COULD WORK.
YOU WILL MAK IT SO.
OKAY. NOW CAN WE GET THE HELL OUT OF HERE BEFORE SOMEONE SEES US TOGETHER?

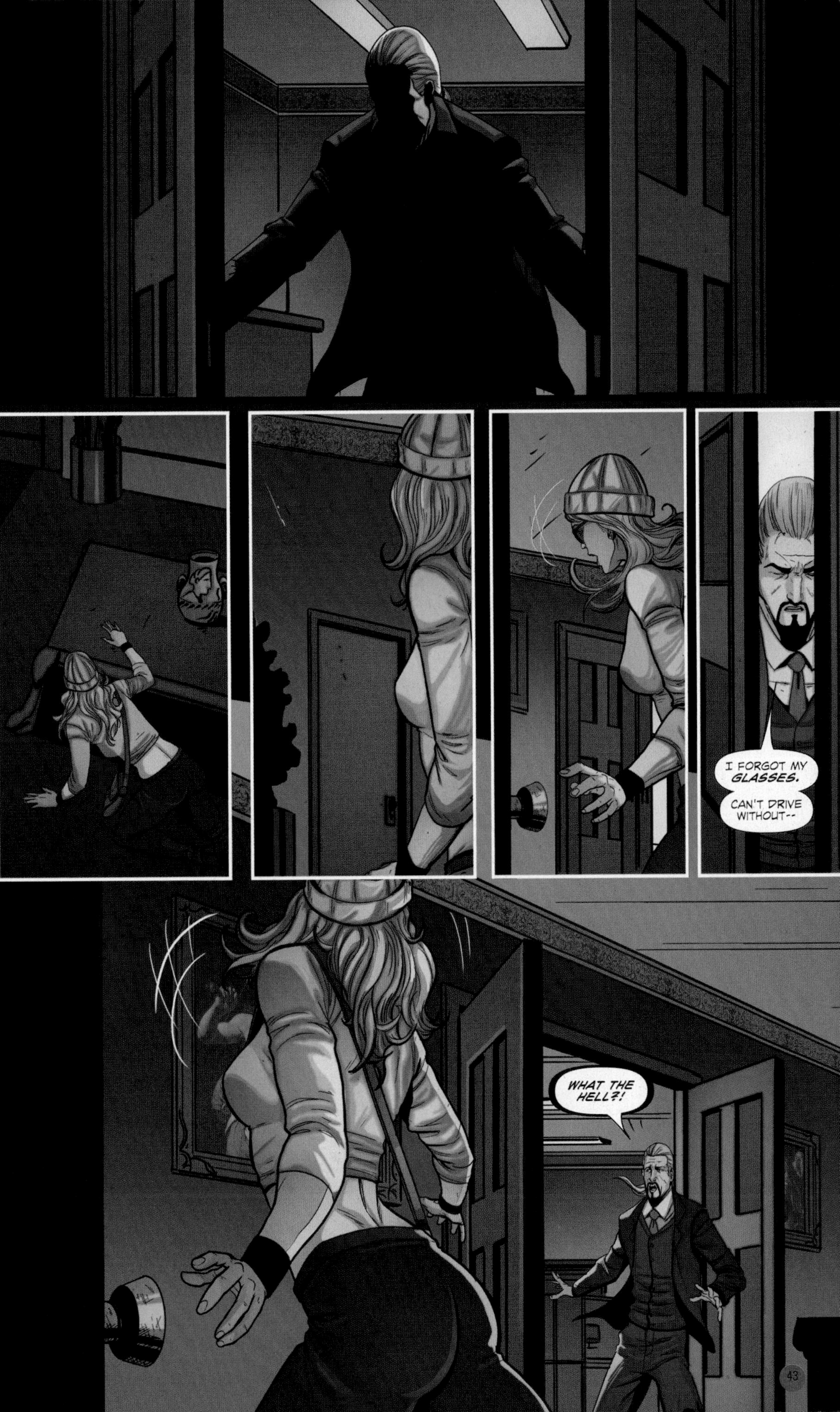
I FORGOT MY GLASSES.
CAN'T DRIVE WITHOUT--
WHAT THE HELL?!

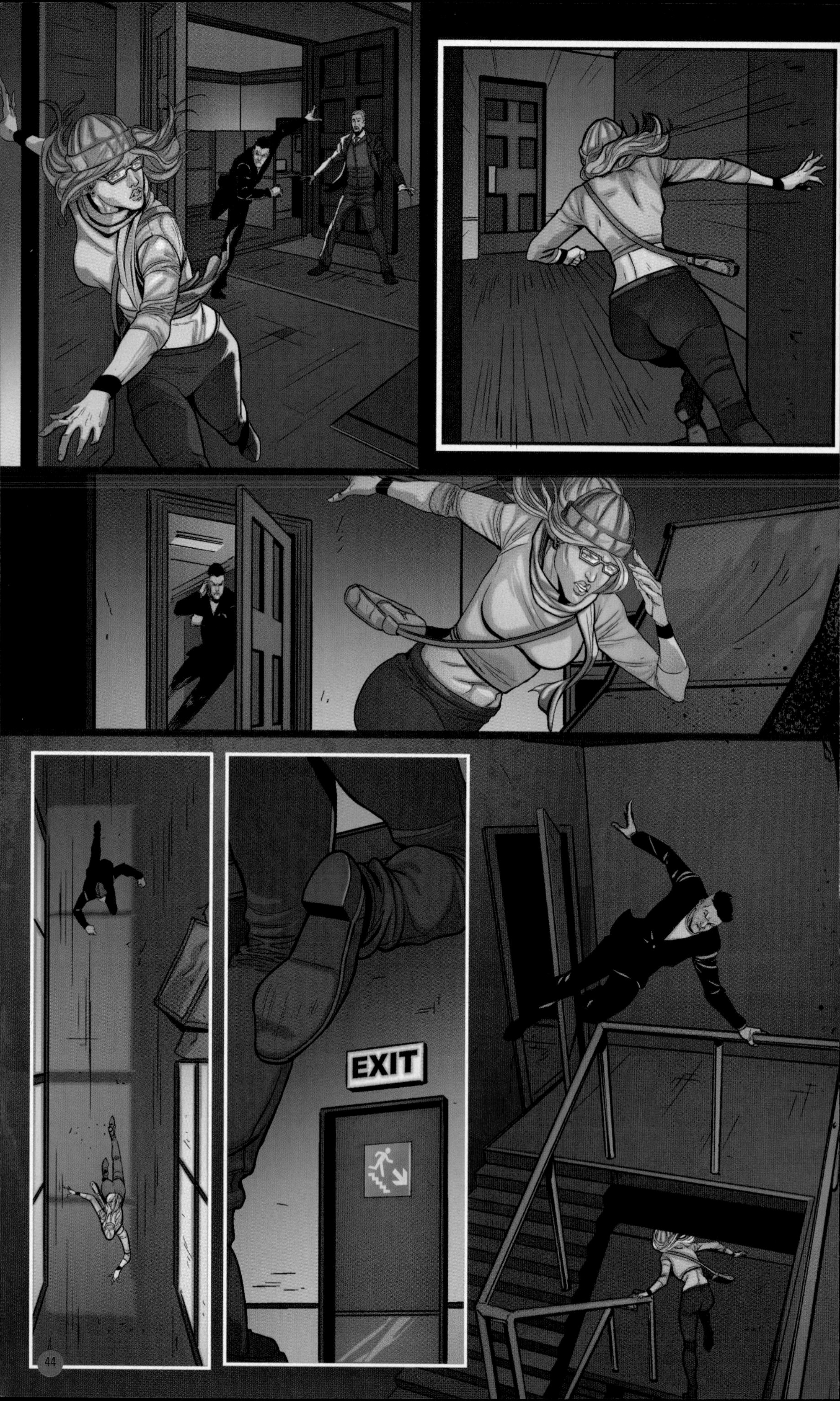

EXIT

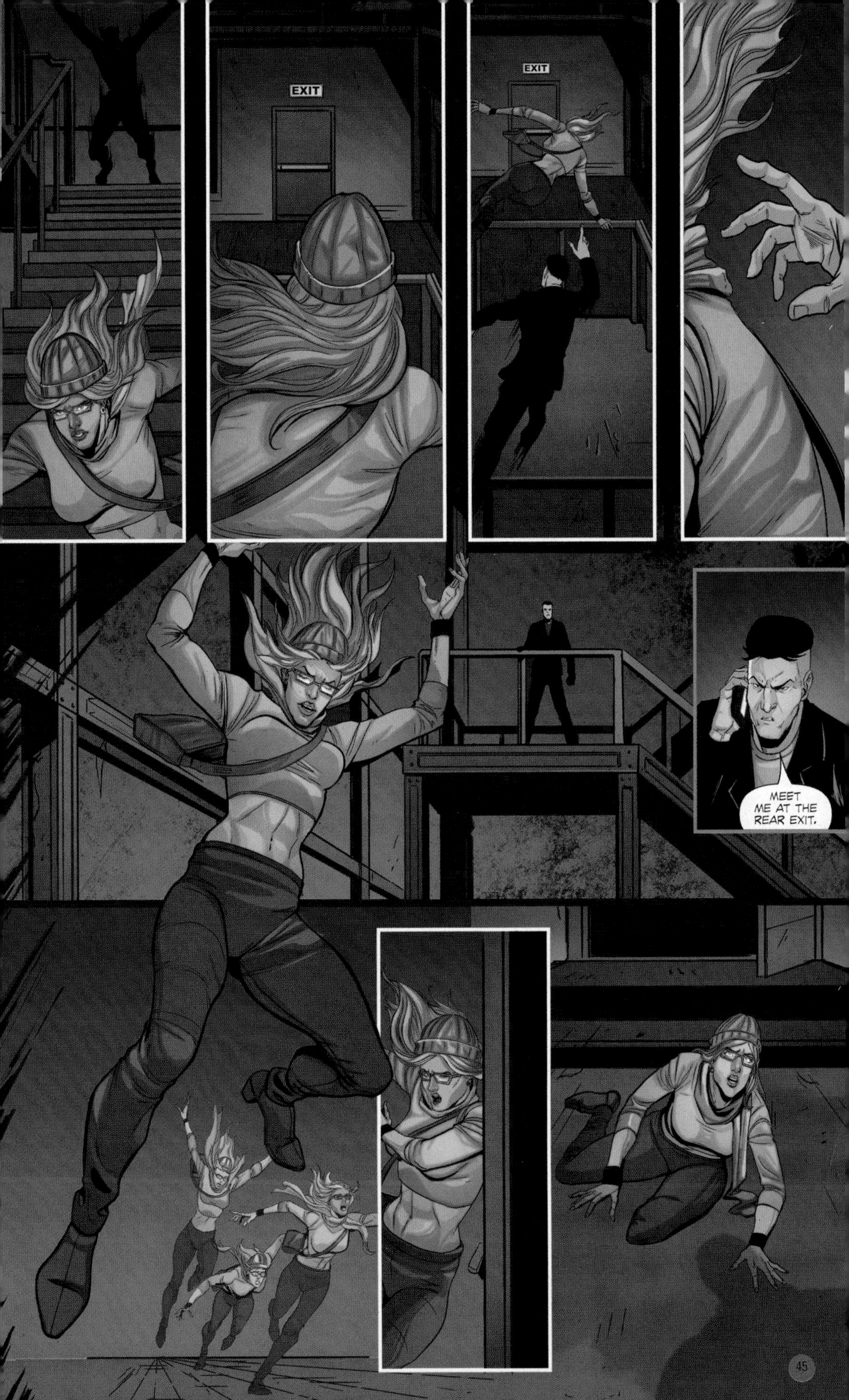
EXIT
EXIT
MEET ME AT THE REAR EXIT.

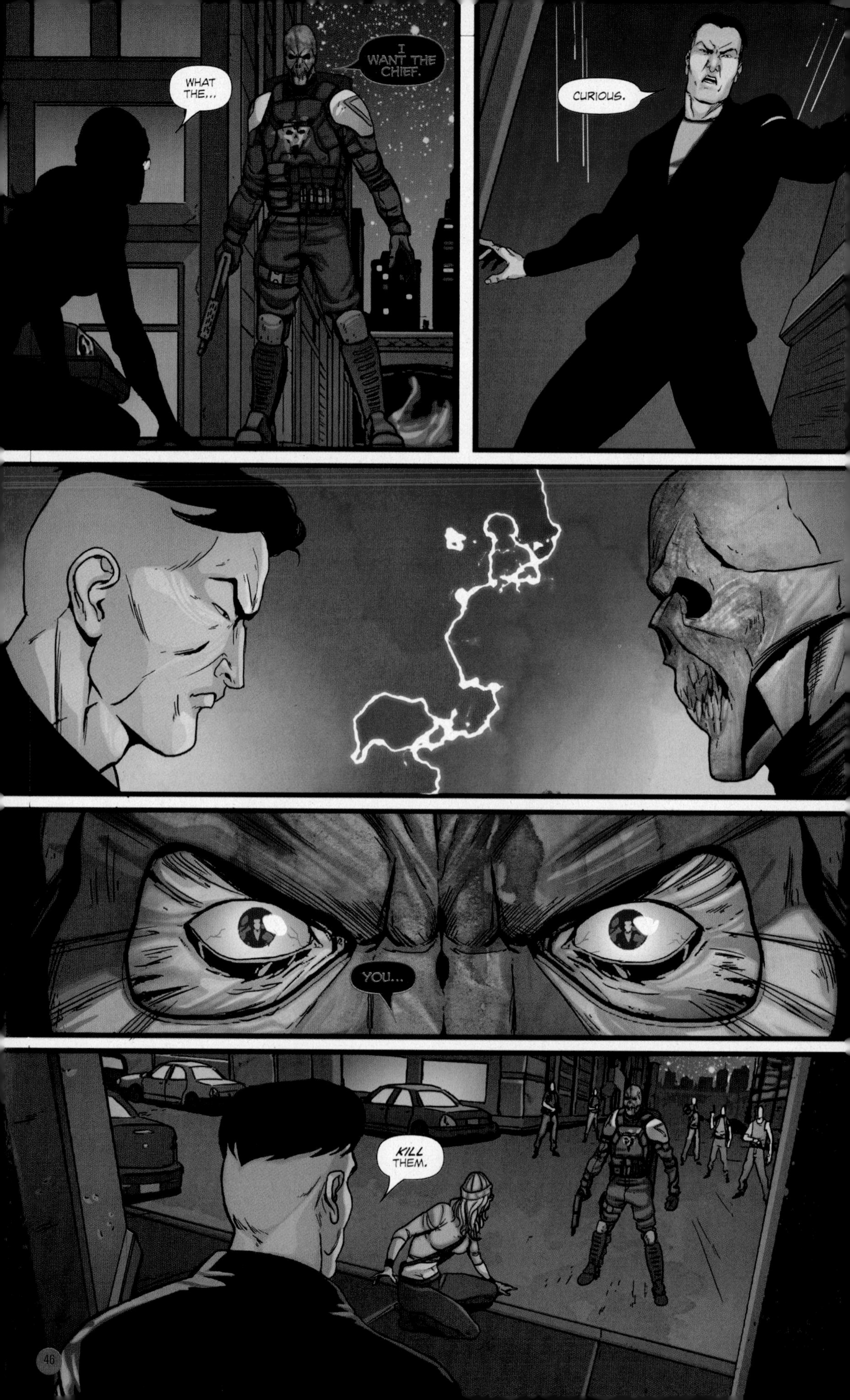
I WANT THE CHIEF.
WHAT THE...
CURIOUS.
YOU...
KILL THEM.

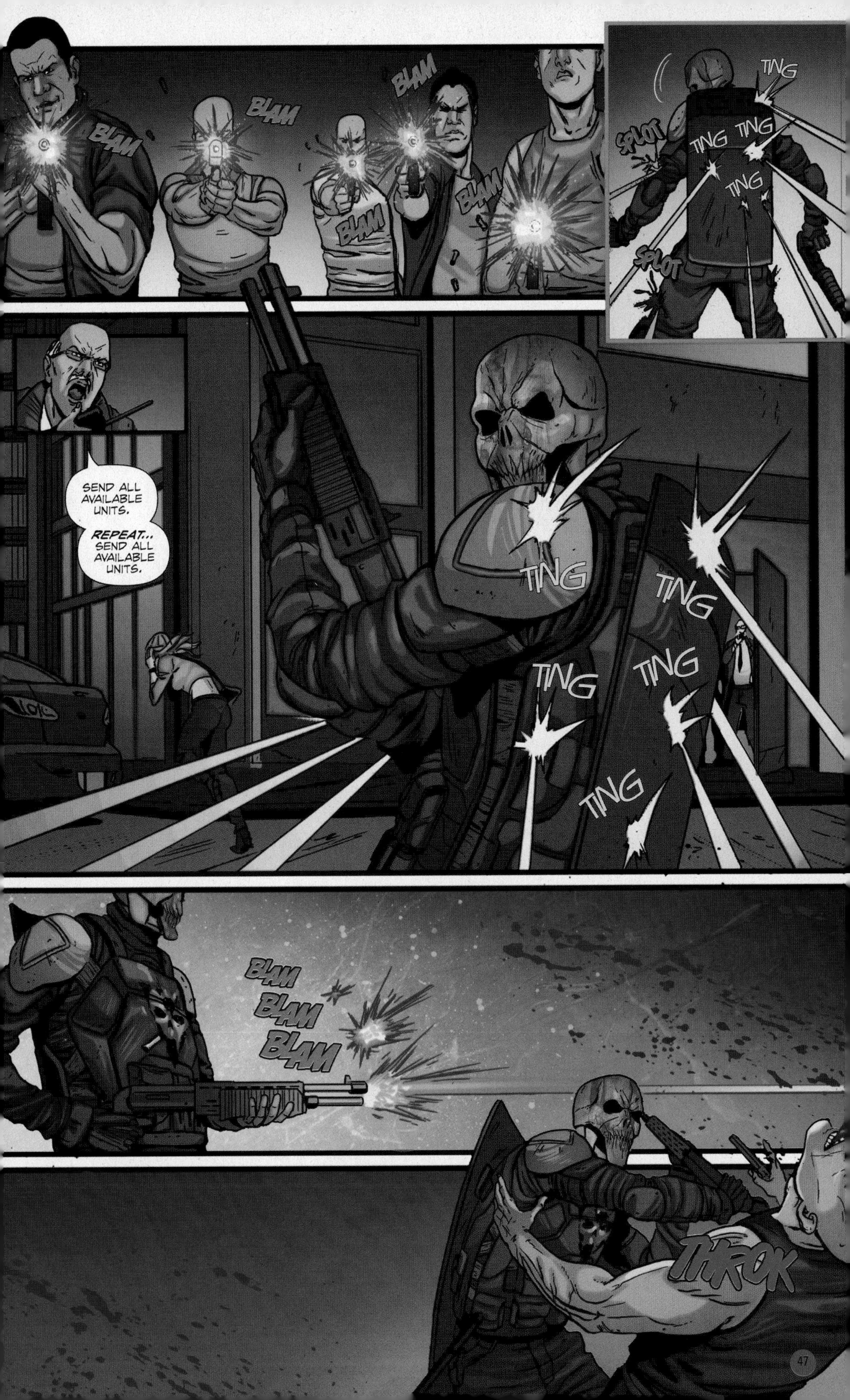
BLAM
BLAM
BLAM
BLAM
BLAM
BLAM
TING
SPLOT
TING TING
TING
SPLOT
SEND ALL AVAILABLE UNITS.
REPEAT... SEND ALL AVAILABLE UNITS.
TING
TING
TING
TING
TING
BLAM
BLAM
BLAM
THROK

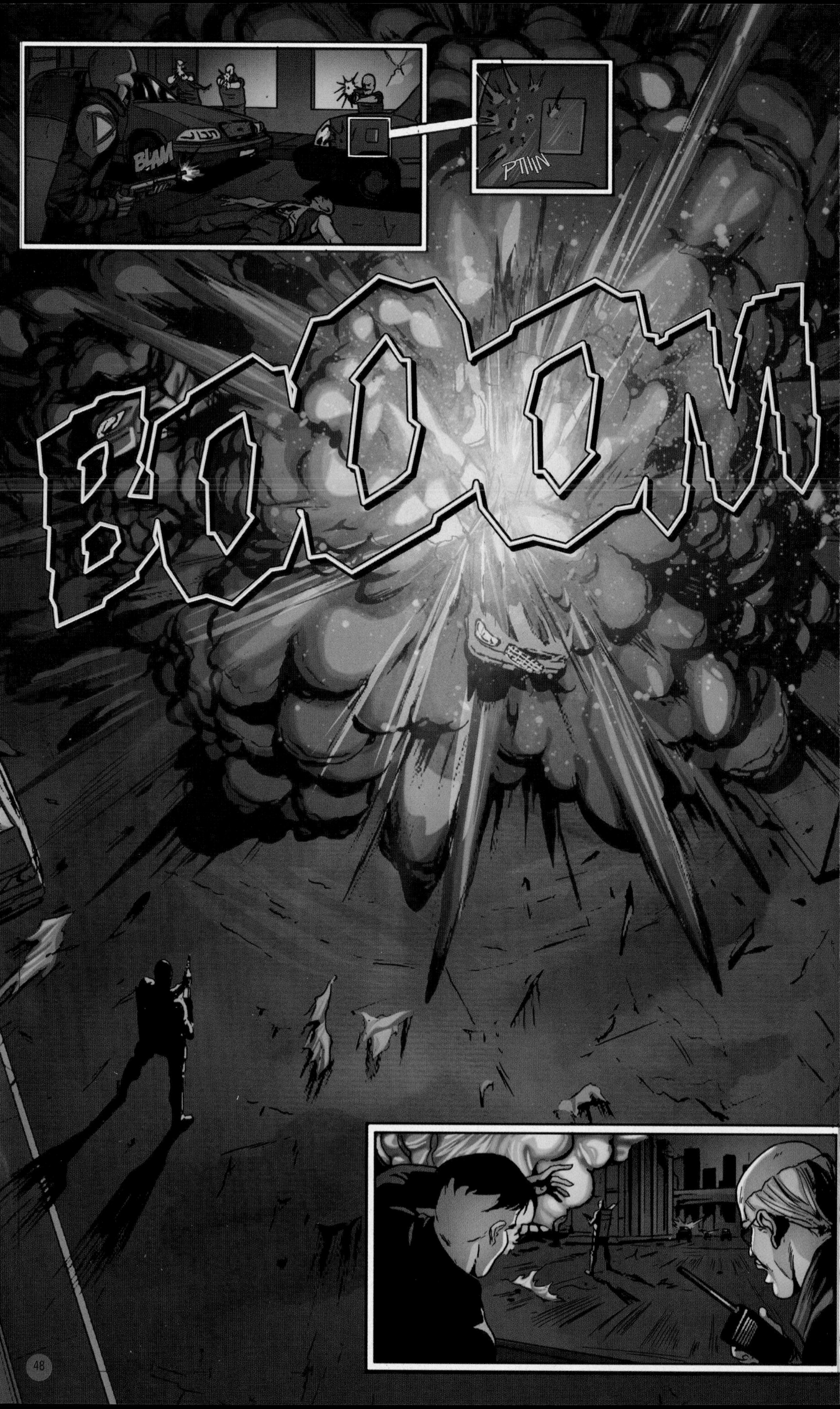
BLAM
PTIIIN
BOOOM

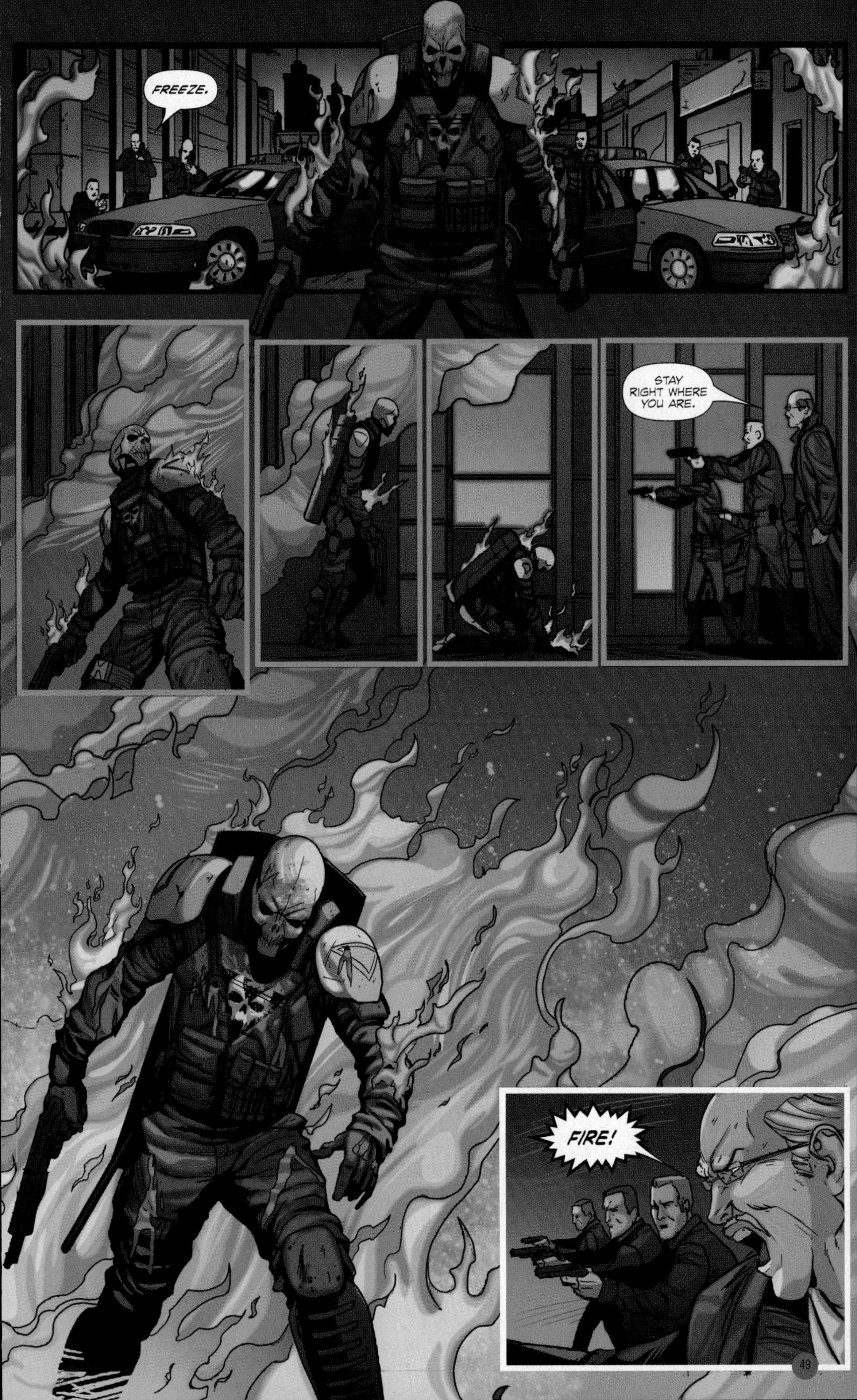
FREEZE.
STAY RIGHT WHERE YOU ARE.
FIRE!

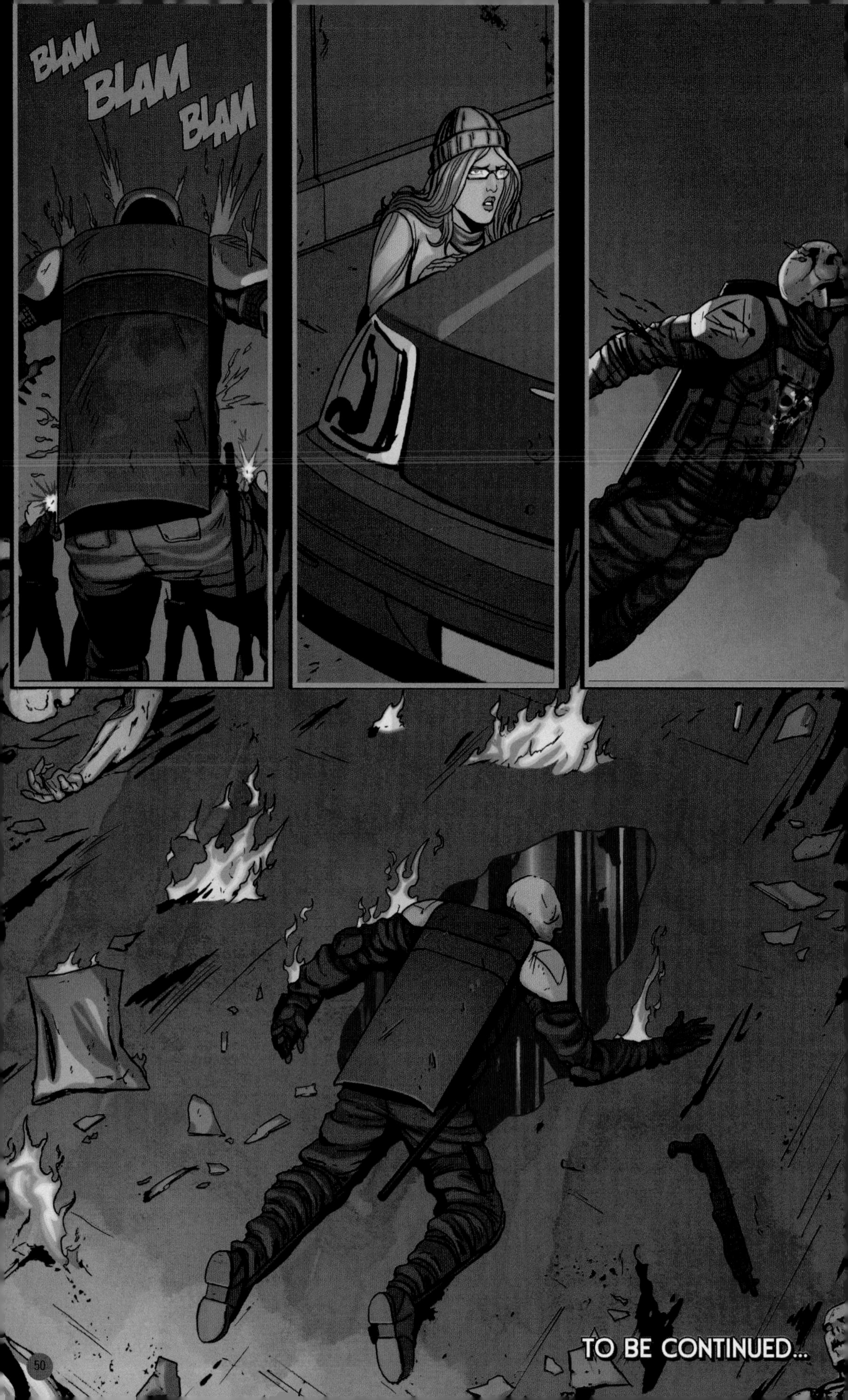
BLAM
BLAM
BLAM
TO BE CONTINUED...

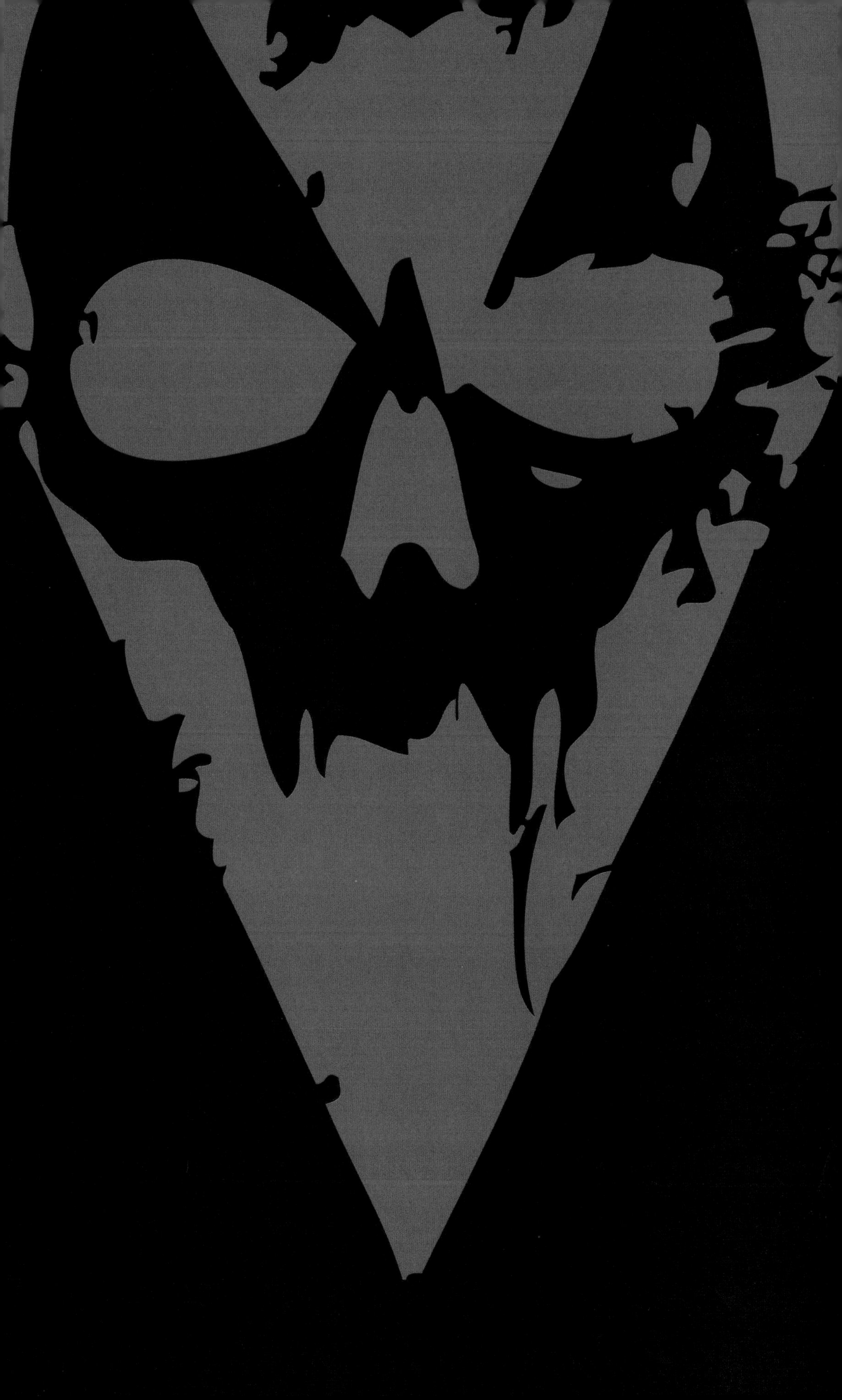

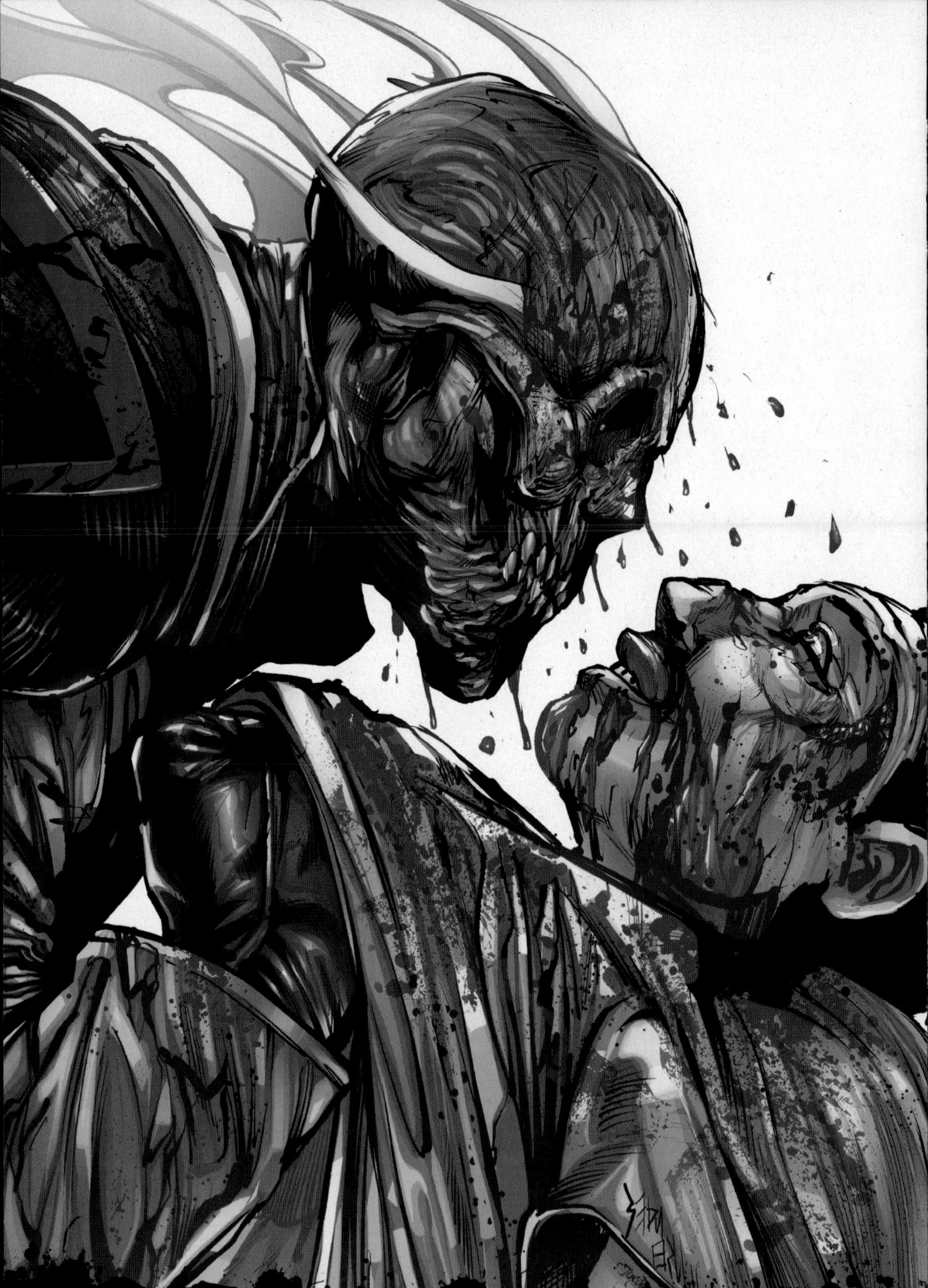

CHAPTER THREE

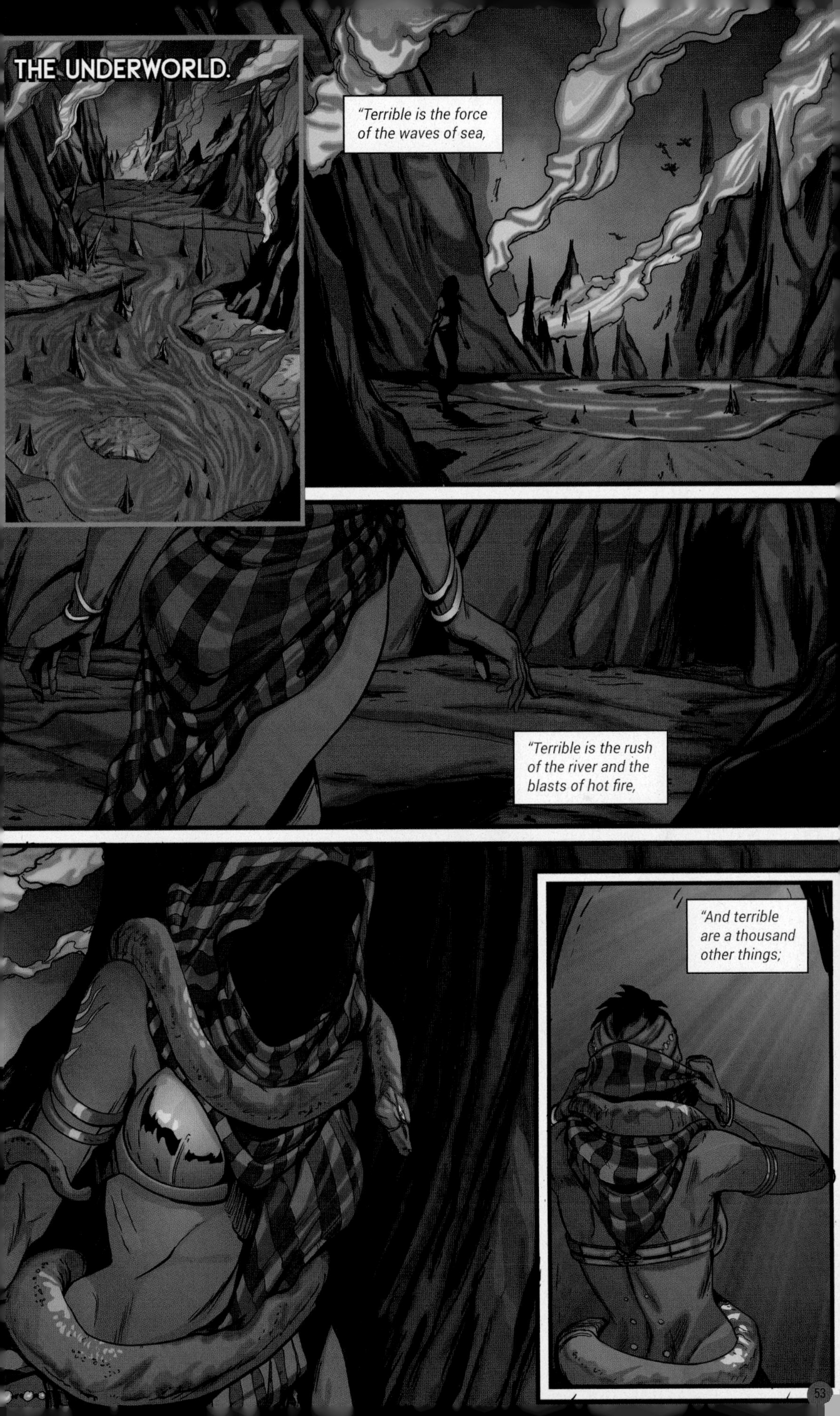
THE UNDERWORLD.
"Terrible is the force of the waves of sea,
"Terrible is the rush of the river and the blasts of hot fire,
"And terrible are a thousand other things;

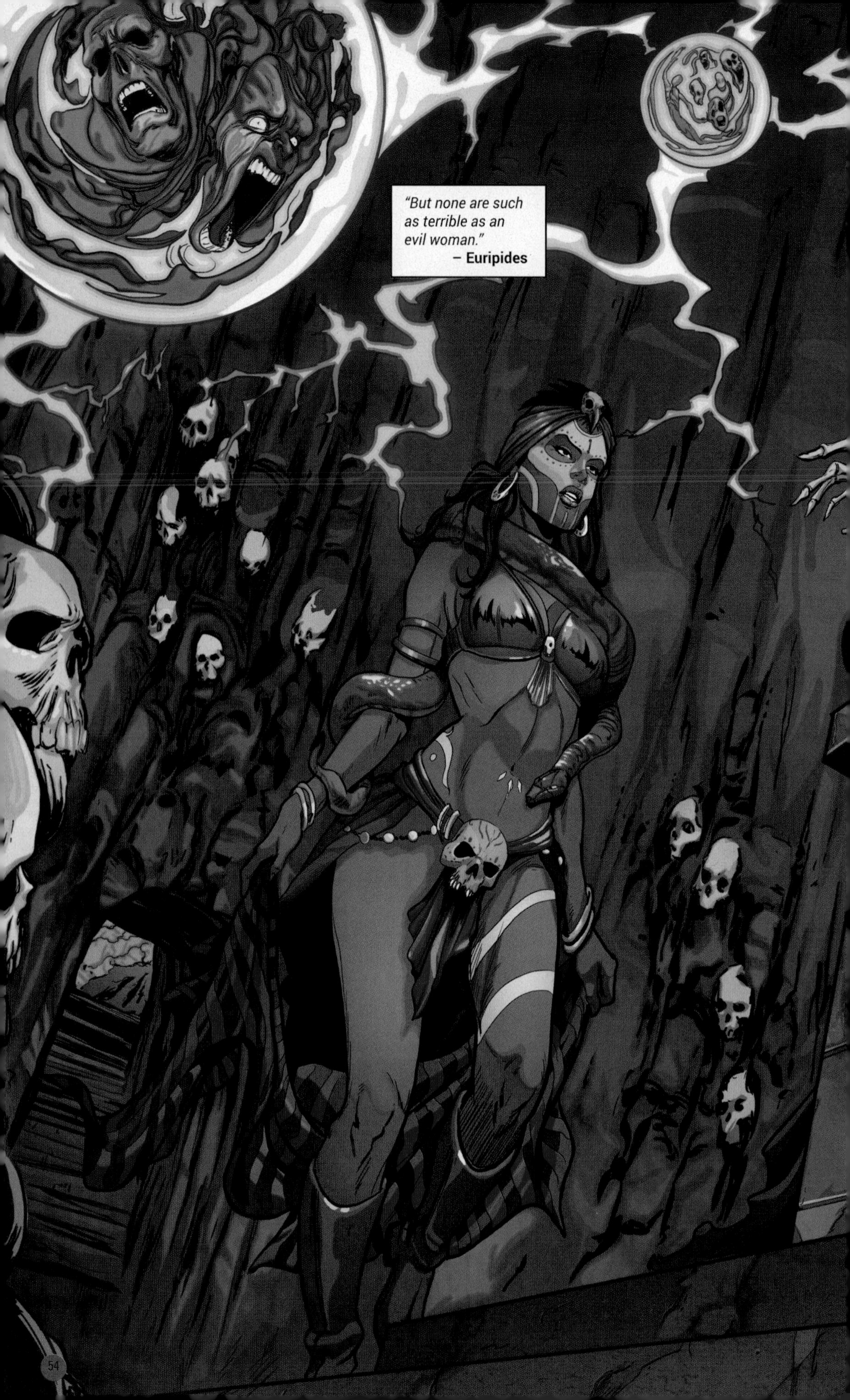
"But none are such as terrible as an evil woman."
– Euripides

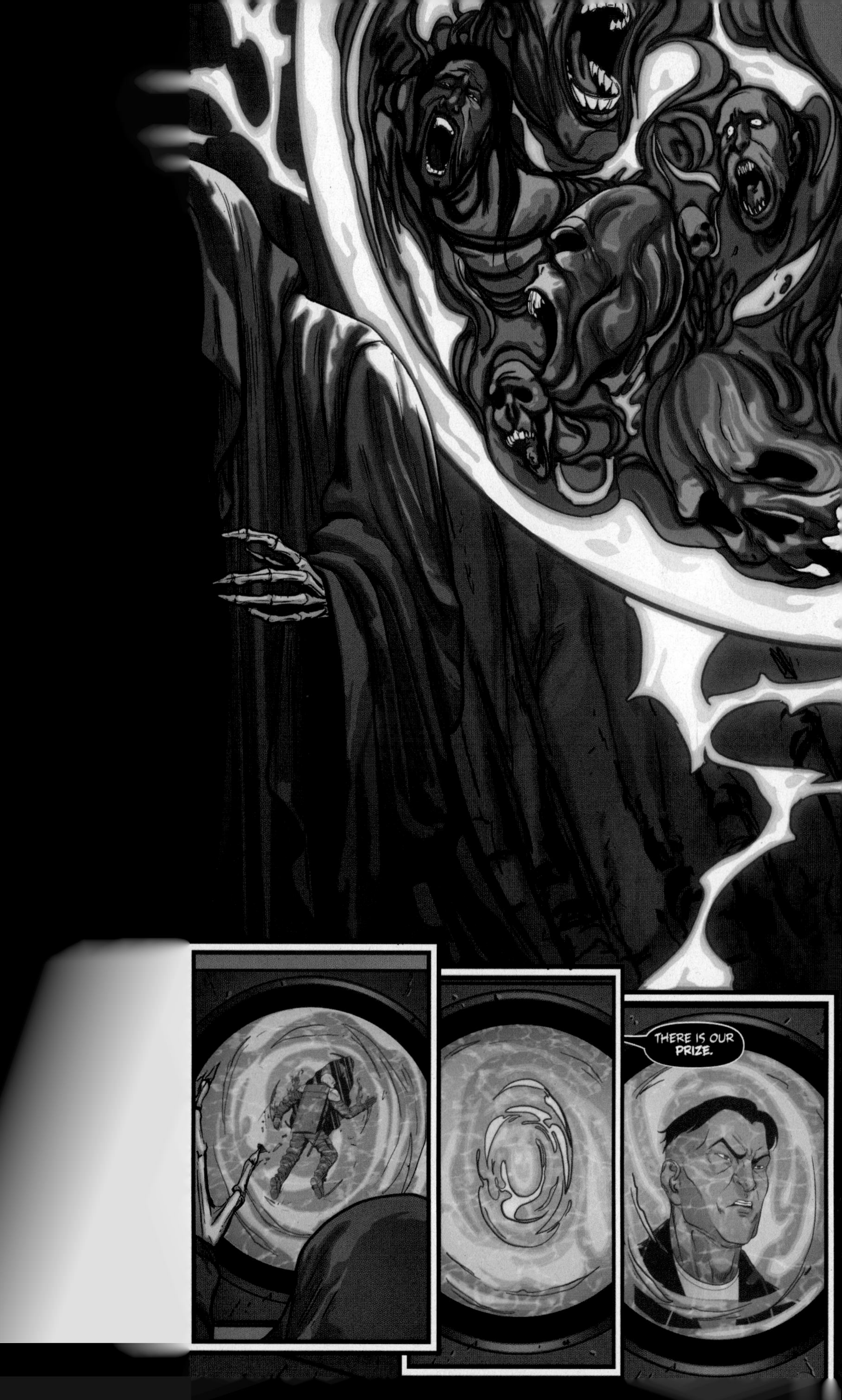
THERE IS OUR PRIZE.

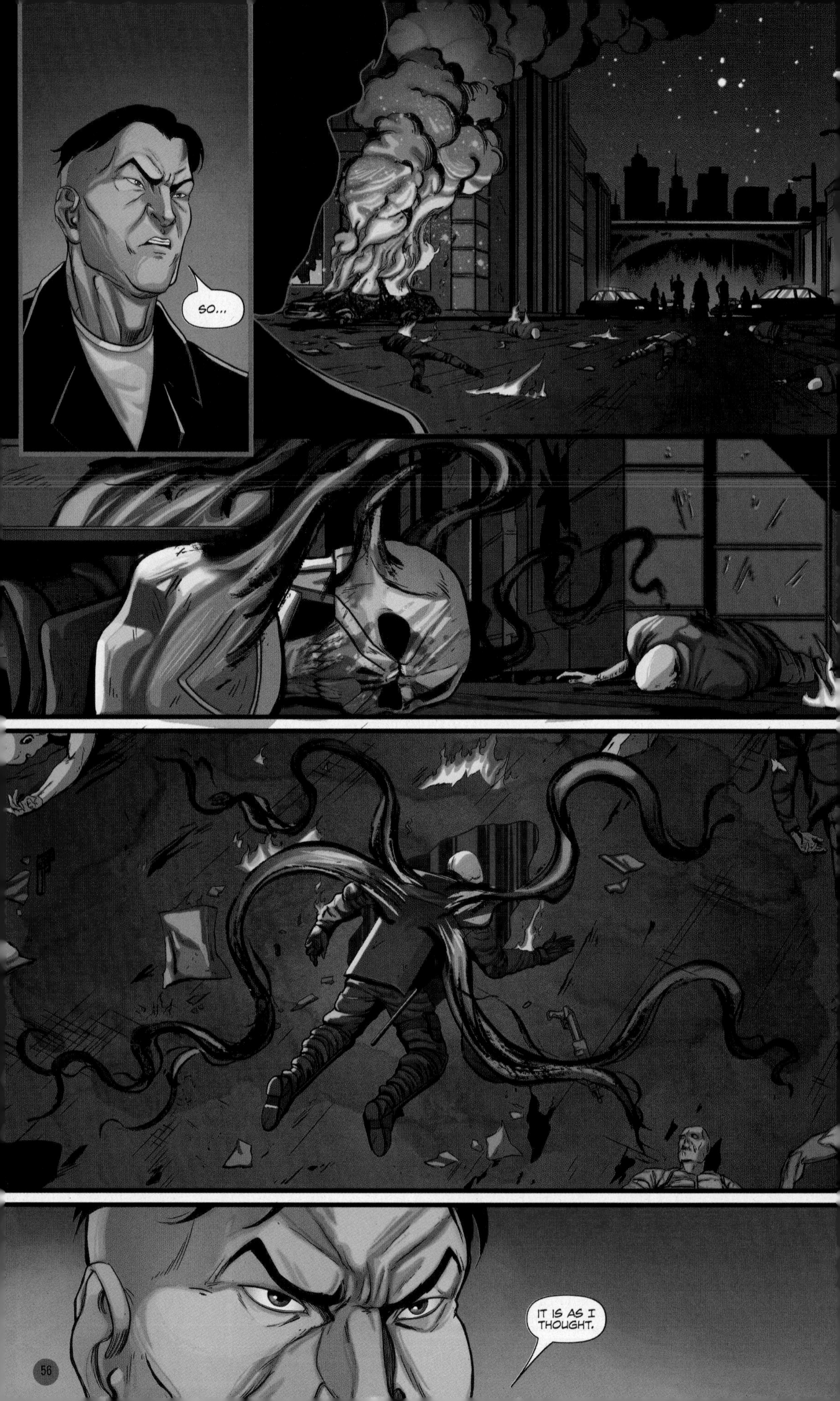
SO...
IT IS AS I THOUGHT.

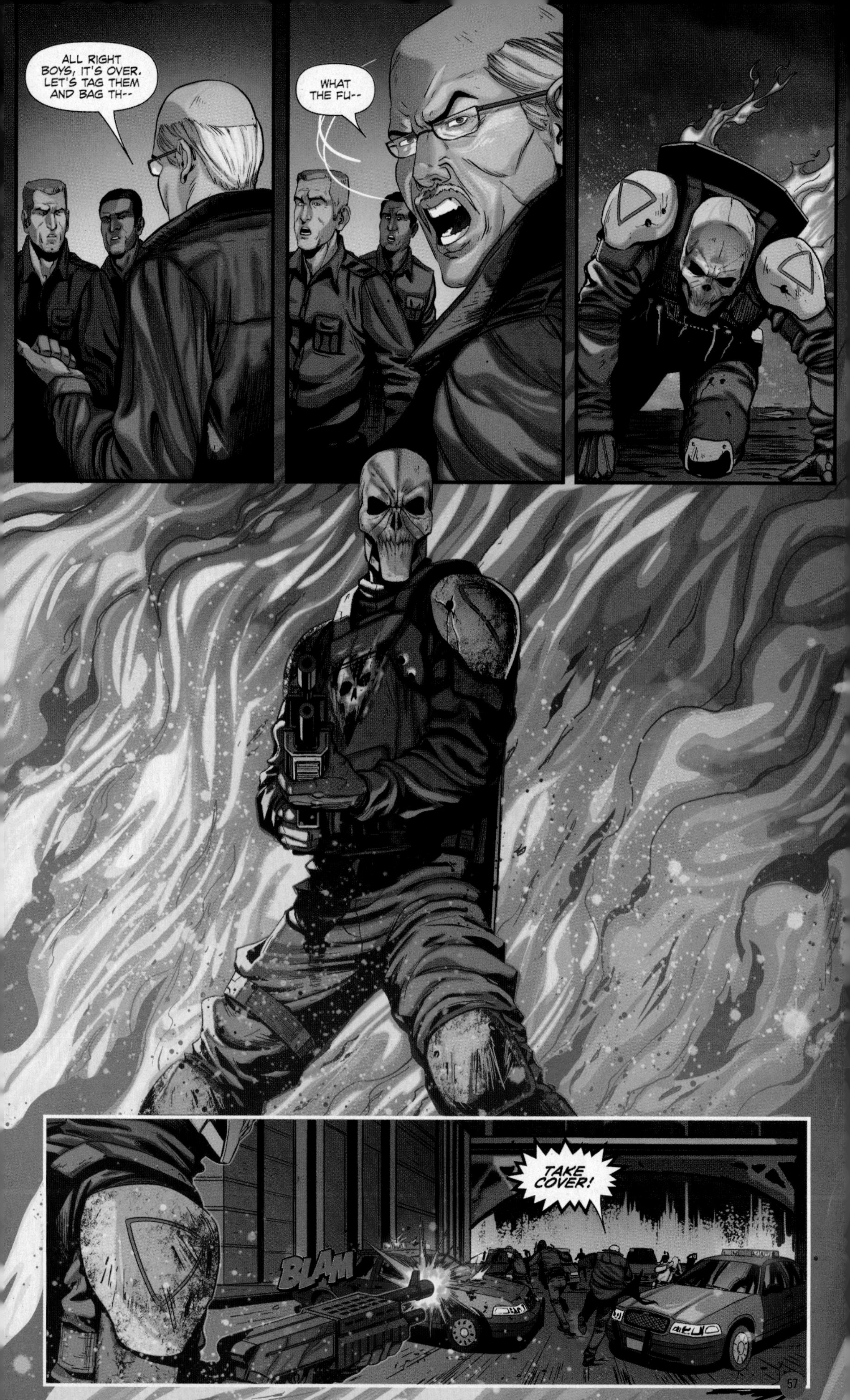

ALL RIGHT BOYS, IT'S OVER. LET'S TAG THEM AND BAG TH--
WHAT THE FU--
TAKE COVER!
BLAM

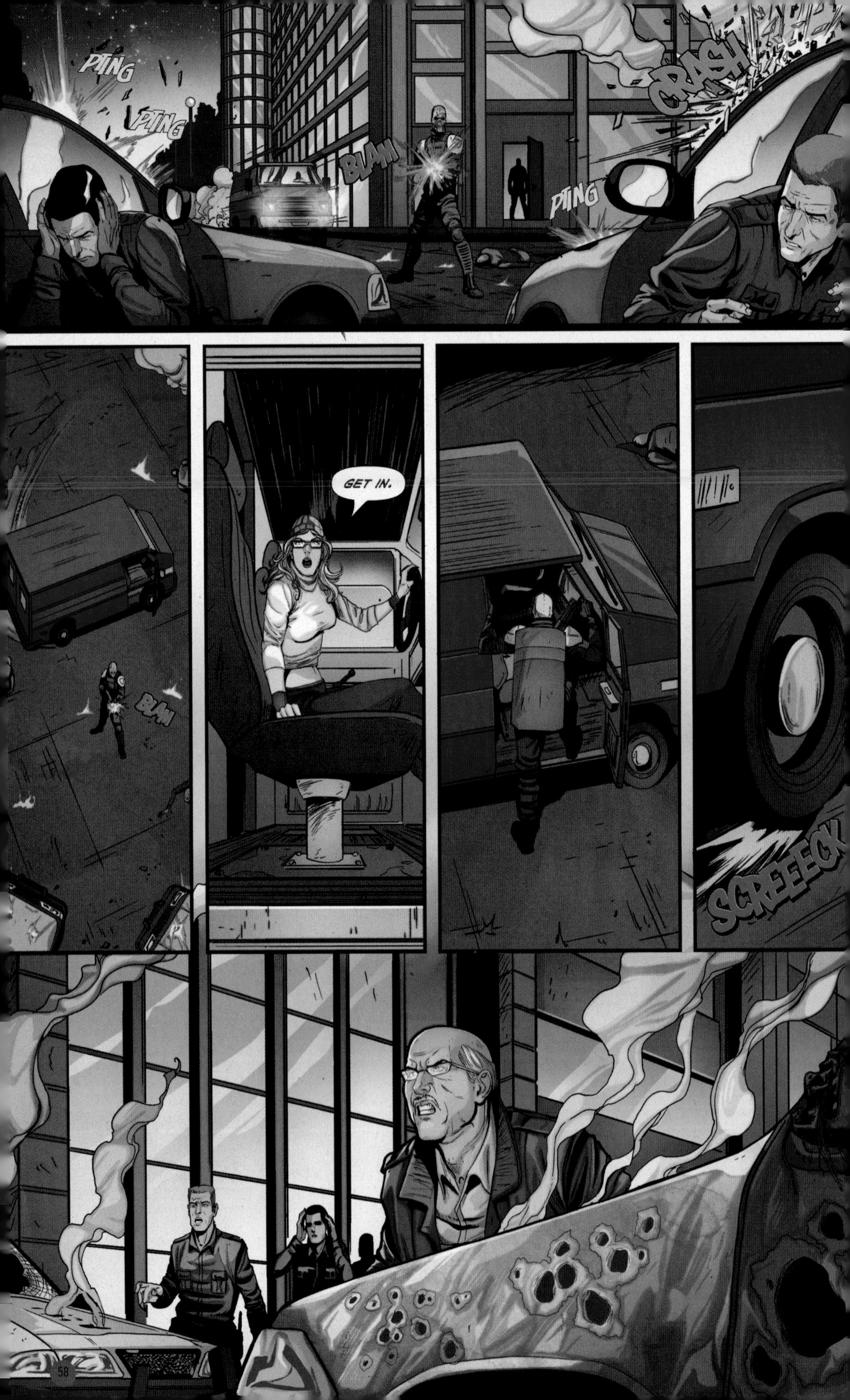
PTING
PTING
BLAM
CRASH
PTING
GET IN.
BLAM
SCREEECK

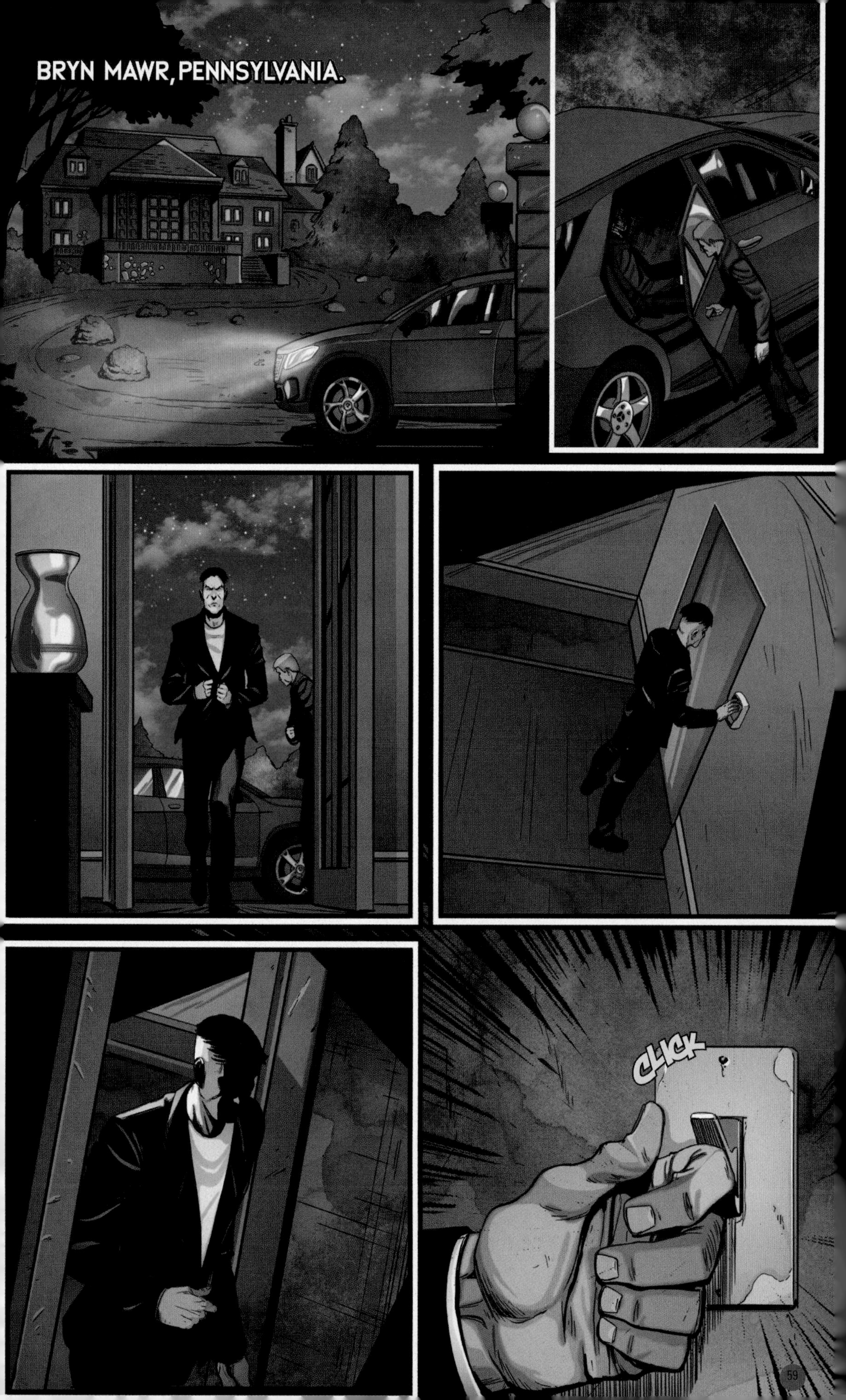
BRYN MAWR, PENNSYLVANIA.
CLICK

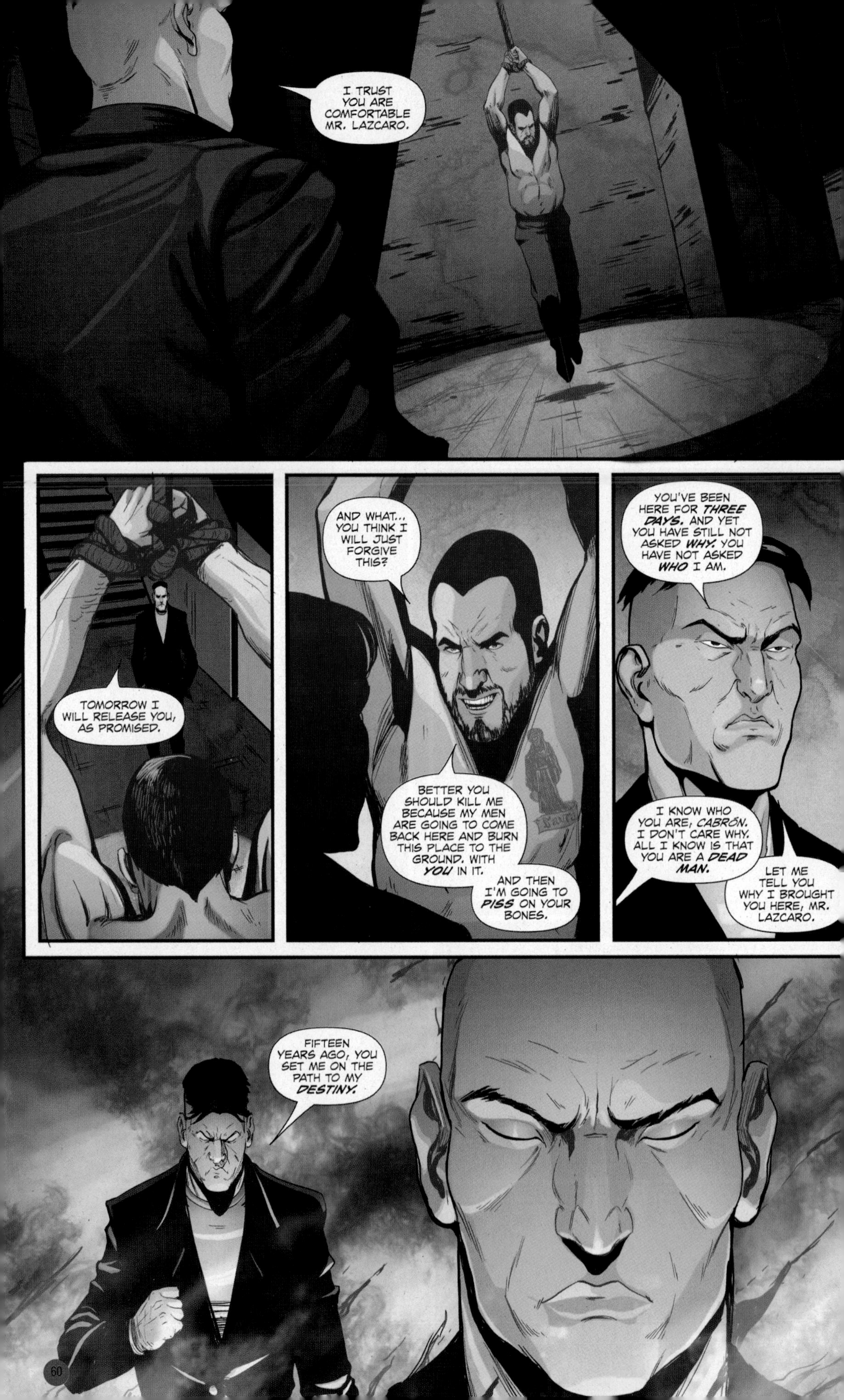
I TRUST YOU ARE COMFORTABLE MR. LAZCARO.
TOMORROW I WILL RELEASE YOU, AS PROMISED.
AND WHAT... YOU THINK I WILL JUST FORGIVE THIS?
BETTER YOU SHOULD KILL ME BECAUSE MY MEN ARE GOING TO COME BACK HERE AND BURN THIS PLACE TO THE GROUND. WITH *YOU* IN IT.
AND THEN I'M GOING TO *PISS* ON YOUR BONES.
YOU'VE BEEN HERE FOR *THREE DAYS.* AND YET YOU HAVE STILL NOT ASKED *WHY.* YOU HAVE NOT ASKED *WHO* I AM.
I KNOW WHO YOU ARE, *CABRÓN.* I DON'T CARE WHY. ALL I KNOW IS THAT YOU ARE A *DEAD MAN.*
LET ME TELL YOU WHY I BROUGHT YOU HERE, MR. LAZCARO.
FIFTEEN YEARS AGO, YOU SET ME ON THE PATH TO MY *DESTINY.*

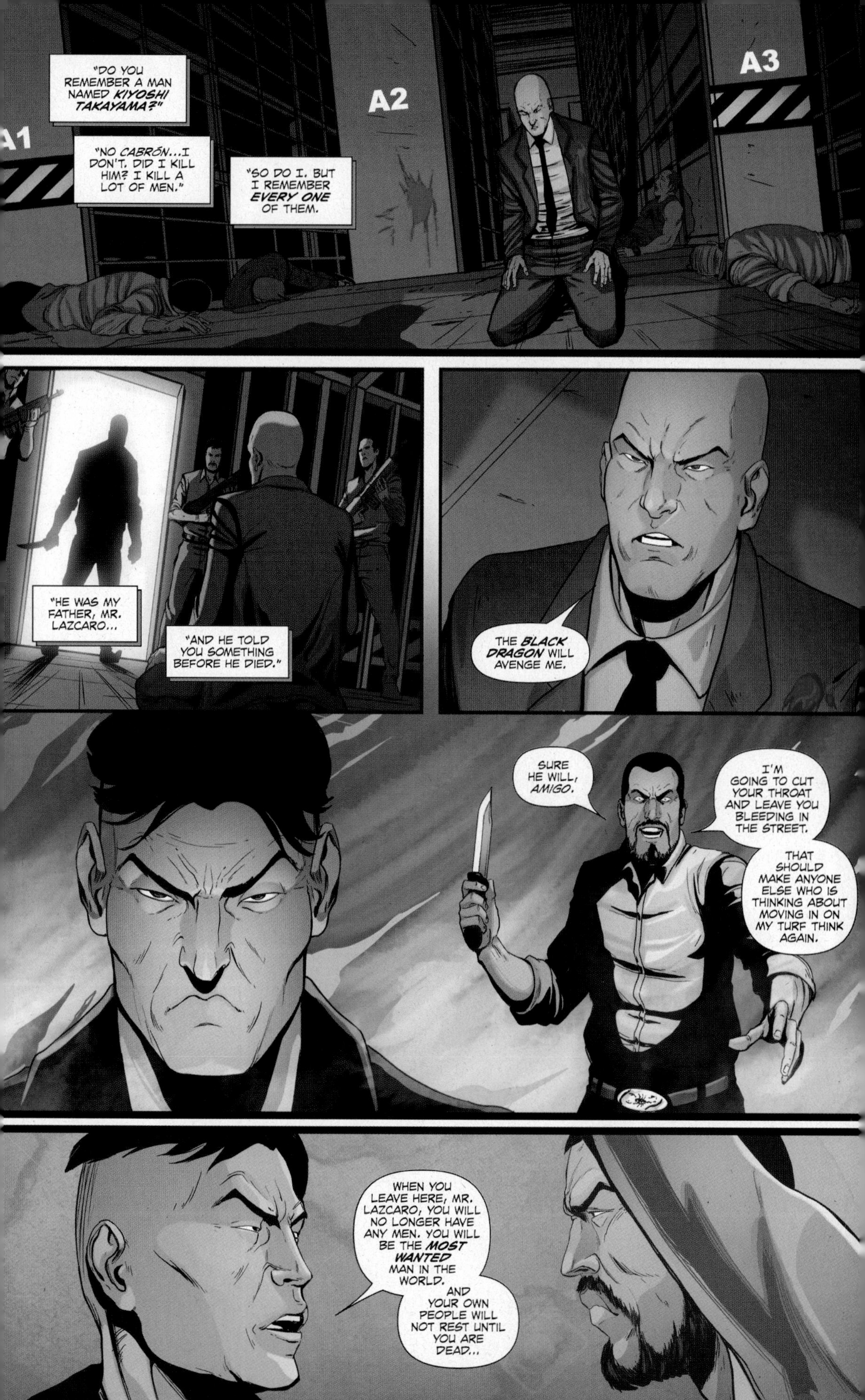
A1
A2
A3
"DO YOU REMEMBER A MAN NAMED KIYOSHI TAKAYAMA?"
"NO CABRÓN...I DON'T. DID I KILL HIM? I KILL A LOT OF MEN."
"SO DO I. BUT I REMEMBER EVERY ONE OF THEM.
"HE WAS MY FATHER, MR. LAZCARO...
"AND HE TOLD YOU SOMETHING BEFORE HE DIED."
THE BLACK DRAGON WILL AVENGE ME.
SURE HE WILL, AMIGO.
I'M GOING TO CUT YOUR THROAT AND LEAVE YOU BLEEDING IN THE STREET.
THAT SHOULD MAKE ANYONE ELSE WHO IS THINKING ABOUT MOVING IN ON MY TURF THINK AGAIN.
WHEN YOU LEAVE HERE, MR. LAZCARO, YOU WILL NO LONGER HAVE ANY MEN. YOU WILL BE THE MOST WANTED MAN IN THE WORLD.
AND YOUR OWN PEOPLE WILL NOT REST UNTIL YOU ARE DEAD...

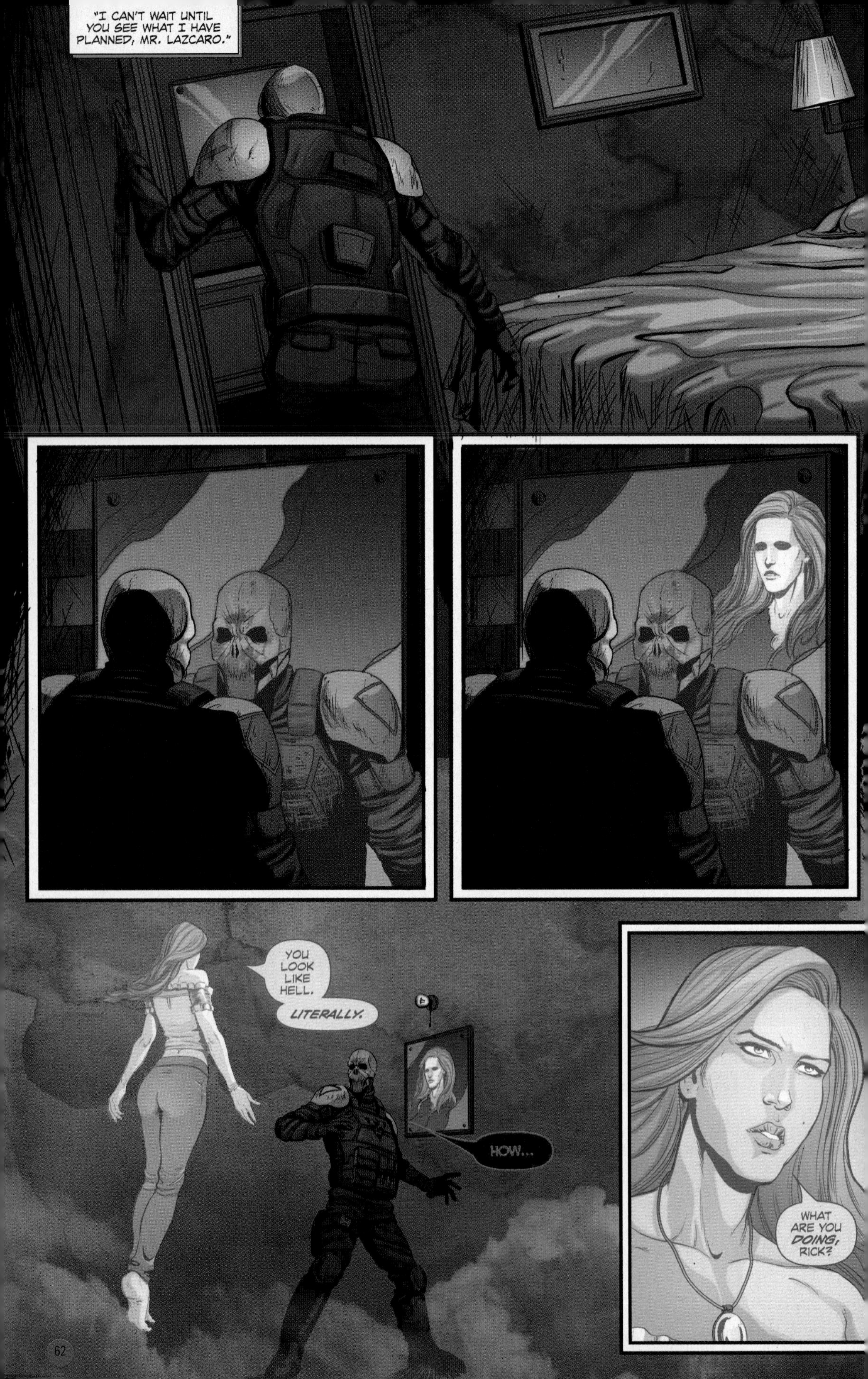
"I CAN'T WAIT UNTIL YOU SEE WHAT I HAVE PLANNED, MR. LAZCARO."
YOU LOOK LIKE HELL.
LITERALLY.
HOW...
WHAT ARE YOU DOING, RICK?

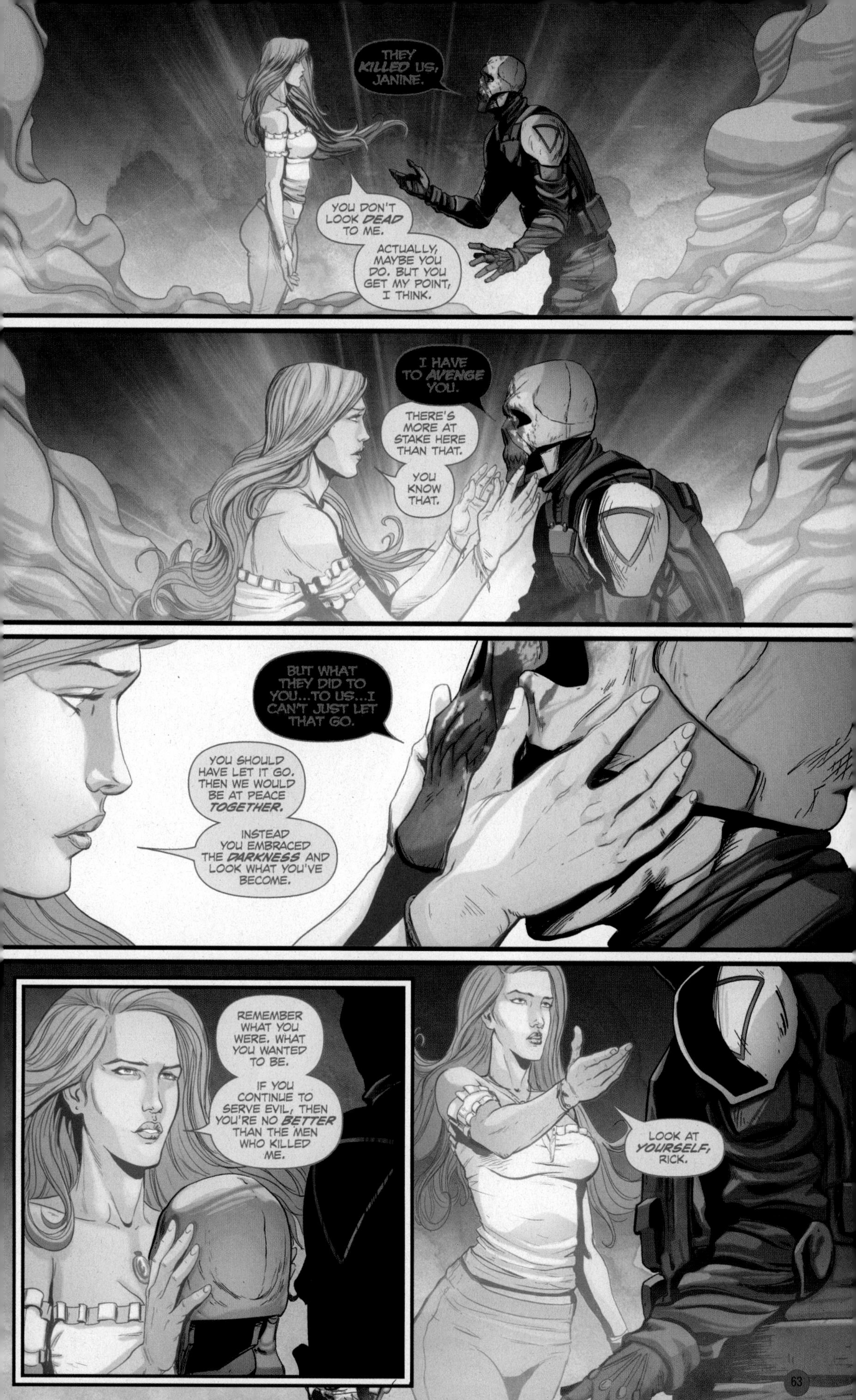

THEY KILLED US, JANINE.
YOU DON'T LOOK DEAD TO ME.
ACTUALLY, MAYBE YOU DO. BUT YOU GET MY POINT, I THINK.
I HAVE TO AVENGE YOU.
THERE'S MORE AT STAKE HERE THAN THAT.
YOU KNOW THAT.
BUT WHAT THEY DID TO YOU...TO US...I CAN'T JUST LET THAT GO.
YOU SHOULD HAVE LET IT GO. THEN WE WOULD BE AT PEACE TOGETHER.
INSTEAD YOU EMBRACED THE DARKNESS AND LOOK WHAT YOU'VE BECOME.
REMEMBER WHAT YOU WERE. WHAT YOU WANTED TO BE.
IF YOU CONTINUE TO SERVE EVIL, THEN YOU'RE NO BETTER THAN THE MEN WHO KILLED ME.
LOOK AT YOURSELF, RICK.

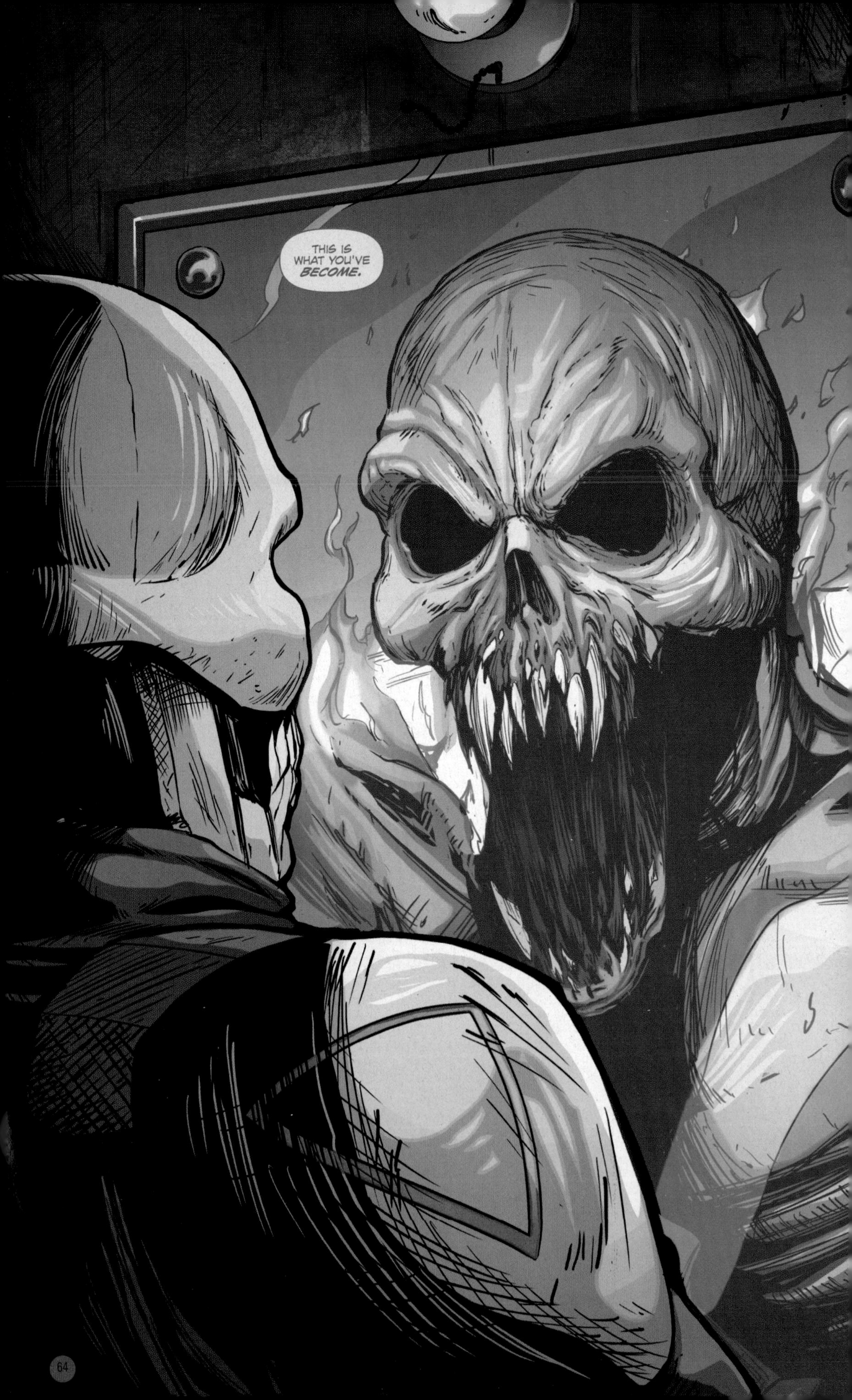
THIS IS WHAT YOU'VE *BECOME.*

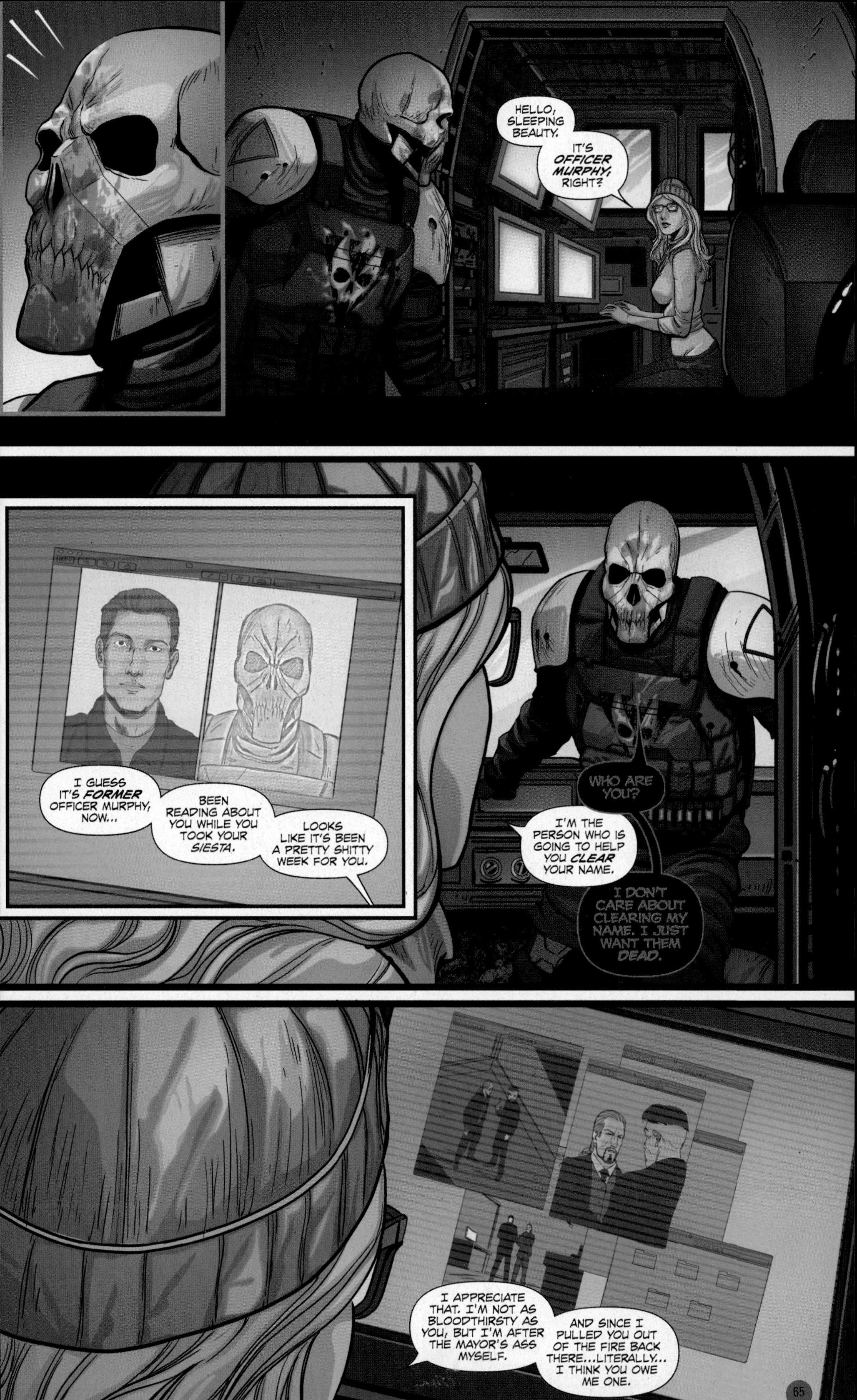
HELLO, SLEEPING BEAUTY.
IT'S **OFFICER MURPHY**, RIGHT?
I GUESS IT'S **FORMER** OFFICER MURPHY, NOW...
BEEN READING ABOUT YOU WHILE YOU TOOK YOUR *SIESTA*.
LOOKS LIKE IT'S BEEN A PRETTY SHITTY WEEK FOR YOU.
WHO ARE YOU?
I'M THE PERSON WHO IS GOING TO HELP YOU **CLEAR** YOUR NAME.
I DON'T CARE ABOUT CLEARING MY NAME. I JUST WANT THEM **DEAD**.
I APPRECIATE THAT. I'M NOT AS BLOODTHIRSTY AS YOU, BUT I'M AFTER THE MAYOR'S ASS MYSELF.
AND SINCE I PULLED YOU OUT OF THE FIRE BACK THERE...LITERALLY... I THINK YOU OWE ME ONE.

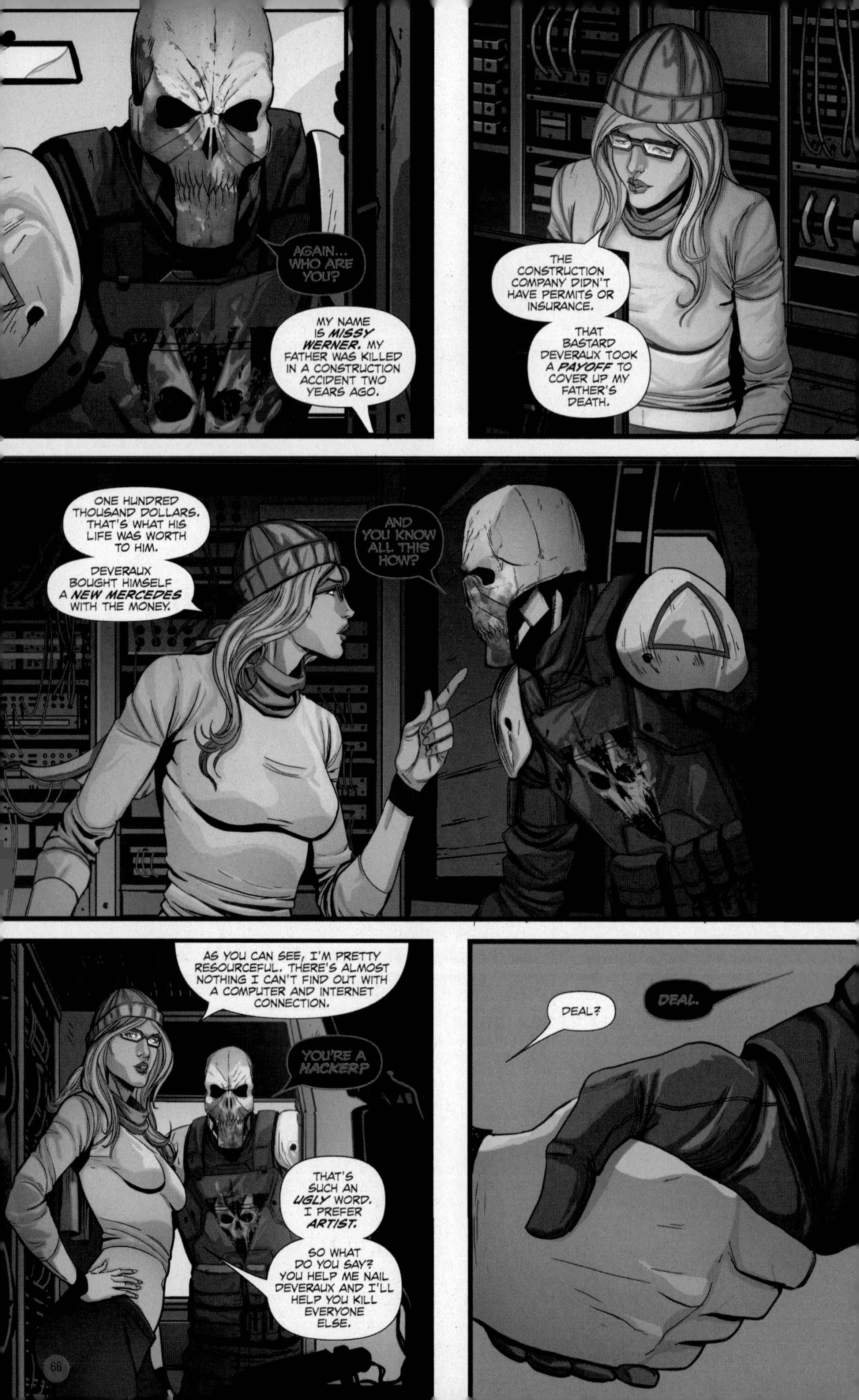
AGAIN... WHO ARE YOU?
MY NAME IS MISSY WERNER. MY FATHER WAS KILLED IN A CONSTRUCTION ACCIDENT TWO YEARS AGO.
THE CONSTRUCTION COMPANY DIDN'T HAVE PERMITS OR INSURANCE.
THAT BASTARD DEVERAUX TOOK A PAYOFF TO COVER UP MY FATHER'S DEATH.
ONE HUNDRED THOUSAND DOLLARS. THAT'S WHAT HIS LIFE WAS WORTH TO HIM.
DEVERAUX BOUGHT HIMSELF A NEW MERCEDES WITH THE MONEY.
AND YOU KNOW ALL THIS HOW?
AS YOU CAN SEE, I'M PRETTY RESOURCEFUL. THERE'S ALMOST NOTHING I CAN'T FIND OUT WITH A COMPUTER AND INTERNET CONNECTION.
YOU'RE A HACKER?
THAT'S SUCH AN UGLY WORD. I PREFER ARTIST.
SO WHAT DO YOU SAY? YOU HELP ME NAIL DEVERAUX AND I'LL HELP YOU KILL EVERYONE ELSE.
DEAL?
DEAL.

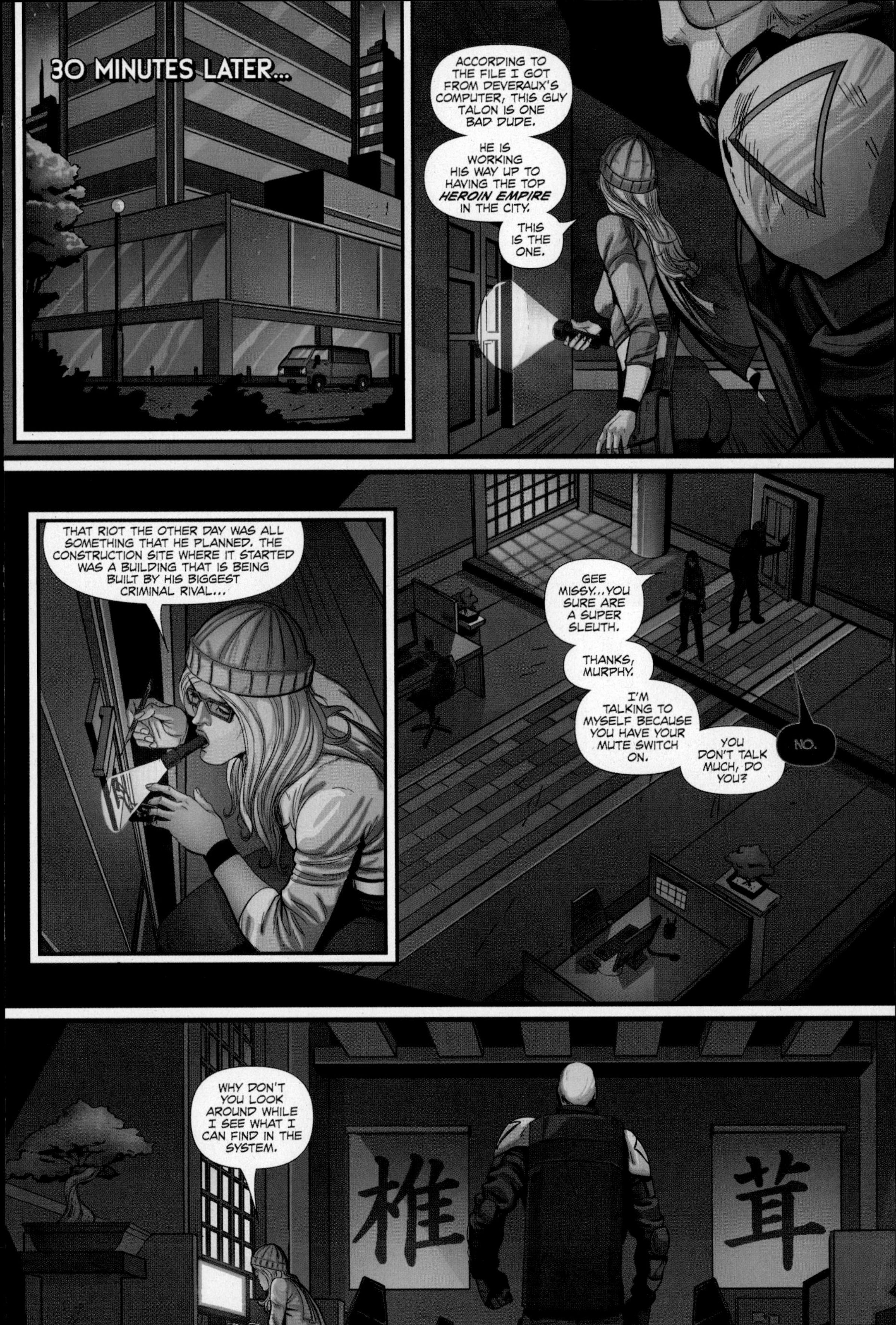
30 MINUTES LATER...
ACCORDING TO THE FILE I GOT FROM DEVERAUX'S COMPUTER, THIS GUY TALON IS ONE BAD DUDE.
HE IS WORKING HIS WAY UP TO HAVING THE TOP ***HEROIN EMPIRE*** IN THE CITY.
THIS IS THE ONE.
THAT RIOT THE OTHER DAY WAS ALL SOMETHING THAT HE PLANNED. THE CONSTRUCTION SITE WHERE IT STARTED WAS A BUILDING THAT IS BEING BUILT BY HIS BIGGEST CRIMINAL RIVAL...
GEE MISSY...YOU SURE ARE A SUPER SLEUTH.
THANKS, MURPHY.
I'M TALKING TO MYSELF BECAUSE YOU HAVE YOUR MUTE SWITCH ON.
YOU DON'T TALK MUCH, DO YOU?
NO.
WHY DON'T YOU LOOK AROUND WHILE I SEE WHAT I CAN FIND IN THE SYSTEM.
椎
茸

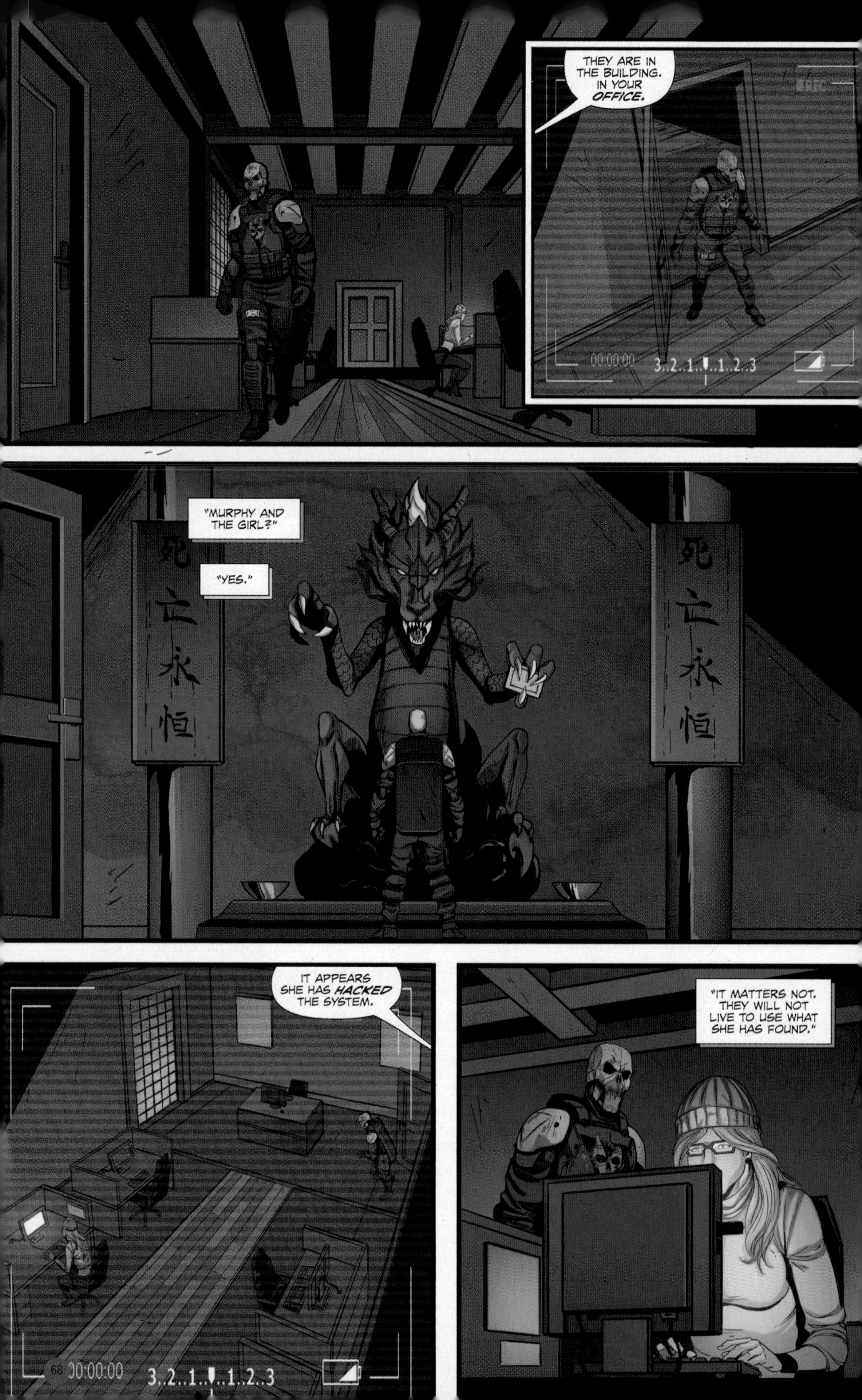
THEY ARE IN THE BUILDING. IN YOUR OFFICE.
REC
00:00:00
3..2..1..1..2..3
"MURPHY AND THE GIRL?"
"YES."
死亡永恒
死亡永恒
IT APPEARS SHE HAS HACKED THE SYSTEM.
00:00:00
3..2..1..1..2..3
"IT MATTERS NOT. THEY WILL NOT LIVE TO USE WHAT SHE HAS FOUND."

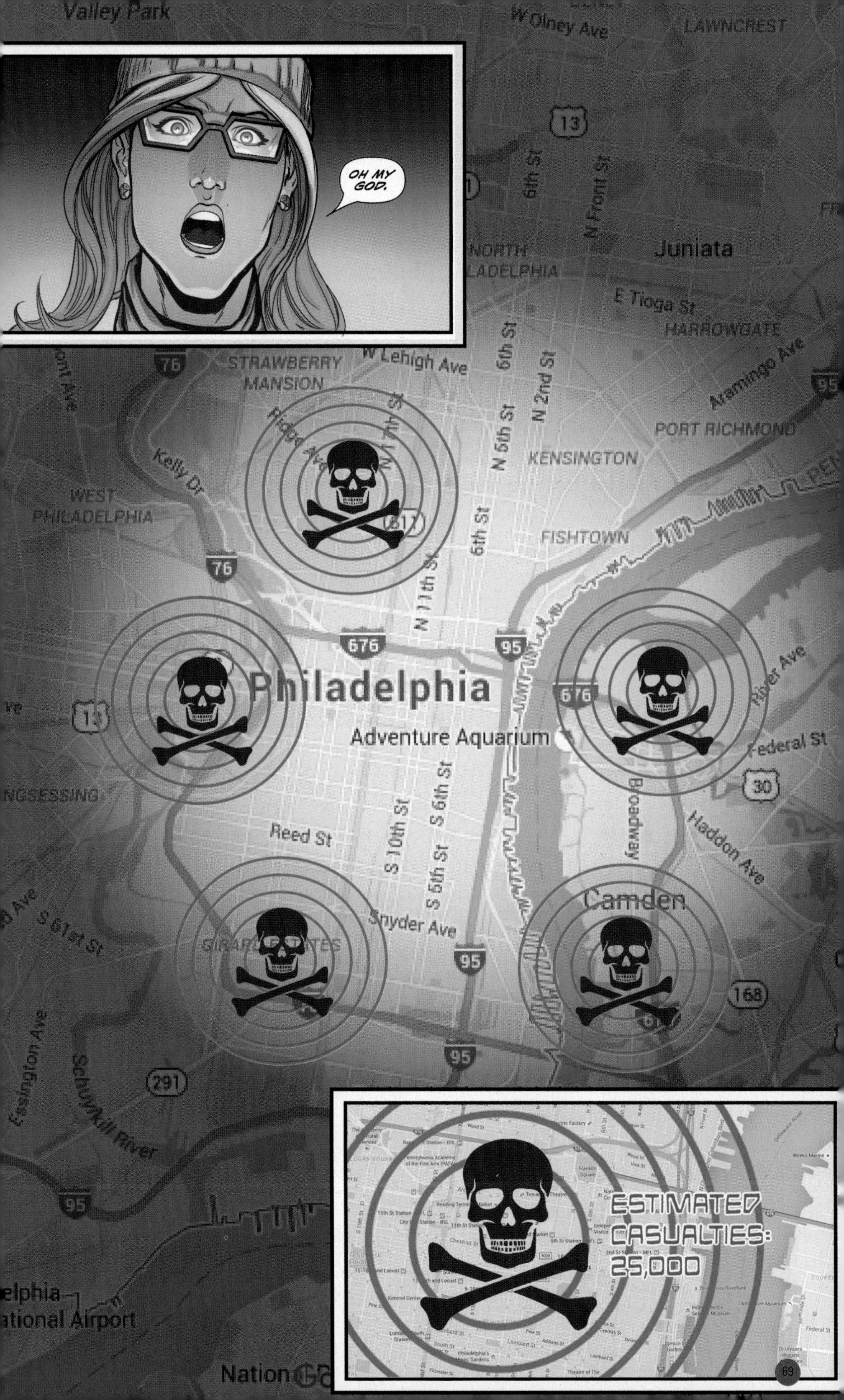
OH MY GOD.
ESTIMATED CASUALTIES: 25,000

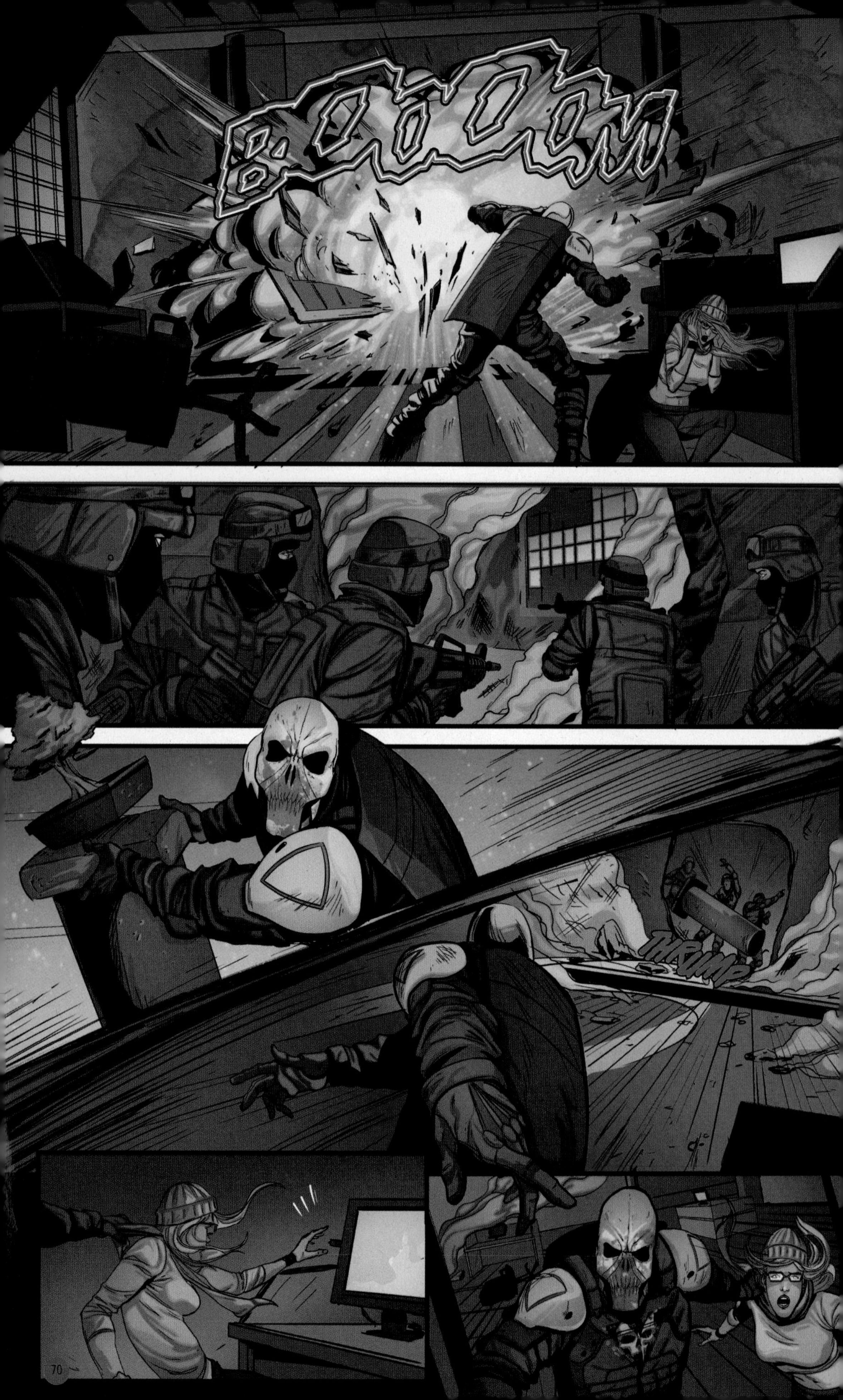
BOOM
THRUMP

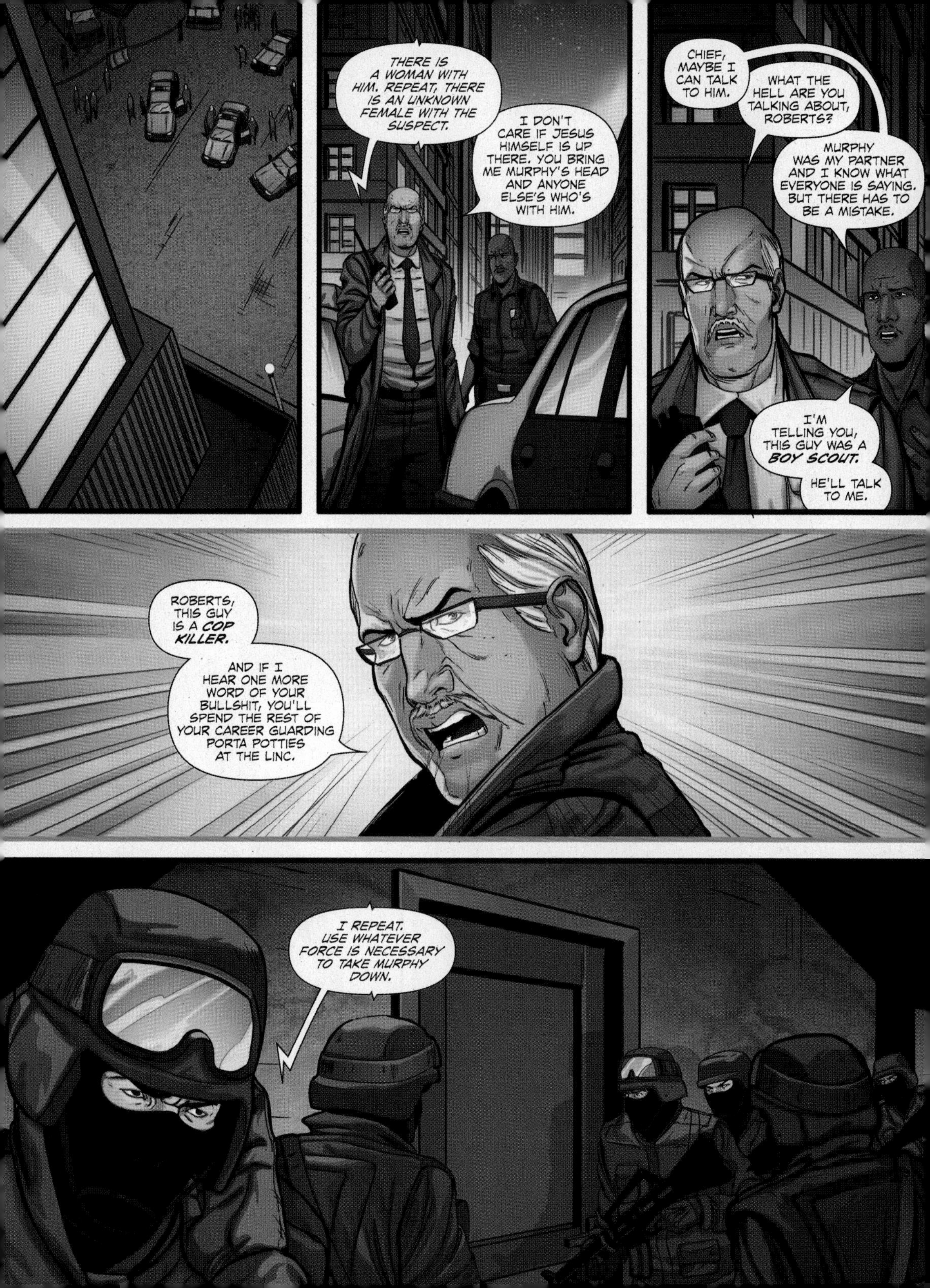
THERE IS A WOMAN WITH HIM. REPEAT, THERE IS AN UNKNOWN FEMALE WITH THE SUSPECT.
I DON'T CARE IF JESUS HIMSELF IS UP THERE. YOU BRING ME MURPHY'S HEAD AND ANYONE ELSE'S WHO'S WITH HIM.
CHIEF, MAYBE I CAN TALK TO HIM.
WHAT THE HELL ARE YOU TALKING ABOUT, ROBERTS?
MURPHY WAS MY PARTNER AND I KNOW WHAT EVERYONE IS SAYING. BUT THERE HAS TO BE A MISTAKE.
I'M TELLING YOU, THIS GUY WAS A BOY SCOUT.
HE'LL TALK TO ME.
ROBERTS, THIS GUY IS A COP KILLER.
AND IF I HEAR ONE MORE WORD OF YOUR BULLSHIT, YOU'LL SPEND THE REST OF YOUR CAREER GUARDING PORTA POTTIES AT THE LINC.
I REPEAT. USE WHATEVER FORCE IS NECESSARY TO TAKE MURPHY DOWN.

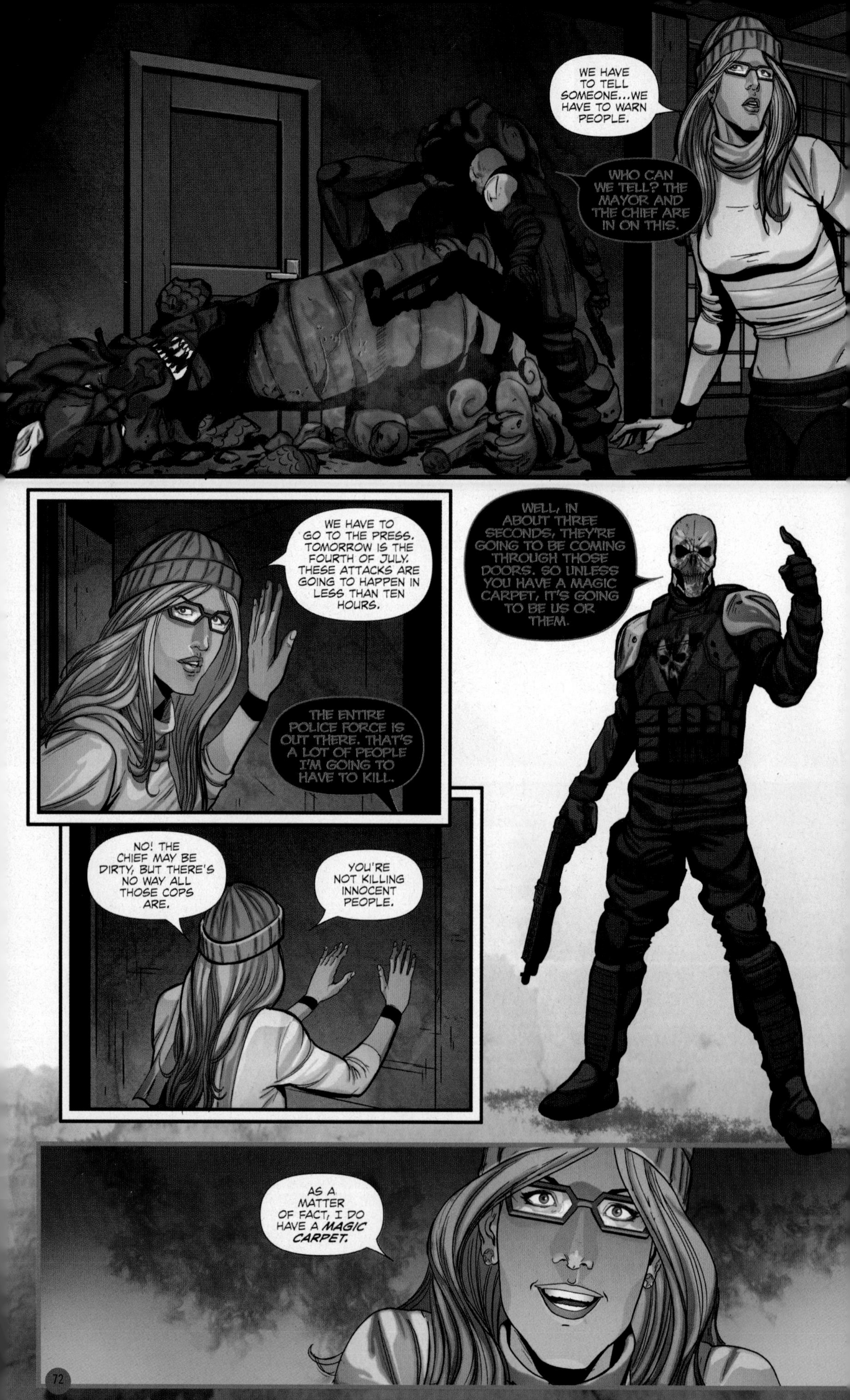
WE HAVE TO TELL SOMEONE...WE HAVE TO WARN PEOPLE.
WHO CAN WE TELL? THE MAYOR AND THE CHIEF ARE IN ON THIS.
WE HAVE TO GO TO THE PRESS. TOMORROW IS THE FOURTH OF JULY. THESE ATTACKS ARE GOING TO HAPPEN IN LESS THAN TEN HOURS.
THE ENTIRE POLICE FORCE IS OUT THERE. THAT'S A LOT OF PEOPLE I'M GOING TO HAVE TO KILL.
NO! THE CHIEF MAY BE DIRTY, BUT THERE'S NO WAY ALL THOSE COPS ARE.
YOU'RE NOT KILLING INNOCENT PEOPLE.
WELL, IN ABOUT THREE SECONDS, THEY'RE GOING TO BE COMING THROUGH THOSE DOORS. SO UNLESS YOU HAVE A MAGIC CARPET, IT'S GOING TO BE US OR THEM.
AS A MATTER OF FACT, I DO HAVE A *MAGIC CARPET.*

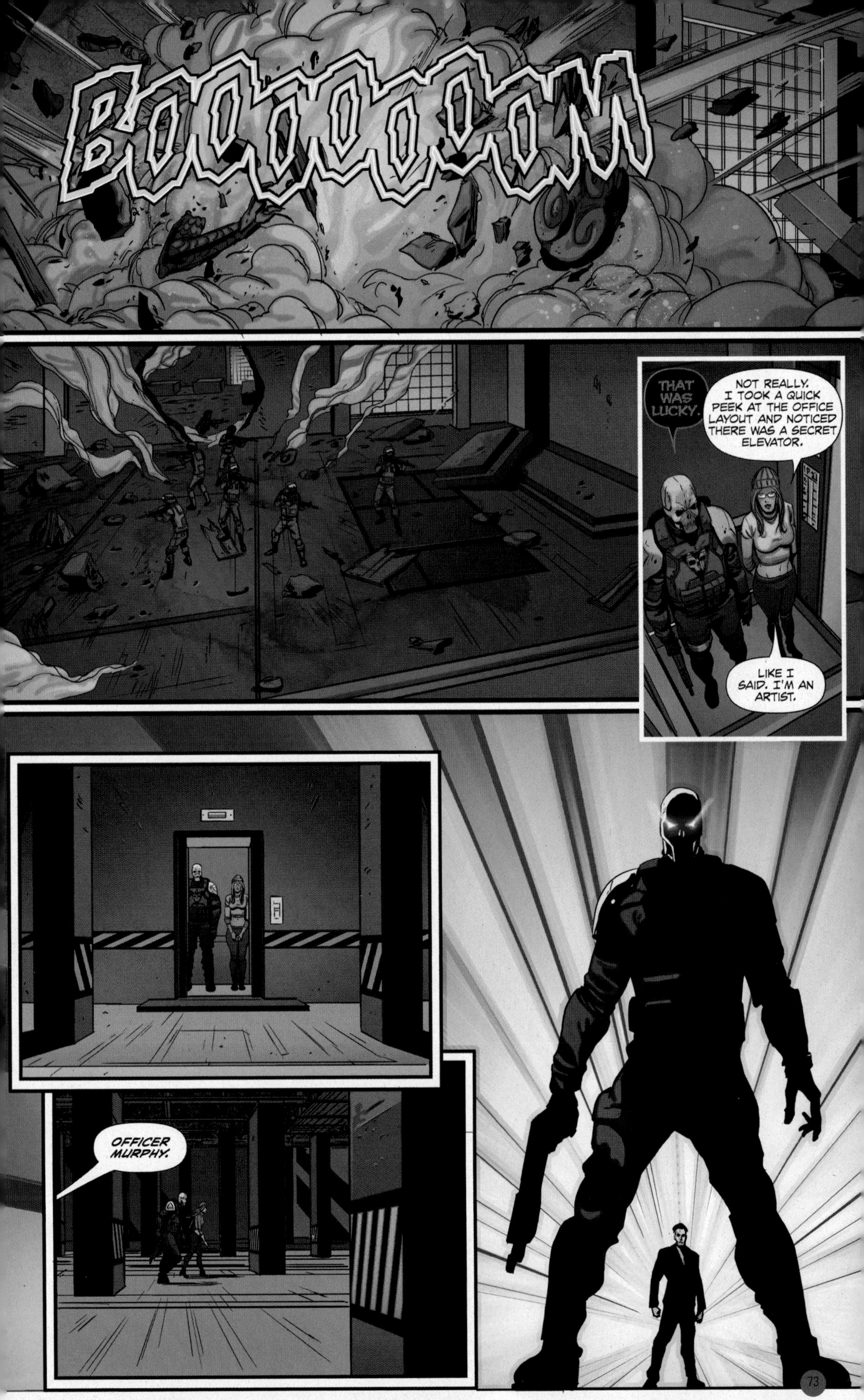
BOOOOOOM
THAT WAS LUCKY.
NOT REALLY. I TOOK A QUICK PEEK AT THE OFFICE LAYOUT AND NOTICED THERE WAS A SECRET ELEVATOR.
LIKE I SAID. I'M AN ARTIST.
OFFICER MURPHY.

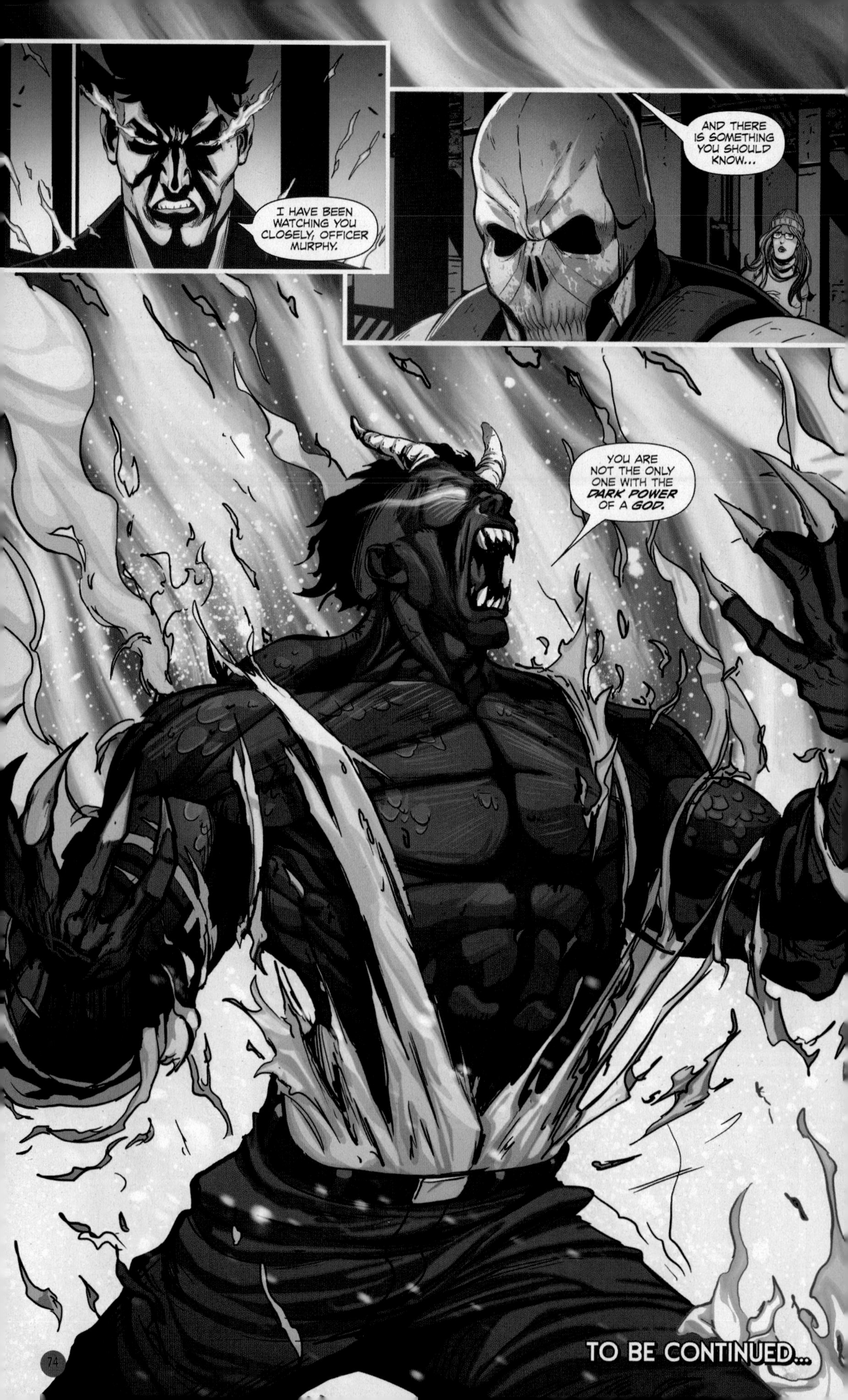
I HAVE BEEN WATCHING YOU CLOSELY, OFFICER MURPHY.
AND THERE IS SOMETHING YOU SHOULD KNOW...
YOU ARE NOT THE ONLY ONE WITH THE DARK POWER OF A GOD.
TO BE CONTINUED...

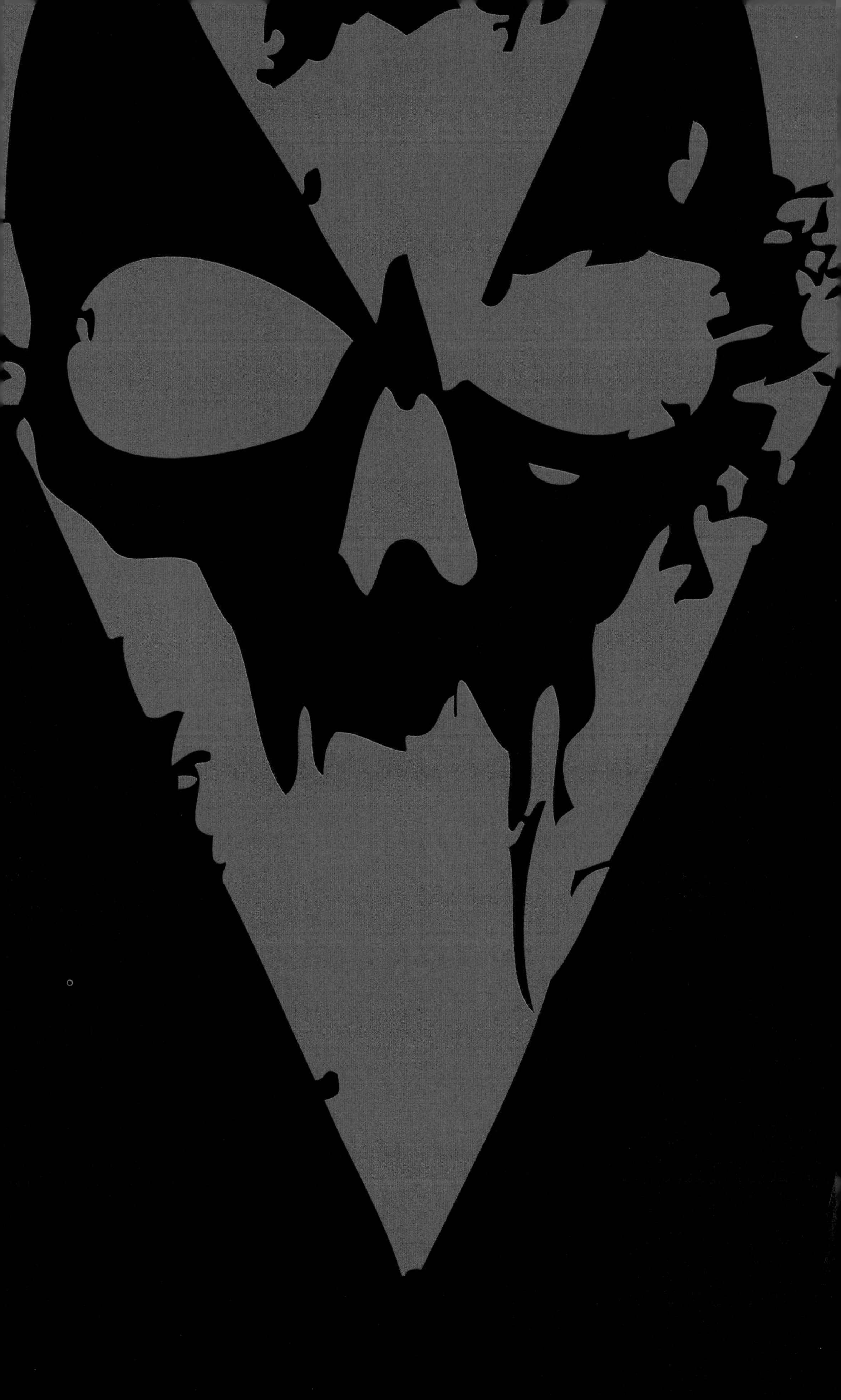

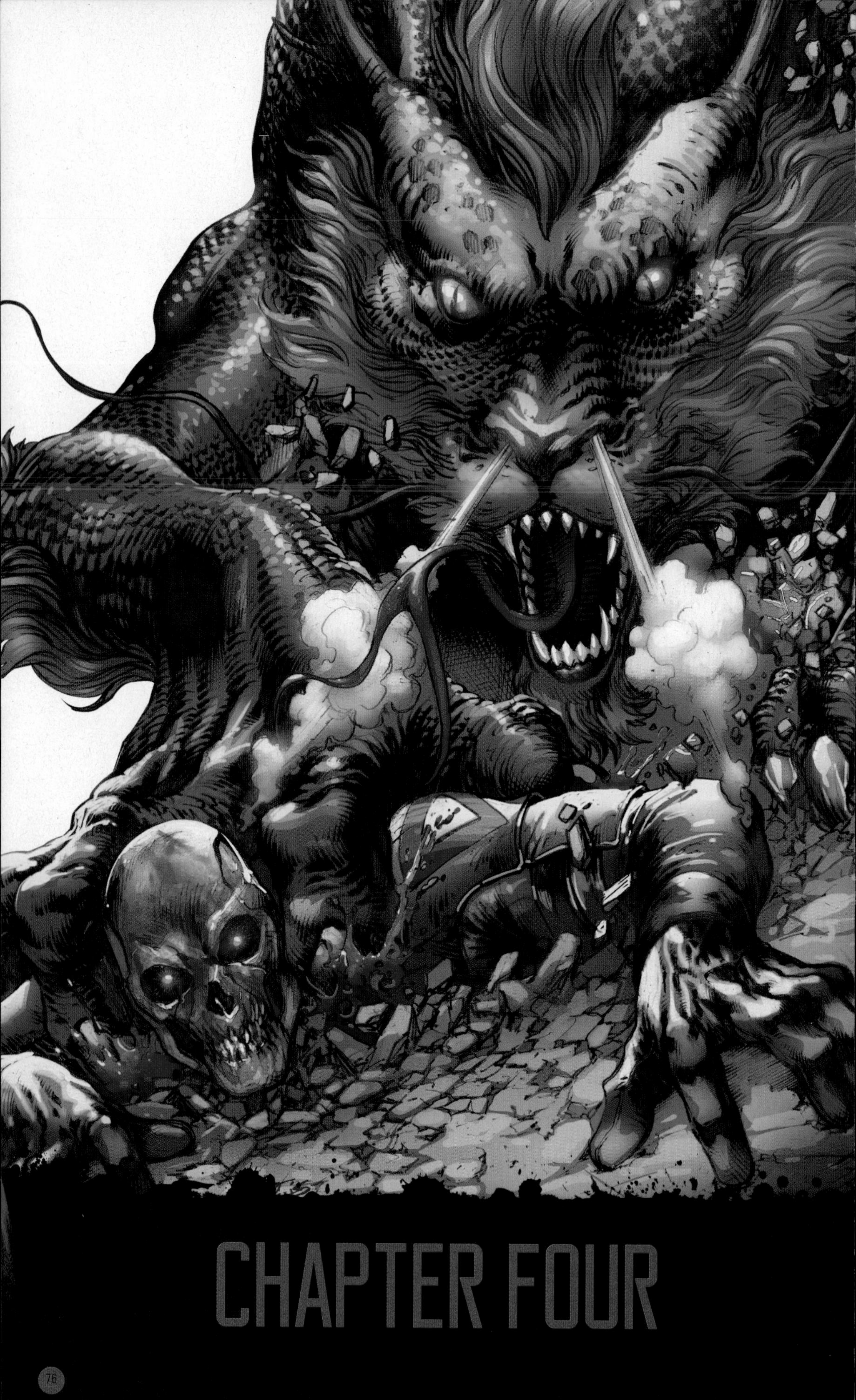

CHAPTER FOUR

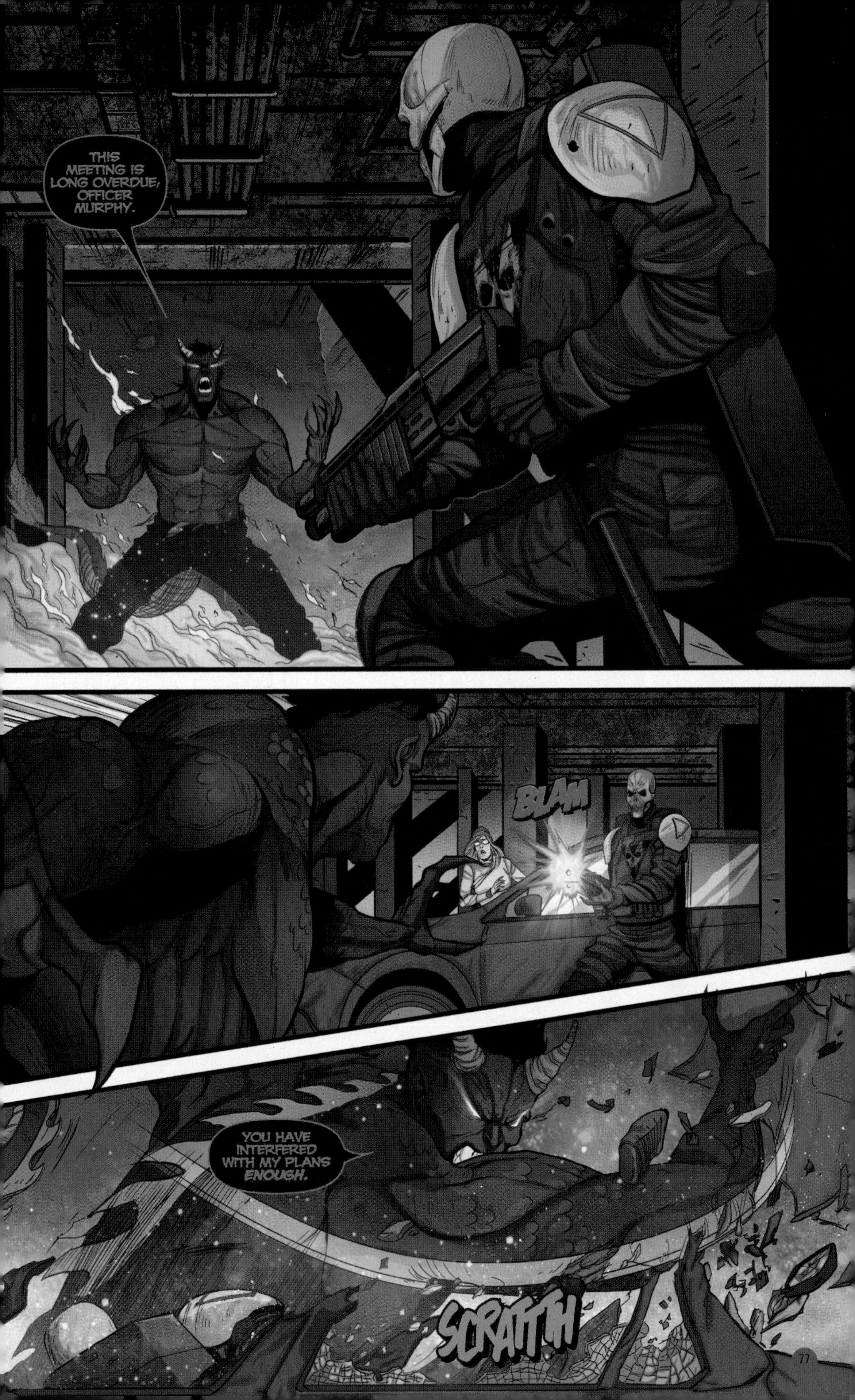
THIS MEETING IS LONG OVERDUE, OFFICER MURPHY.
BLAM
YOU HAVE INTERFERED WITH MY PLANS ENOUGH.
SCRATTTH

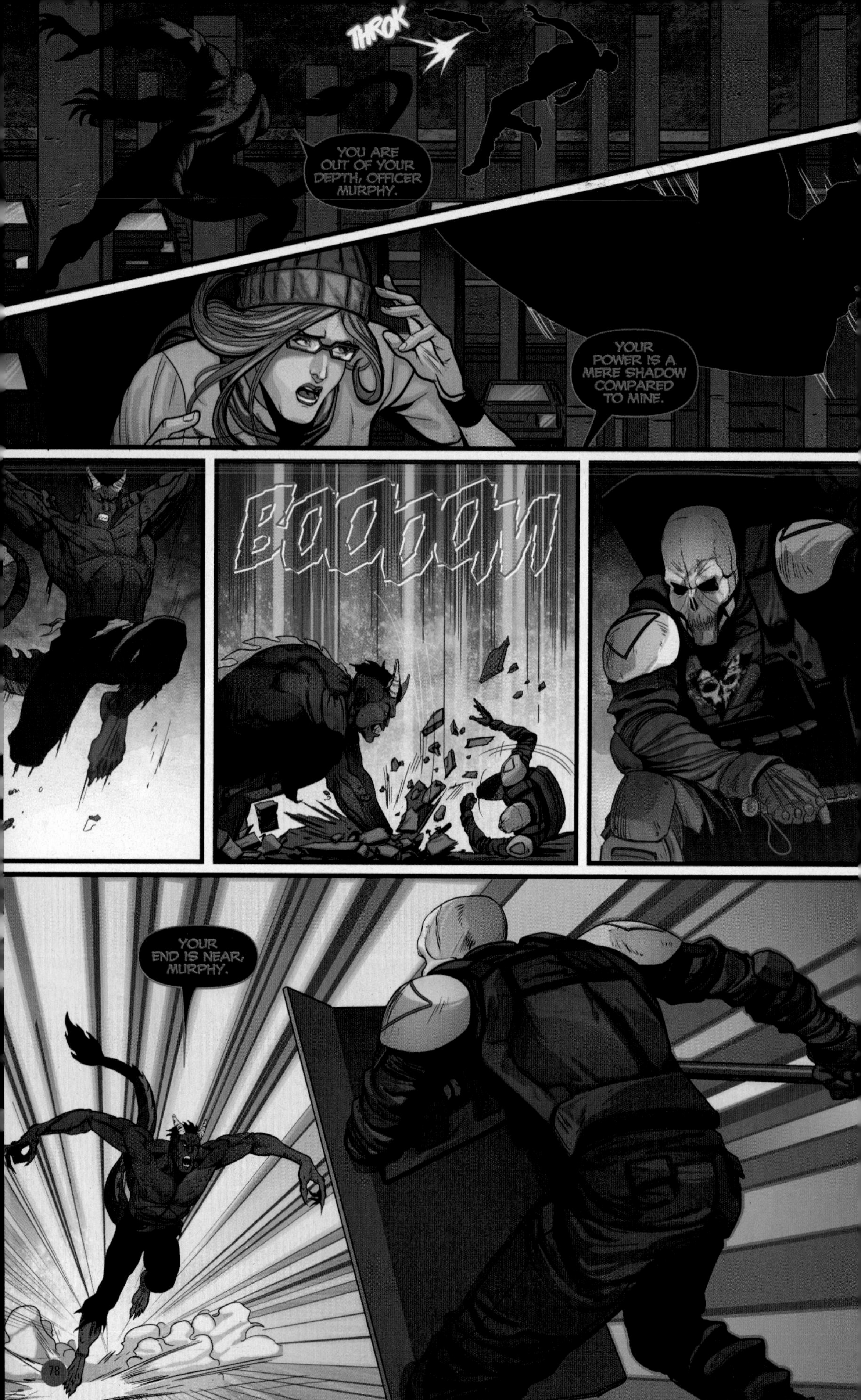
THROK
YOU ARE OUT OF YOUR DEPTH, OFFICER MURPHY.
YOUR POWER IS A MERE SHADOW COMPARED TO MINE.
BOOOOM
YOUR END IS NEAR, MURPHY.

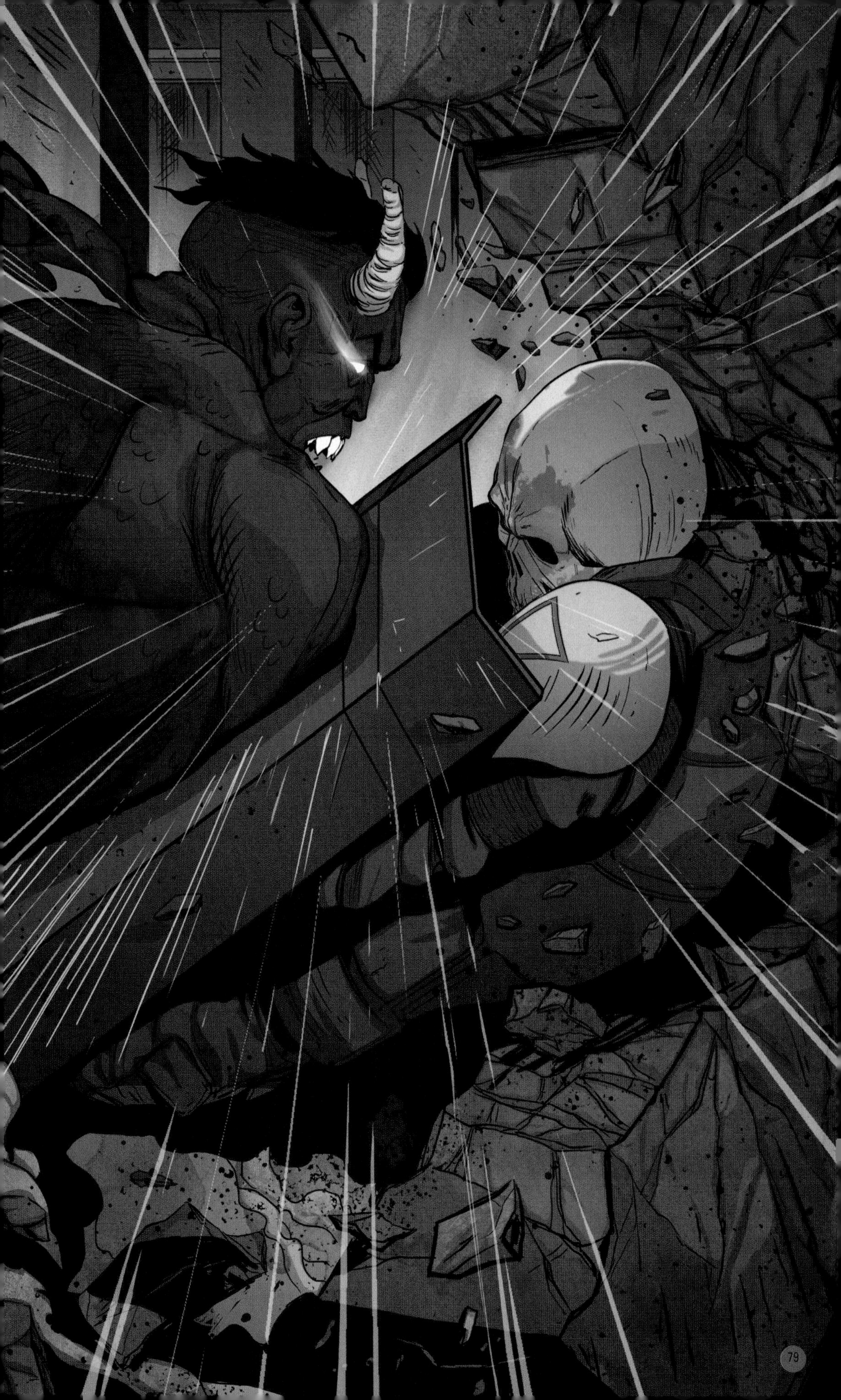

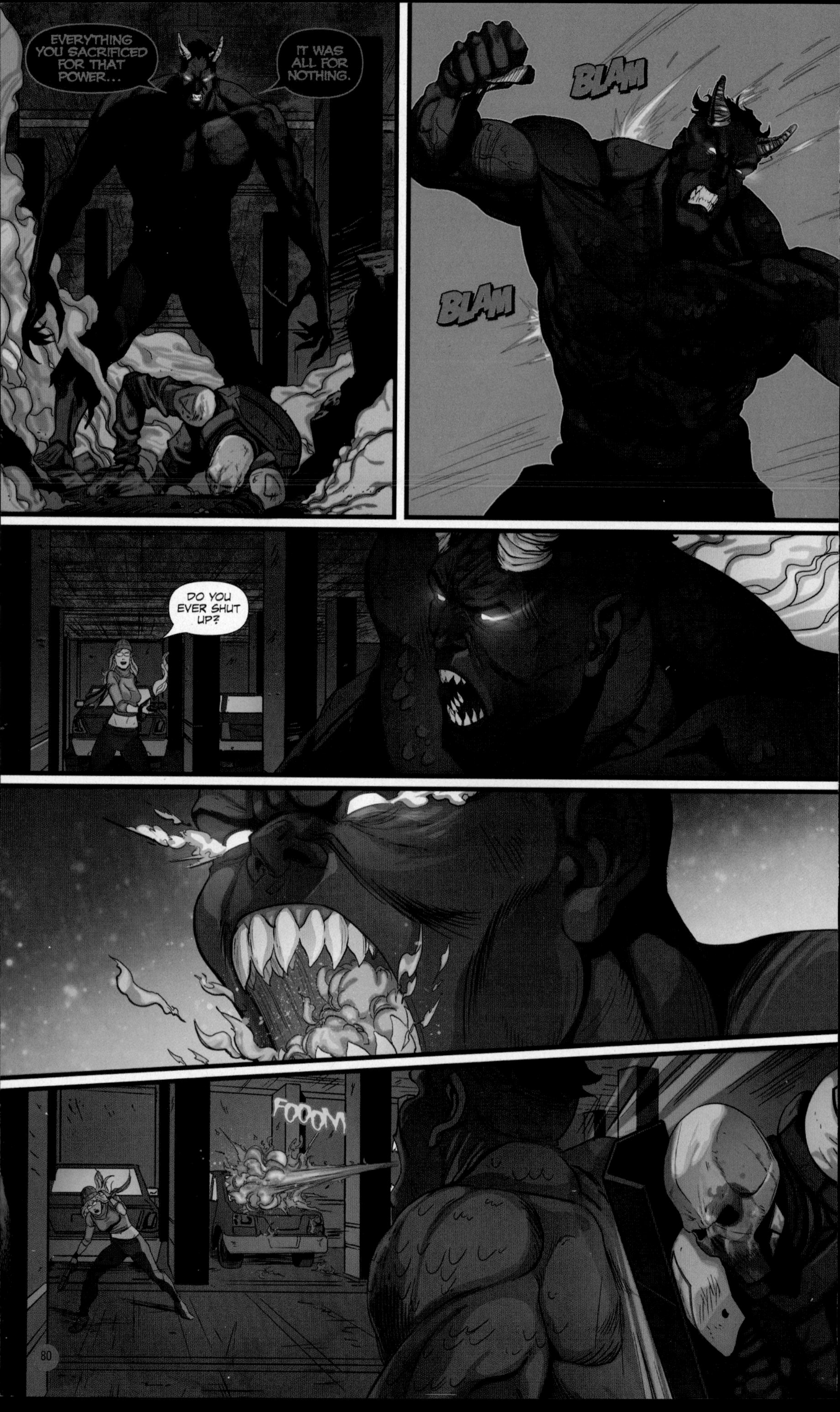
EVERYTHING YOU SACRIFICED FOR THAT POWER...
IT WAS ALL FOR NOTHING.
BLAM
BLAM
DO YOU EVER SHUT UP?
FOOOM

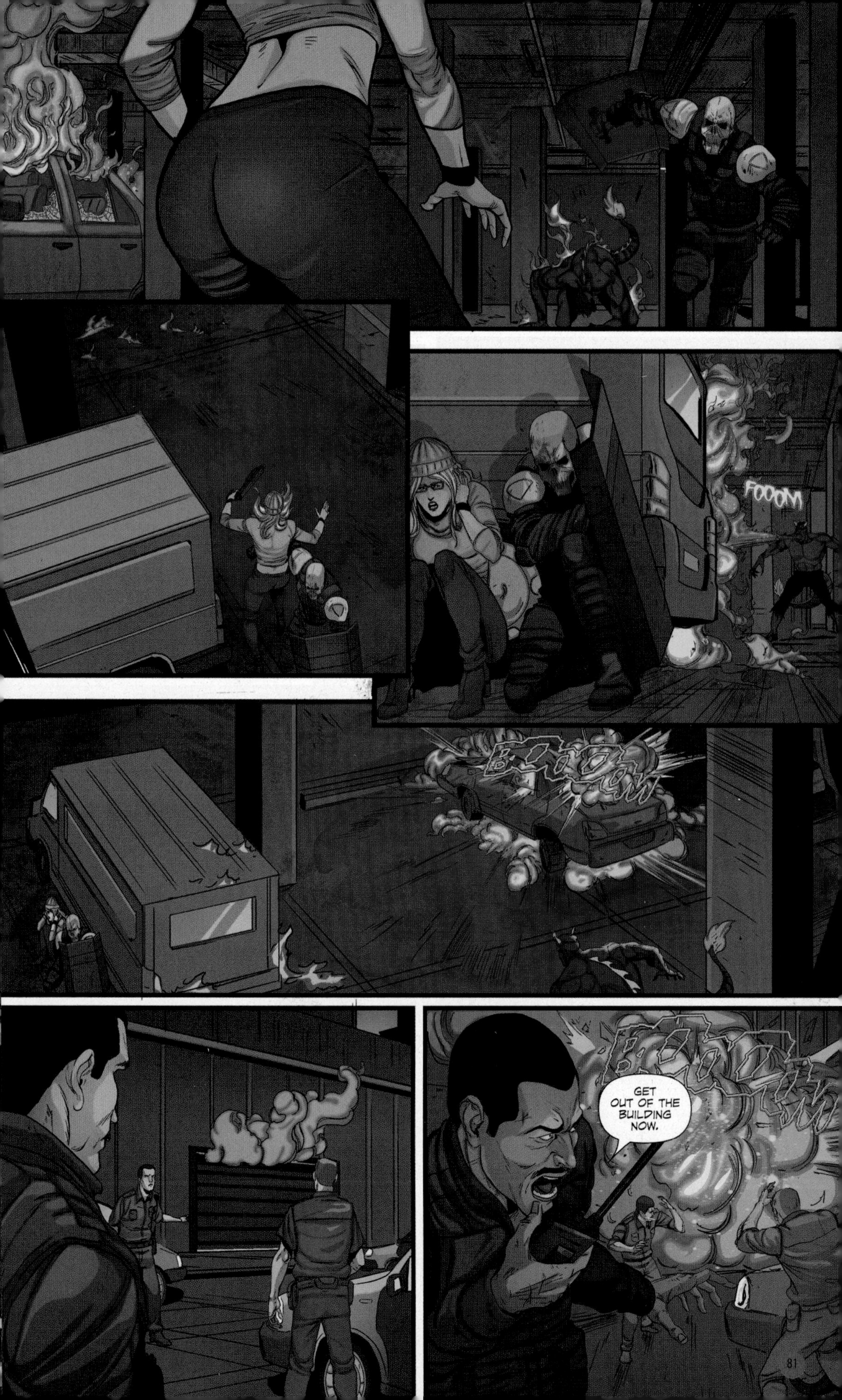
FOOOM
GET OUT OF THE BUILDING NOW.

DON'T YOU HAVE AN APARTMENT OR HOUSE WE CAN GO TO?

NO.

YOU LIVE IN THIS VAN?

YES. DO YOU HAVE A PROBLEM WITH THAT?

NO.

GOOD. DO YOU EVER TAKE THAT MASK OFF?

NO. I GUESS I DON'T.

I HAVEN'T REALLY HAD TIME TO THINK ABOUT IT.

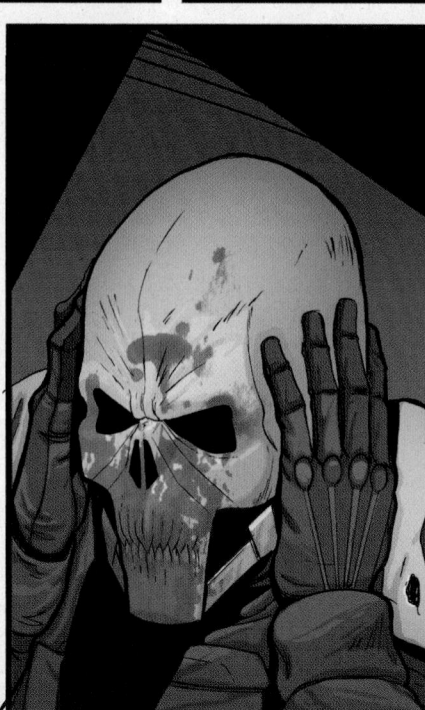

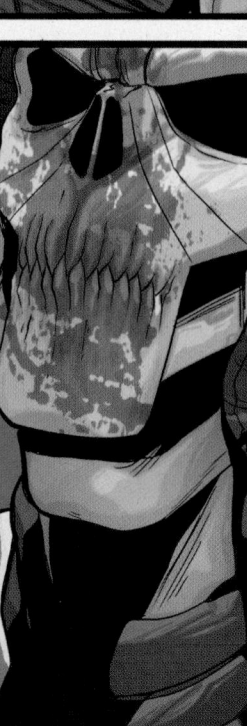

84

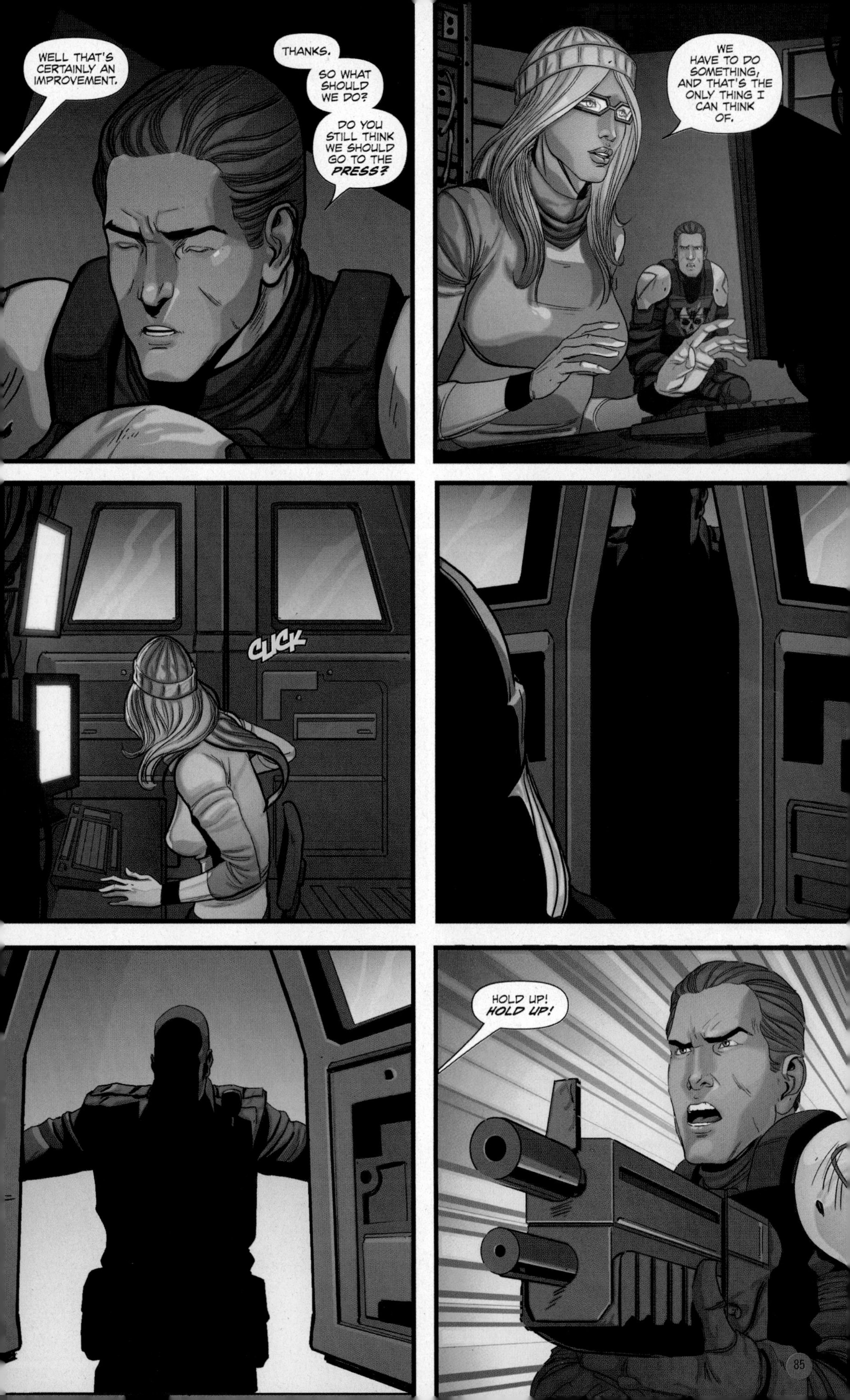
WELL THAT'S CERTAINLY AN IMPROVEMENT.
THANKS.
SO WHAT SHOULD WE DO?
DO YOU STILL THINK WE SHOULD GO TO THE PRESS?
WE HAVE TO DO SOMETHING, AND THAT'S THE ONLY THING I CAN THINK OF.
CLICK
HOLD UP! HOLD UP!

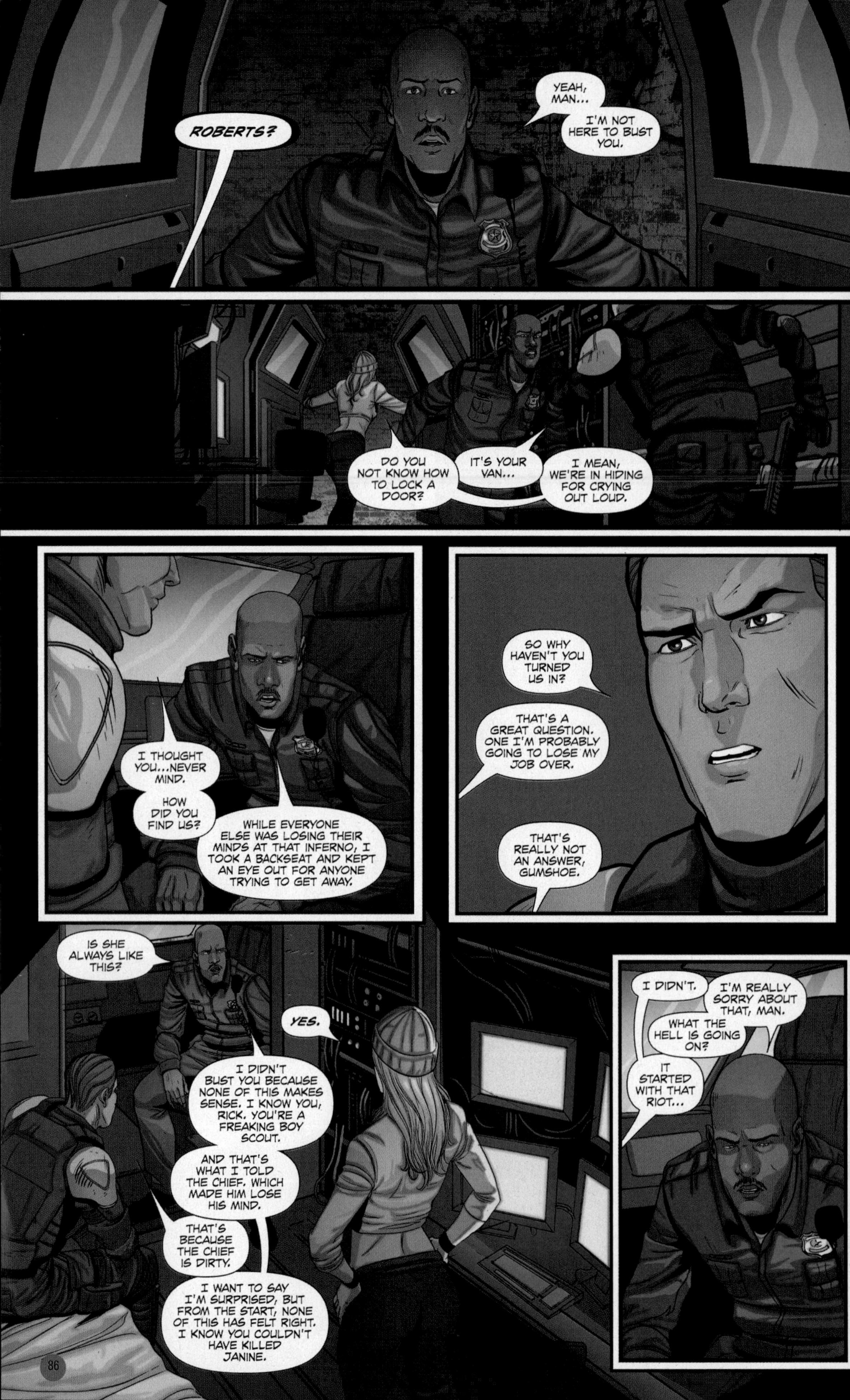
ROBERTS?
YEAH, MAN...
I'M NOT HERE TO BUST YOU.
DO YOU NOT KNOW HOW TO LOCK A DOOR?
IT'S YOUR VAN...
I MEAN, WE'RE IN HIDING FOR CRYING OUT LOUD.
I THOUGHT YOU...NEVER MIND.
HOW DID YOU FIND US?
WHILE EVERYONE ELSE WAS LOSING THEIR MINDS AT THAT INFERNO, I TOOK A BACKSEAT AND KEPT AN EYE OUT FOR ANYONE TRYING TO GET AWAY.
SO WHY HAVEN'T YOU TURNED US IN?
THAT'S A GREAT QUESTION. ONE I'M PROBABLY GOING TO LOSE MY JOB OVER.
THAT'S REALLY NOT AN ANSWER, GUMSHOE.
IS SHE ALWAYS LIKE THIS?
YES.
I DIDN'T BUST YOU BECAUSE NONE OF THIS MAKES SENSE. I KNOW YOU, RICK. YOU'RE A FREAKING BOY SCOUT.
AND THAT'S WHAT I TOLD THE CHIEF. WHICH MADE HIM LOSE HIS MIND.
THAT'S BECAUSE THE CHIEF IS DIRTY.
I WANT TO SAY I'M SURPRISED, BUT FROM THE START, NONE OF THIS HAS FELT RIGHT. I KNOW YOU COULDN'T HAVE KILLED JANINE.
I DIDN'T.
I'M REALLY SORRY ABOUT THAT, MAN.
WHAT THE HELL IS GOING ON?
IT STARTED WITH THAT RIOT...

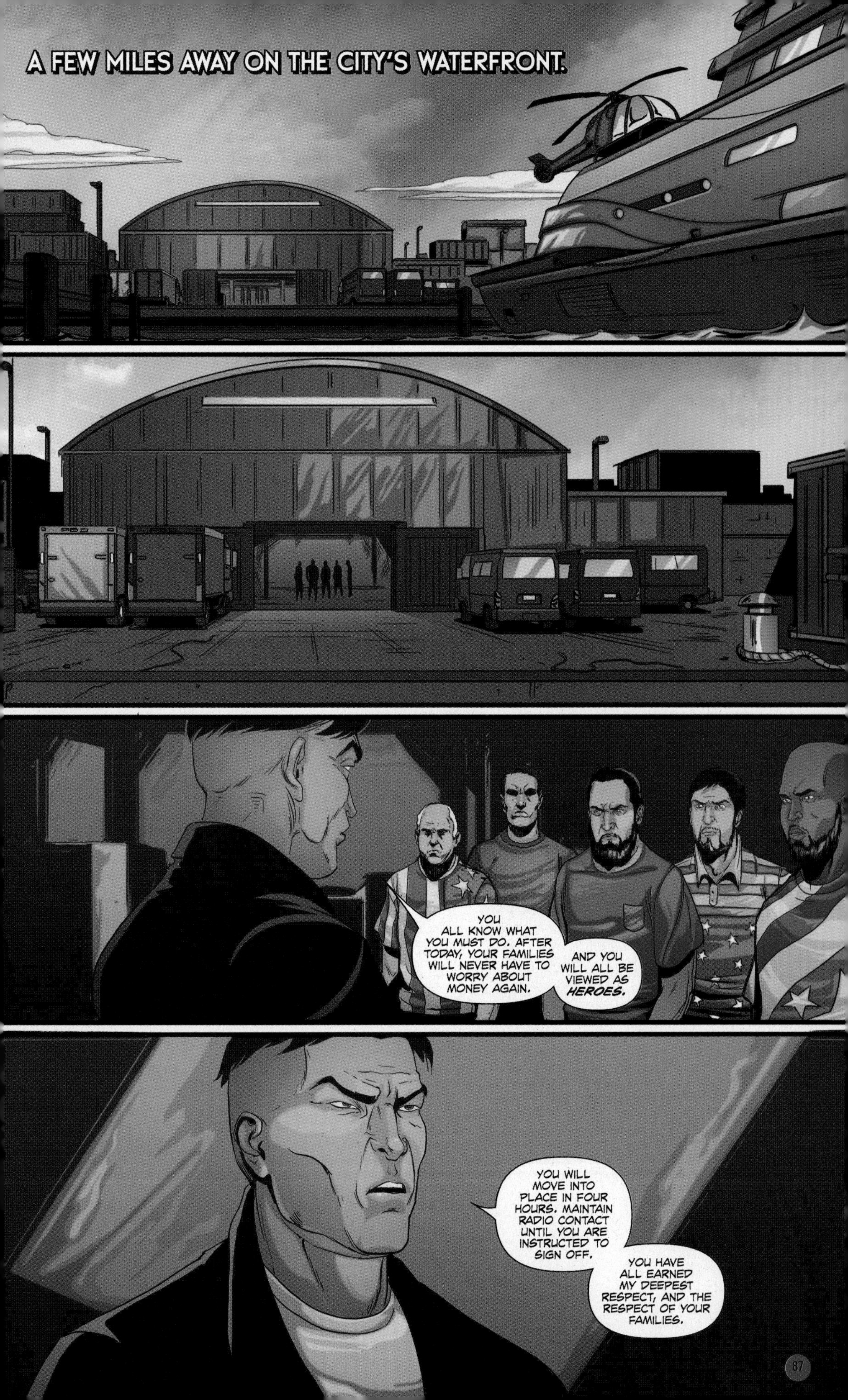
A FEW MILES AWAY ON THE CITY'S WATERFRONT.
YOU ALL KNOW WHAT YOU MUST DO. AFTER TODAY, YOUR FAMILIES WILL NEVER HAVE TO WORRY ABOUT MONEY AGAIN.
AND YOU WILL ALL BE VIEWED AS *HEROES.*
YOU WILL MOVE INTO PLACE IN FOUR HOURS. MAINTAIN RADIO CONTACT UNTIL YOU ARE INSTRUCTED TO SIGN OFF.
YOU HAVE ALL EARNED MY DEEPEST RESPECT, AND THE RESPECT OF YOUR FAMILIES.

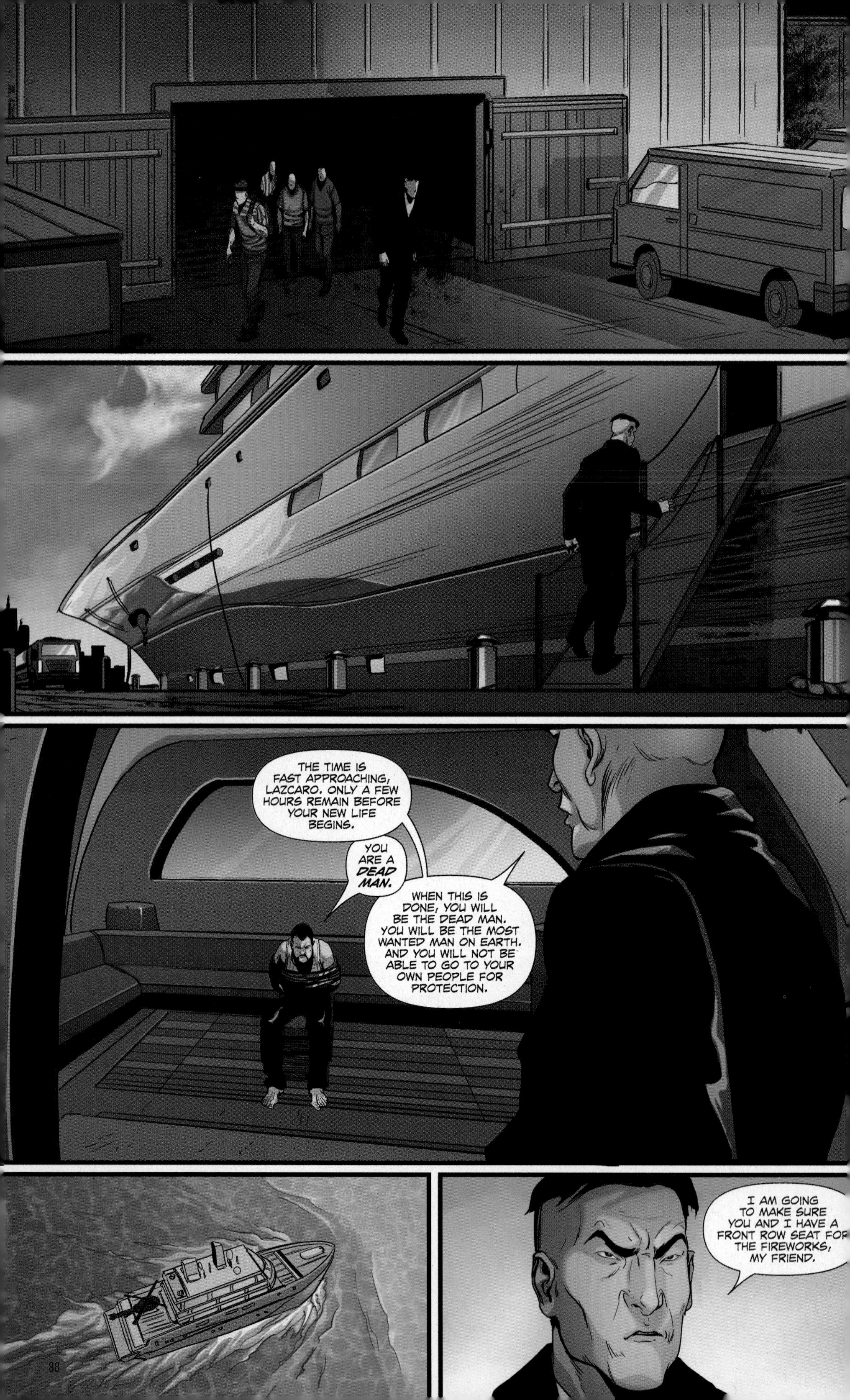
THE TIME IS FAST APPROACHING, LAZCARO. ONLY A FEW HOURS REMAIN BEFORE YOUR NEW LIFE BEGINS.
YOU ARE A *DEAD MAN.*
WHEN THIS IS DONE, YOU WILL BE THE DEAD MAN. YOU WILL BE THE MOST WANTED MAN ON EARTH. AND YOU WILL NOT BE ABLE TO GO TO YOUR OWN PEOPLE FOR PROTECTION.
I AM GOING TO MAKE SURE YOU AND I HAVE A FRONT ROW SEAT FOR THE FIREWORKS, MY FRIEND.

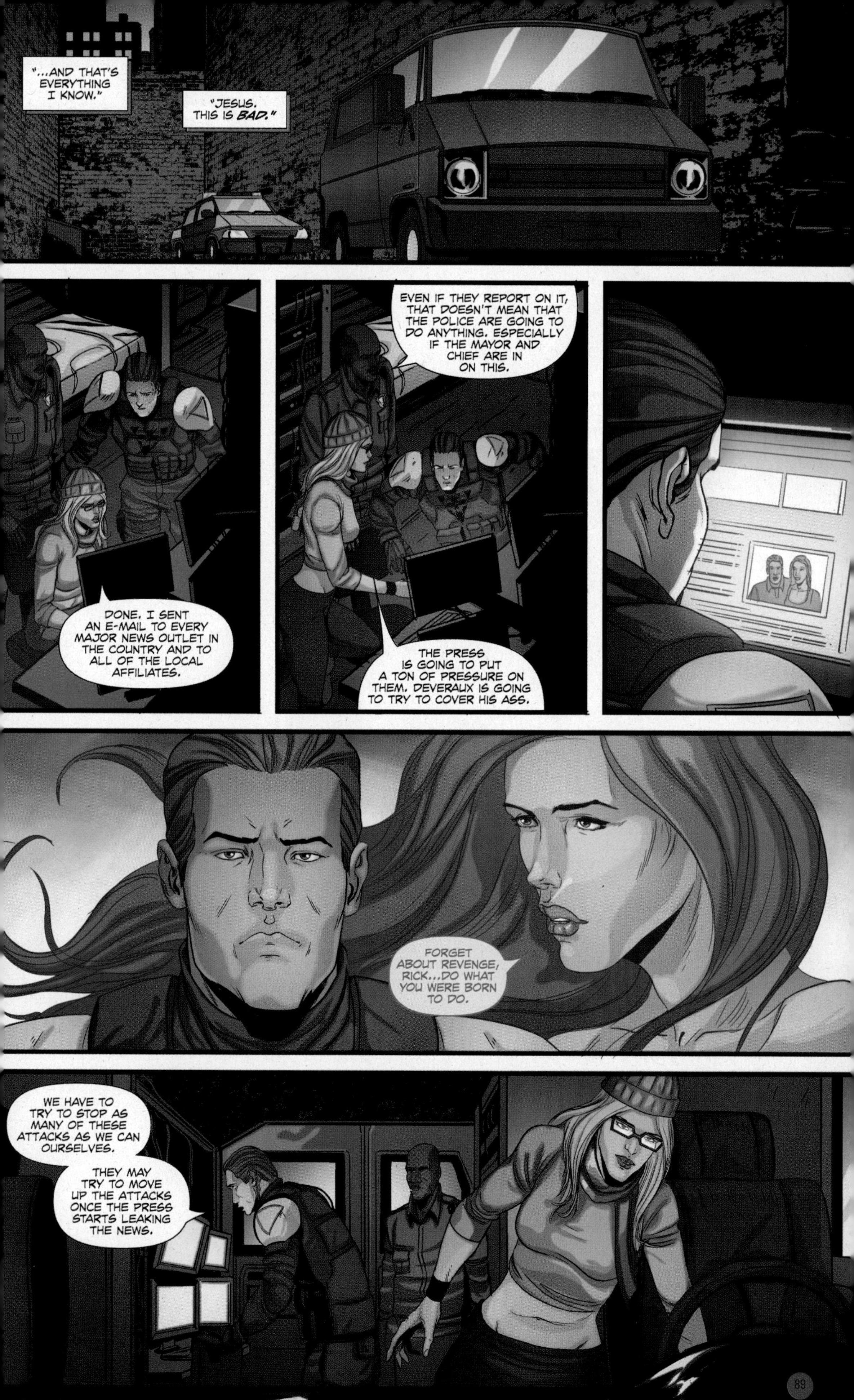
"...AND THAT'S EVERYTHING I KNOW."
"JESUS. THIS IS BAD."
DONE. I SENT AN E-MAIL TO EVERY MAJOR NEWS OUTLET IN THE COUNTRY AND TO ALL OF THE LOCAL AFFILIATES.
EVEN IF THEY REPORT ON IT, THAT DOESN'T MEAN THAT THE POLICE ARE GOING TO DO ANYTHING. ESPECIALLY IF THE MAYOR AND CHIEF ARE IN ON THIS.
THE PRESS IS GOING TO PUT A TON OF PRESSURE ON THEM. DEVERAUX IS GOING TO TRY TO COVER HIS ASS.
FORGET ABOUT REVENGE, RICK...DO WHAT YOU WERE BORN TO DO.
WE HAVE TO TRY TO STOP AS MANY OF THESE ATTACKS AS WE CAN OURSELVES.
THEY MAY TRY TO MOVE UP THE ATTACKS ONCE THE PRESS STARTS LEAKING THE NEWS.

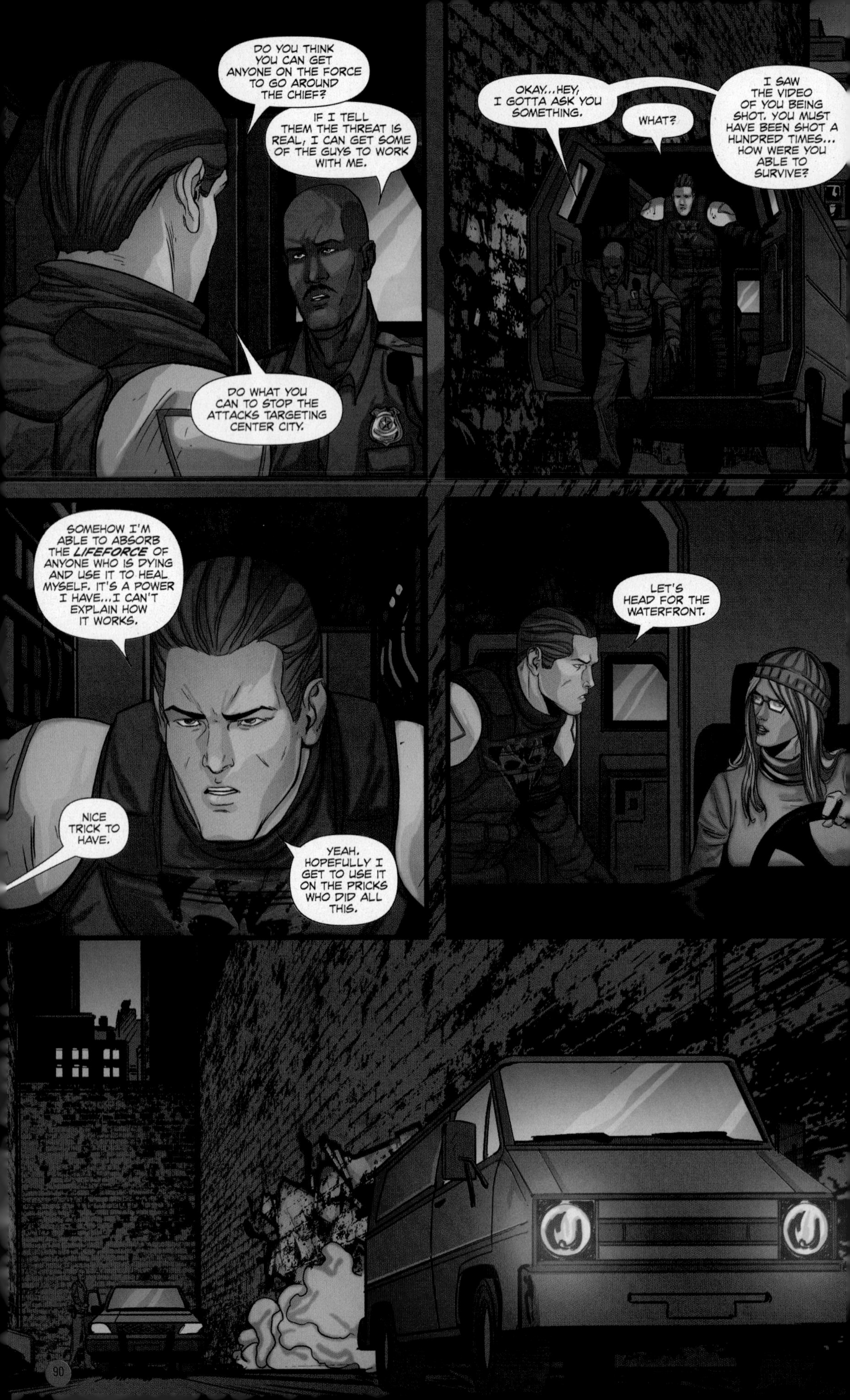
DO YOU THINK YOU CAN GET ANYONE ON THE FORCE TO GO AROUND THE CHIEF?
IF I TELL THEM THE THREAT IS REAL, I CAN GET SOME OF THE GUYS TO WORK WITH ME.
DO WHAT YOU CAN TO STOP THE ATTACKS TARGETING CENTER CITY.
OKAY...HEY, I GOTTA ASK YOU SOMETHING.
WHAT?
I SAW THE VIDEO OF YOU BEING SHOT. YOU MUST HAVE BEEN SHOT A HUNDRED TIMES... HOW WERE YOU ABLE TO SURVIVE?
SOMEHOW I'M ABLE TO ABSORB THE *LIFEFORCE* OF ANYONE WHO IS DYING AND USE IT TO HEAL MYSELF. IT'S A POWER I HAVE...I CAN'T EXPLAIN HOW IT WORKS.
NICE TRICK TO HAVE.
YEAH. HOPEFULLY I GET TO USE IT ON THE PRICKS WHO DID ALL THIS.
LET'S HEAD FOR THE WATERFRONT.

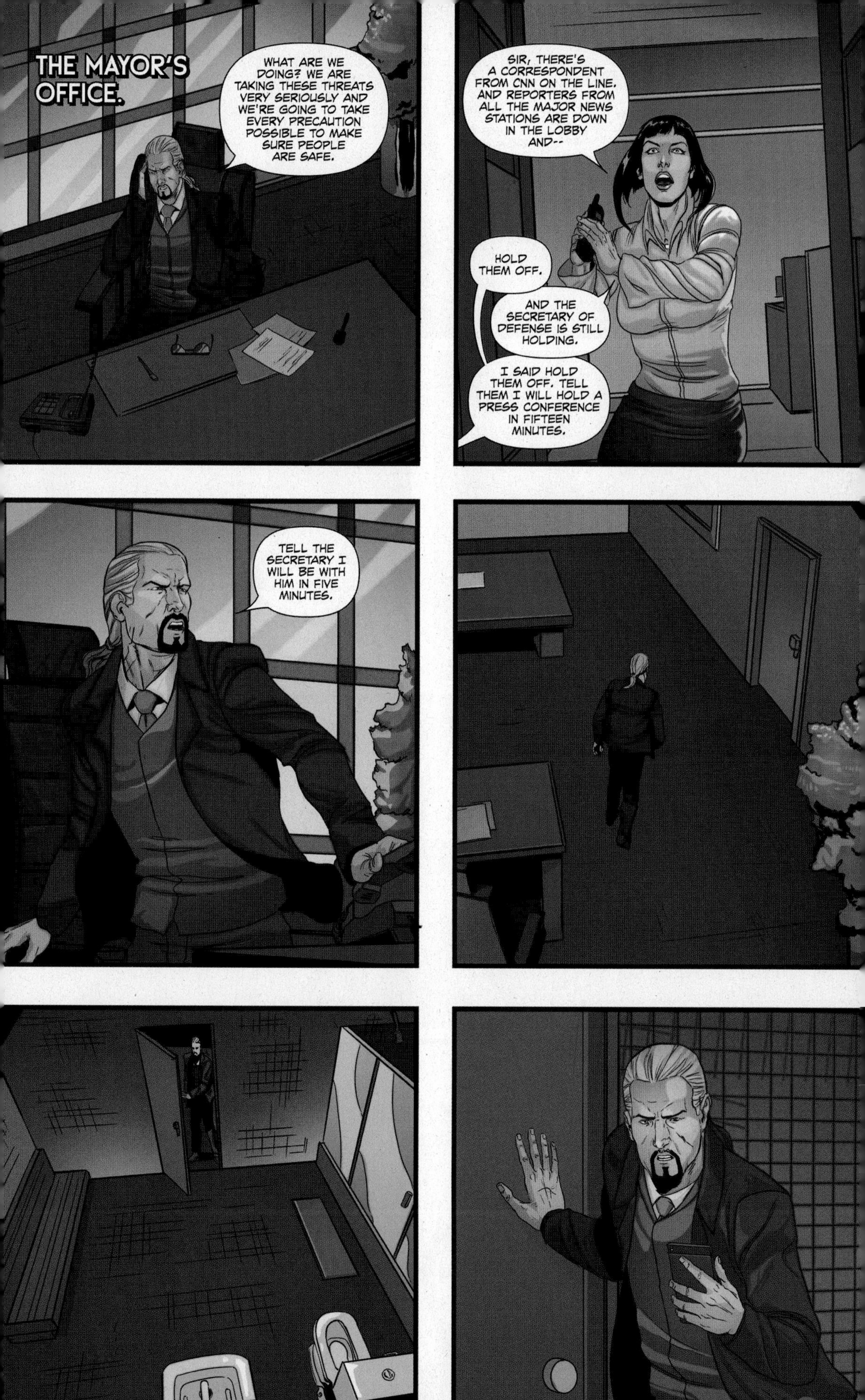
THE MAYOR'S OFFICE.
WHAT ARE WE DOING? WE ARE TAKING THESE THREATS VERY SERIOUSLY AND WE'RE GOING TO TAKE EVERY PRECAUTION POSSIBLE TO MAKE SURE PEOPLE ARE SAFE.
SIR, THERE'S A CORRESPONDENT FROM CNN ON THE LINE. AND REPORTERS FROM ALL THE MAJOR NEWS STATIONS ARE DOWN IN THE LOBBY AND--
HOLD THEM OFF.
AND THE SECRETARY OF DEFENSE IS STILL HOLDING.
I SAID HOLD THEM OFF. TELL THEM I WILL HOLD A PRESS CONFERENCE IN FIFTEEN MINUTES.
TELL THE SECRETARY I WILL BE WITH HIM IN FIVE MINUTES.

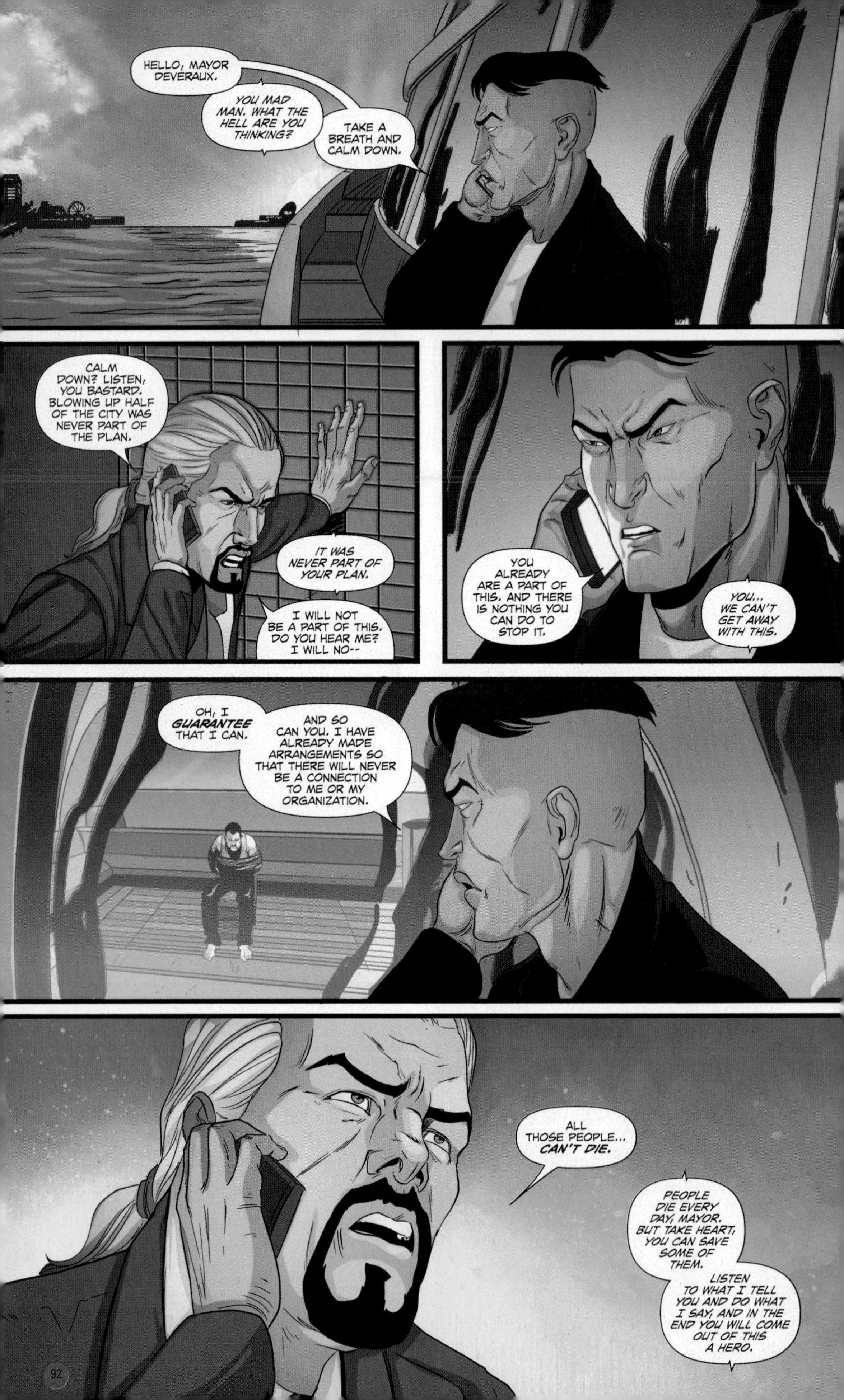
HELLO, MAYOR DEVERAUX.
YOU MAD MAN. WHAT THE HELL ARE YOU THINKING?
TAKE A BREATH AND CALM DOWN.
CALM DOWN? LISTEN, YOU BASTARD. BLOWING UP HALF OF THE CITY WAS NEVER PART OF THE PLAN.
IT WAS NEVER PART OF YOUR PLAN.
I WILL NOT BE A PART OF THIS. DO YOU HEAR ME? I WILL NO--
YOU ALREADY ARE A PART OF THIS. AND THERE IS NOTHING YOU CAN DO TO STOP IT.
YOU... WE CAN'T GET AWAY WITH THIS.
OH, I GUARANTEE THAT I CAN.
AND SO CAN YOU. I HAVE ALREADY MADE ARRANGEMENTS SO THAT THERE WILL NEVER BE A CONNECTION TO ME OR MY ORGANIZATION.
ALL THOSE PEOPLE... CAN'T DIE.
PEOPLE DIE EVERY DAY, MAYOR. BUT TAKE HEART, YOU CAN SAVE SOME OF THEM.
LISTEN TO WHAT I TELL YOU AND DO WHAT I SAY, AND IN THE END YOU WILL COME OUT OF THIS A HERO.

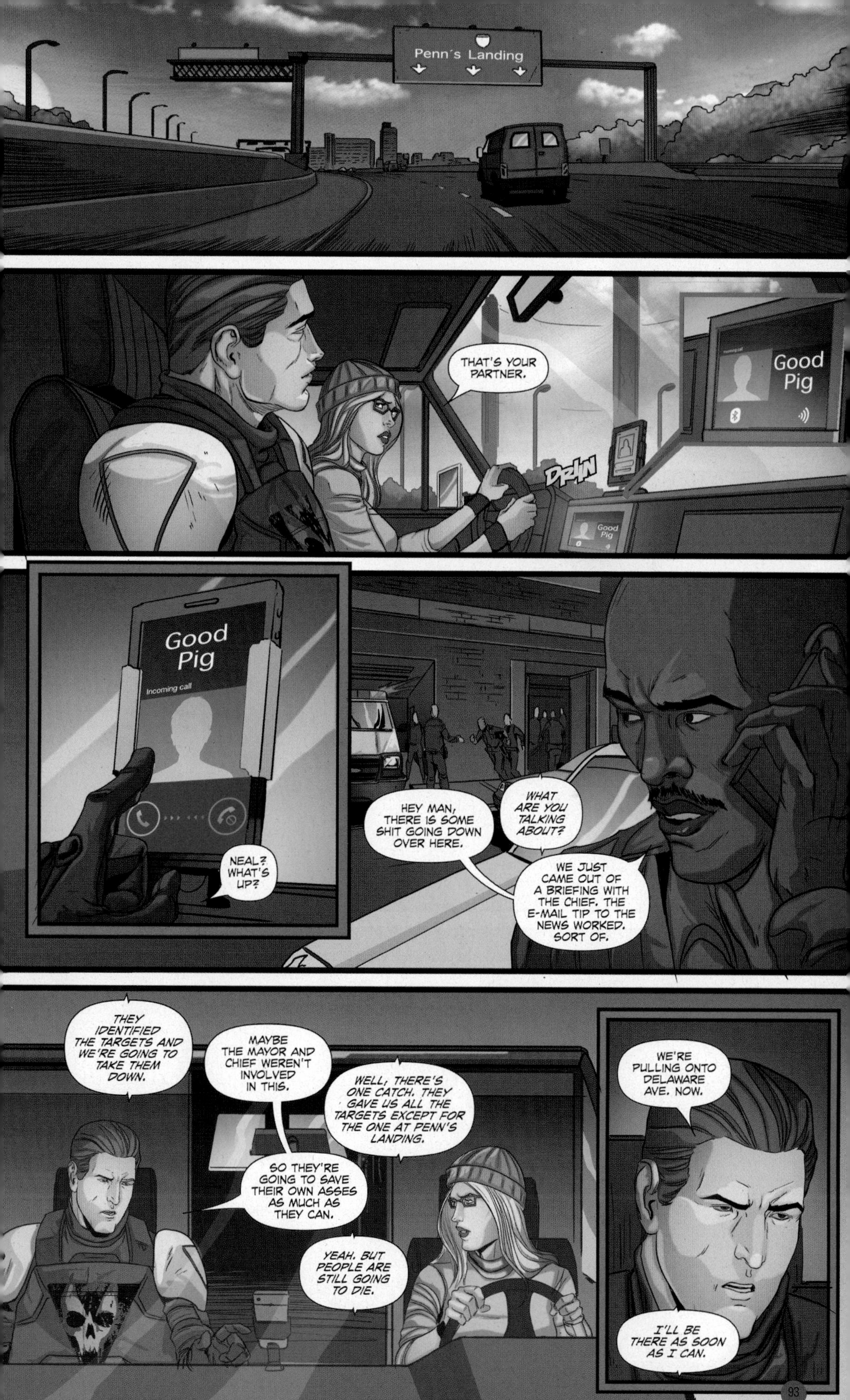
Penn's Landing
THAT'S YOUR PARTNER.
Good Pig
DRHN
Good Pig
Incoming call
NEAL? WHAT'S UP?
HEY MAN, THERE IS SOME SHIT GOING DOWN OVER HERE.
WHAT ARE YOU TALKING ABOUT?
WE JUST CAME OUT OF A BRIEFING WITH THE CHIEF. THE E-MAIL TIP TO THE NEWS WORKED. SORT OF.
THEY IDENTIFIED THE TARGETS AND WE'RE GOING TO TAKE THEM DOWN.
MAYBE THE MAYOR AND CHIEF WEREN'T INVOLVED IN THIS.
WELL, THERE'S ONE CATCH. THEY GAVE US ALL THE TARGETS EXCEPT FOR THE ONE AT PENN'S LANDING.
SO THEY'RE GOING TO SAVE THEIR OWN ASSES AS MUCH AS THEY CAN.
YEAH. BUT PEOPLE ARE STILL GOING TO DIE.
WE'RE PULLING ONTO DELAWARE AVE. NOW.
I'LL BE THERE AS SOON AS I CAN.

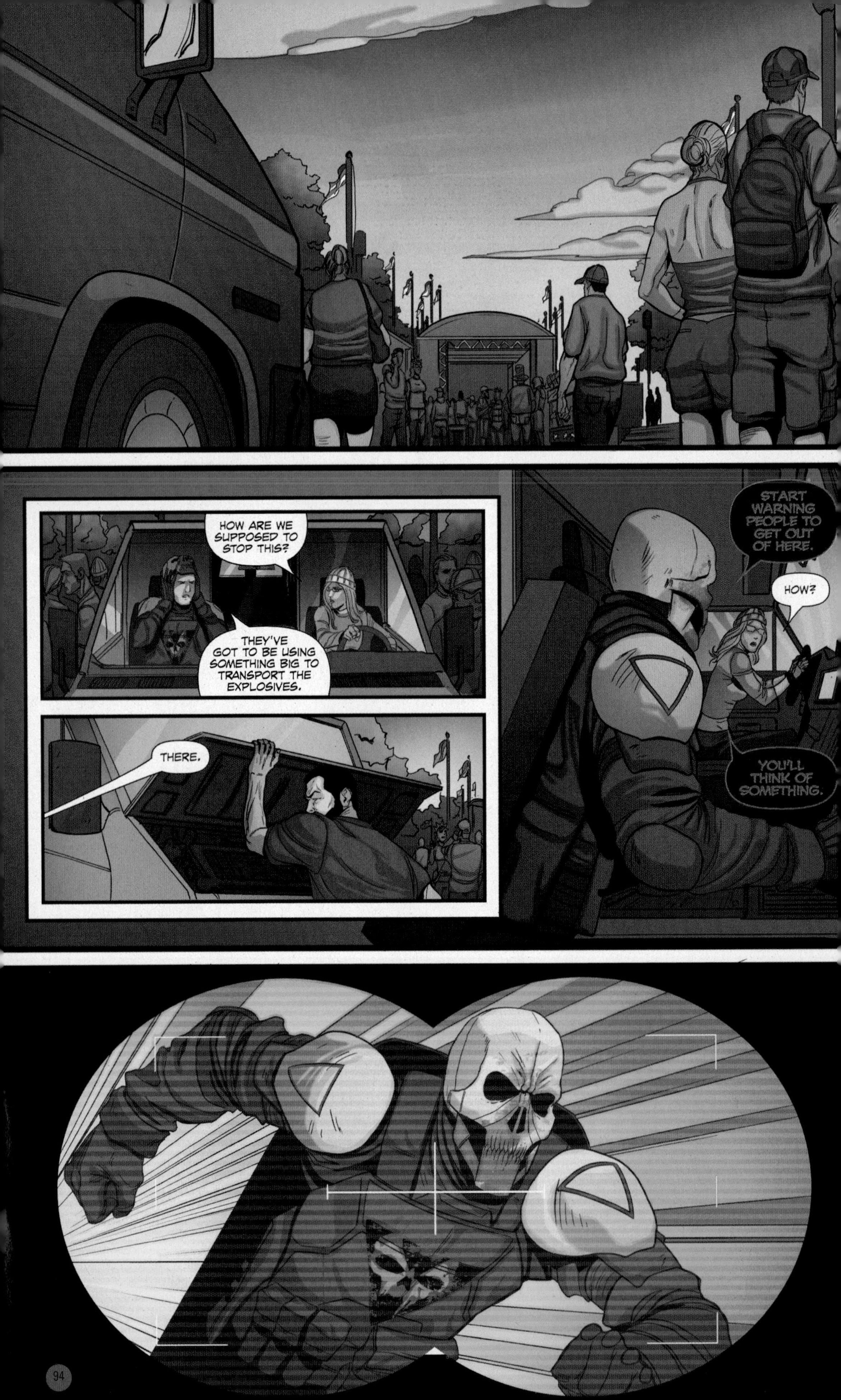
HOW ARE WE SUPPOSED TO STOP THIS?
THEY'VE GOT TO BE USING SOMETHING BIG TO TRANSPORT THE EXPLOSIVES.
THERE.
START WARNING PEOPLE TO GET OUT OF HERE.
HOW?
YOU'LL THINK OF SOMETHING.

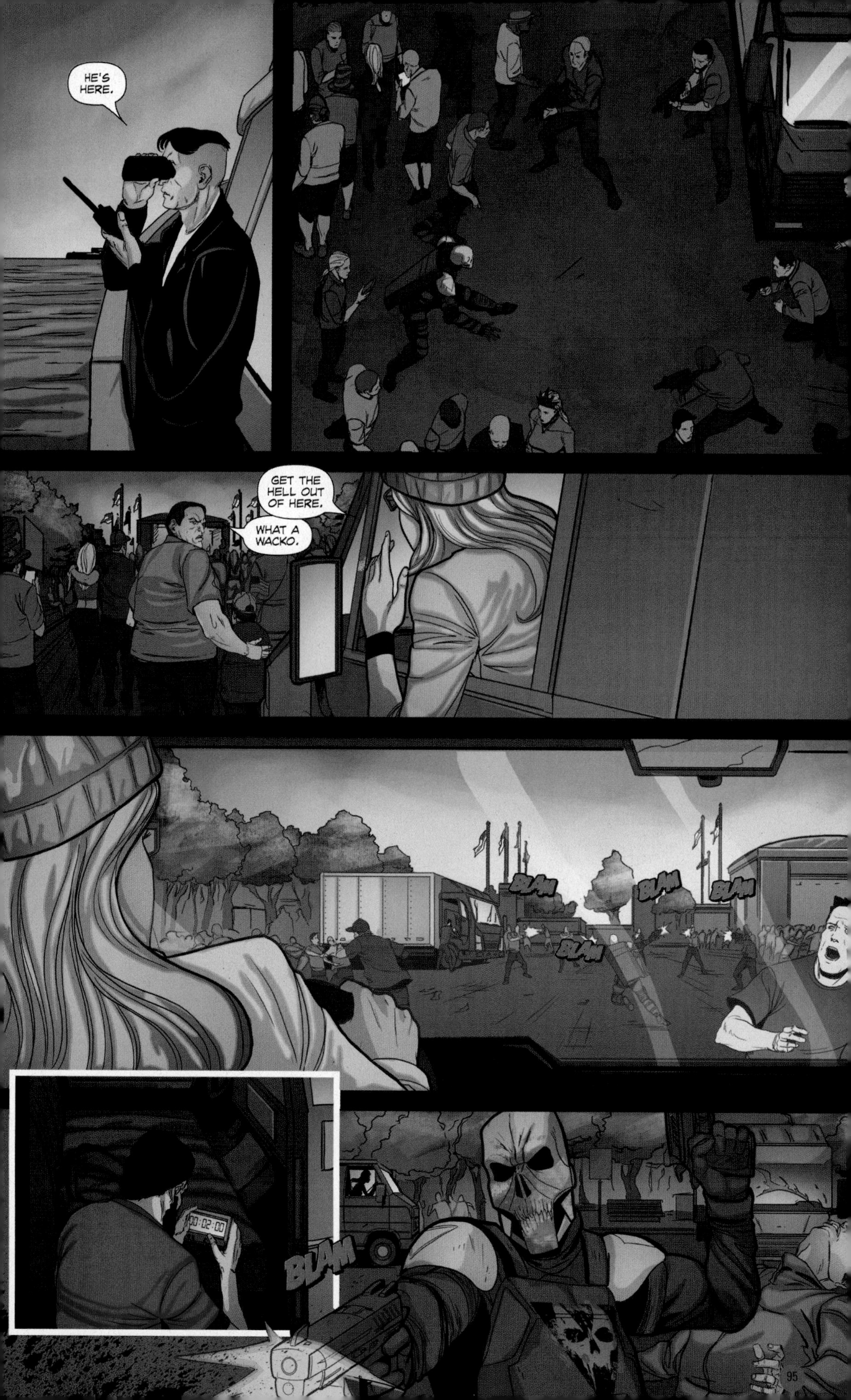
HE'S HERE.
GET THE HELL OUT OF HERE.
WHAT A WACKO.
BLAM
BLAM
BLAM
BLAM
00:02:00
BLAM

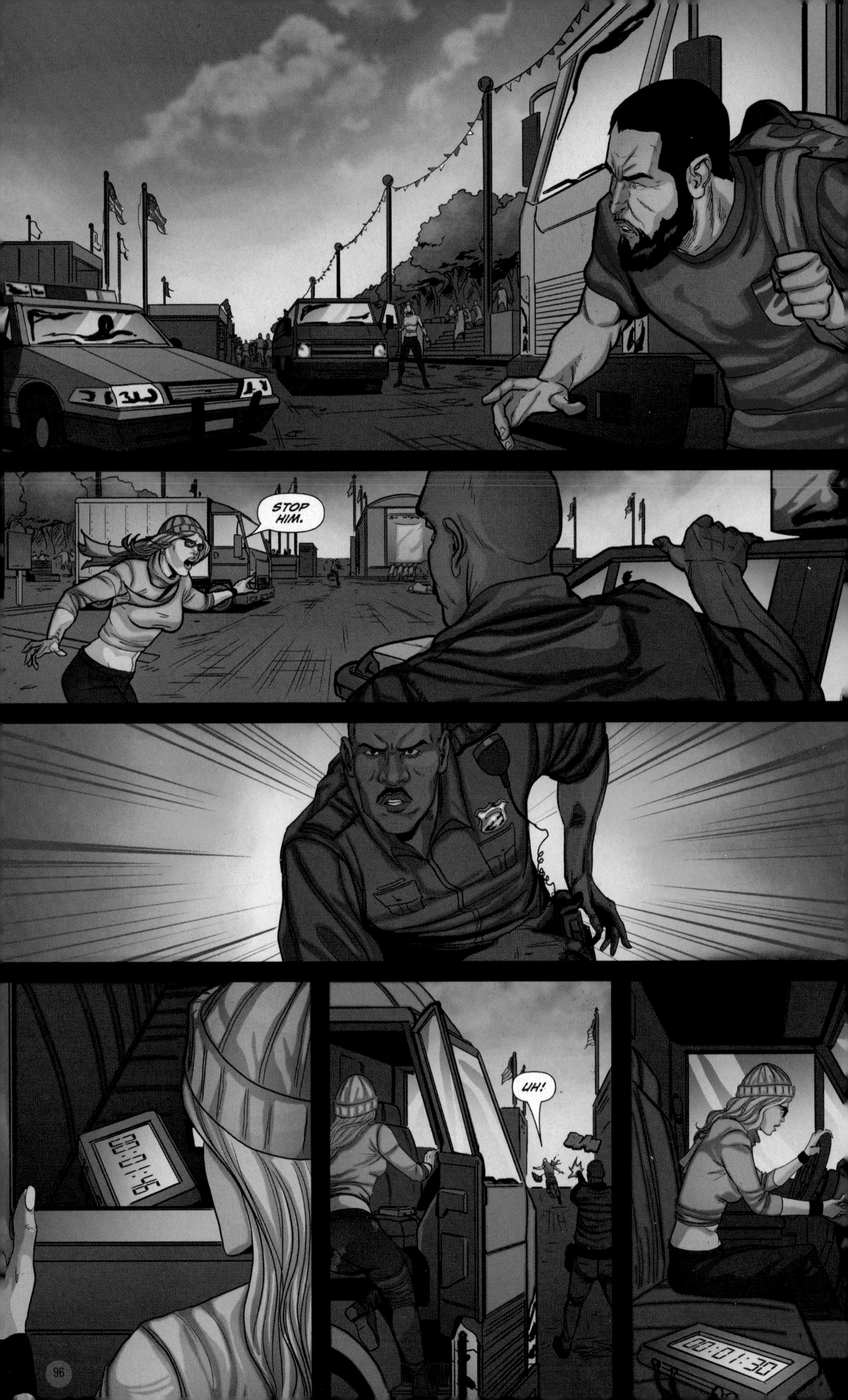
STOP HIM.
UH!
00:01:45
00:01:30

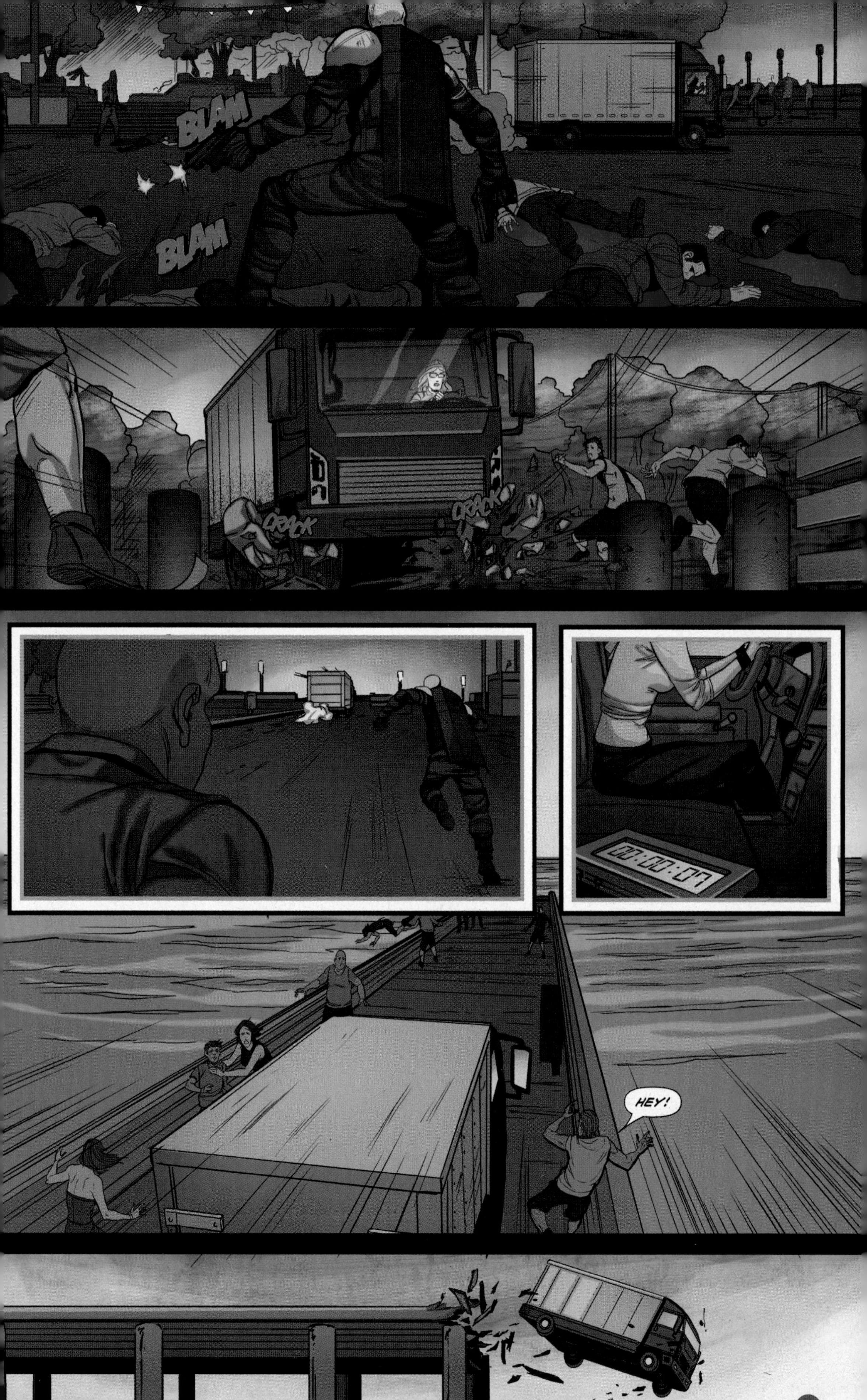
BLAM
BLAM
CRACK
CRACK
00:00:07
HEY!

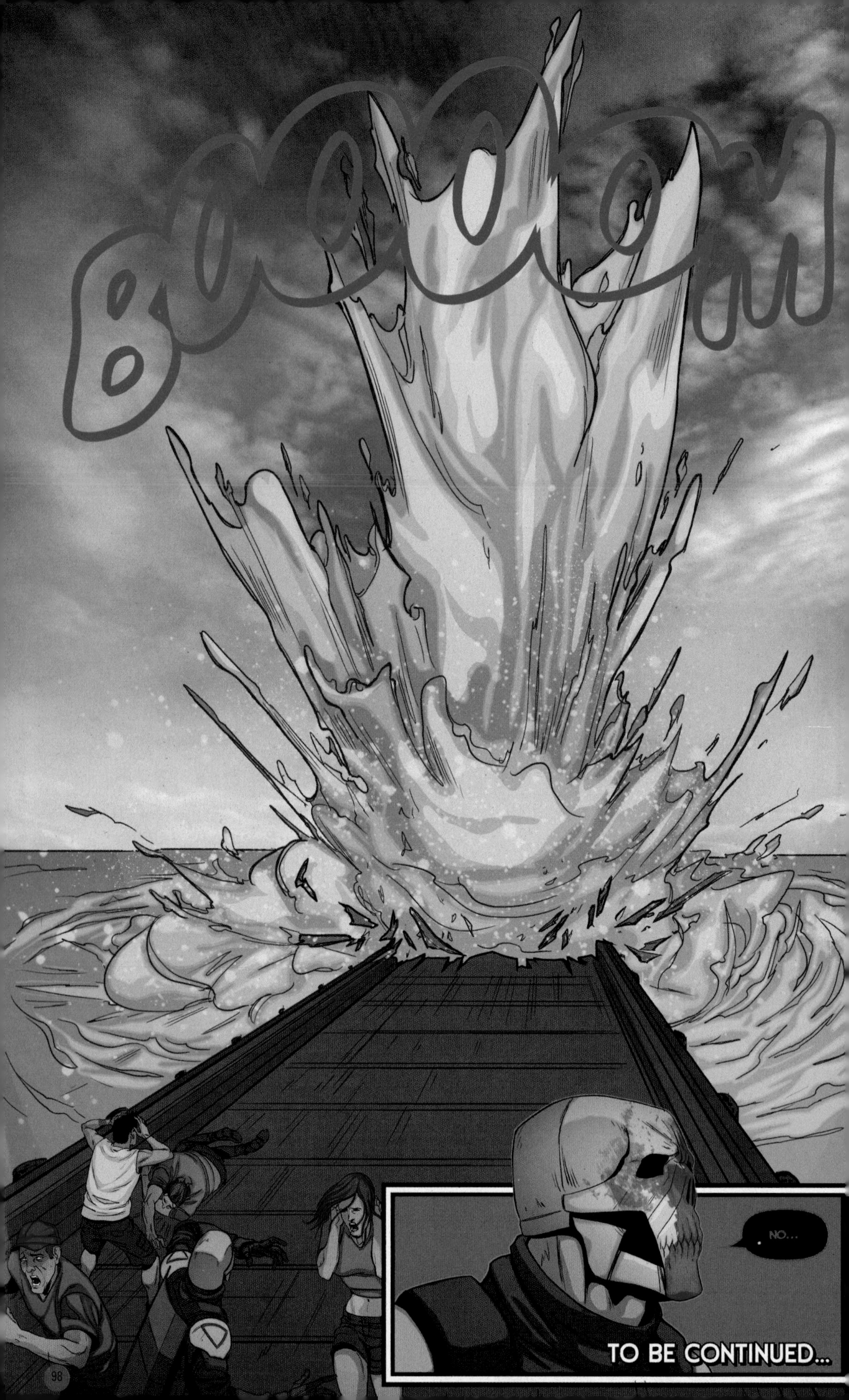
BOOOOOM
NO...
TO BE CONTINUED...

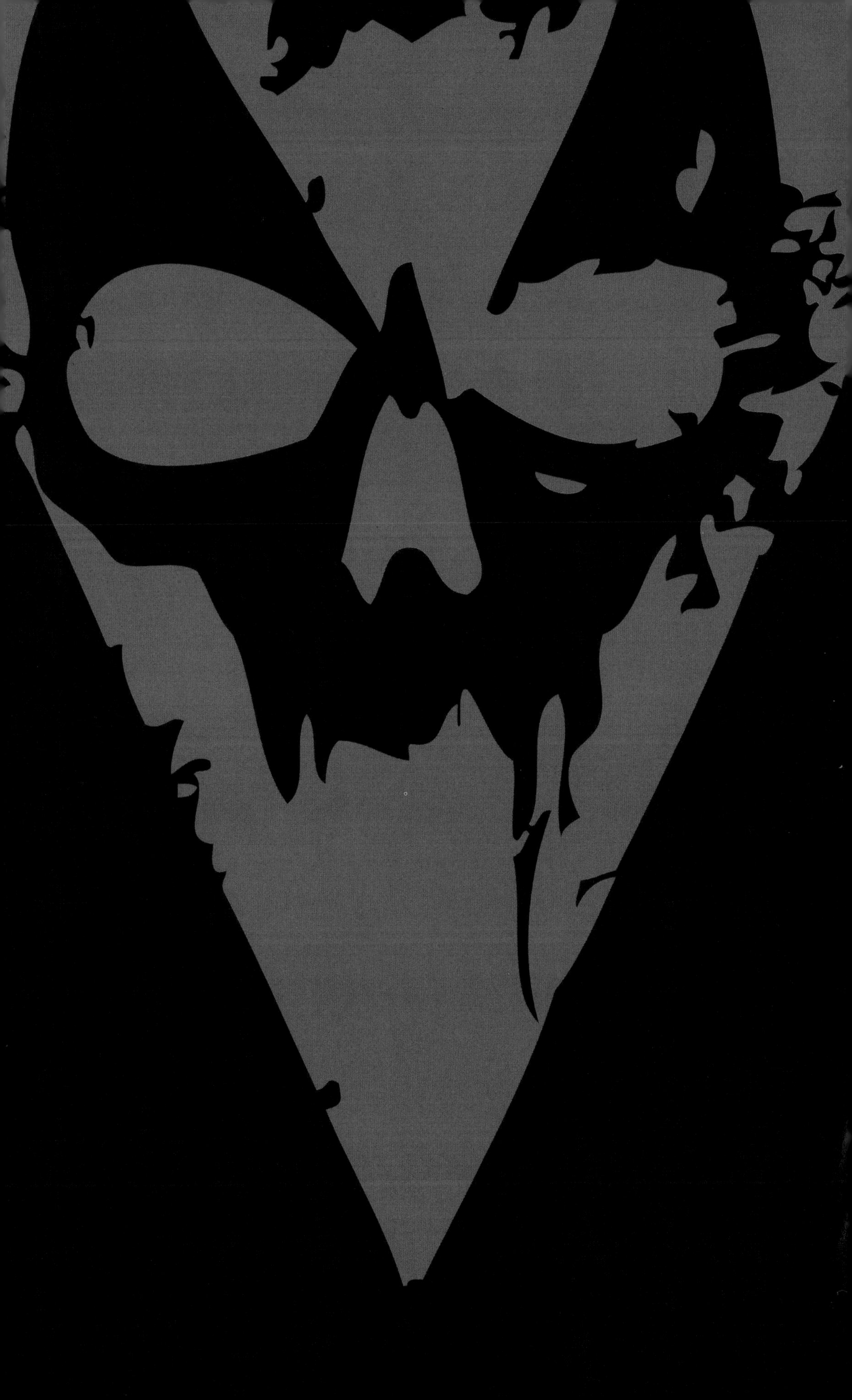

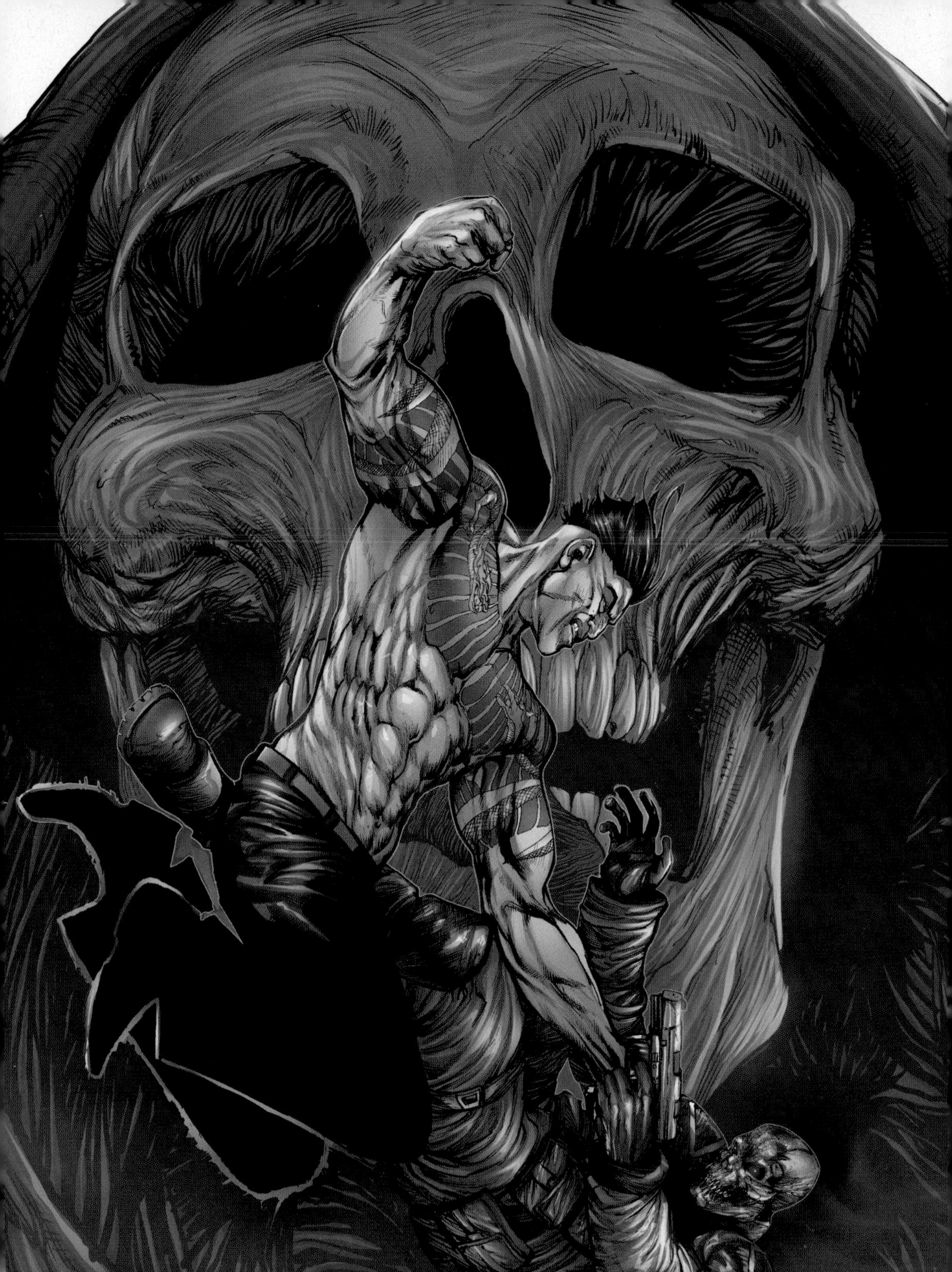

CHAPTER FIVE

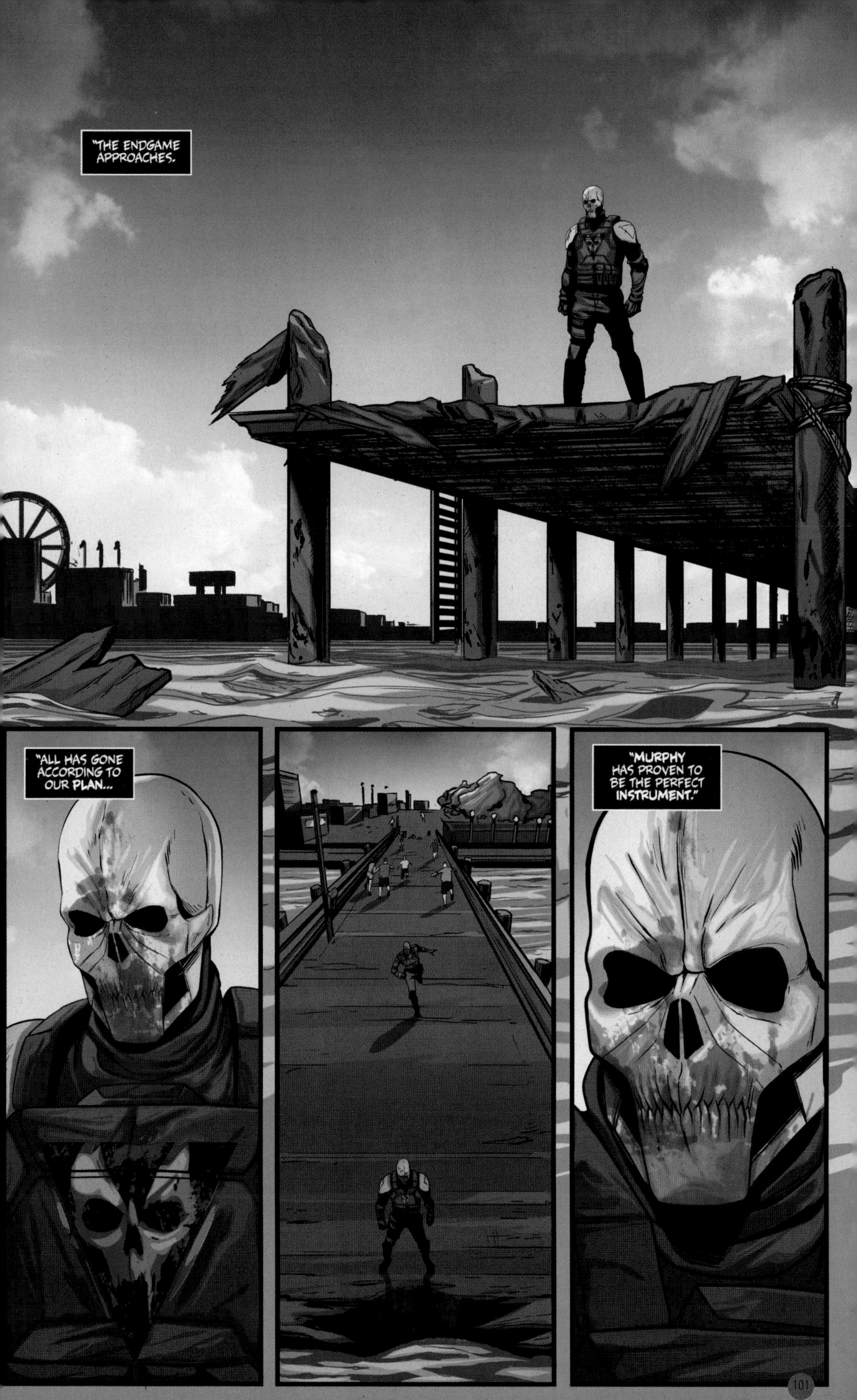
"THE ENDGAME APPROACHES.
"ALL HAS GONE ACCORDING TO OUR **PLAN**...
"MURPHY HAS PROVEN TO BE THE PERFECT **INSTRUMENT**."

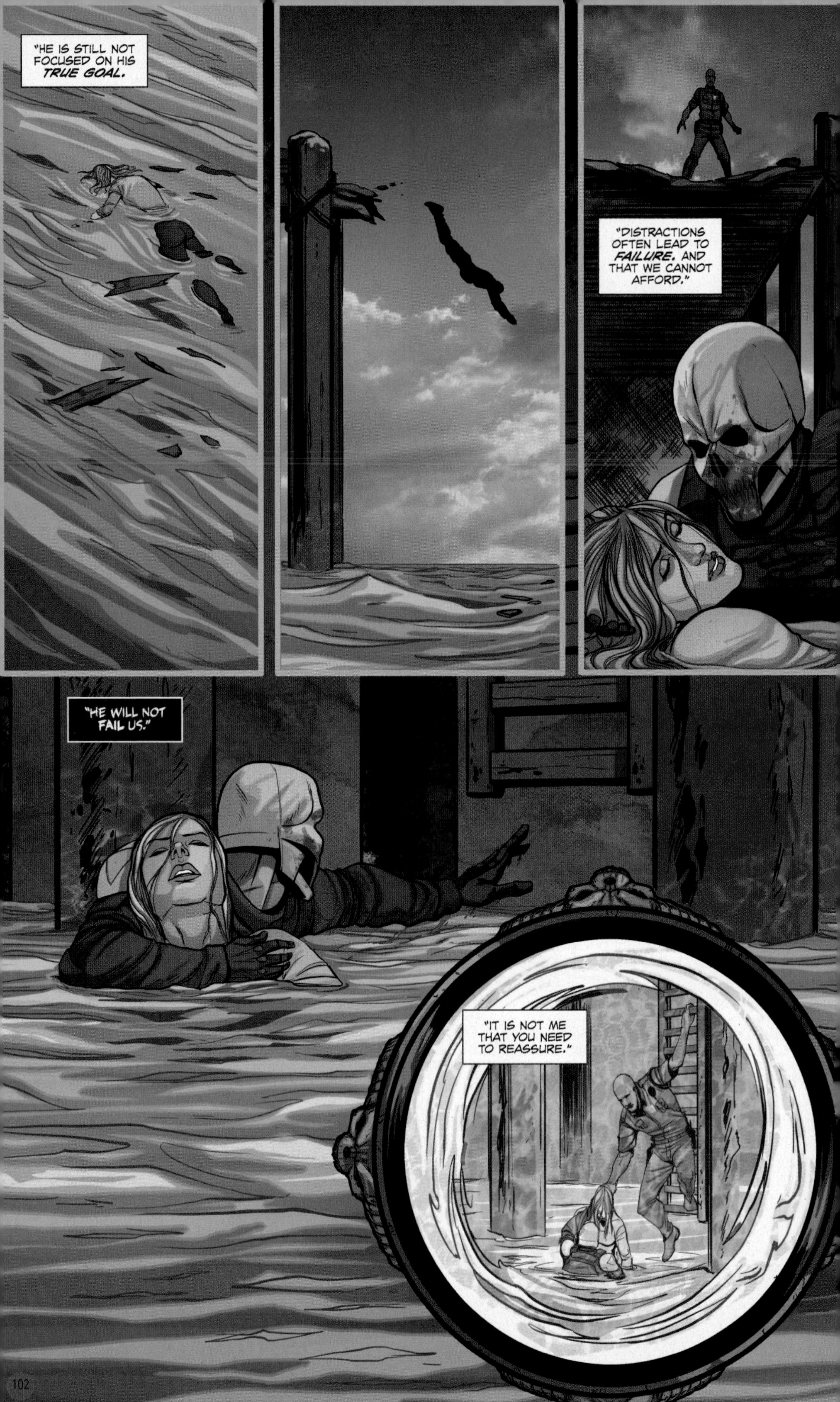
"HE IS STILL NOT FOCUSED ON HIS TRUE GOAL.
"DISTRACTIONS OFTEN LEAD TO FAILURE. AND THAT WE CANNOT AFFORD."
"HE WILL NOT FAIL US."
"IT IS NOT ME THAT YOU NEED TO REASSURE."

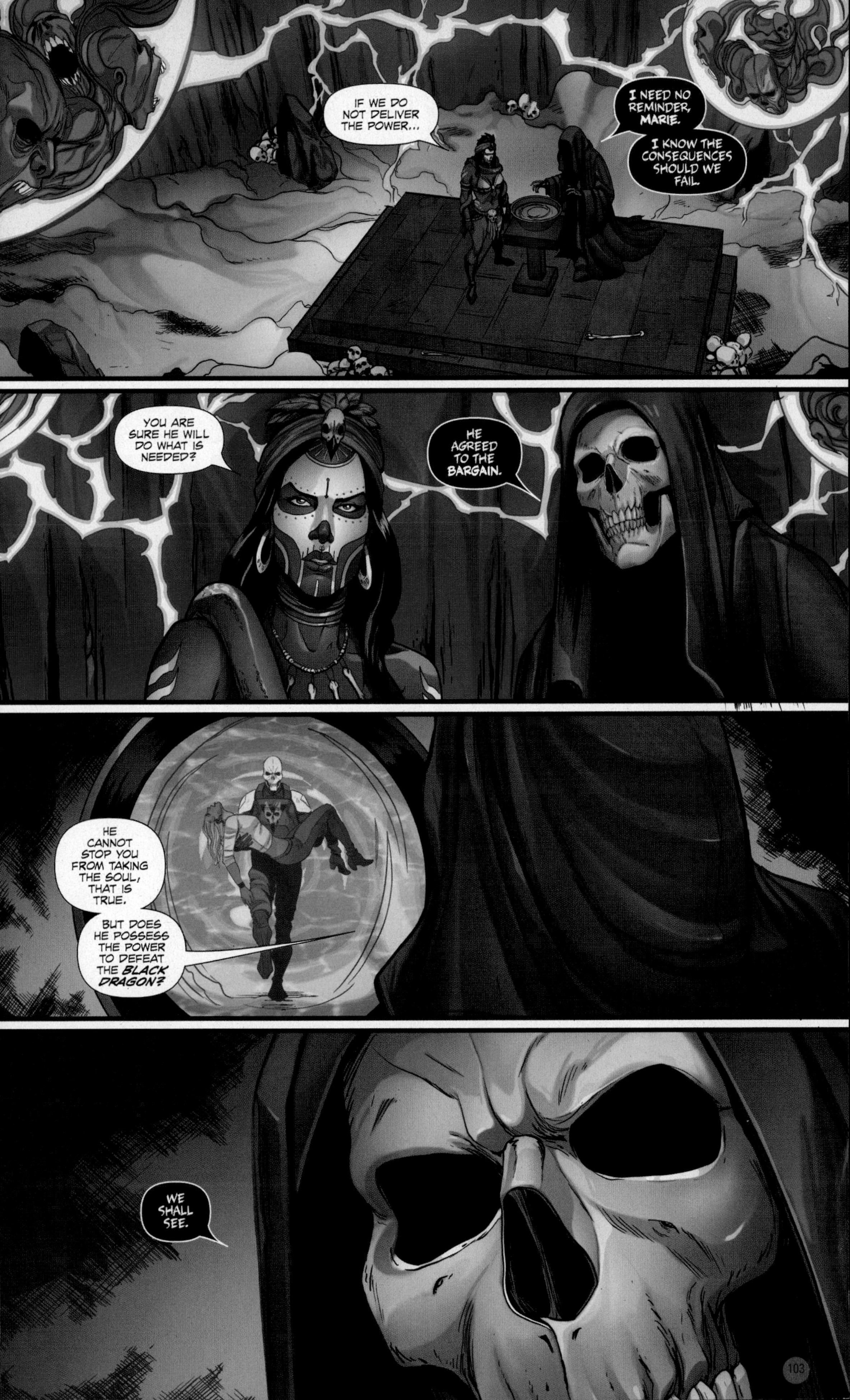
IF WE DO NOT DELIVER THE POWER...
I NEED NO REMINDER, MARIE.
I KNOW THE CONSEQUENCES SHOULD WE FAIL.
YOU ARE SURE HE WILL DO WHAT IS NEEDED?
HE AGREED TO THE BARGAIN.
HE CANNOT STOP YOU FROM TAKING THE SOUL, THAT IS TRUE.
BUT DOES HE POSSESS THE POWER TO DEFEAT THE BLACK DRAGON?
WE SHALL SEE.

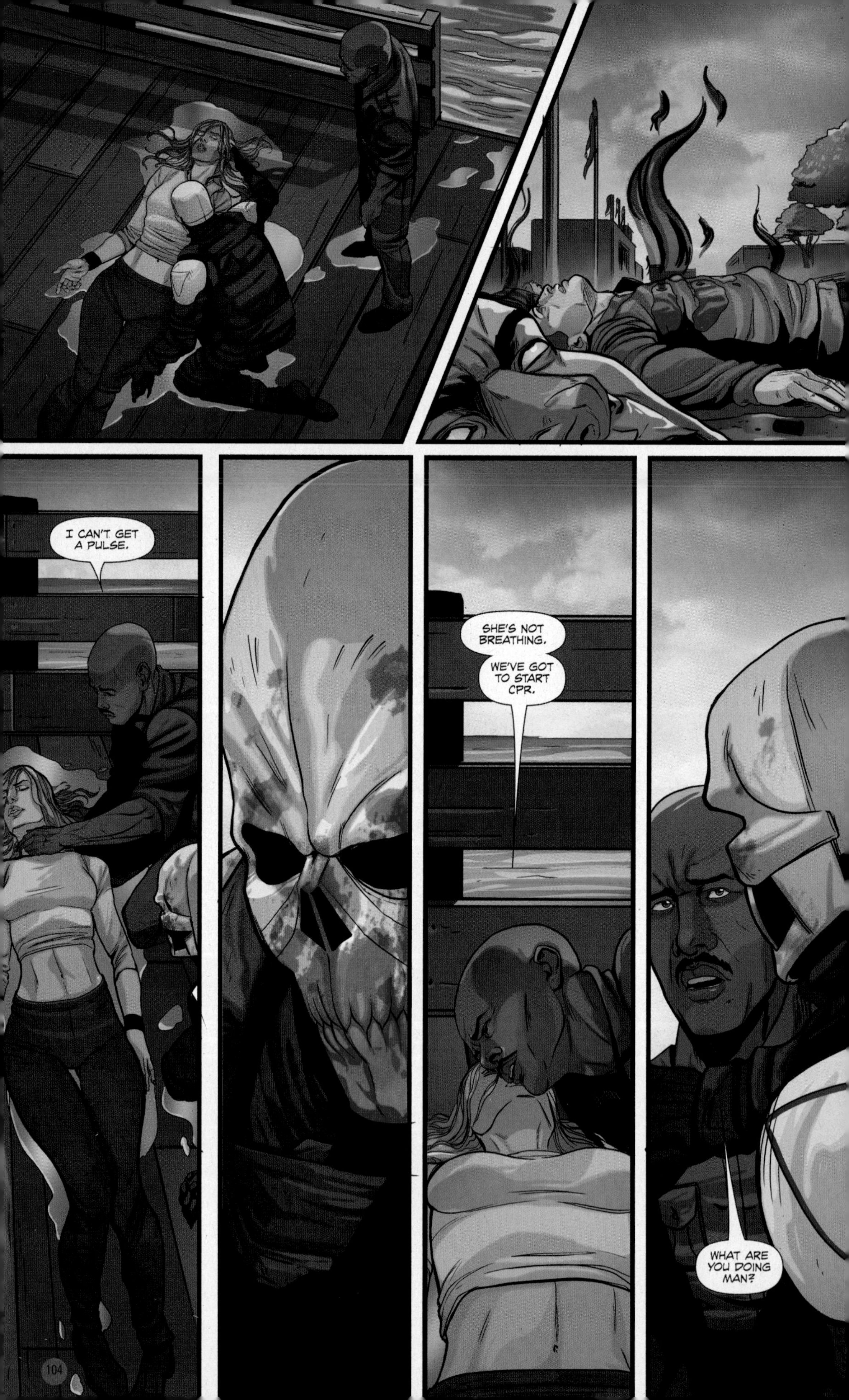
I CAN'T GET A PULSE.
SHE'S NOT BREATHING.
WE'VE GOT TO START CPR.
WHAT ARE YOU DOING MAN?

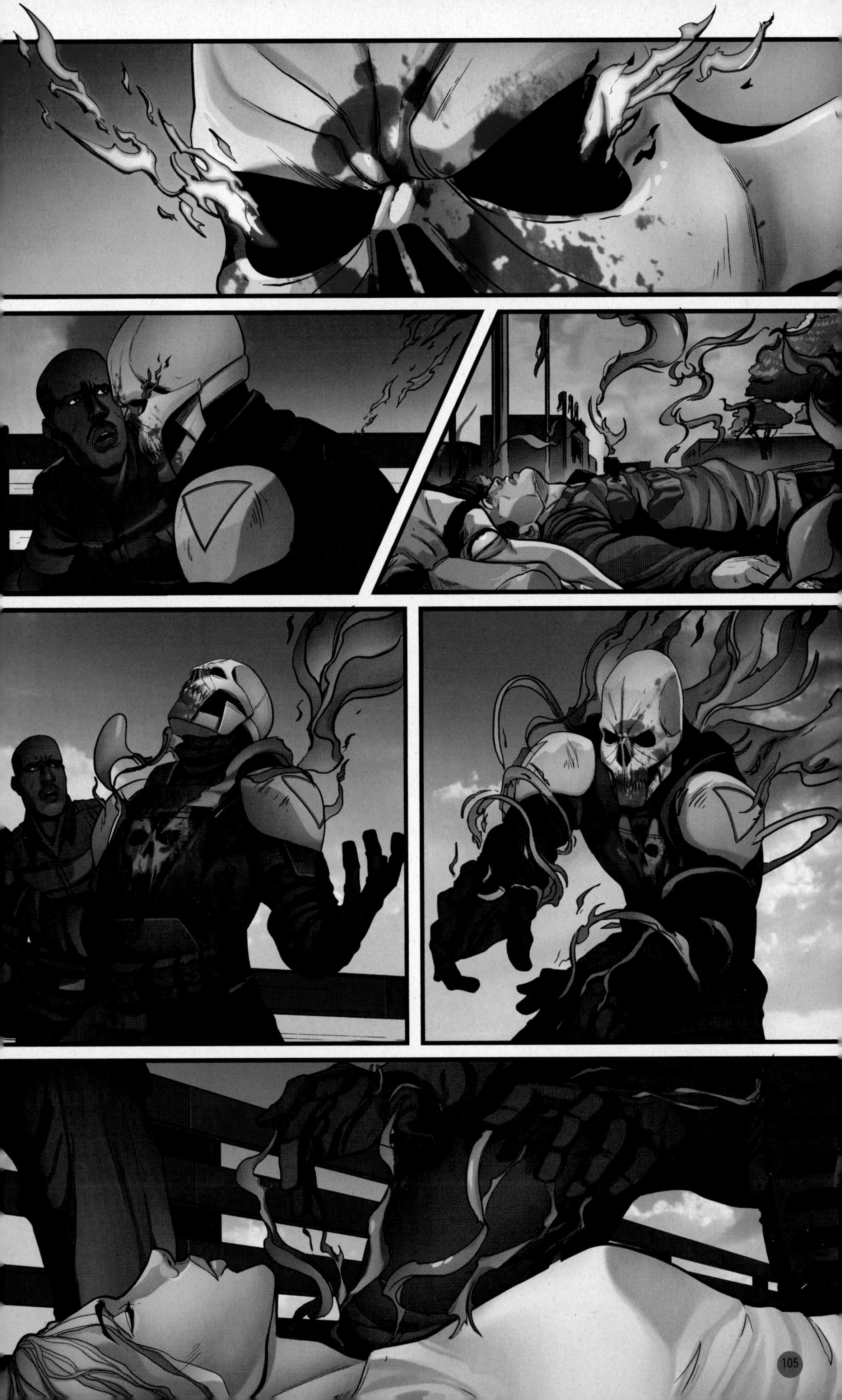

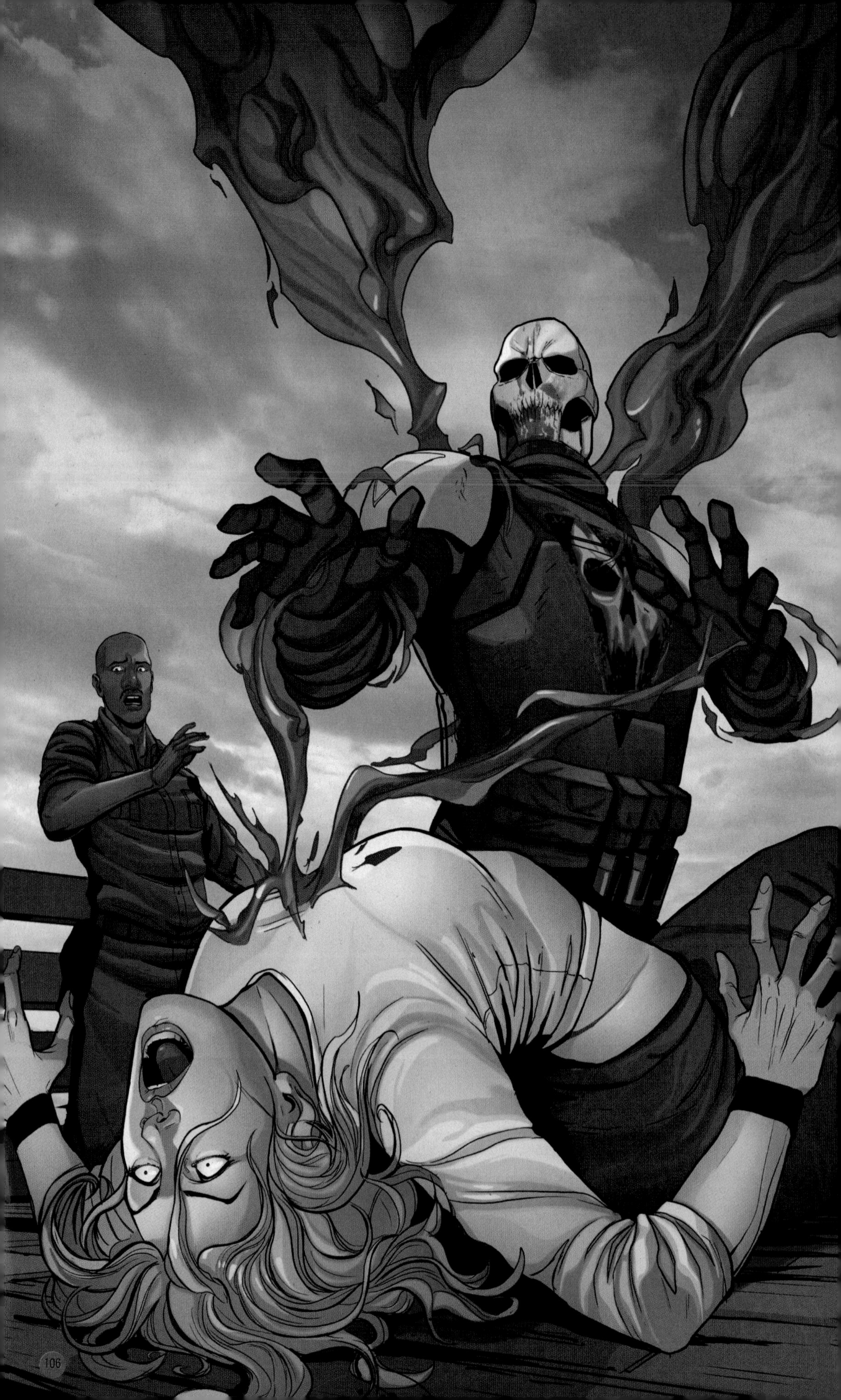

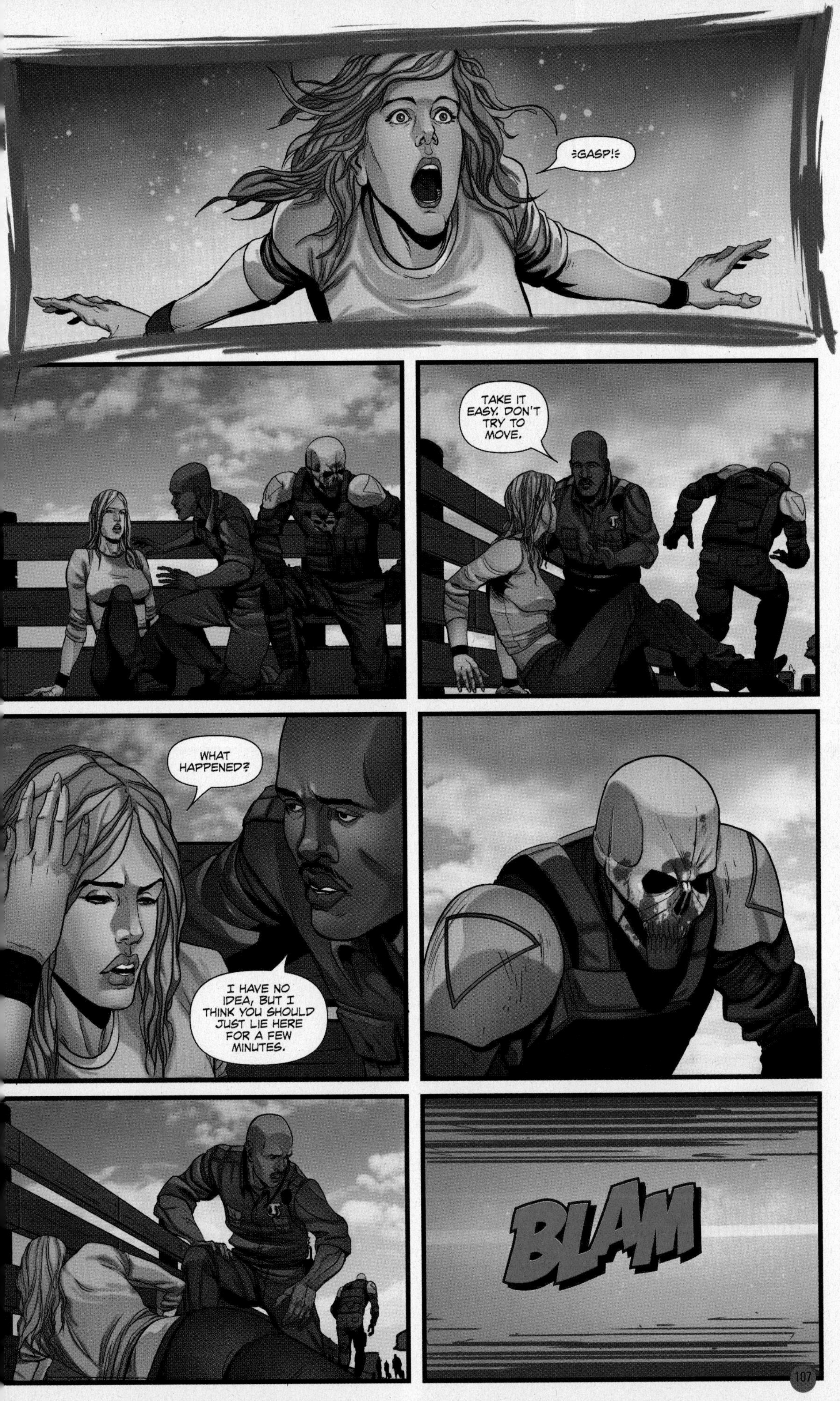

≥GASP!≤
TAKE IT EASY. DON'T TRY TO MOVE.
WHAT HAPPENED?
I HAVE NO IDEA, BUT I THINK YOU SHOULD JUST LIE HERE FOR A FEW MINUTES.
BLAM

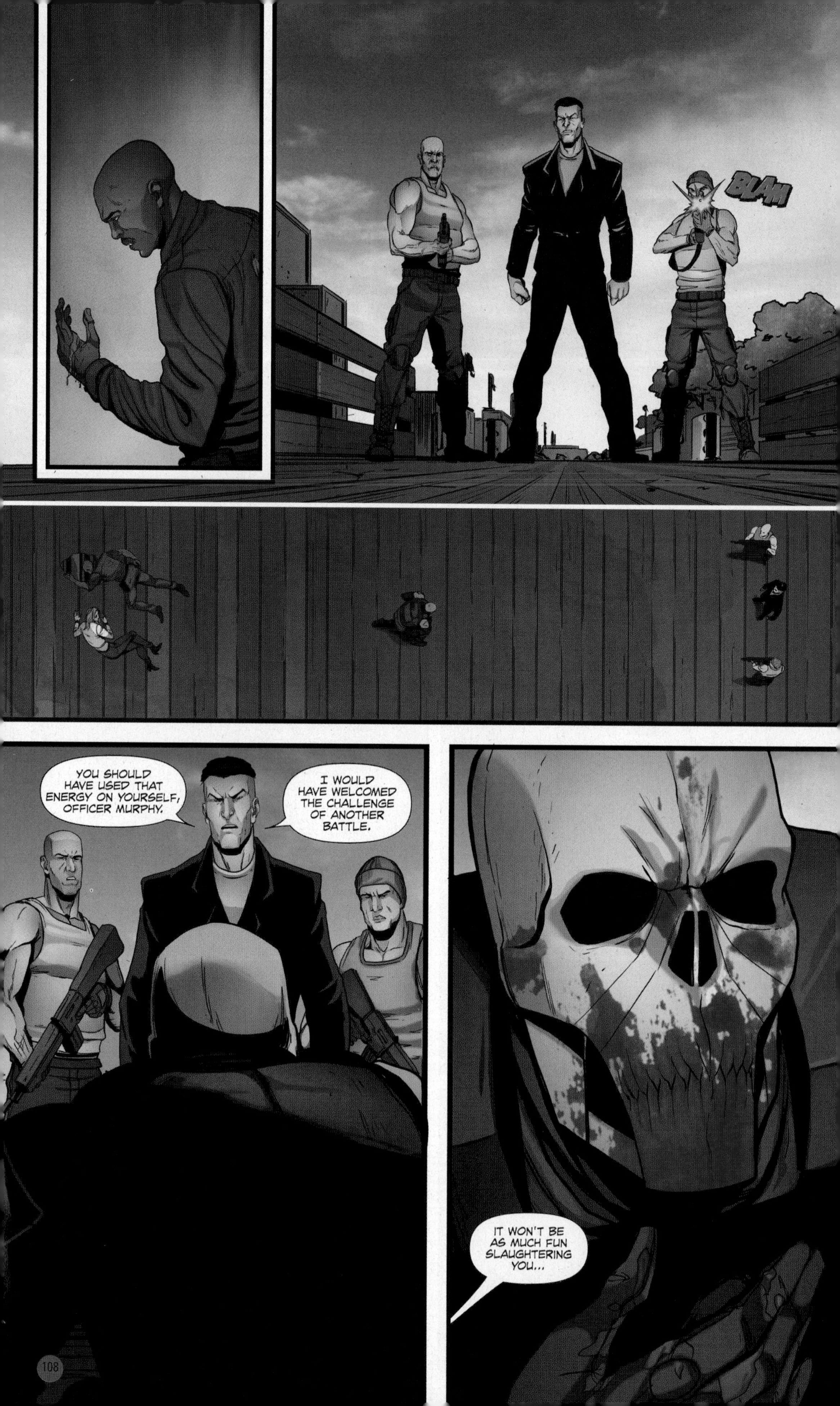
BLAM
YOU SHOULD HAVE USED THAT ENERGY ON YOURSELF, OFFICER MURPHY.
I WOULD HAVE WELCOMED THE CHALLENGE OF ANOTHER BATTLE.
IT WON'T BE AS MUCH FUN SLAUGHTERING YOU...

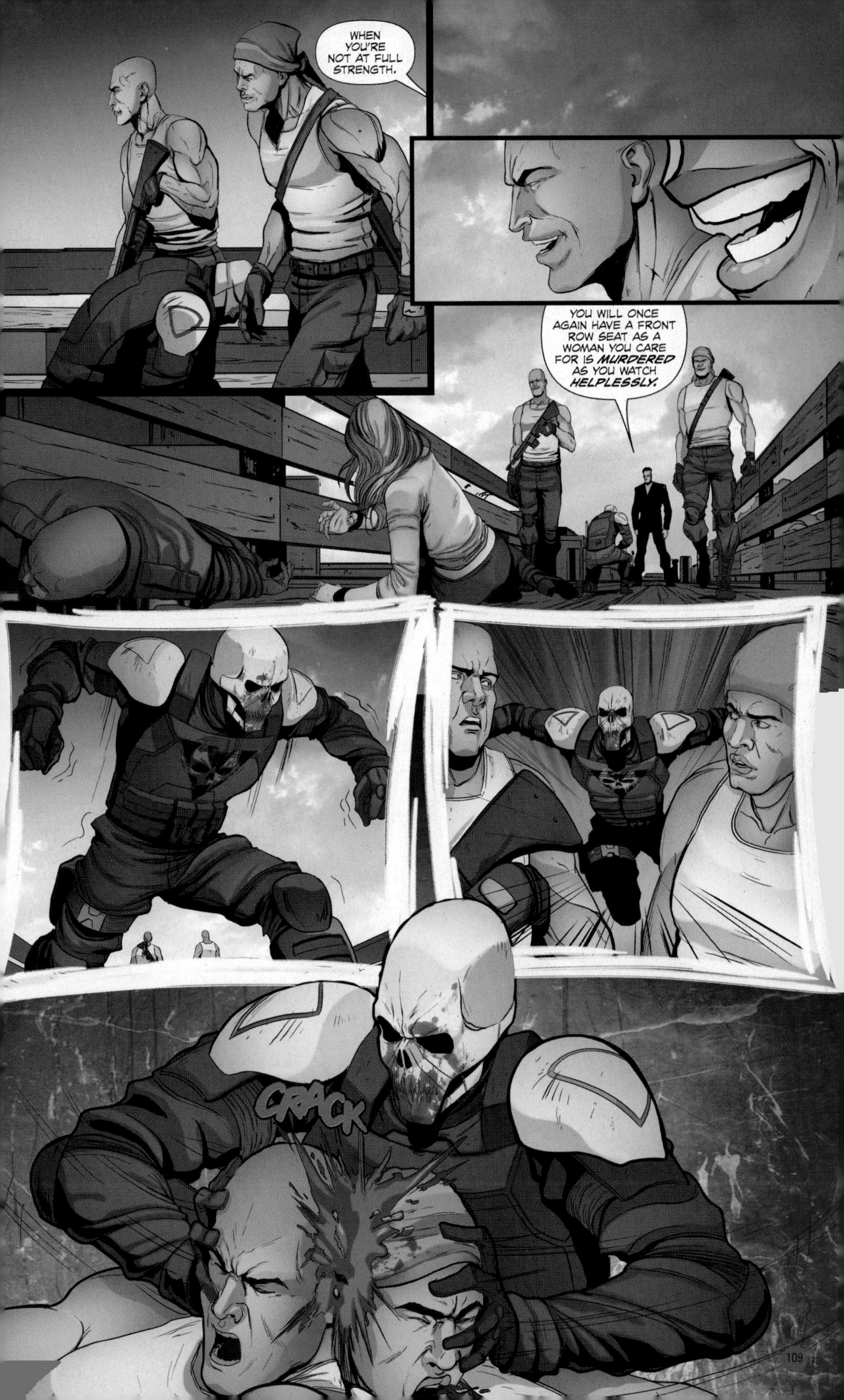
WHEN YOU'RE NOT AT FULL STRENGTH.
YOU WILL ONCE AGAIN HAVE A FRONT ROW SEAT AS A WOMAN YOU CARE FOR IS MURDERED AS YOU WATCH HELPLESSLY.
CRACK

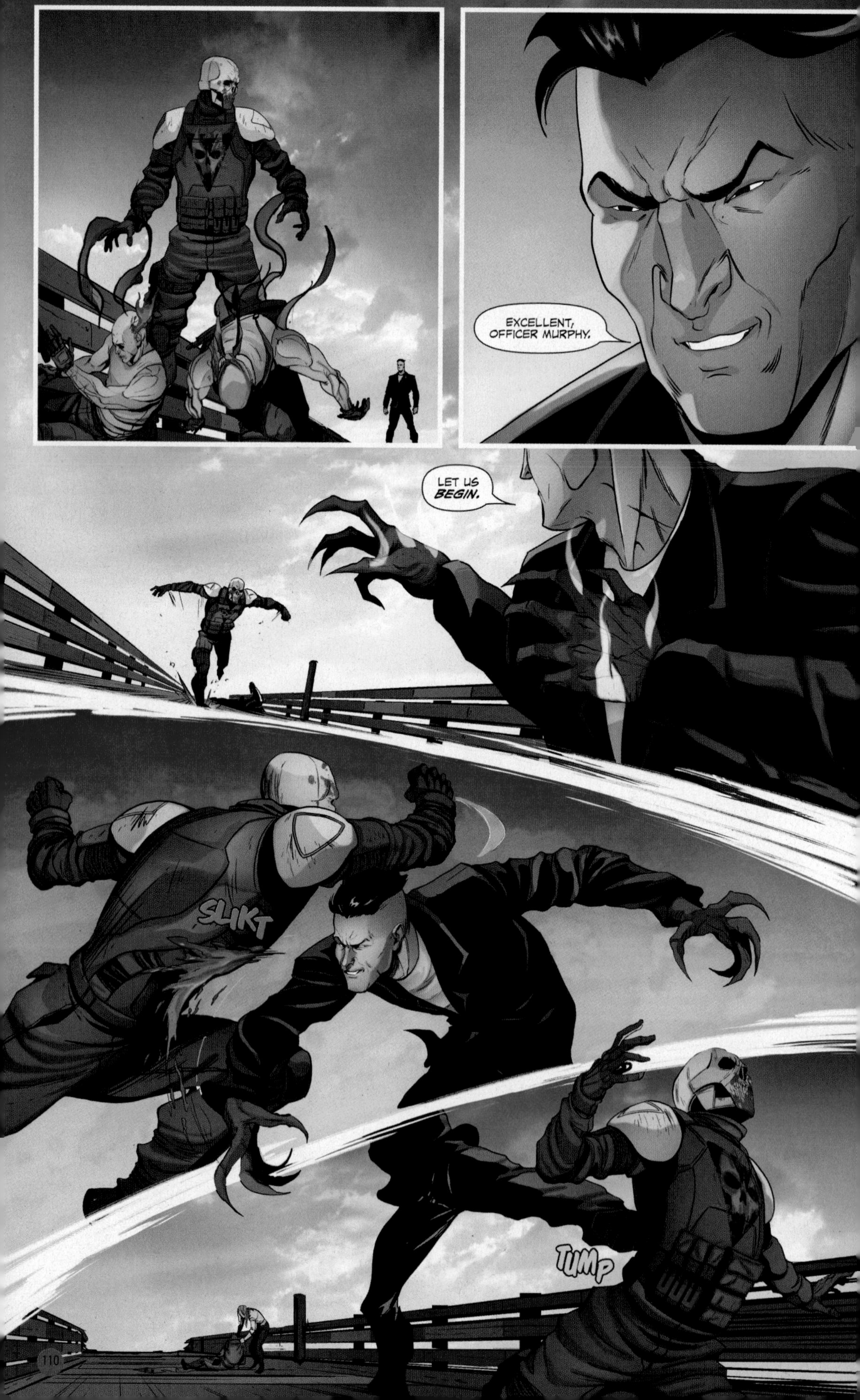
EXCELLENT, OFFICER MURPHY.
LET US BEGIN.
SLIKT
TUMP

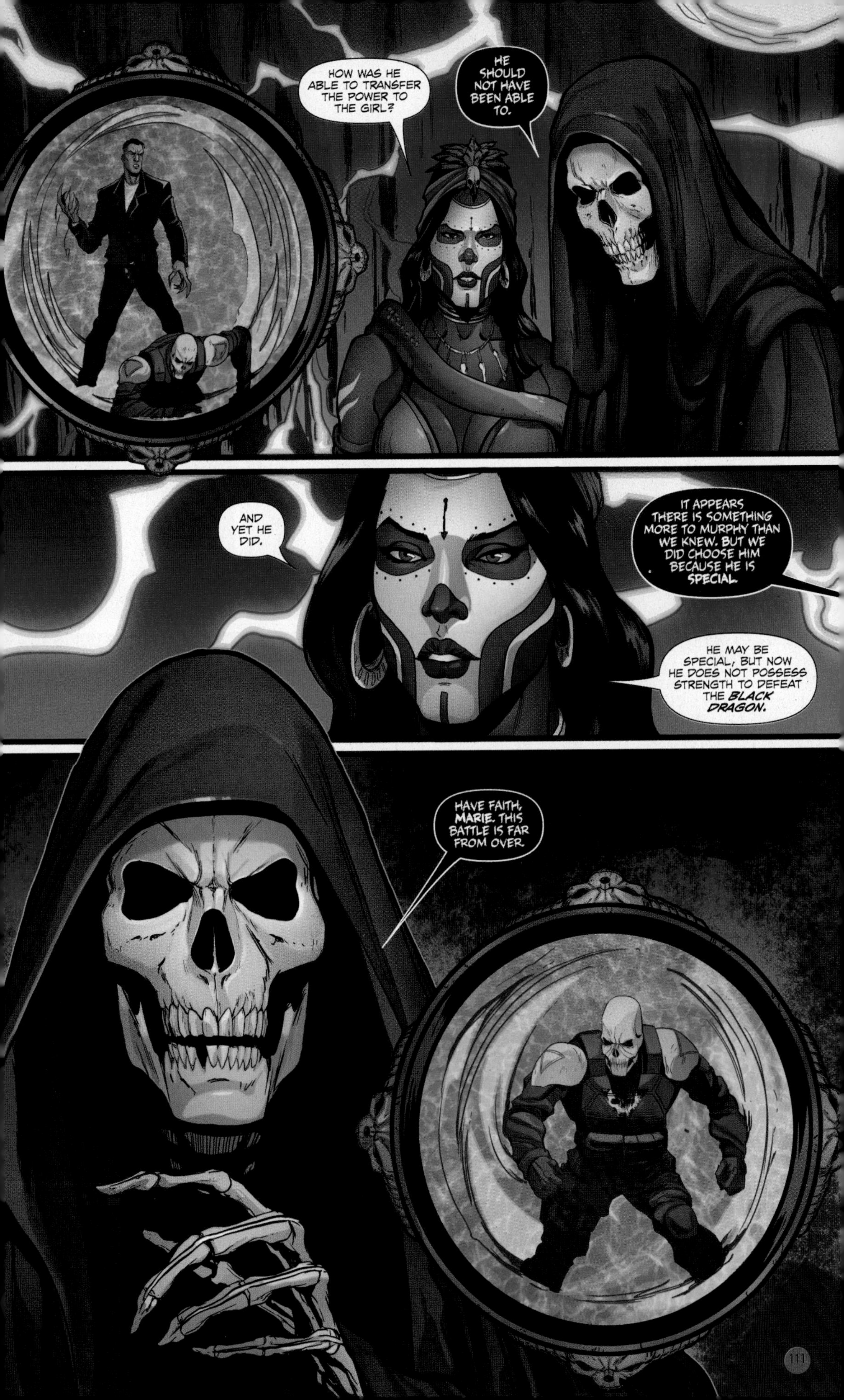
HOW WAS HE ABLE TO TRANSFER THE POWER TO THE GIRL?
HE SHOULD NOT HAVE BEEN ABLE TO.
AND YET HE DID.
IT APPEARS THERE IS SOMETHING MORE TO MURPHY THAN WE KNEW. BUT WE DID CHOOSE HIM BECAUSE HE IS SPECIAL.
HE MAY BE SPECIAL, BUT NOW HE DOES NOT POSSESS STRENGTH TO DEFEAT THE BLACK DRAGON.
HAVE FAITH, MARIE. THIS BATTLE IS FAR FROM OVER.

I MUST GIVE YOU CREDIT, MURPHY. YOU REFUSE TO BE BEATEN EASILY.

THAT'S QUITE A CHANGE FROM THE FIRST TIME WE MET.

DID I *STRIKE* A CHORD?

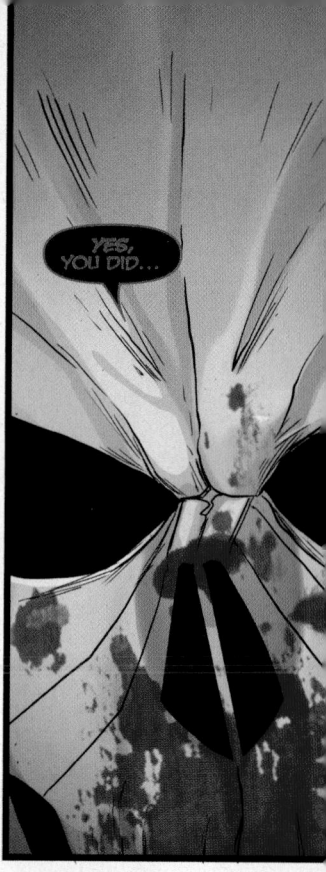

YES, YOU DID...

NOW LET ME *REPAY* YOU...

CRACK

112

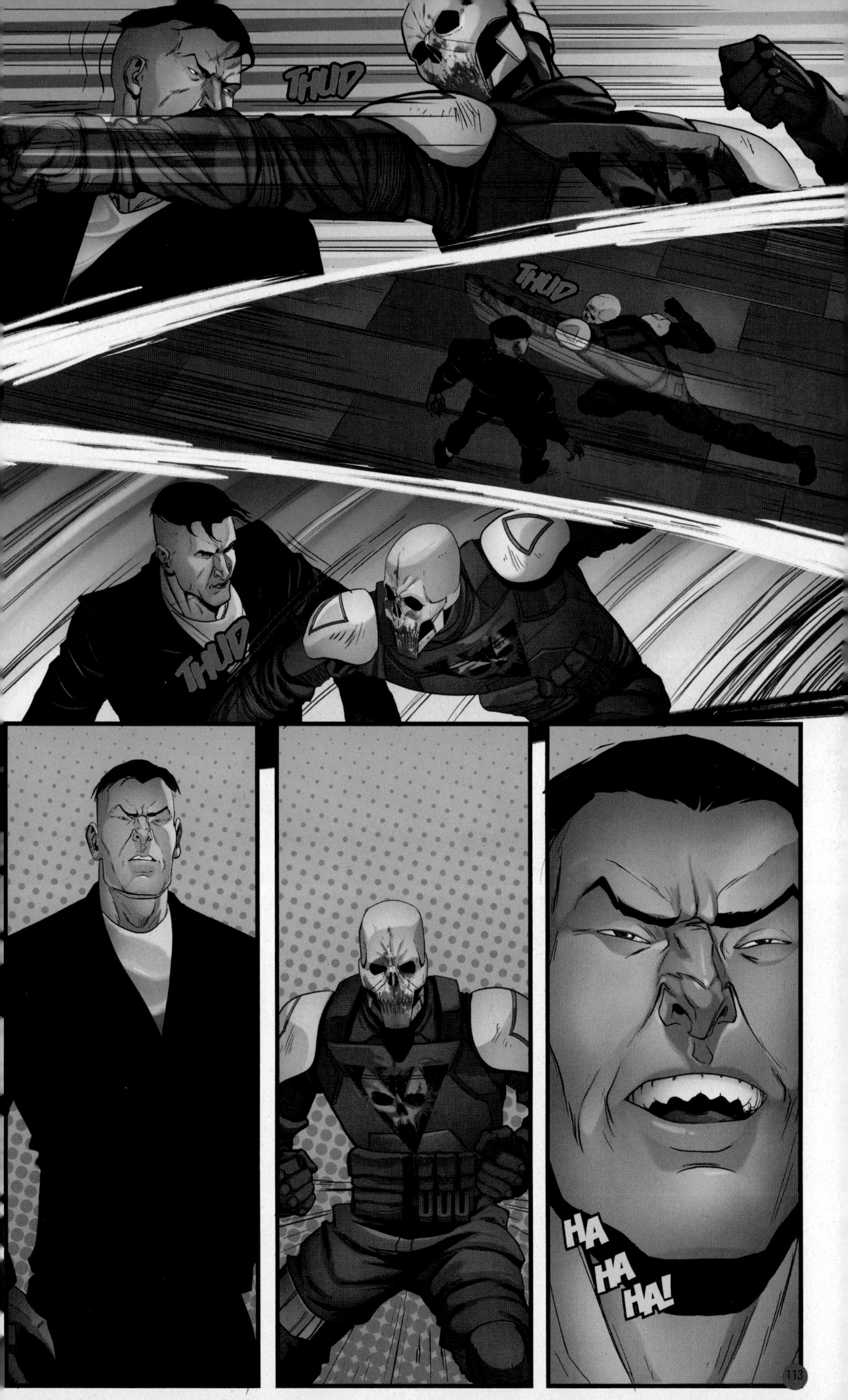
THUD
THUD
THUD
HA
HA
HA!

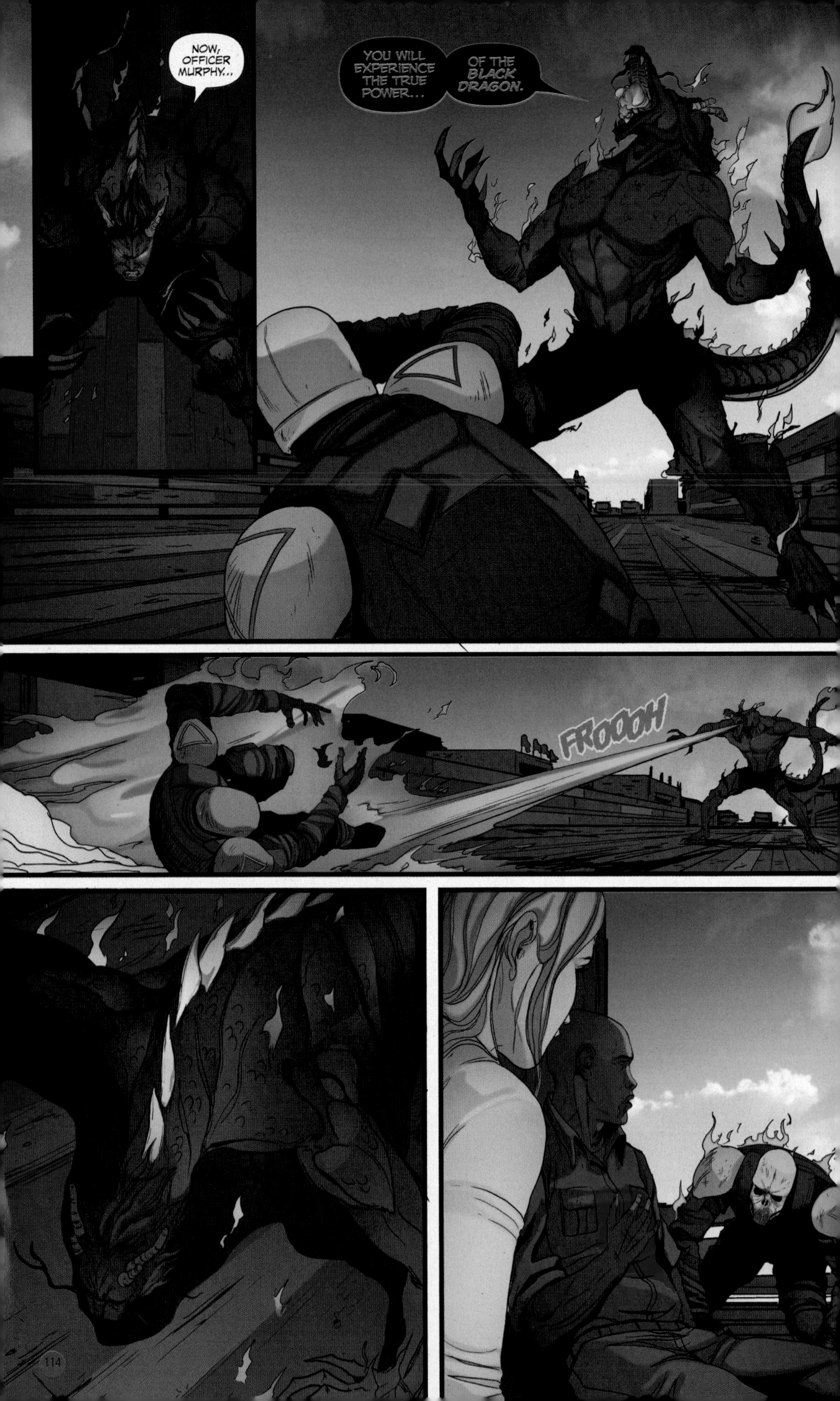
NOW, OFFICER MURPHY...
YOU WILL EXPERIENCE THE TRUE POWER...
OF THE BLACK DRAGON.
FROOOH

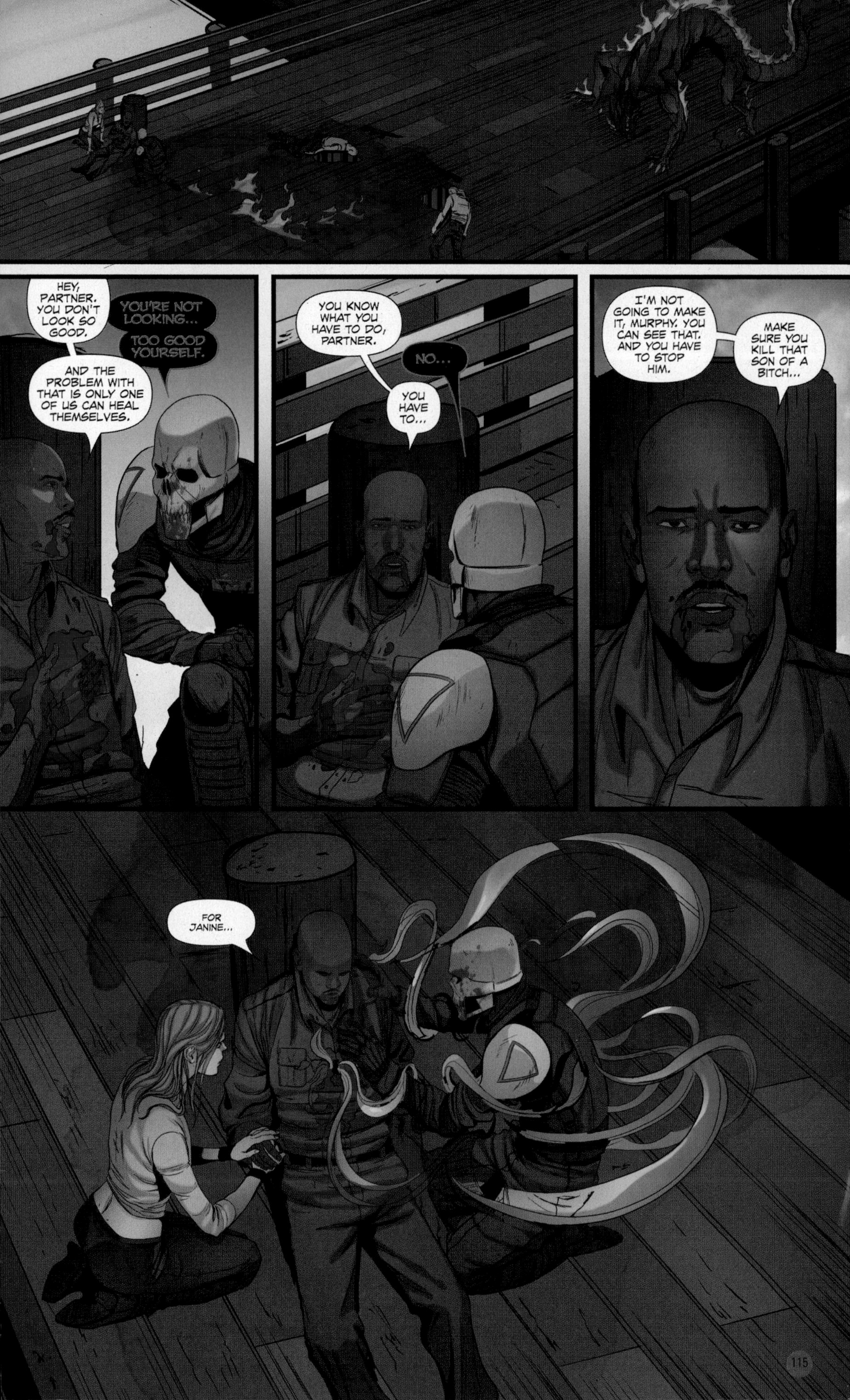
HEY, PARTNER. YOU DON'T LOOK SO GOOD.
YOU'RE NOT LOOKING...
TOO GOOD YOURSELF.
AND THE PROBLEM WITH THAT IS ONLY ONE OF US CAN HEAL THEMSELVES.
YOU KNOW WHAT YOU HAVE TO DO, PARTNER.
NO...
YOU HAVE TO...
I'M NOT GOING TO MAKE IT, MURPHY. YOU CAN SEE THAT. AND YOU HAVE TO STOP HIM.
MAKE SURE YOU KILL THAT SON OF A BITCH...
FOR JANINE...

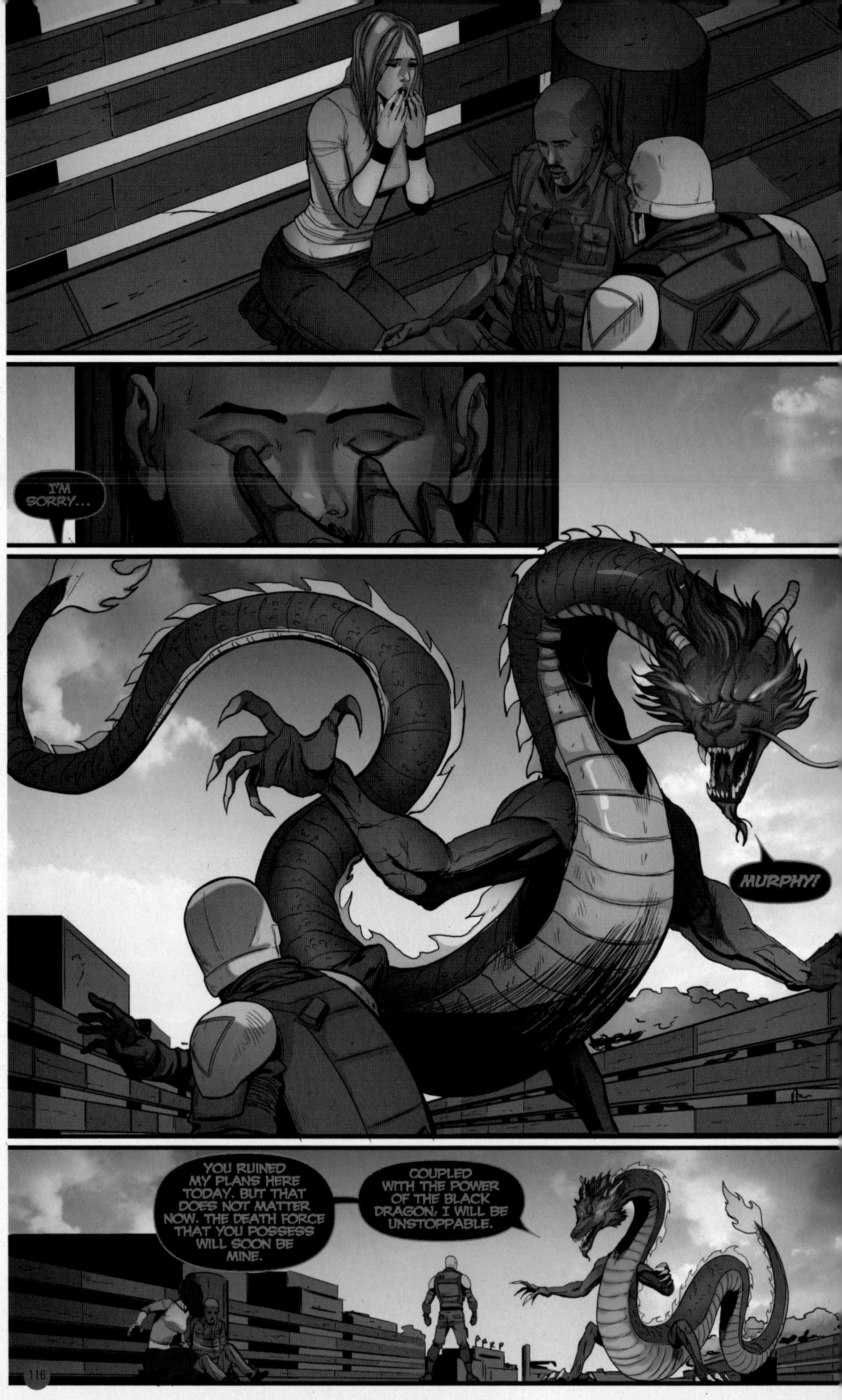
I'M SORRY...
MURPHY!
YOU RUINED MY PLANS HERE TODAY. BUT THAT DOES NOT MATTER NOW. THE DEATH FORCE THAT YOU POSSESS WILL SOON BE MINE.
COUPLED WITH THE POWER OF THE BLACK DRAGON, I WILL BE UNSTOPPABLE.

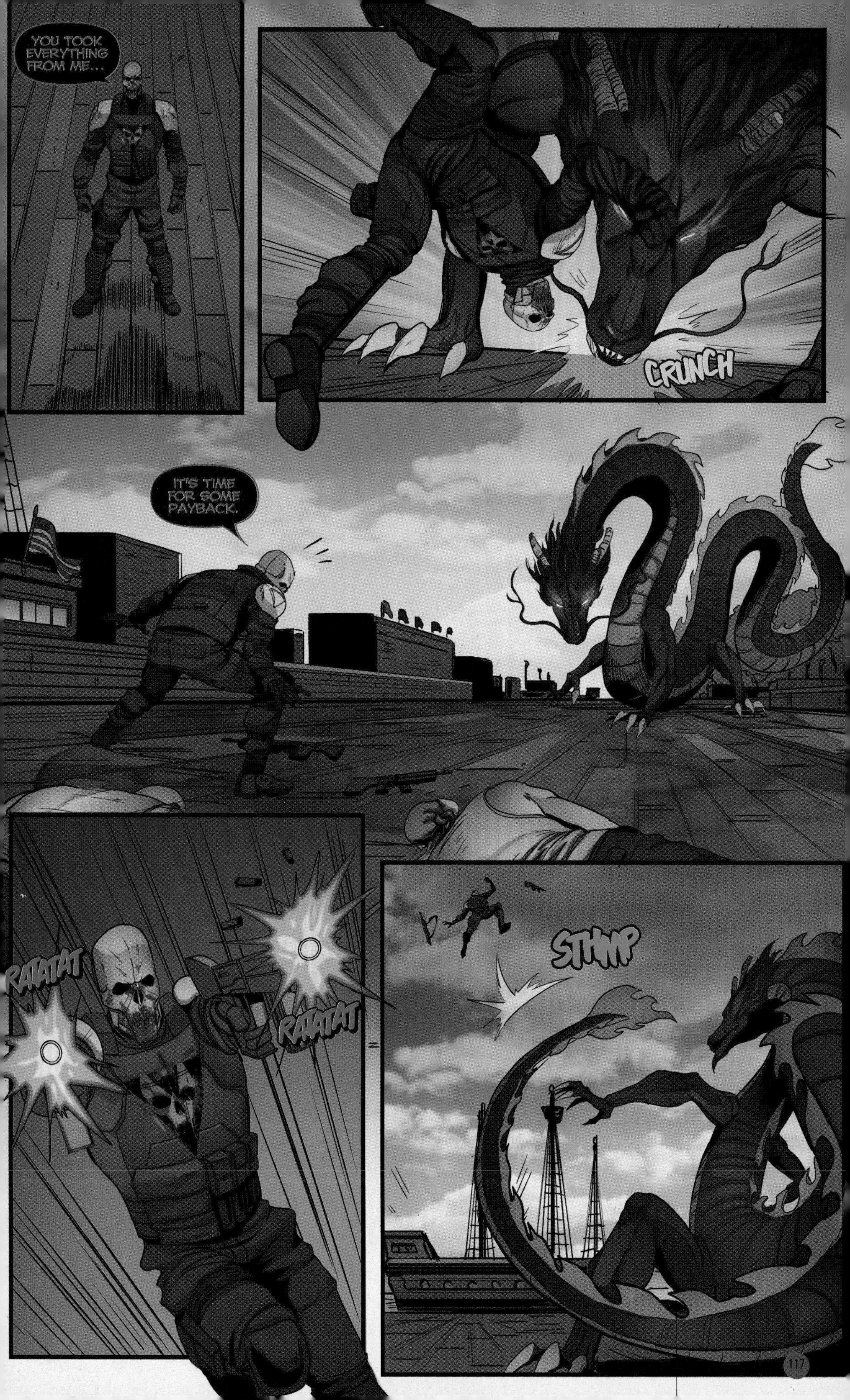

YOU TOOK EVERYTHING FROM ME...
CRUNCH
IT'S TIME FOR SOME PAYBACK.
RATATAT
RATATAT
STHMP

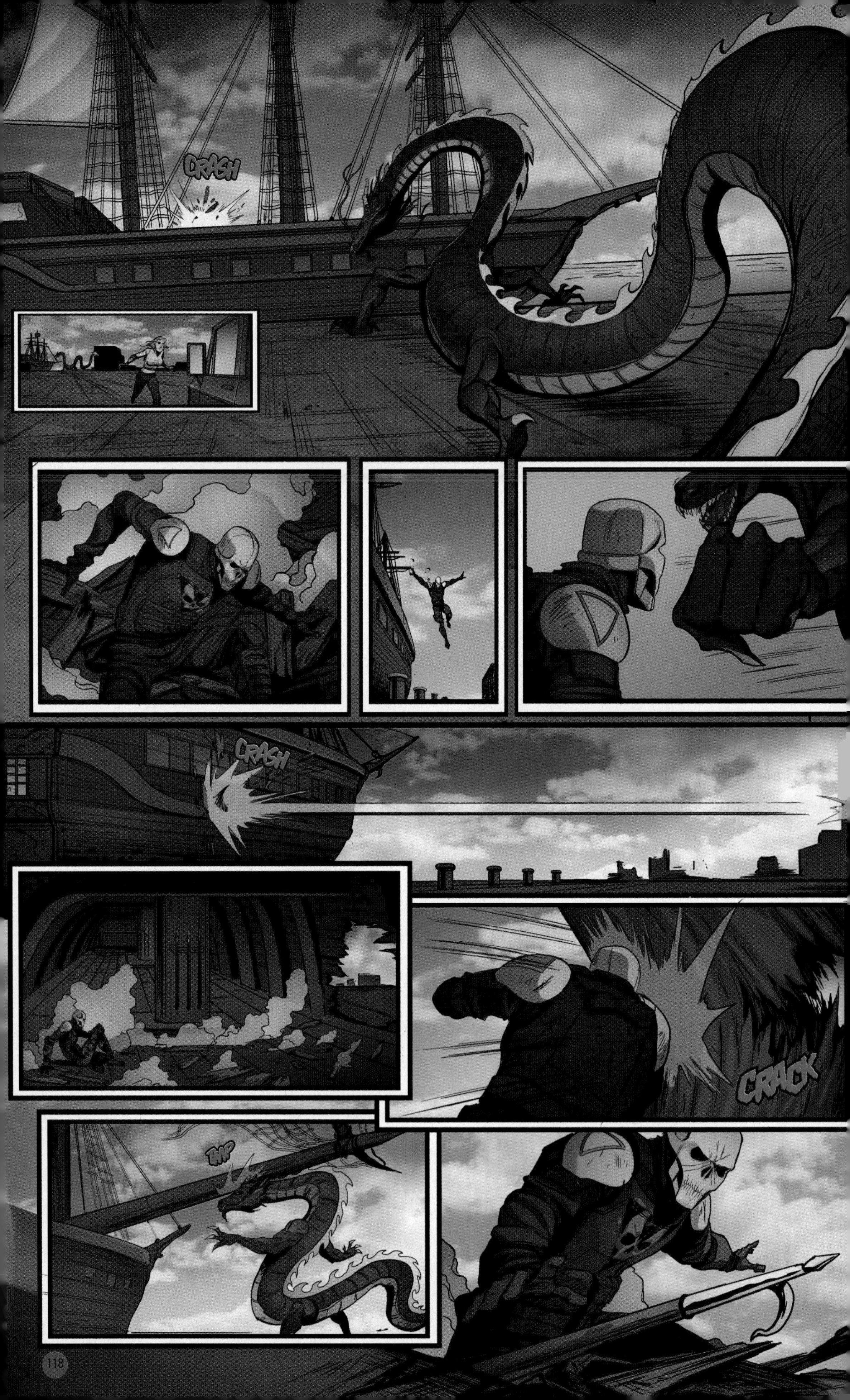
CRASH
CRASH
CRACK
TMP

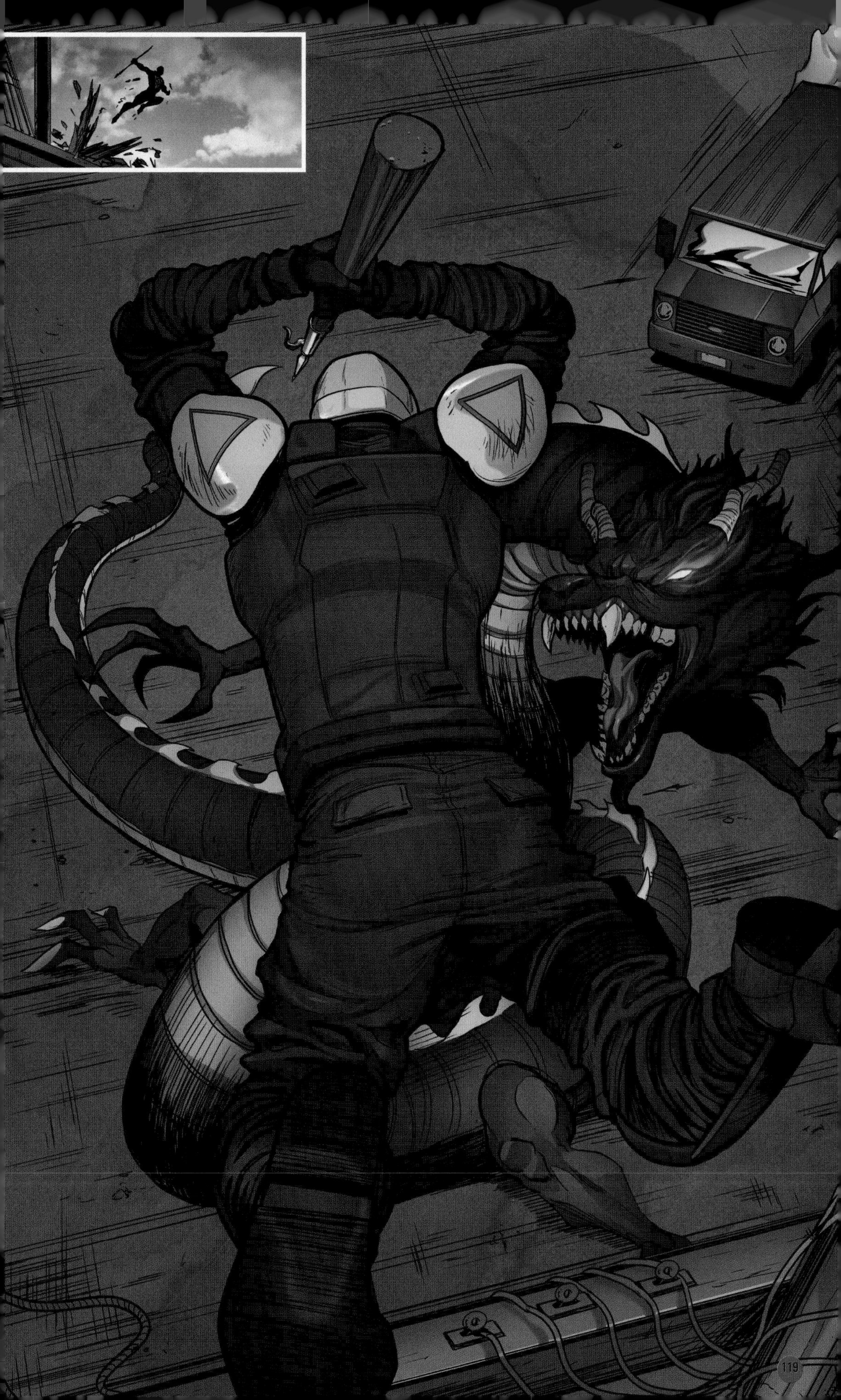

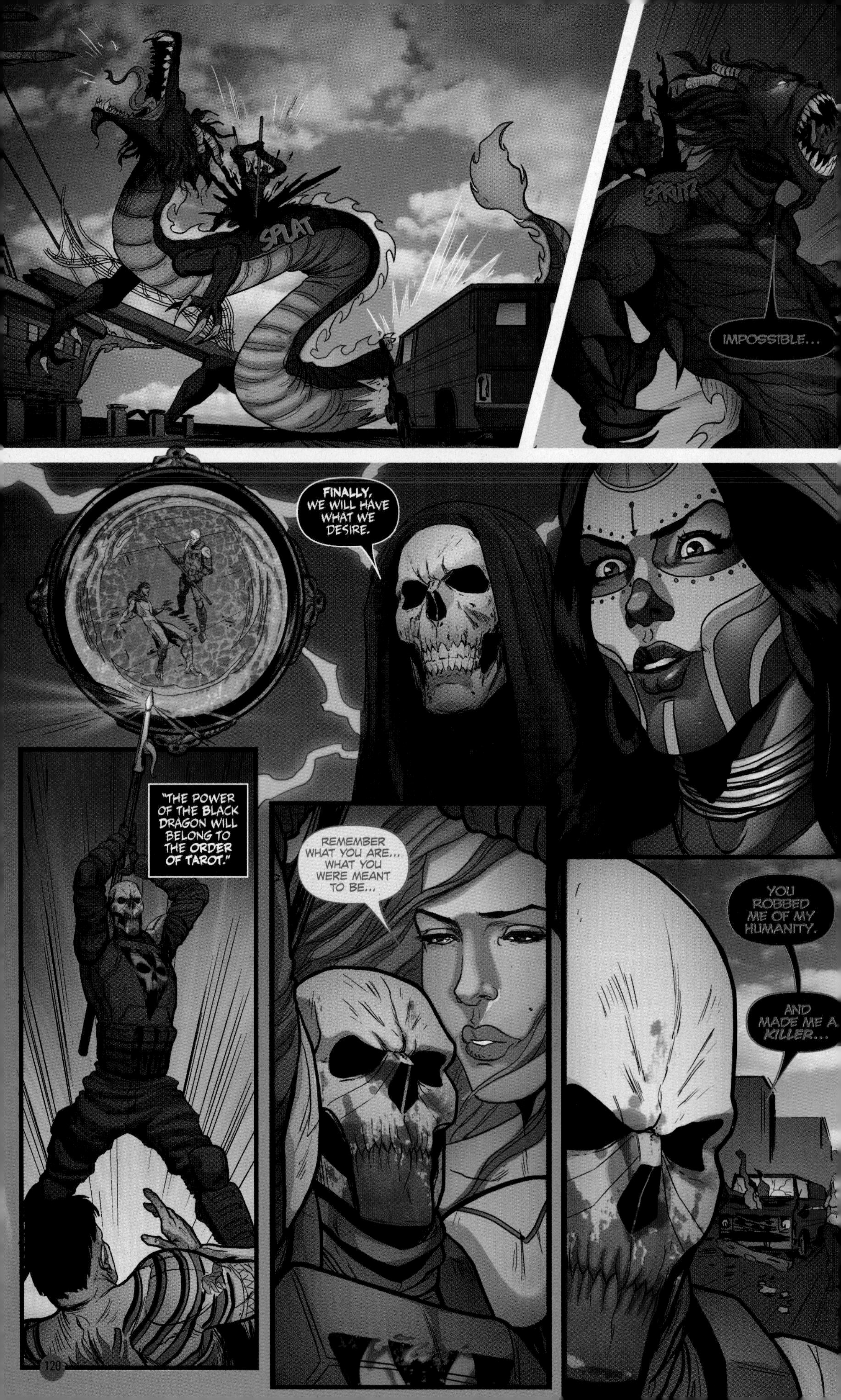
SPLAT
SPRITZ
IMPOSSIBLE...
FINALLY, WE WILL HAVE WHAT WE DESIRE.
"THE POWER OF THE BLACK DRAGON WILL BELONG TO THE ORDER OF TAROT."
REMEMBER WHAT YOU ARE... WHAT YOU WERE MEANT TO BE...
YOU ROBBED ME OF MY HUMANITY.
AND MADE ME A KILLER...

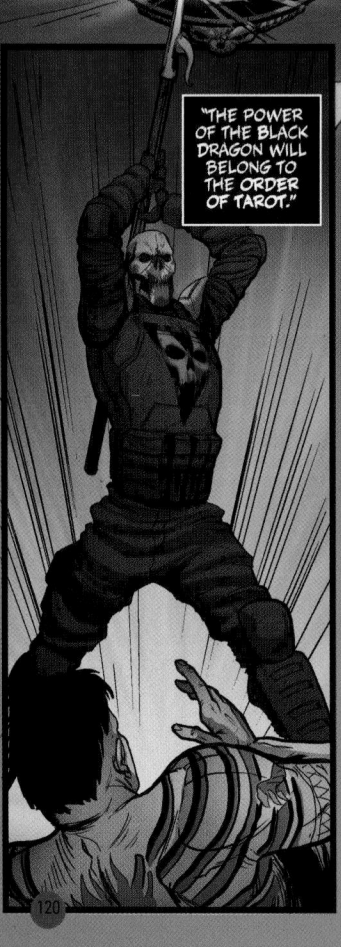

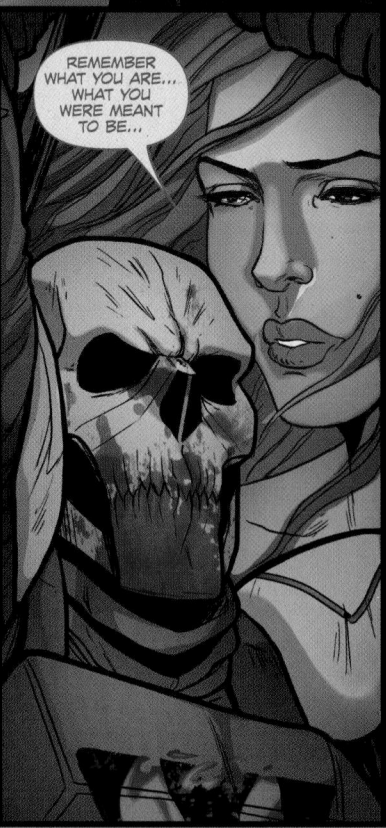

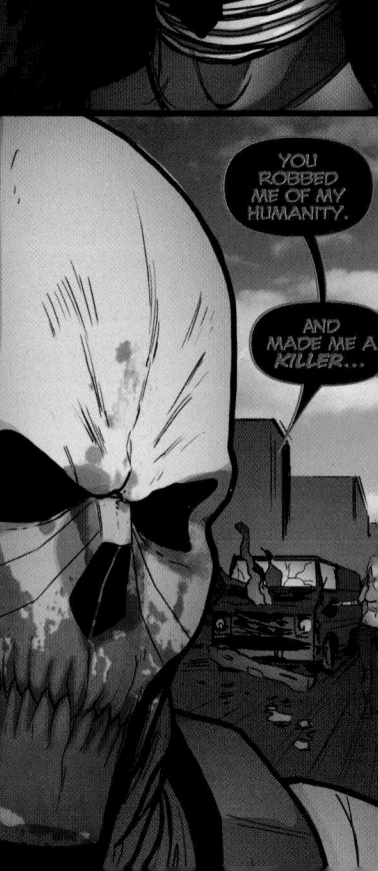

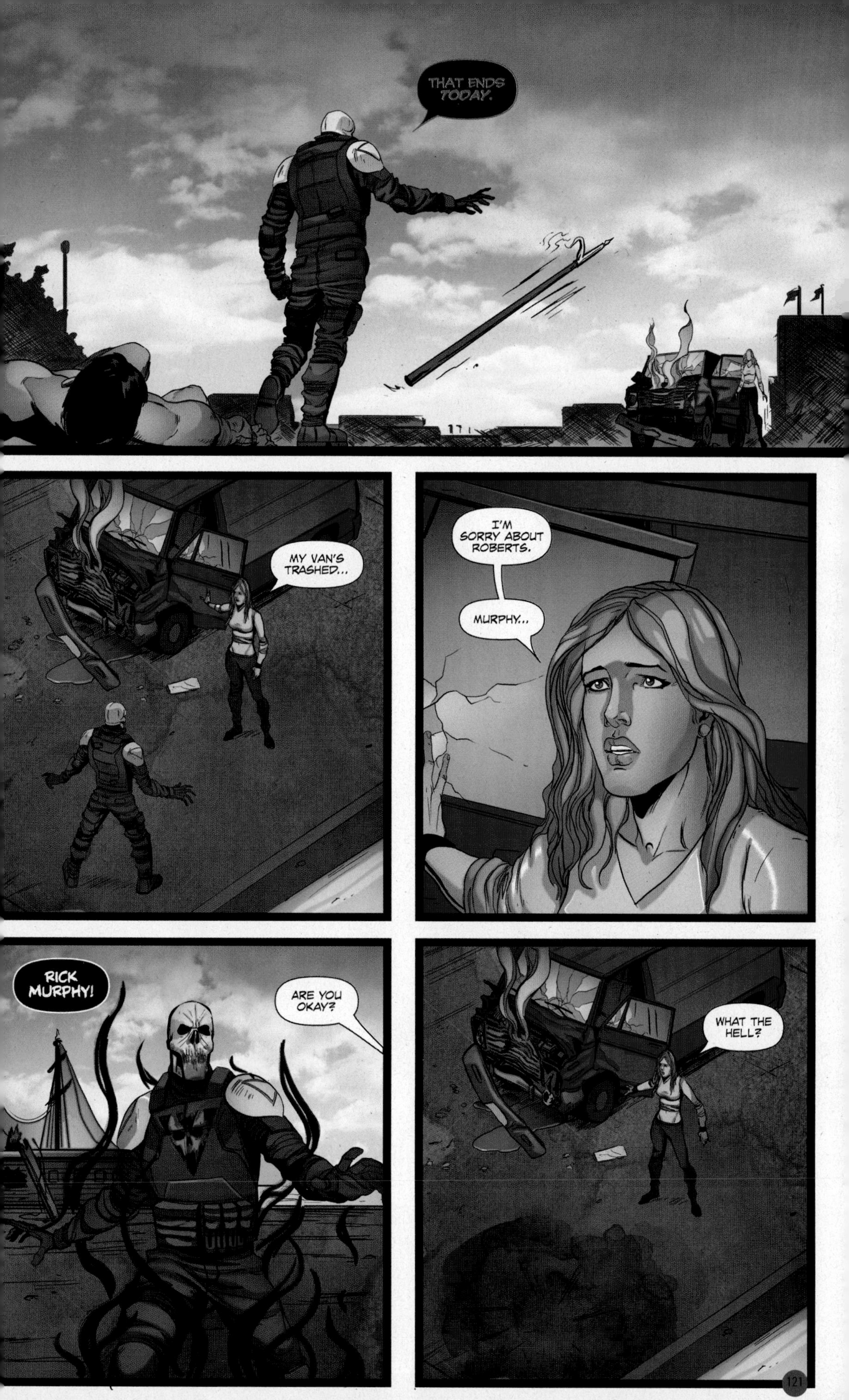
THAT ENDS TODAY.
MY VAN'S TRASHED...
I'M SORRY ABOUT ROBERTS.
MURPHY...
RICK MURPHY!
ARE YOU OKAY?
WHAT THE HELL?

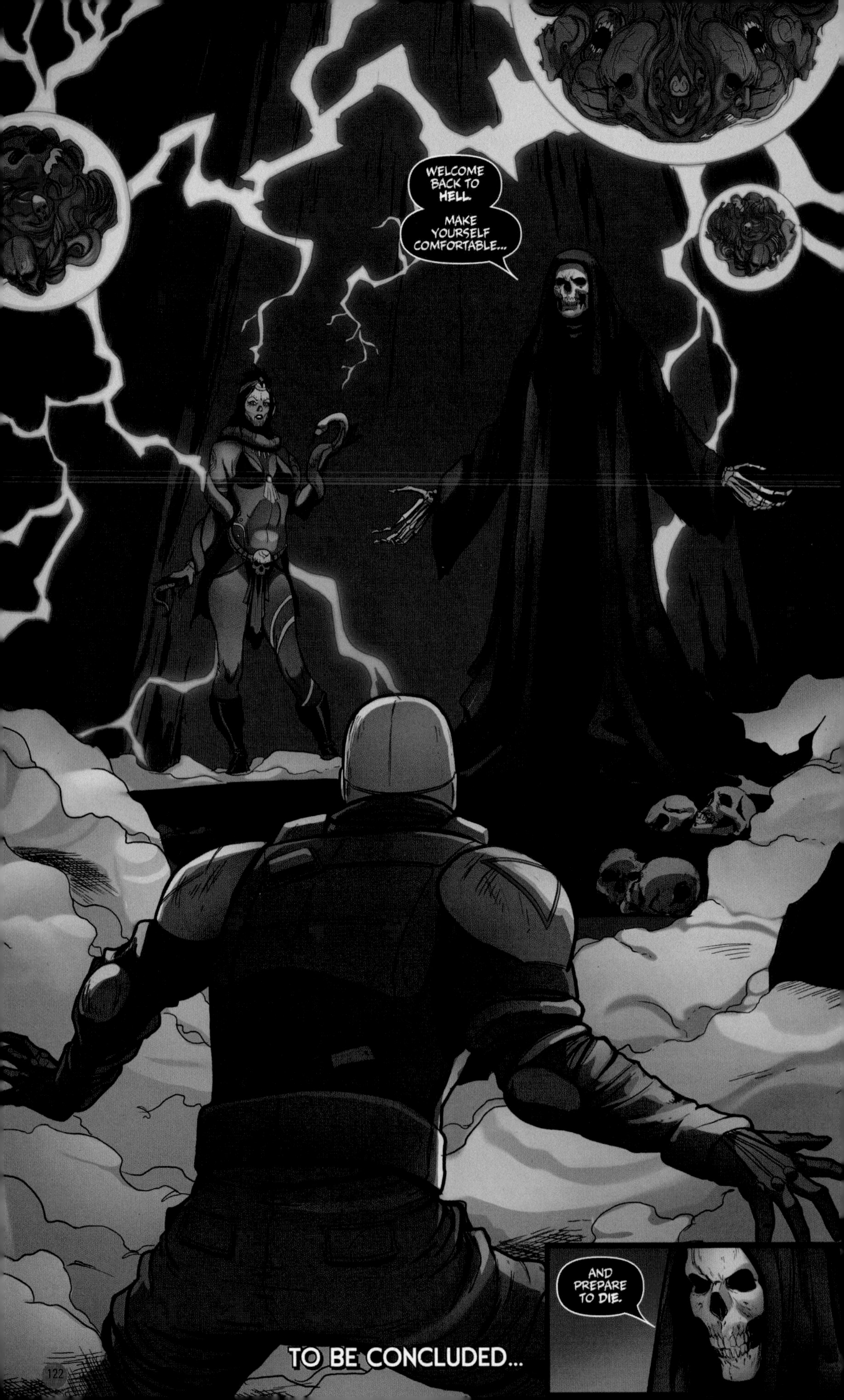
WELCOME BACK TO HELL.
MAKE YOURSELF COMFORTABLE...
AND PREPARE TO DIE.
TO BE CONCLUDED...

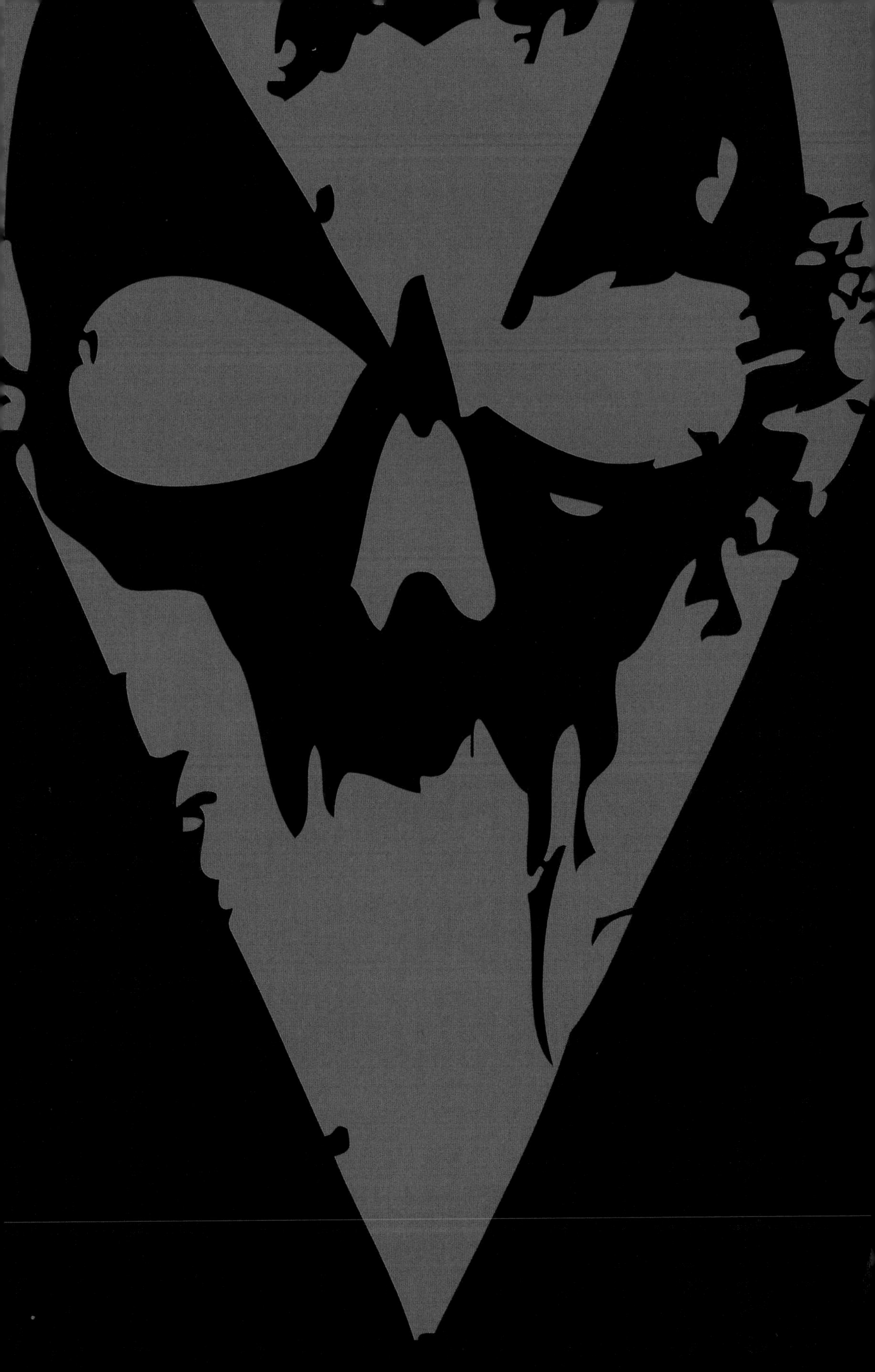

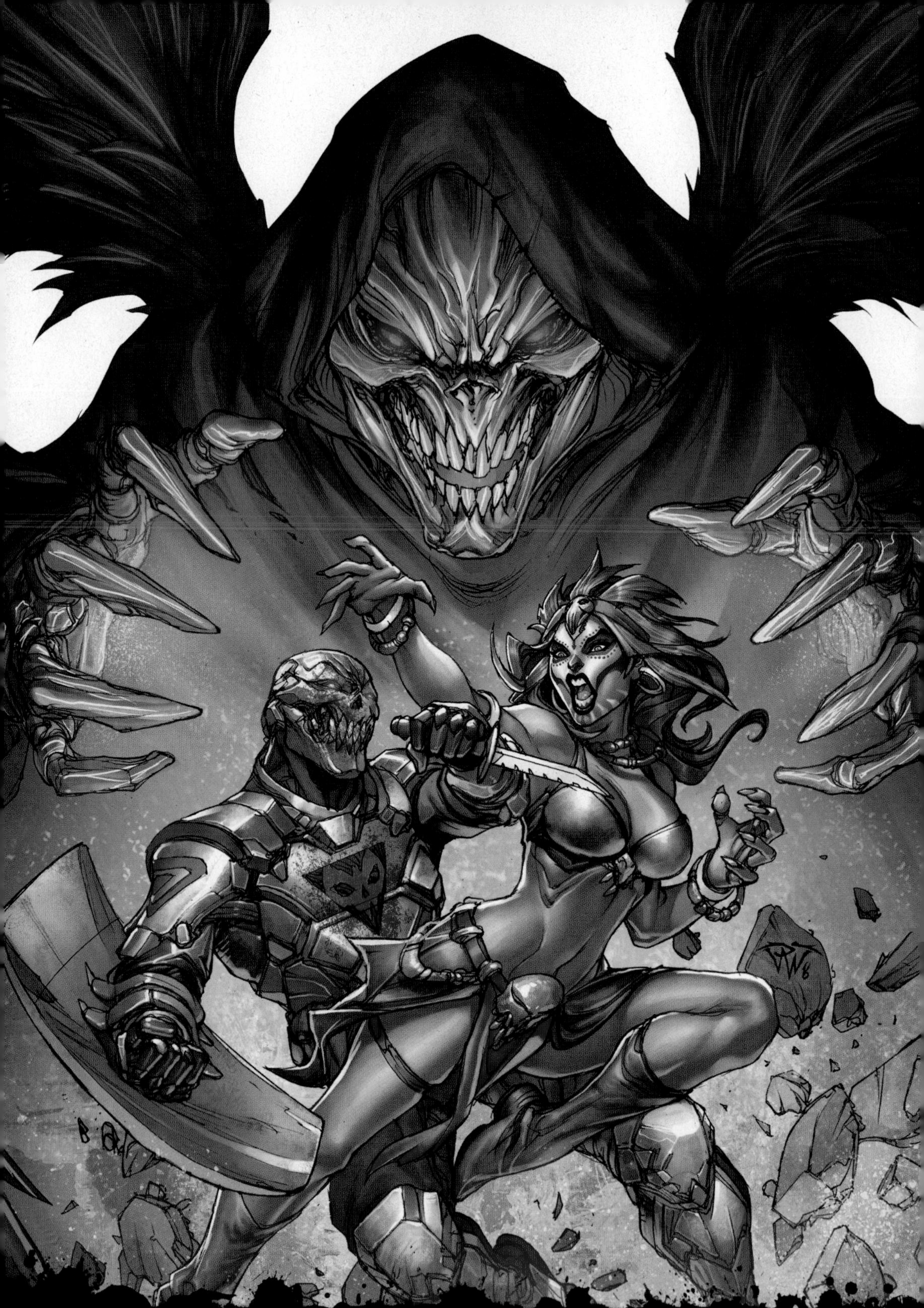

CHAPTER SIX

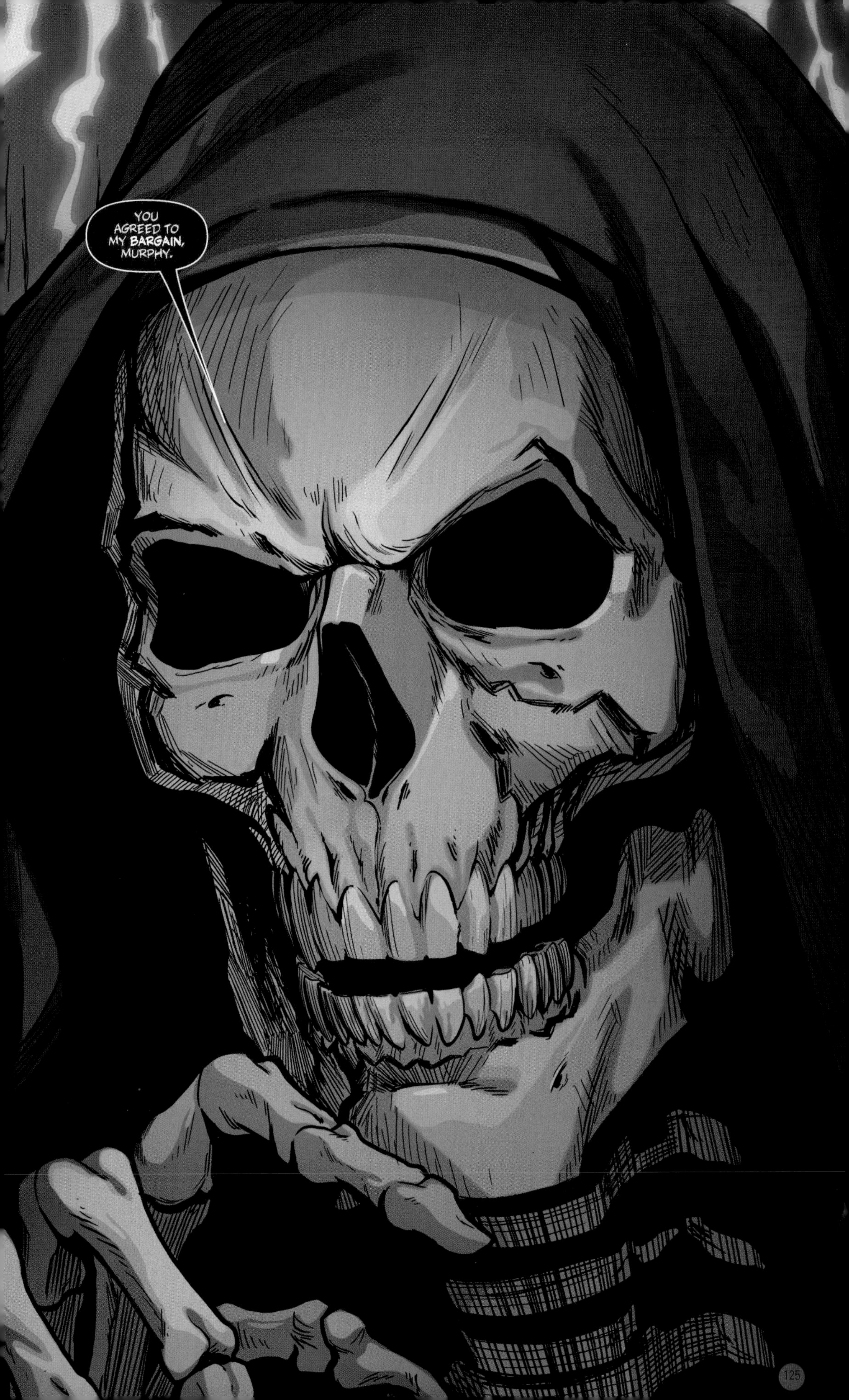
YOU AGREED TO MY BARGAIN, MURPHY.

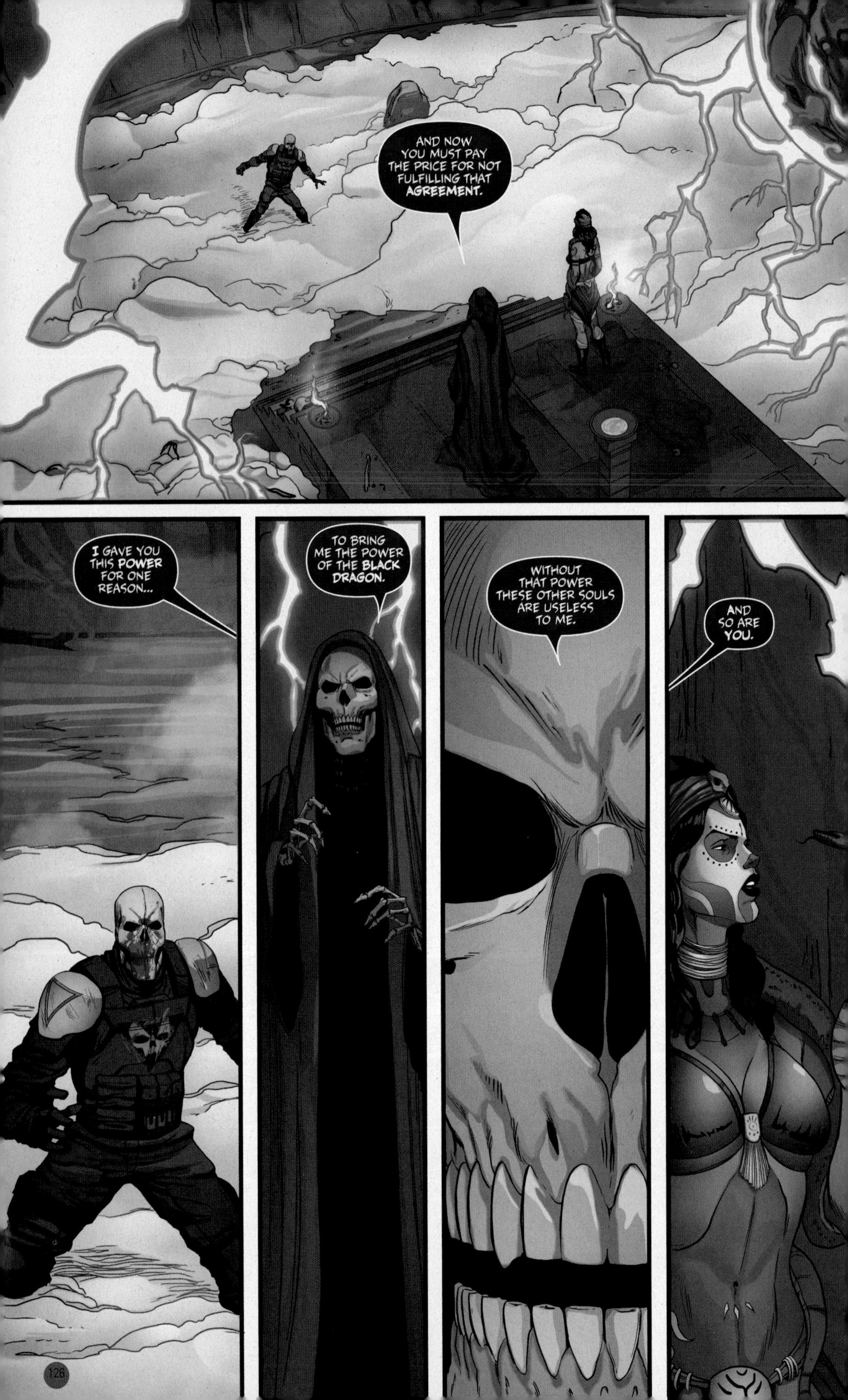
AND NOW YOU MUST PAY THE PRICE FOR NOT FULFILLING THAT AGREEMENT.
I GAVE YOU THIS POWER FOR ONE REASON...
TO BRING ME THE POWER OF THE BLACK DRAGON.
WITHOUT THAT POWER THESE OTHER SOULS ARE USELESS TO ME.
AND SO ARE YOU.

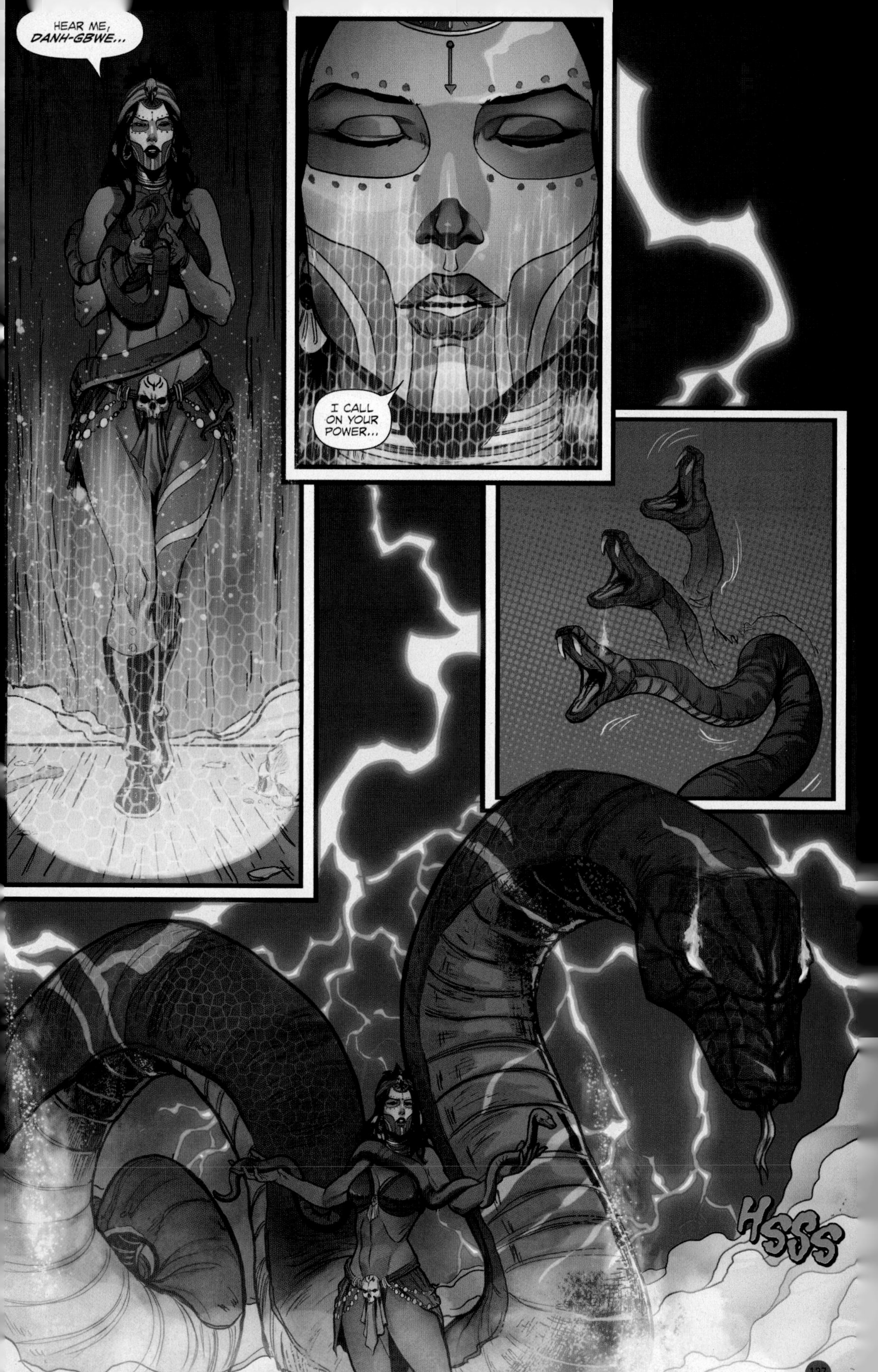
HEAR ME, DANH-GBWE...
I CALL ON YOUR POWER...
HSSS

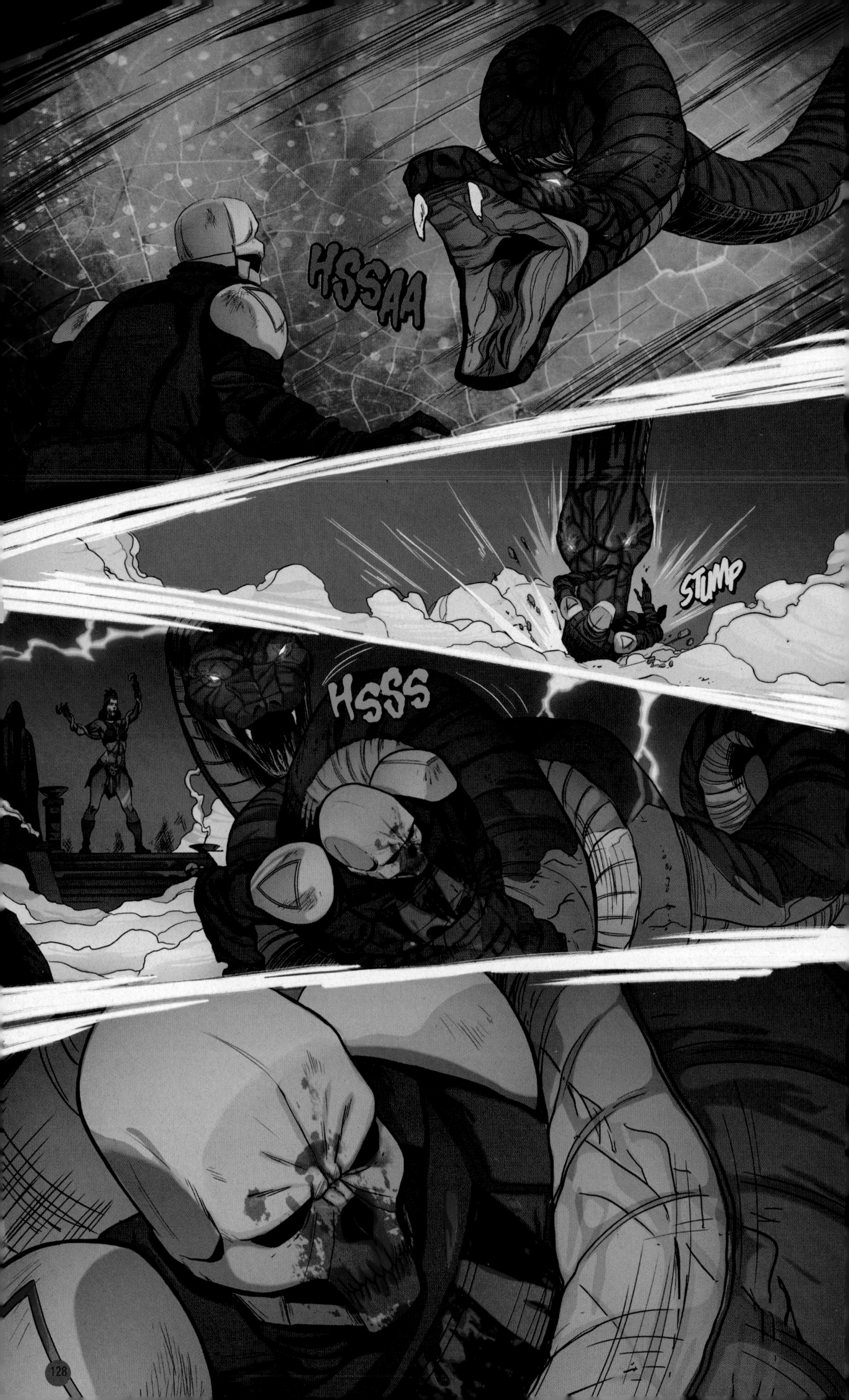
HSSAA
STUMP
HSSS

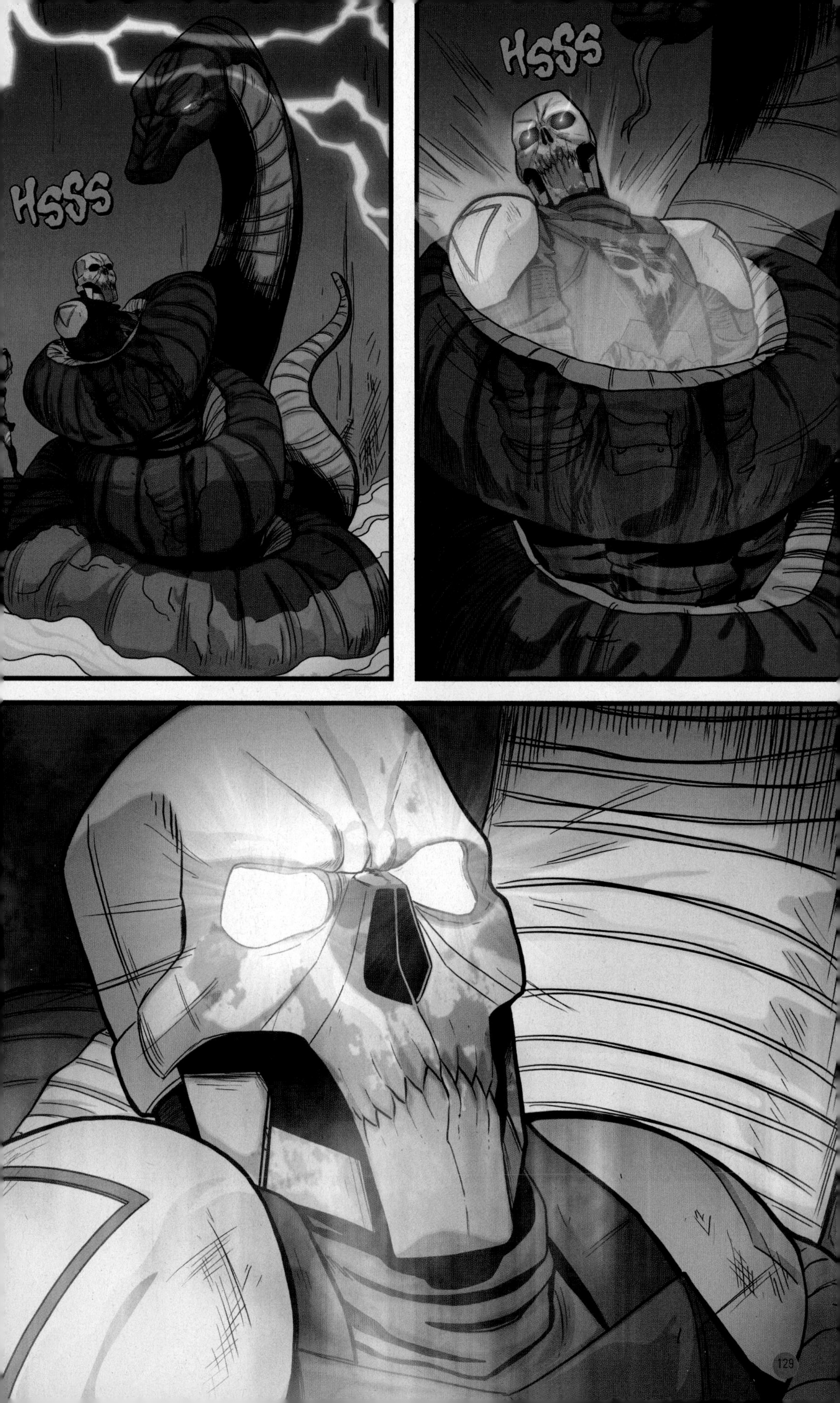
HSSS
HSSS

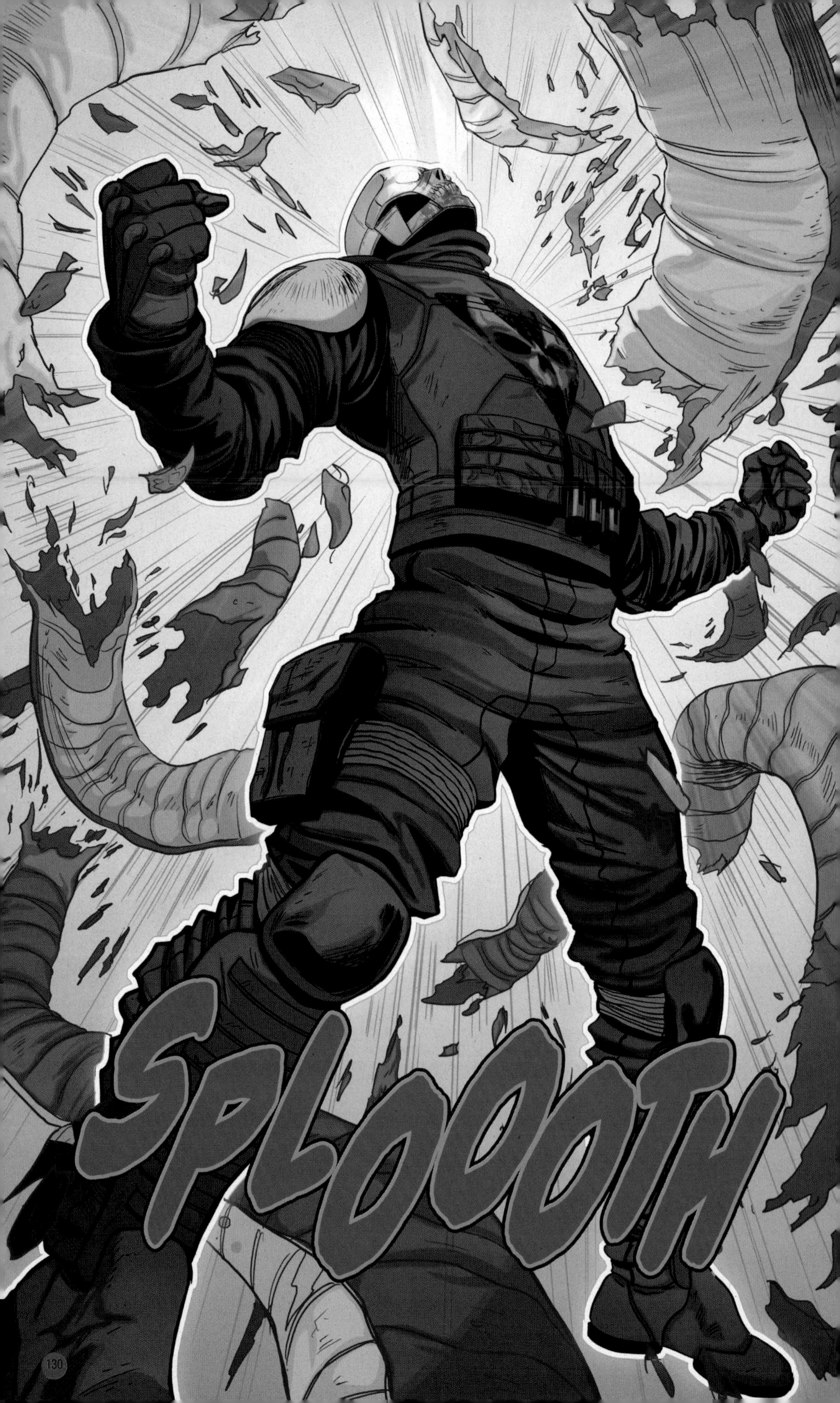
SPLOOOTH

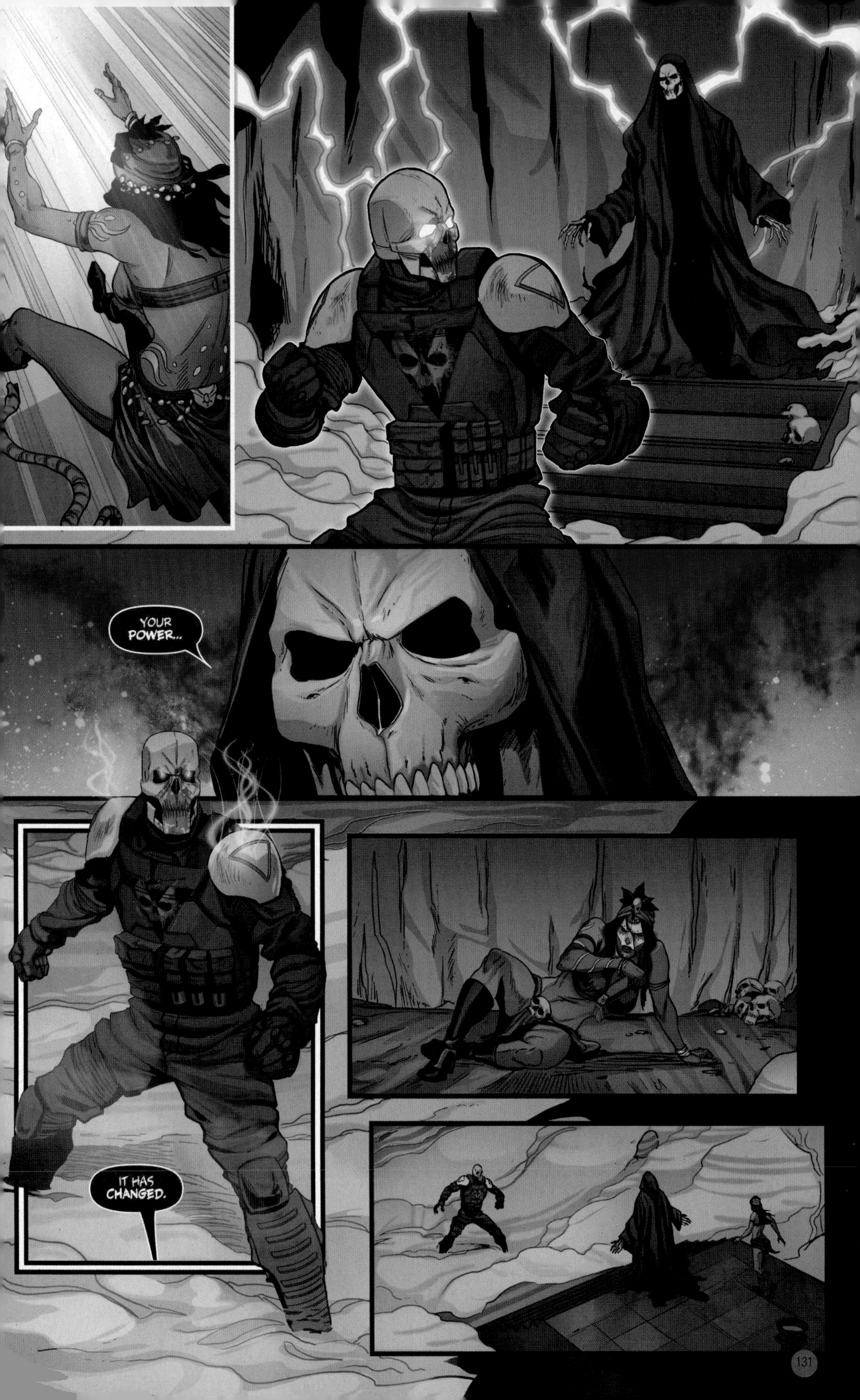
YOUR POWER...
IT HAS CHANGED.

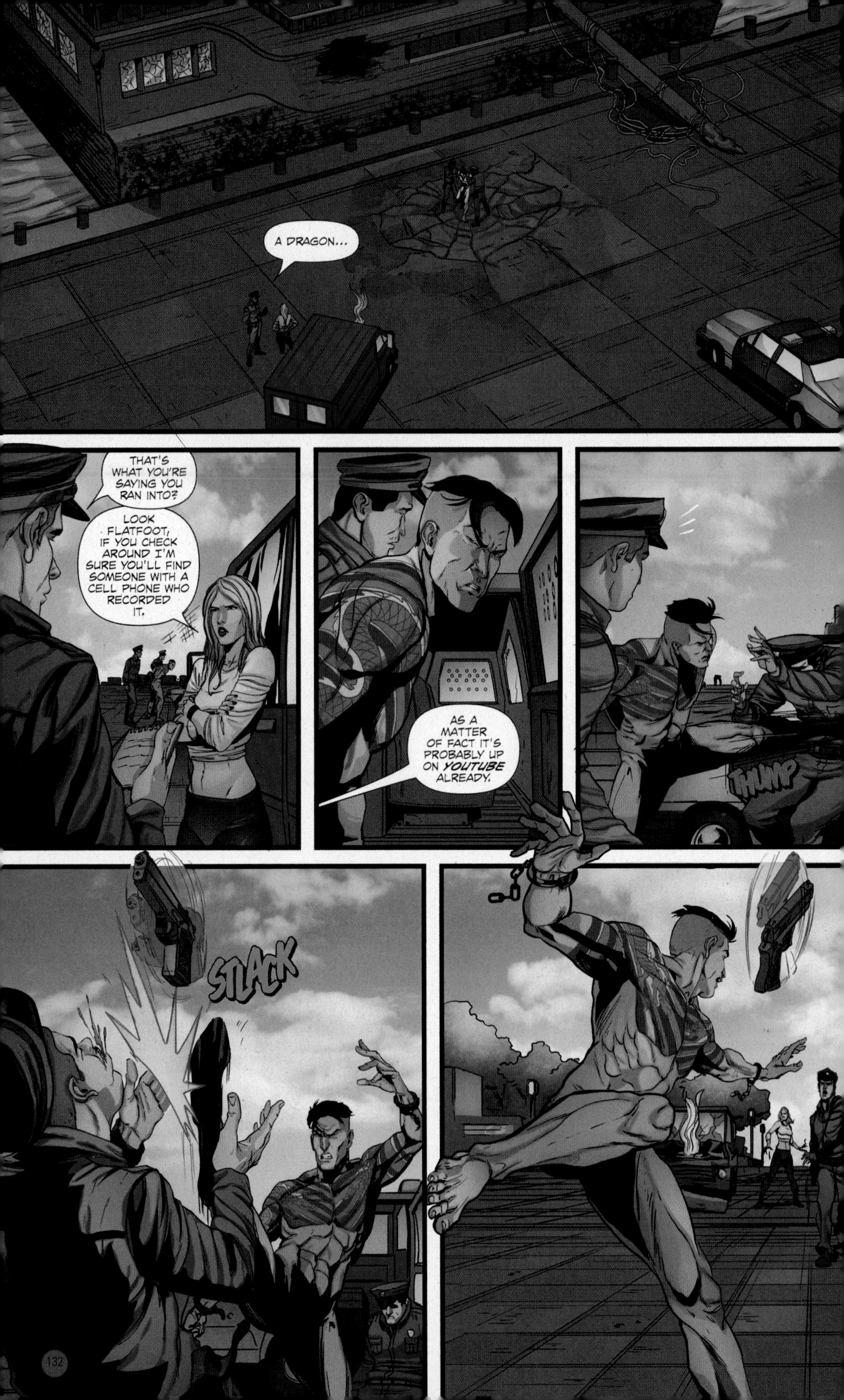
A DRAGON...
THAT'S WHAT YOU'RE SAYING YOU RAN INTO?
LOOK FLATFOOT, IF YOU CHECK AROUND I'M SURE YOU'LL FIND SOMEONE WITH A CELL PHONE WHO RECORDED IT.
AS A MATTER OF FACT IT'S PROBABLY UP ON YOUTUBE ALREADY.
THUMP
STLACK

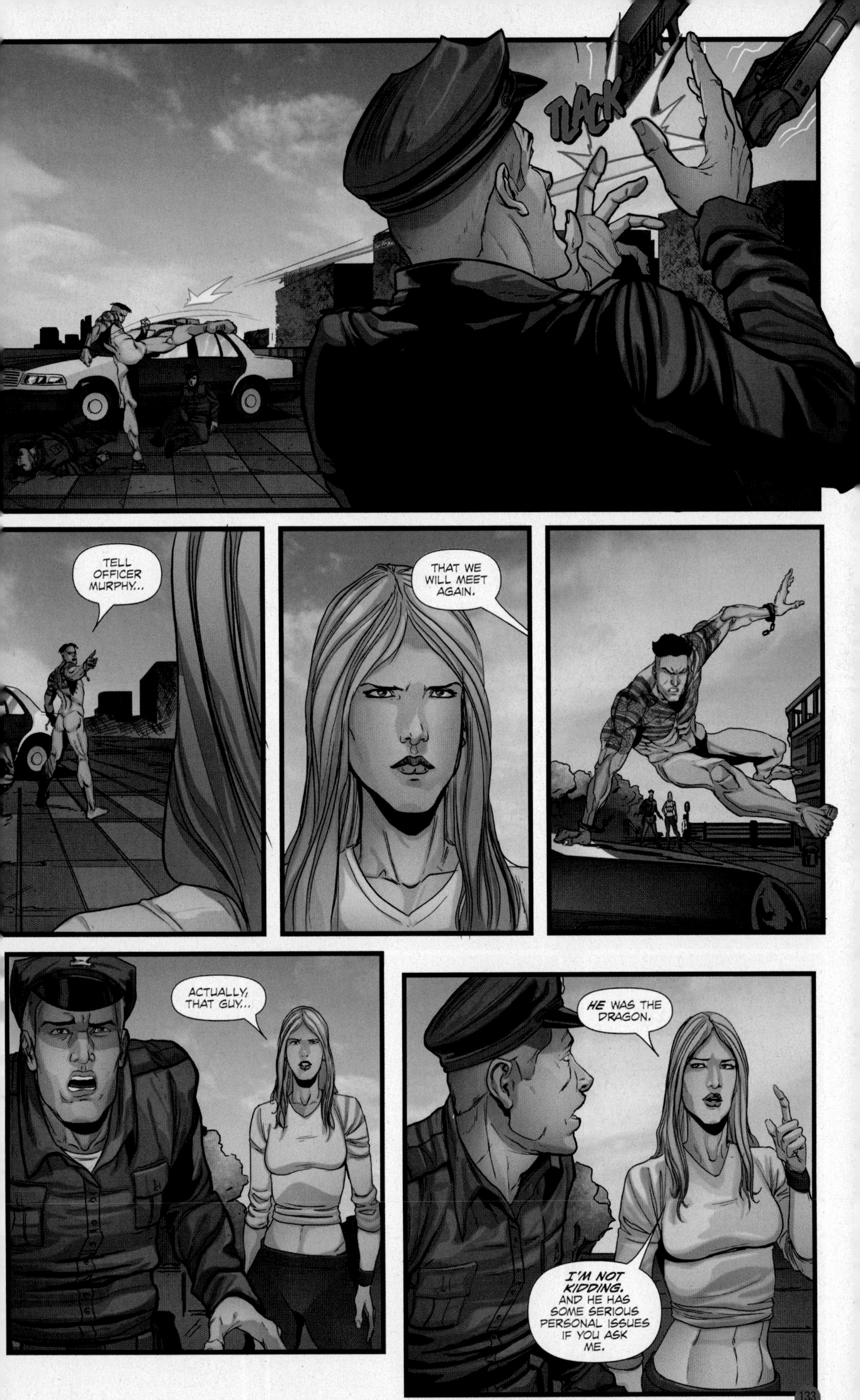
TLACK
TELL OFFICER MURPHY...
THAT WE WILL MEET AGAIN.
ACTUALLY, THAT GUY...
HE WAS THE DRAGON.
I'M NOT KIDDING. AND HE HAS SOME SERIOUS PERSONAL ISSUES IF YOU ASK ME.

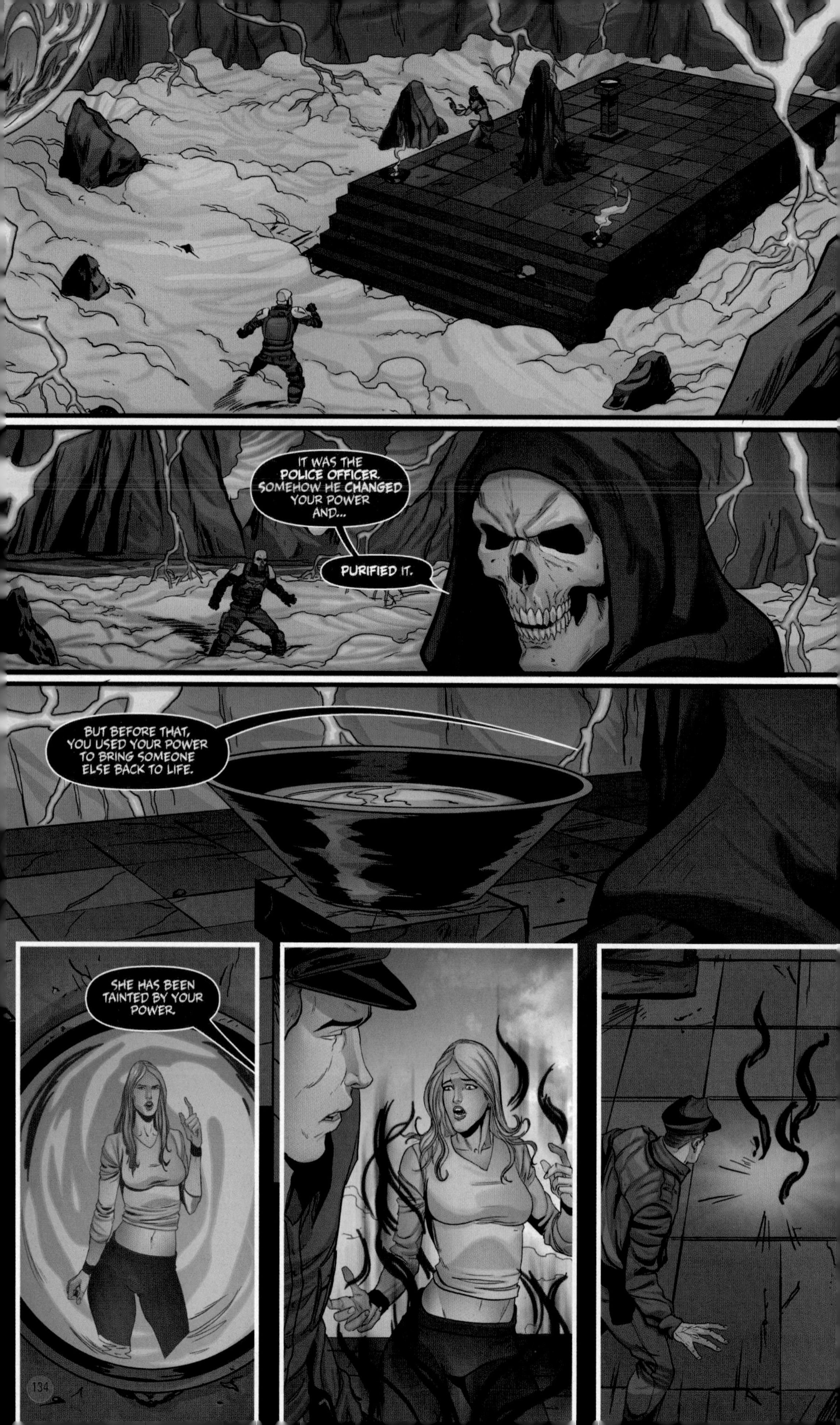
IT WAS THE POLICE OFFICER. SOMEHOW HE CHANGED YOUR POWER AND...
PURIFIED IT.
BUT BEFORE THAT, YOU USED YOUR POWER TO BRING SOMEONE ELSE BACK TO LIFE.
SHE HAS BEEN TAINTED BY YOUR POWER.

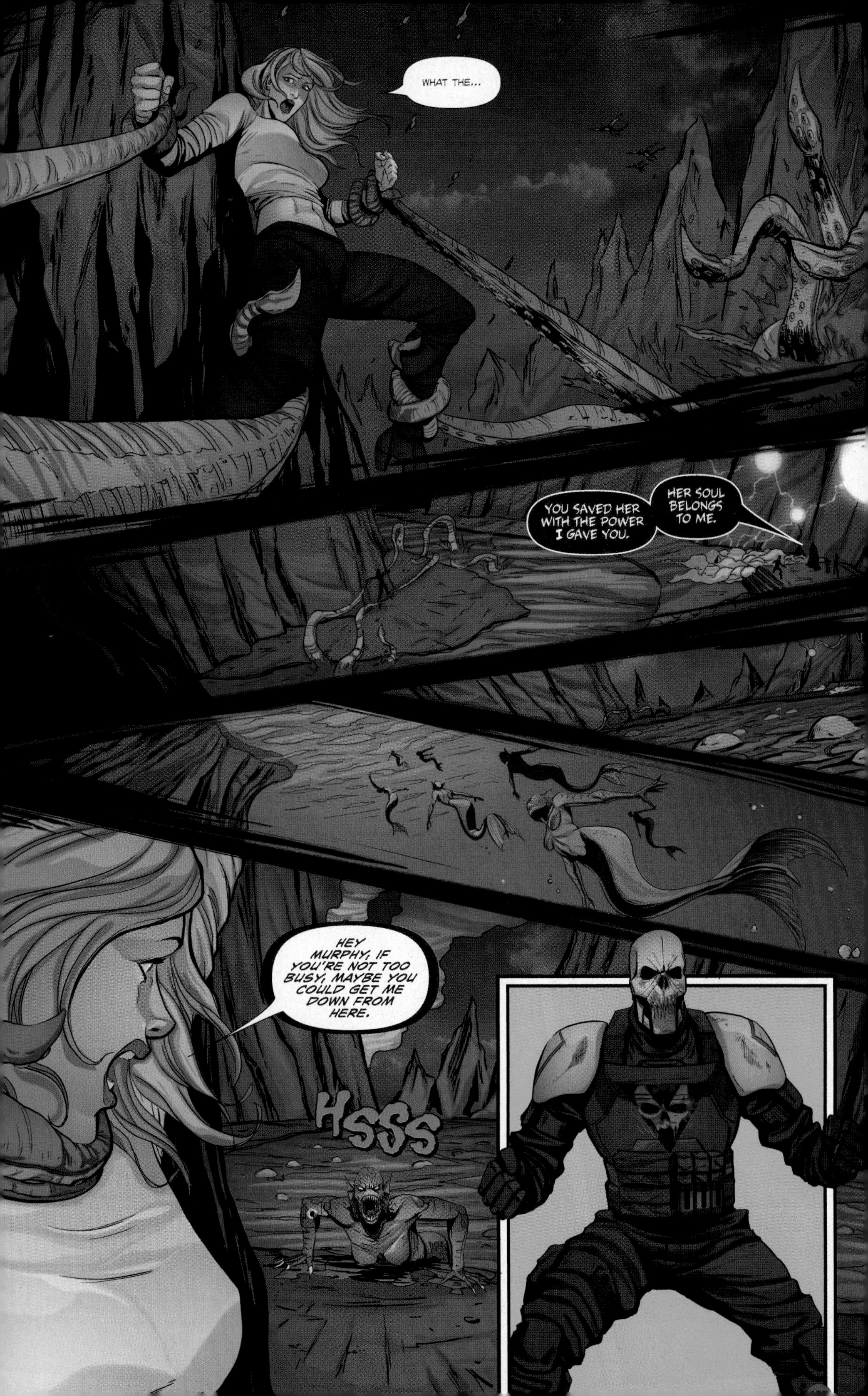
WHAT THE...
YOU SAVED HER WITH THE POWER I GAVE YOU.
HER SOUL BELONGS TO ME.
HEY MURPHY, IF YOU'RE NOT TOO BUSY, MAYBE YOU COULD GET ME DOWN FROM HERE.
HSSS

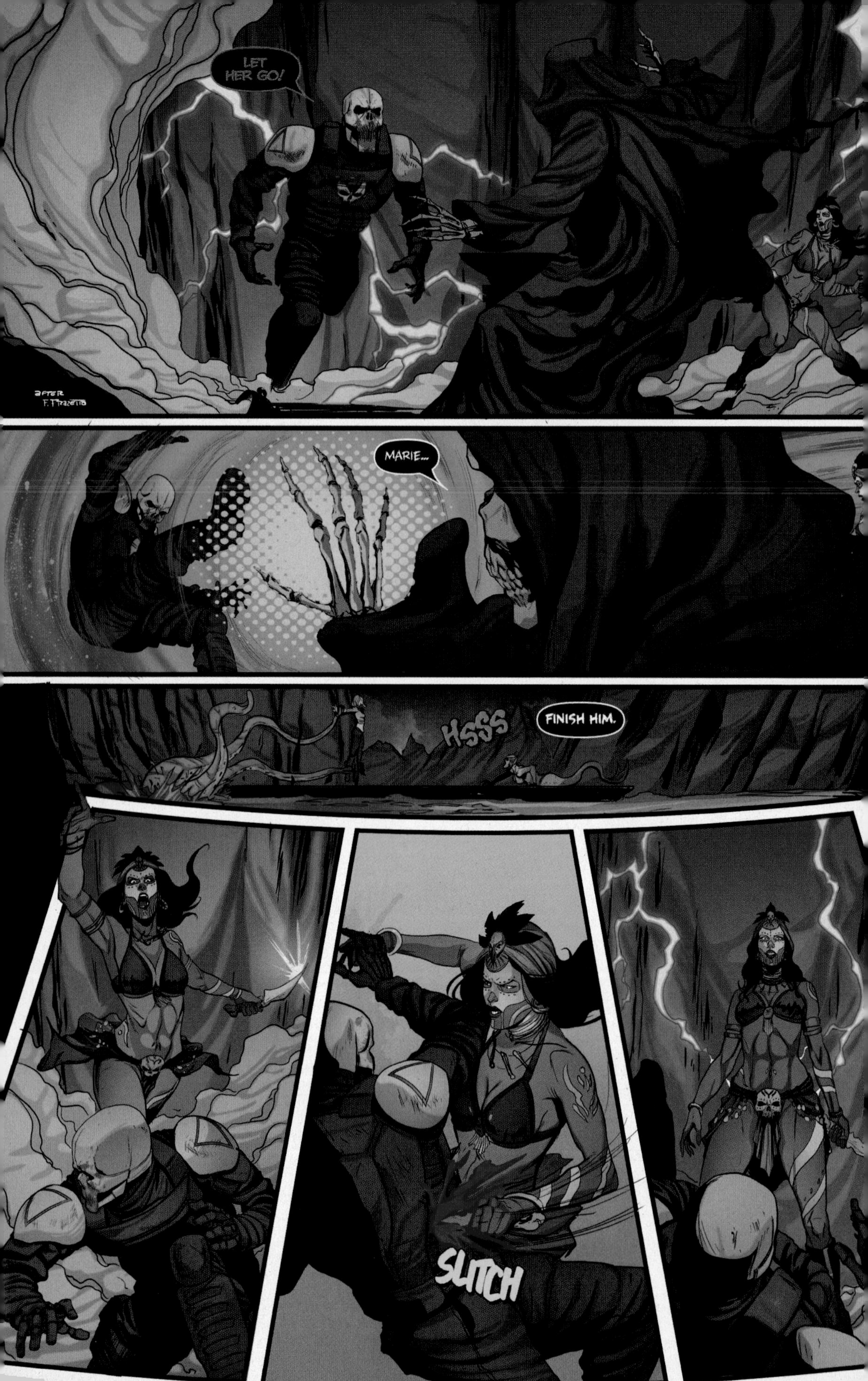
LET HER GO!
after F. Frazetta
MARIE...
HSSS
FINISH HIM.
SLITCH

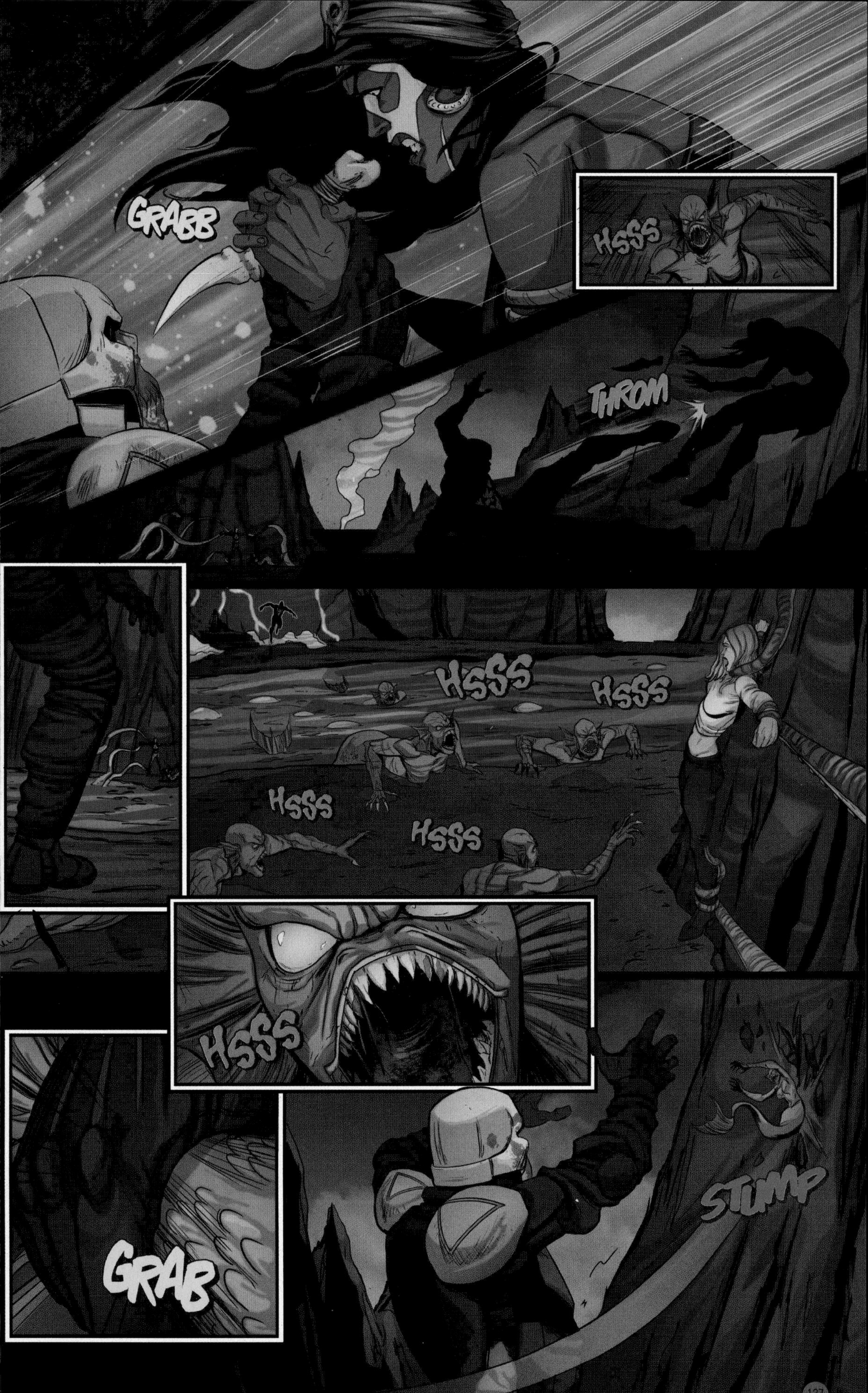
GRABB
HSSS
THROM
HSSS
HSSS
HSSS
HSSS
HSSS
GRAB
STUMP

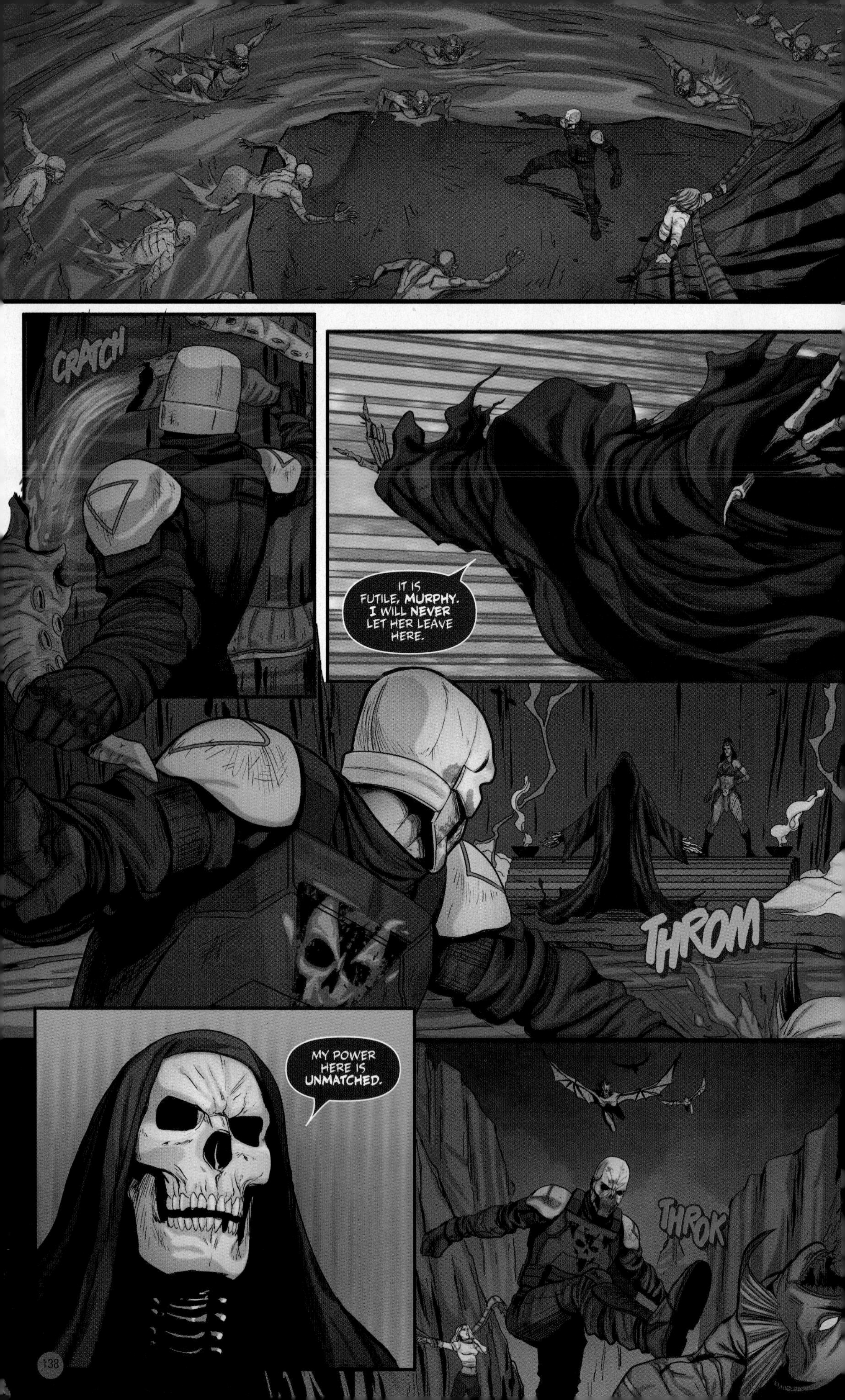
CRATCH
IT IS FUTILE, MURPHY. I WILL NEVER LET HER LEAVE HERE.
THROM
MY POWER HERE IS UNMATCHED.
THROK

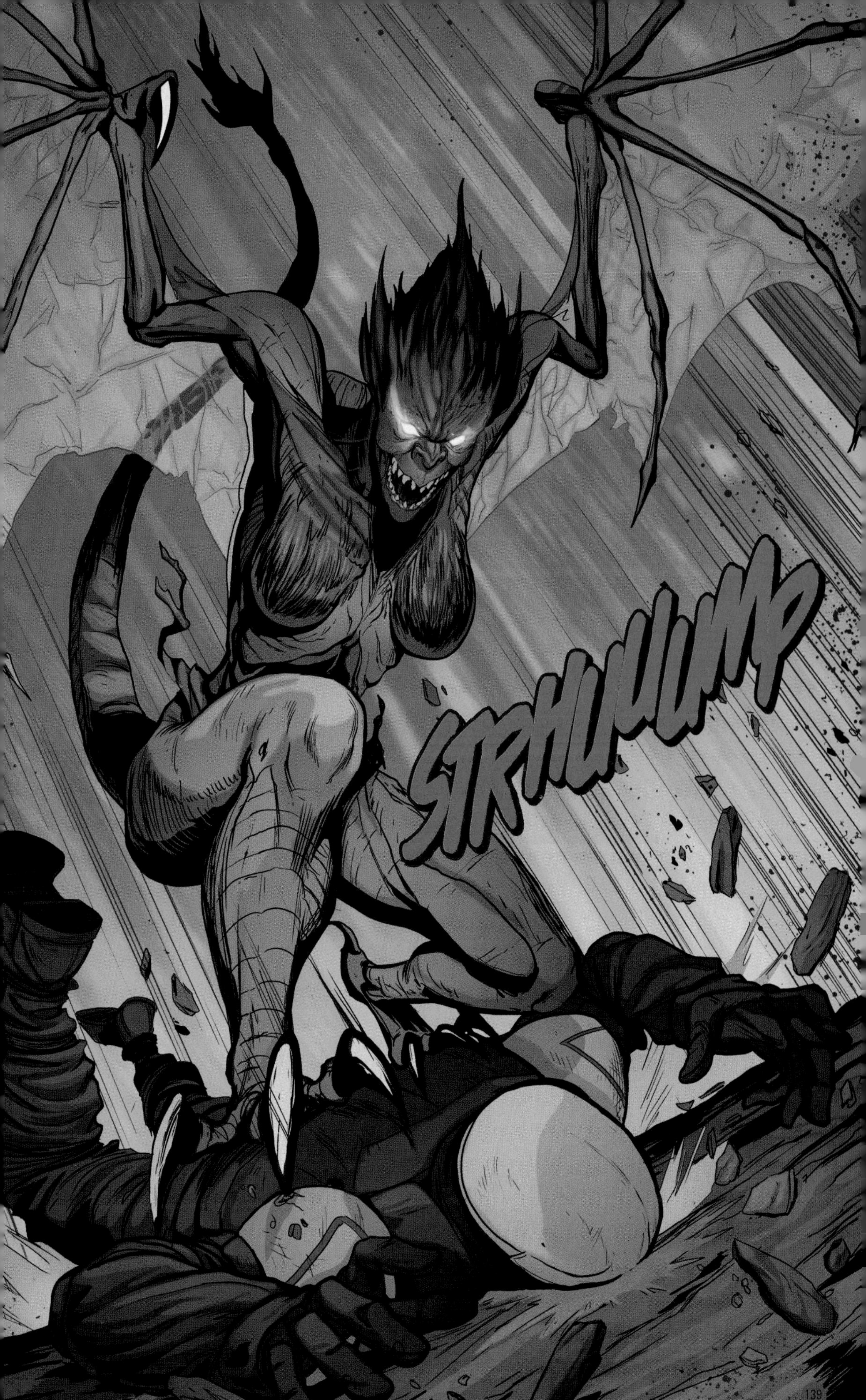
STRHUUUMP

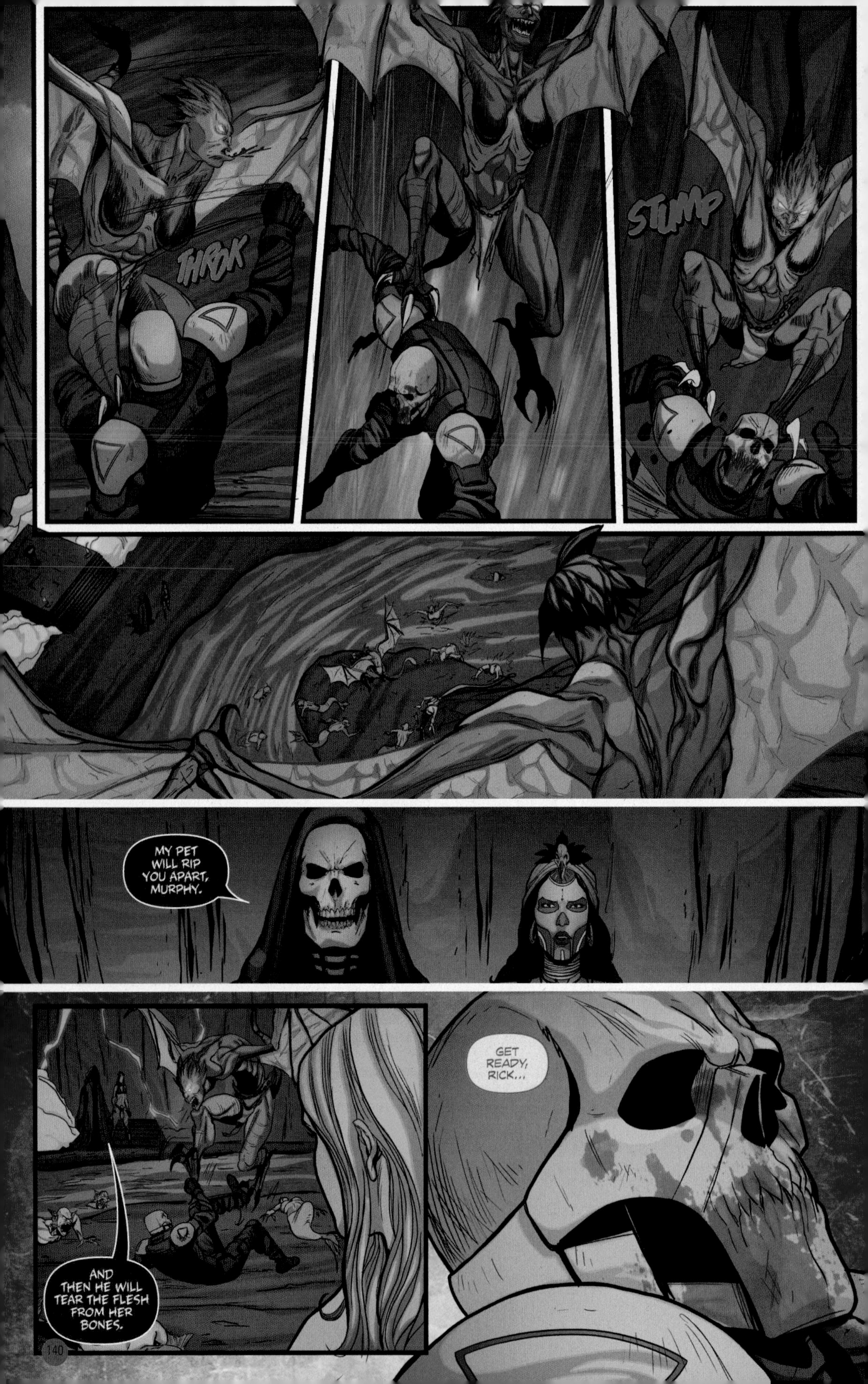
THROK
STUMP
MY PET WILL RIP YOU APART, MURPHY.
GET READY, RICK...
AND THEN HE WILL TEAR THE FLESH FROM HER BONES.

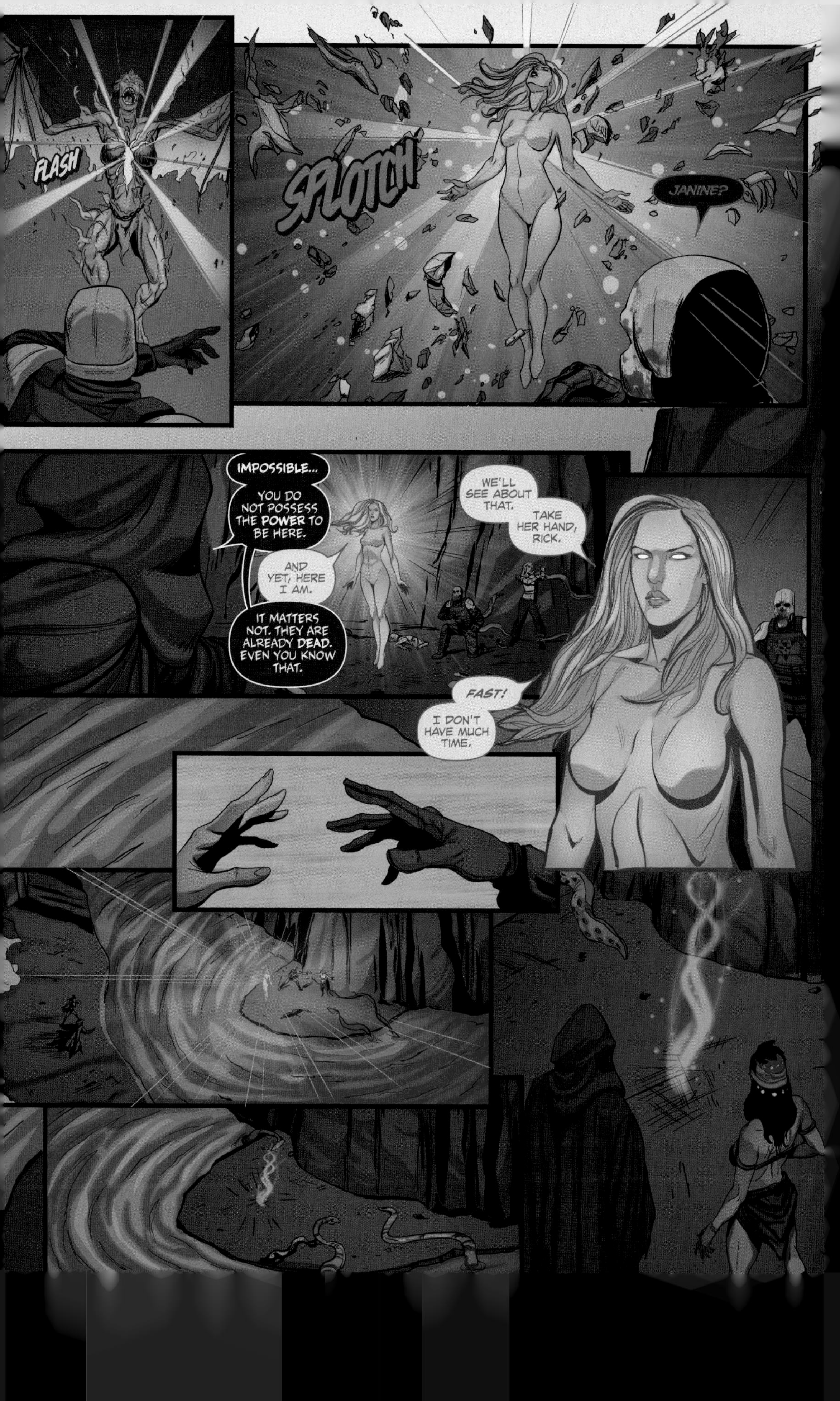
FLASH
SPLOTCH
JANINE?
IMPOSSIBLE...
YOU DO NOT POSSESS THE POWER TO BE HERE.
AND YET, HERE I AM.
IT MATTERS NOT. THEY ARE ALREADY DEAD. EVEN YOU KNOW THAT.
WE'LL SEE ABOUT THAT.
TAKE HER HAND, RICK.
FAST!
I DON'T HAVE MUCH TIME.

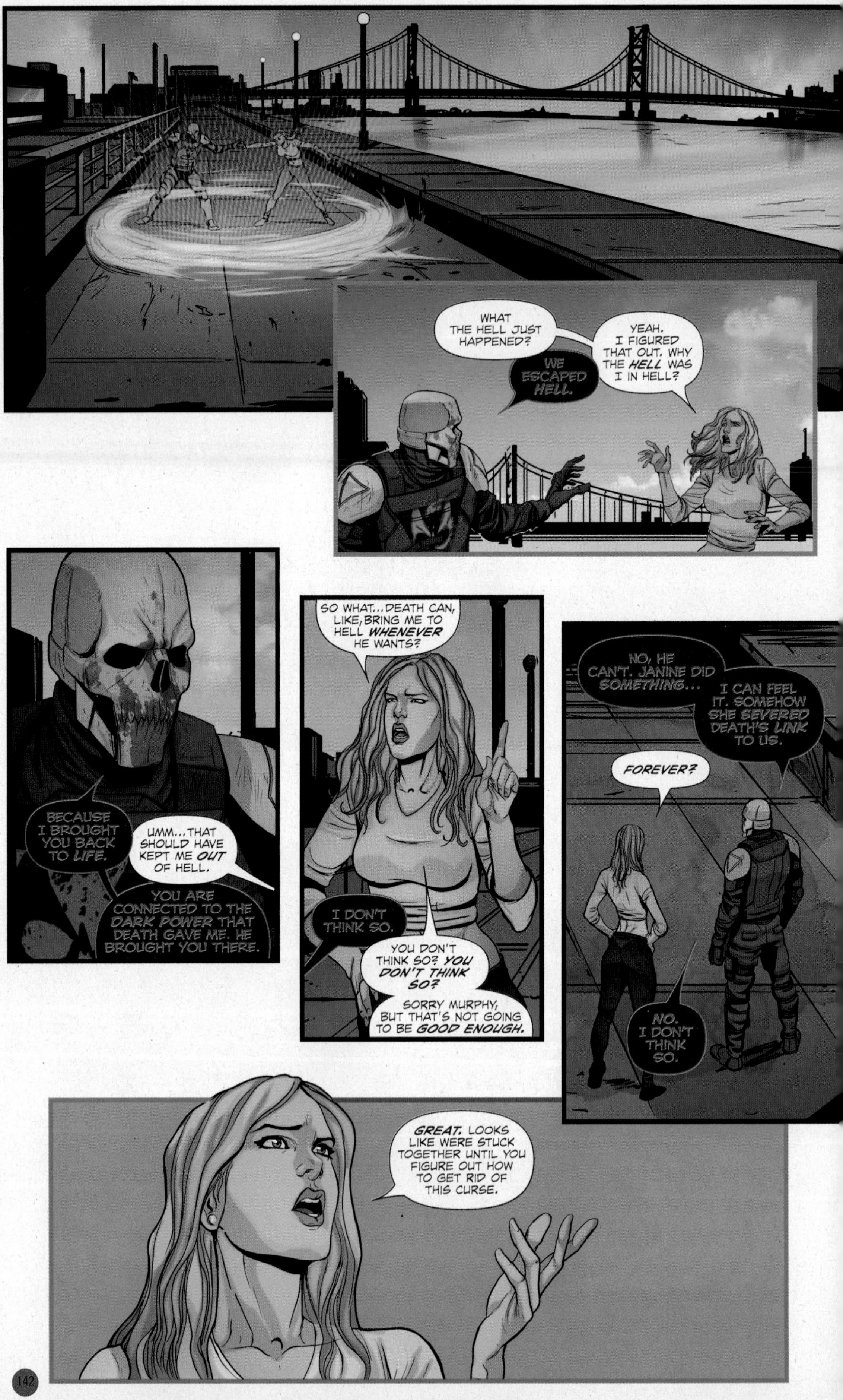

WHAT THE HELL JUST HAPPENED?
WE ESCAPED HELL.
YEAH. I FIGURED THAT OUT. WHY THE HELL WAS I IN HELL?
BECAUSE I BROUGHT YOU BACK TO LIFE.
UMM...THAT SHOULD HAVE KEPT ME OUT OF HELL.
YOU ARE CONNECTED TO THE DARK POWER THAT DEATH GAVE ME. HE BROUGHT YOU THERE.
SO WHAT...DEATH CAN, LIKE, BRING ME TO HELL WHENEVER HE WANTS?
I DON'T THINK SO.
YOU DON'T THINK SO? YOU DON'T THINK SO?
SORRY MURPHY, BUT THAT'S NOT GOING TO BE GOOD ENOUGH.
NO, HE CAN'T. JANINE DID SOMETHING...
I CAN FEEL IT. SOMEHOW SHE SEVERED DEATH'S LINK TO US.
FOREVER?
NO. I DON'T THINK SO.
GREAT. LOOKS LIKE WERE STUCK TOGETHER UNTIL YOU FIGURE OUT HOW TO GET RID OF THIS CURSE.

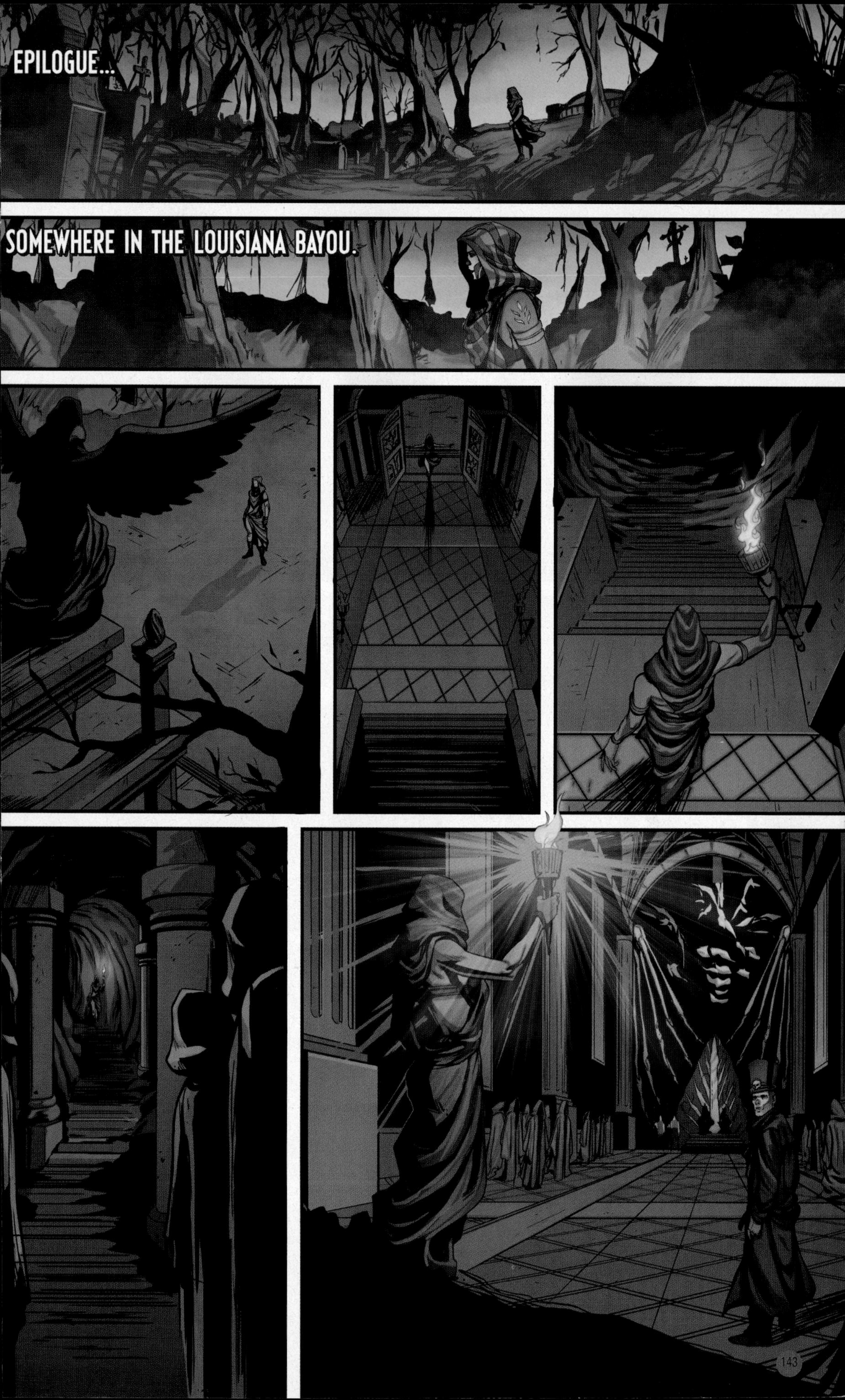
EPILOGUE...
SOMEWHERE IN THE LOUISIANA BAYOU.

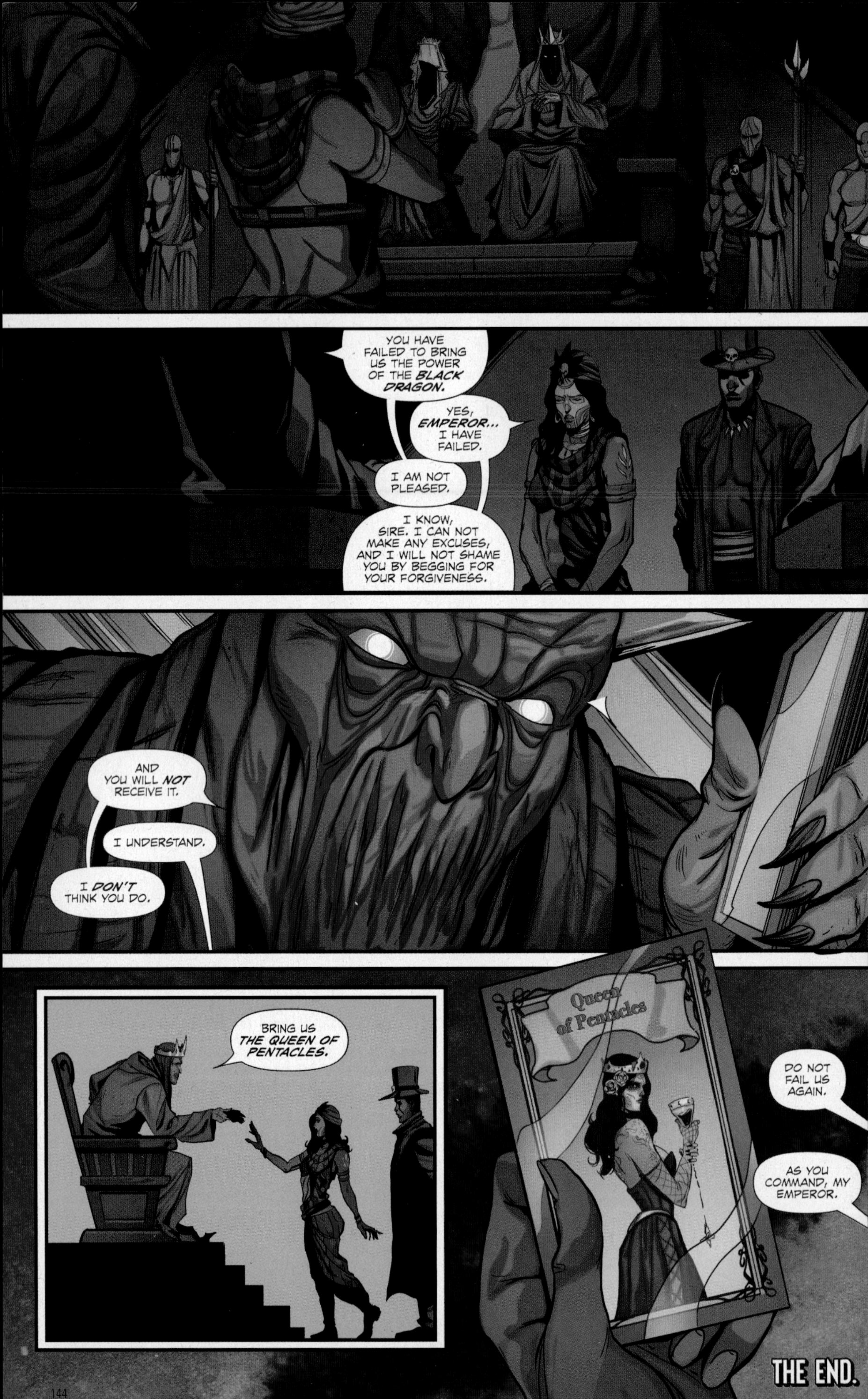
YOU HAVE FAILED TO BRING US THE POWER OF THE BLACK DRAGON.
YES, EMPEROR... I HAVE FAILED.
I AM NOT PLEASED.
I KNOW, SIRE. I CAN NOT MAKE ANY EXCUSES, AND I WILL NOT SHAME YOU BY BEGGING FOR YOUR FORGIVENESS.
AND YOU WILL NOT RECEIVE IT.
I UNDERSTAND.
I DON'T THINK YOU DO.
BRING US THE QUEEN OF PENTACLES.
Queen of Pentacles
DO NOT FAIL US AGAIN.
AS YOU COMMAND, MY EMPEROR.
THE END.

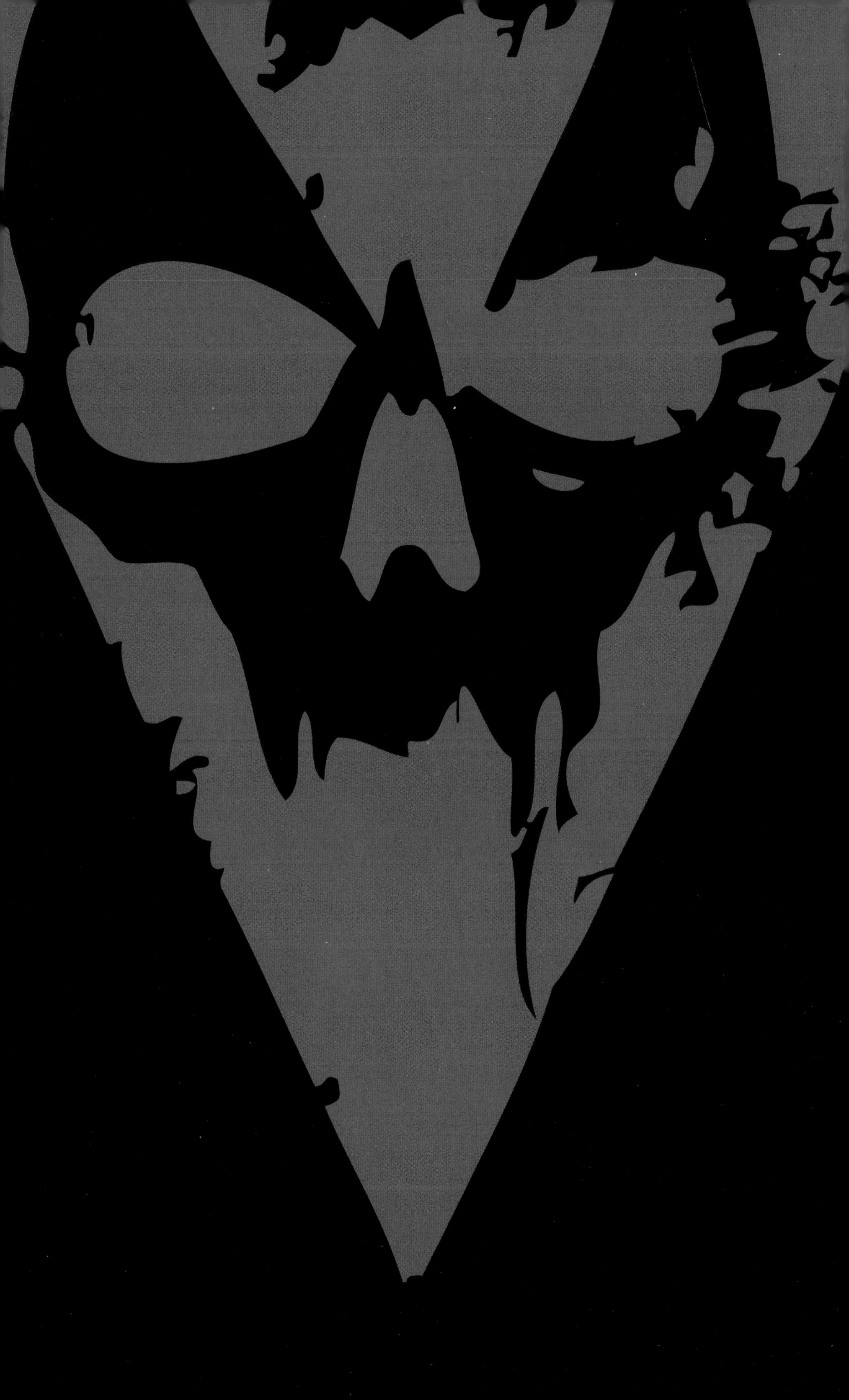

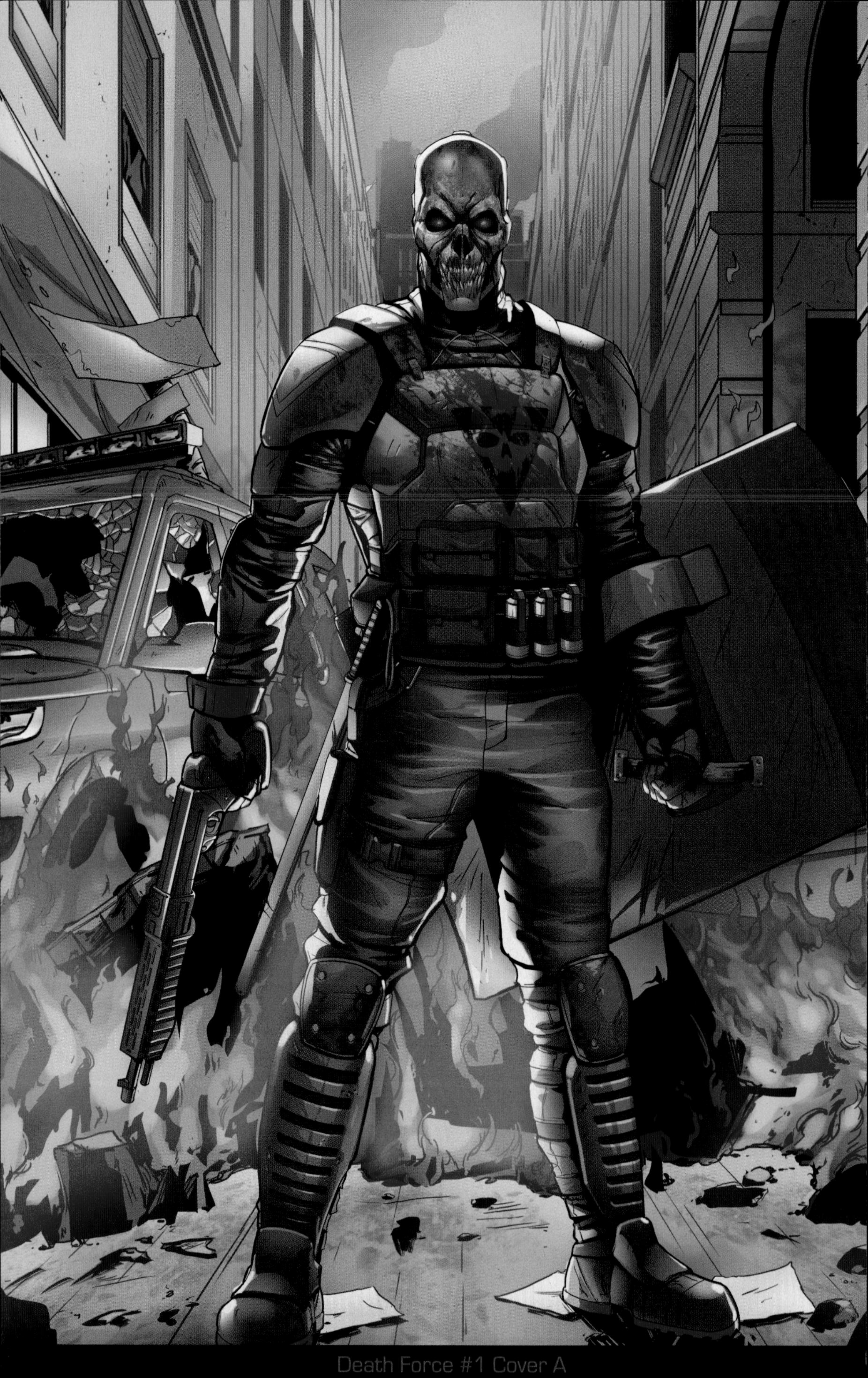

Death Force #1 Cover A

ARTWORK BY MARC ROSETE • COLORS BY GROSTIETA

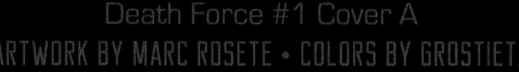

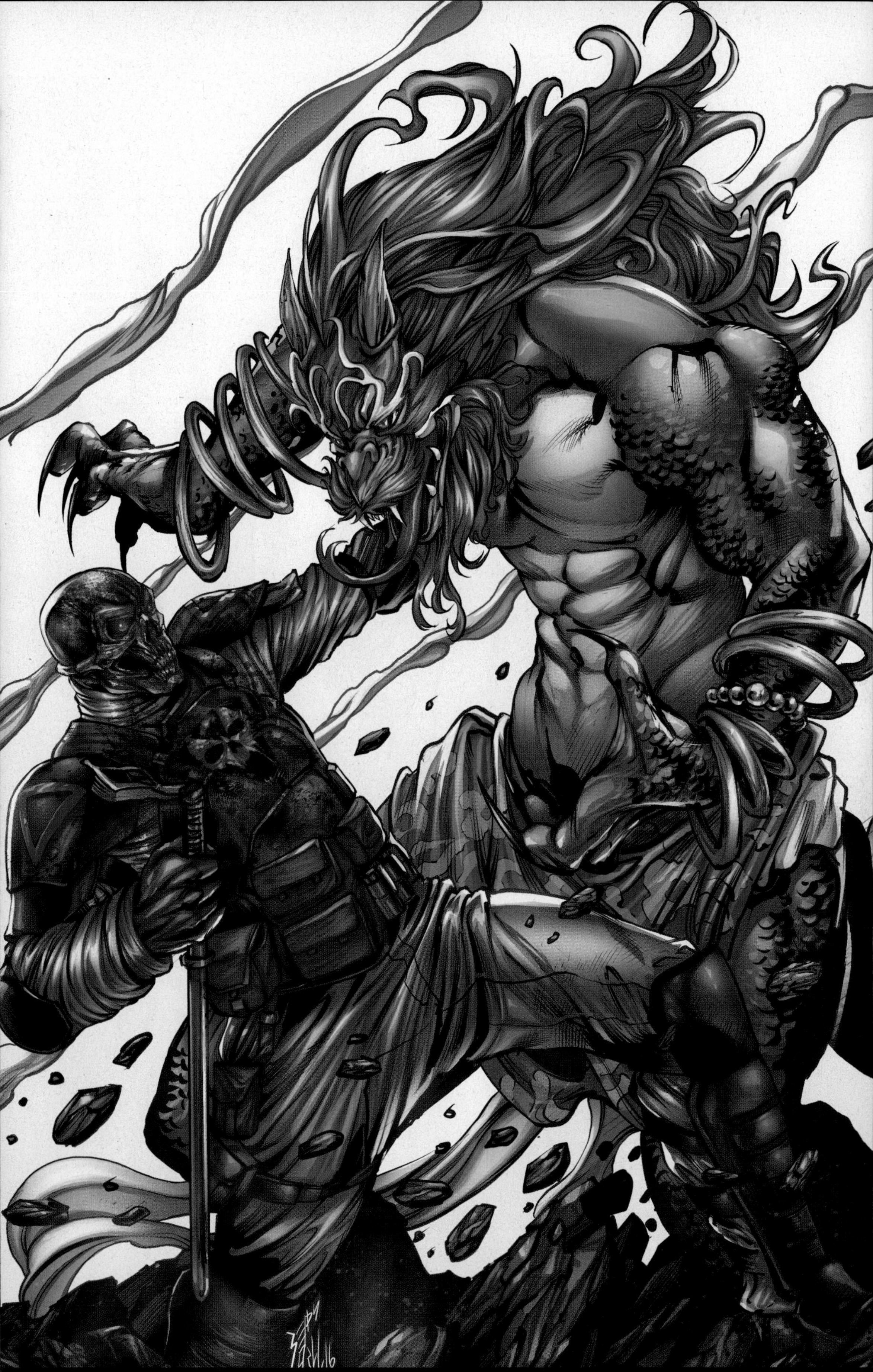

Death Force #1 Cover B

ARTWORK BY SEAN HILL • COLORS BY JORGE CORTES

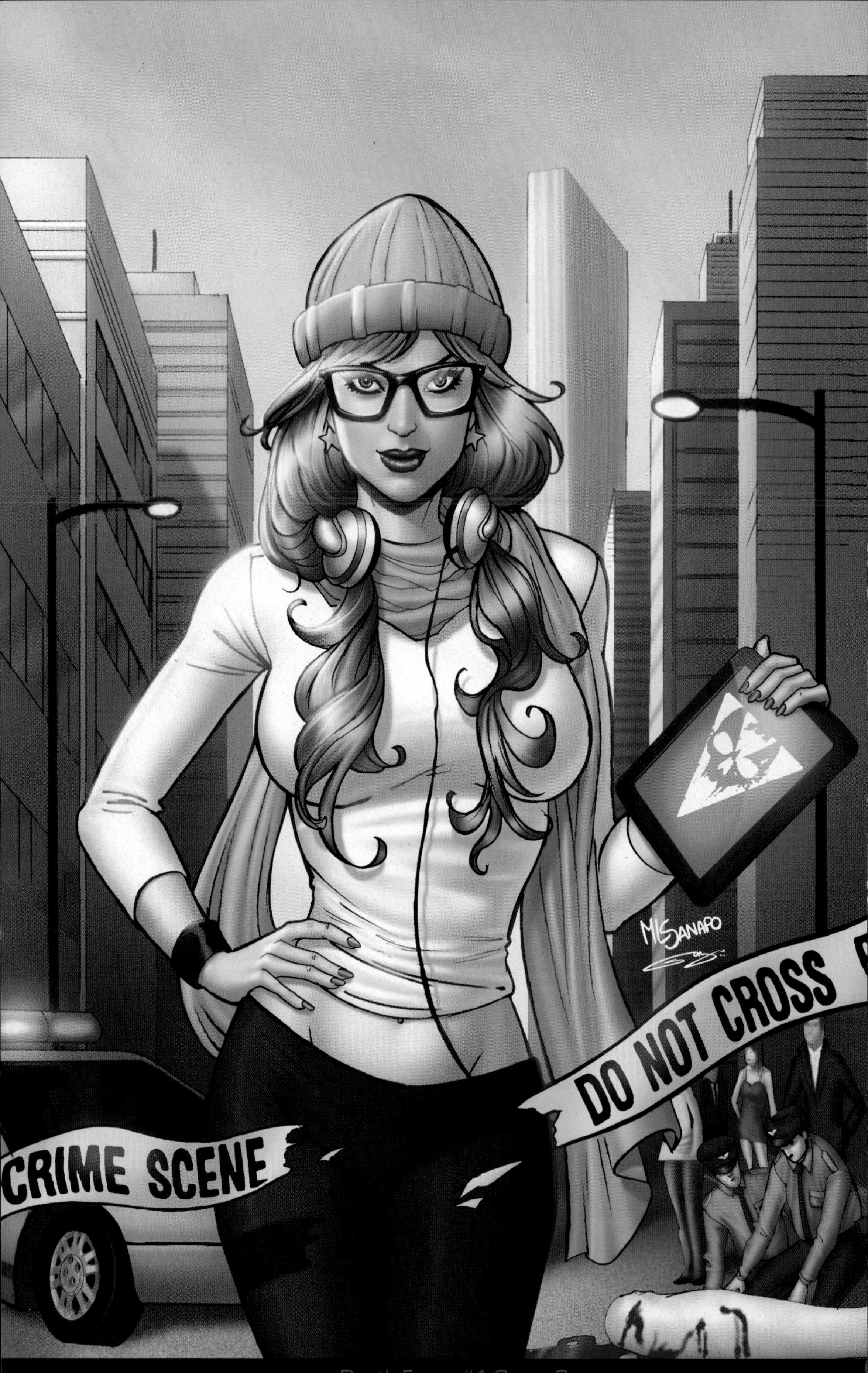
CRIME SCENE
DO NOT CROSS
M L SANAPO

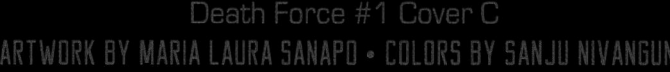

Death Force #1 Cover C
ARTWORK BY MARIA LAURA SANAPO • COLORS BY SANJU NIVANGUNE

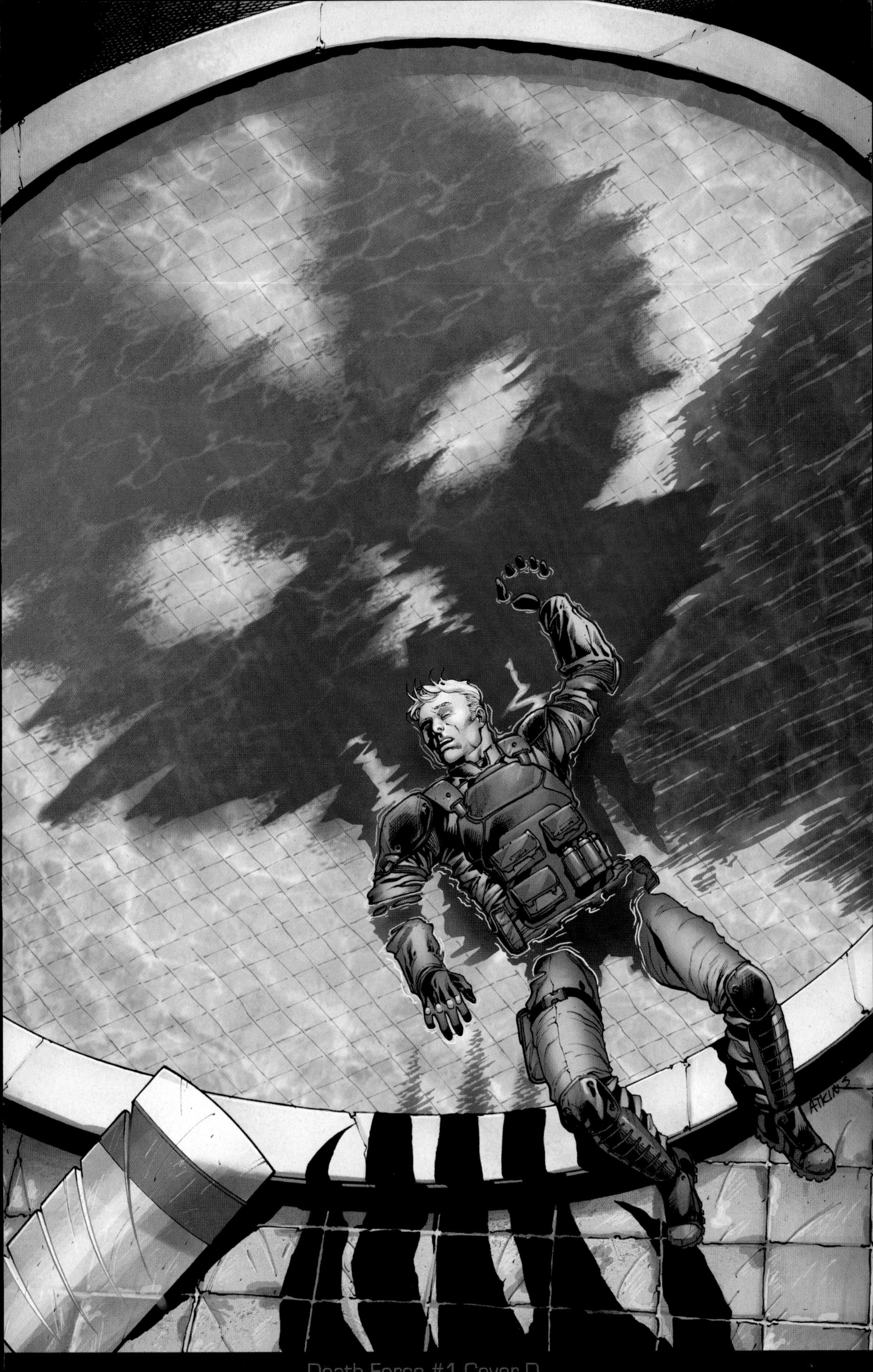
ATKINS

Death Force #1 Cover D

ARTWORK BY ROBERT ATKINS • COLORS BY WES HARTMAN

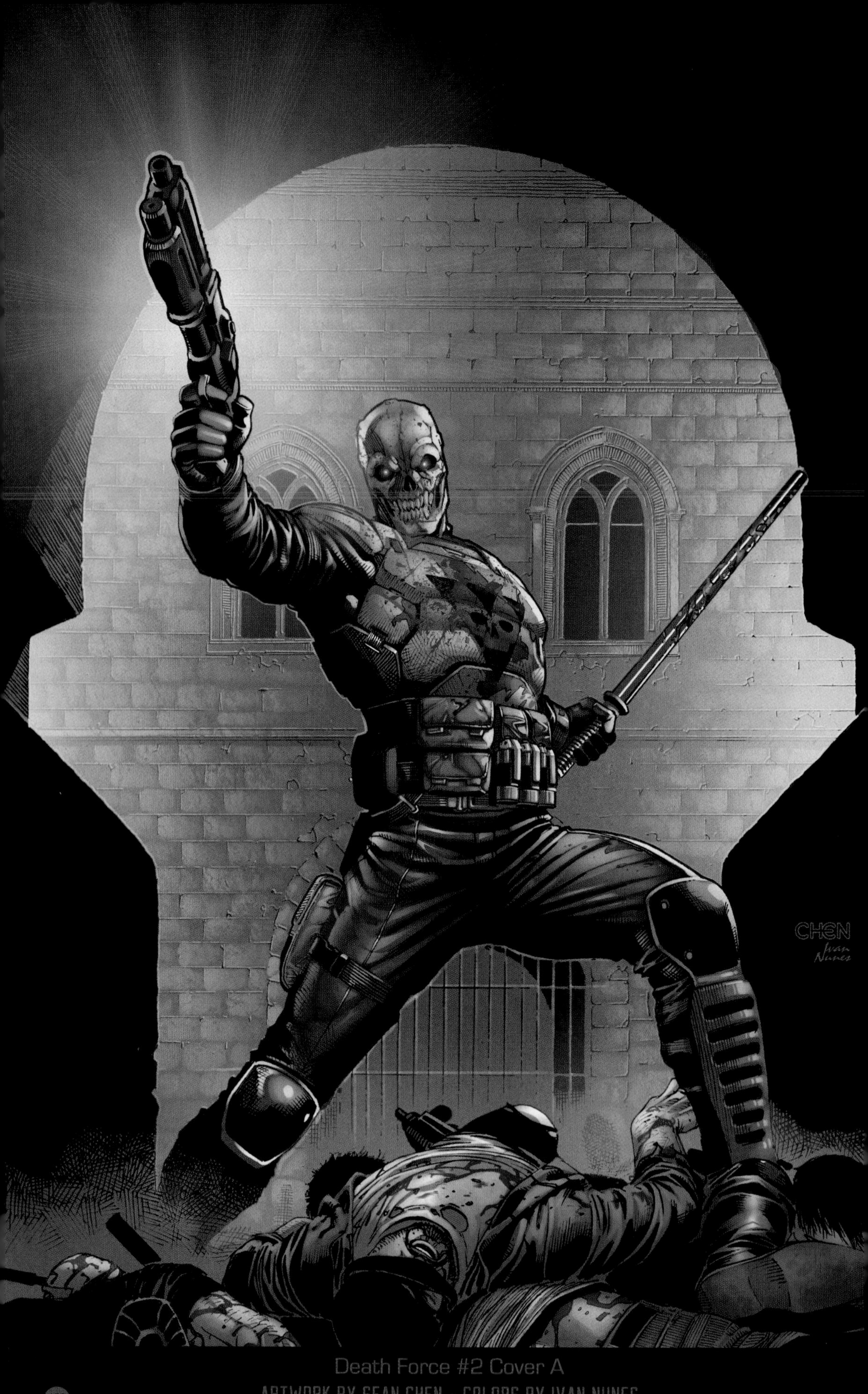
CHEN
Ivan Nunes

Death Force #2 Cover A

ARTWORK BY SEAN CHEN • COLORS BY IVAN NUNES

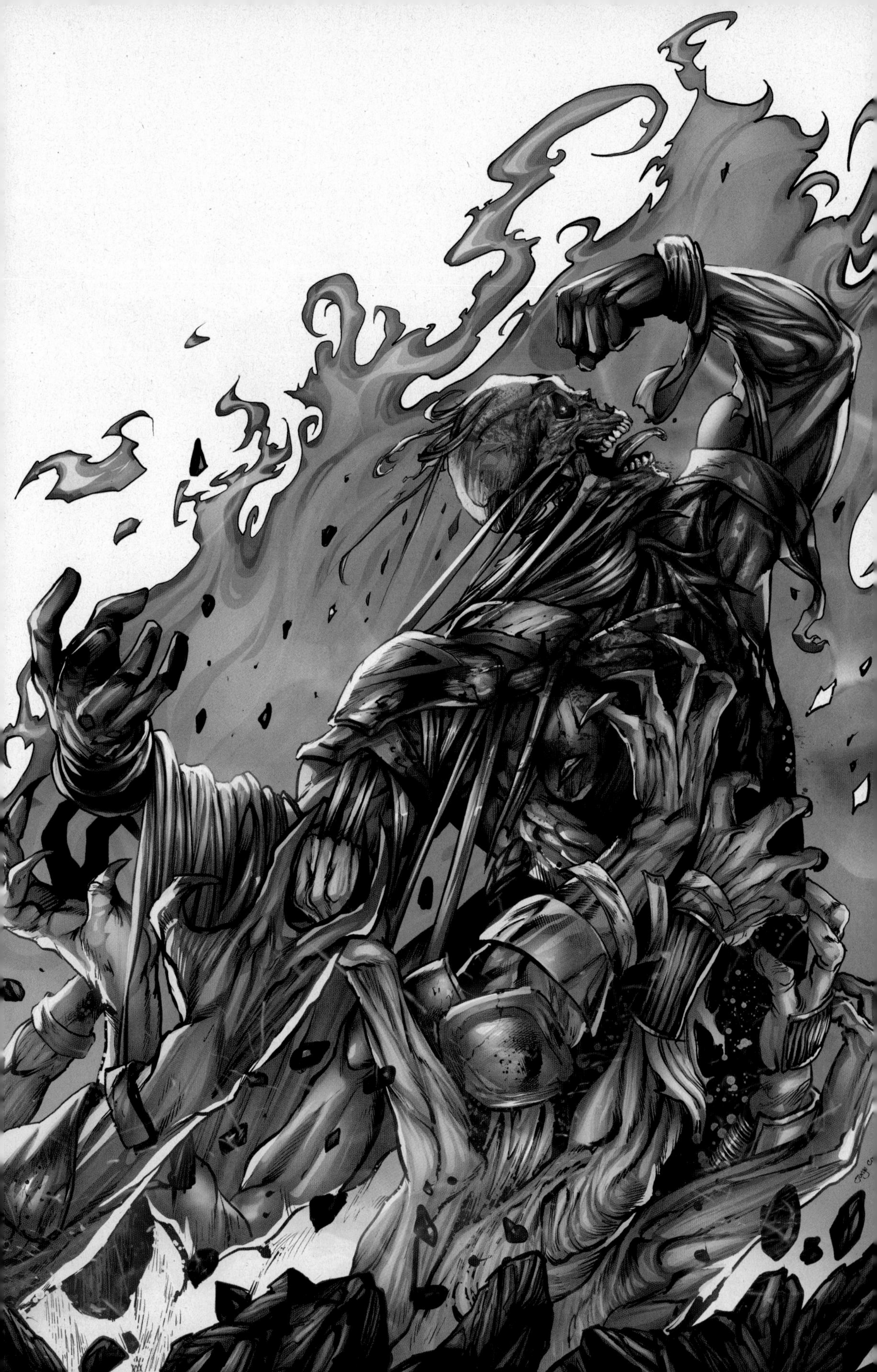

Death Force #2 Cover B

ARTWORK BY SEAN HILL • COLORS BY JORGE CORTES

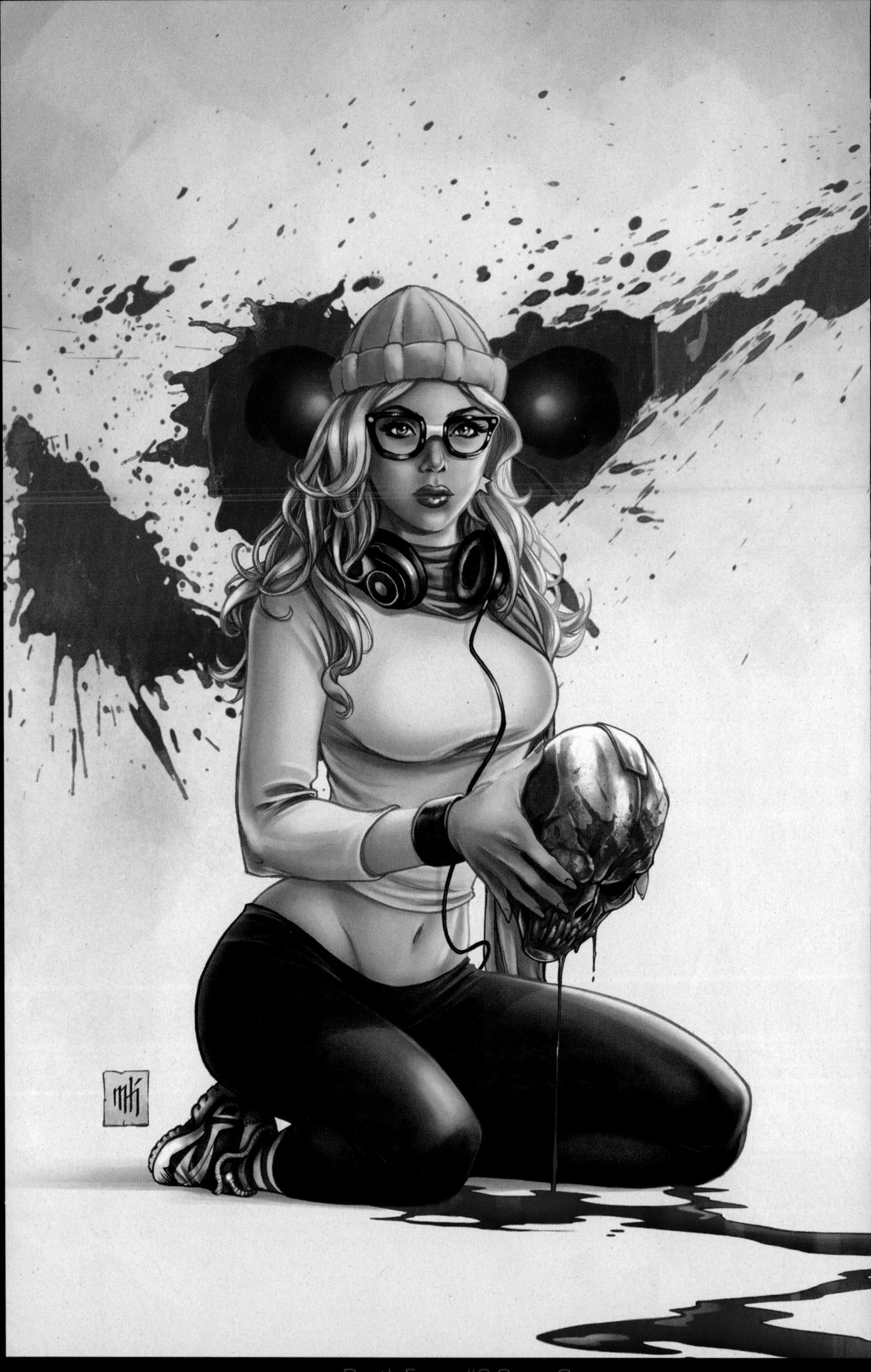

Death Force #2 Cover C
ARTWORK BY MIKE KROME

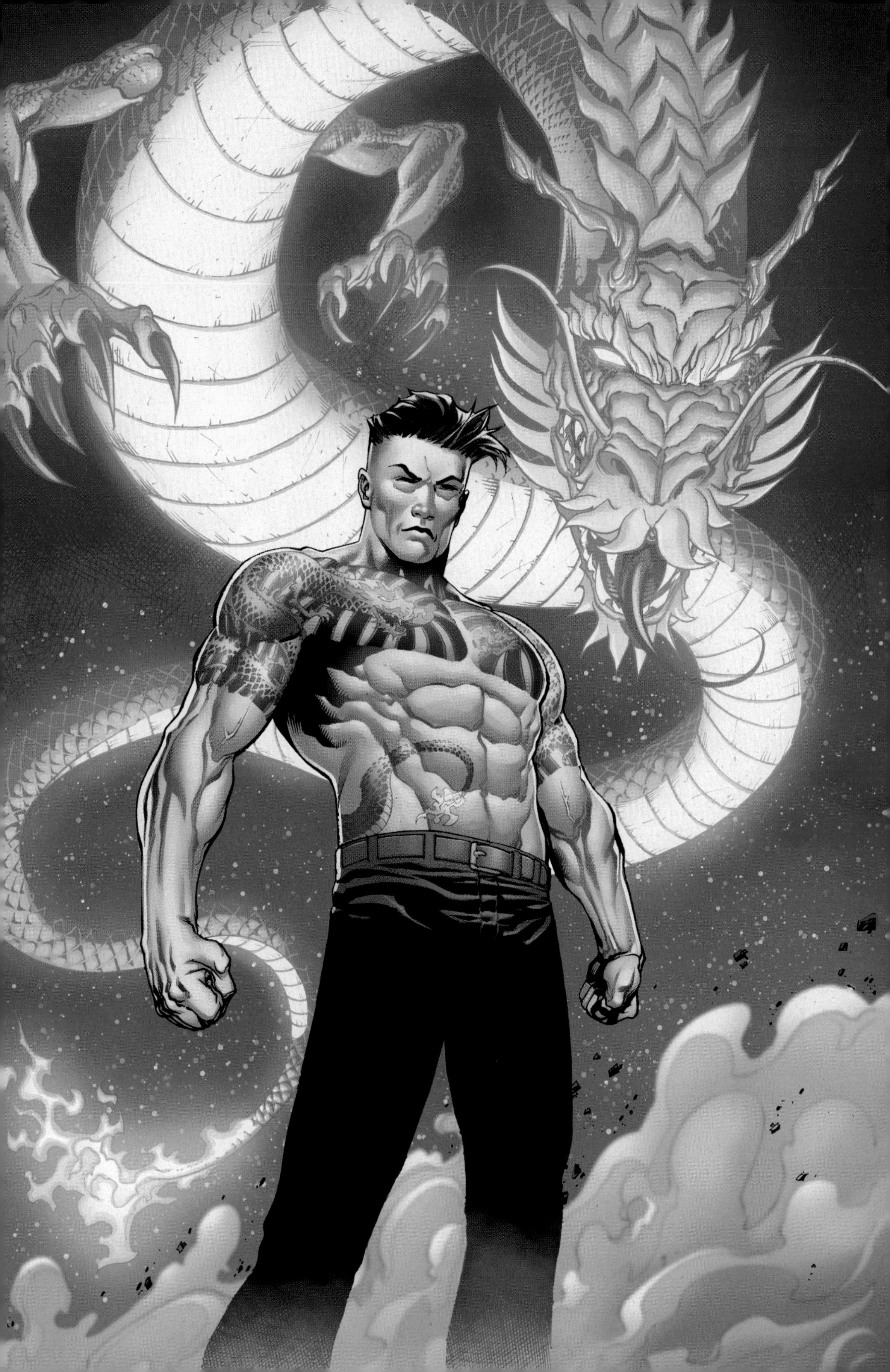

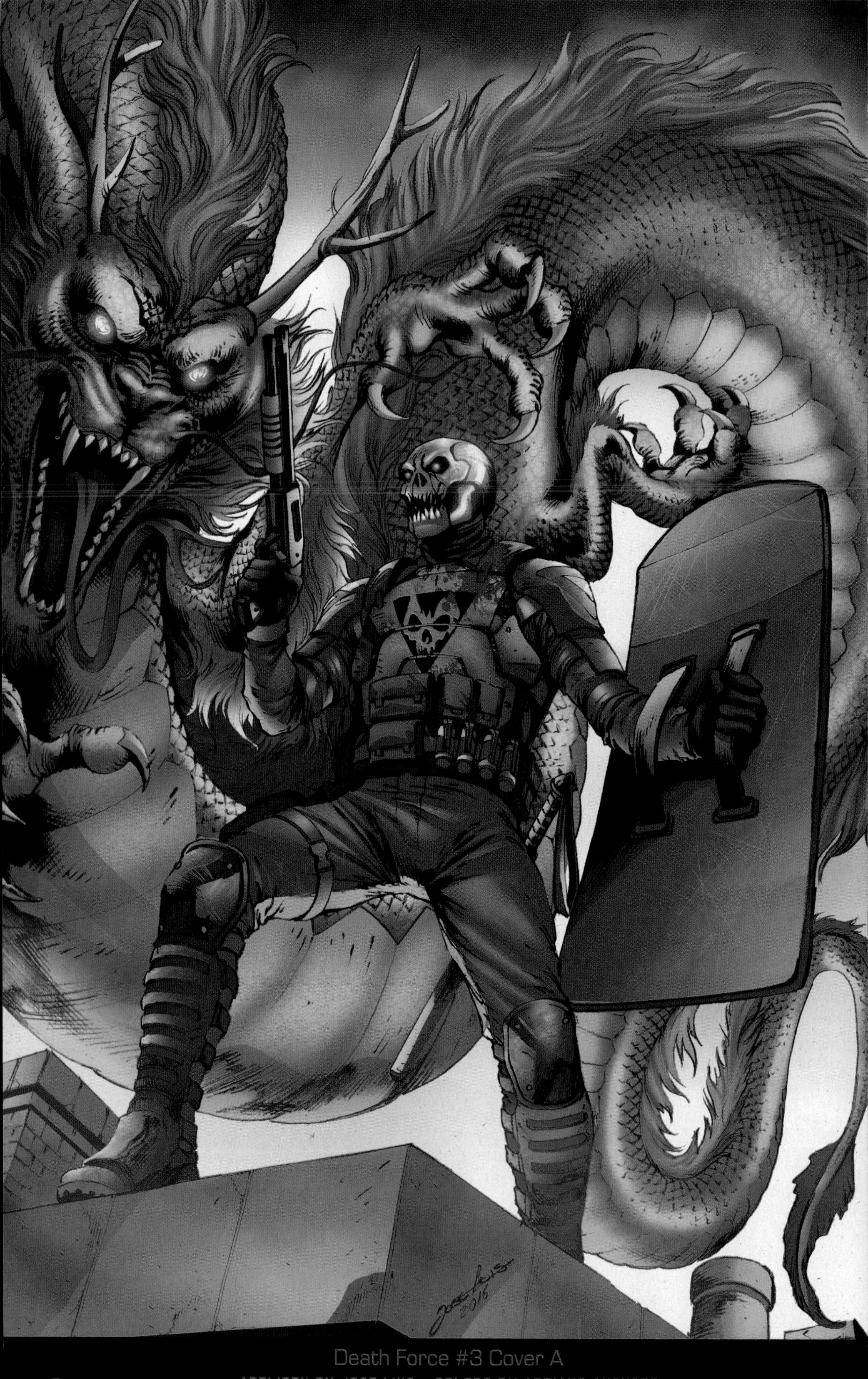

Death Force #3 Cover A

ARTWORK BY JOSE LUIS • COLORS BY ADRIANO AUGUSTO

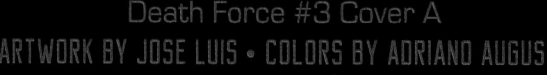

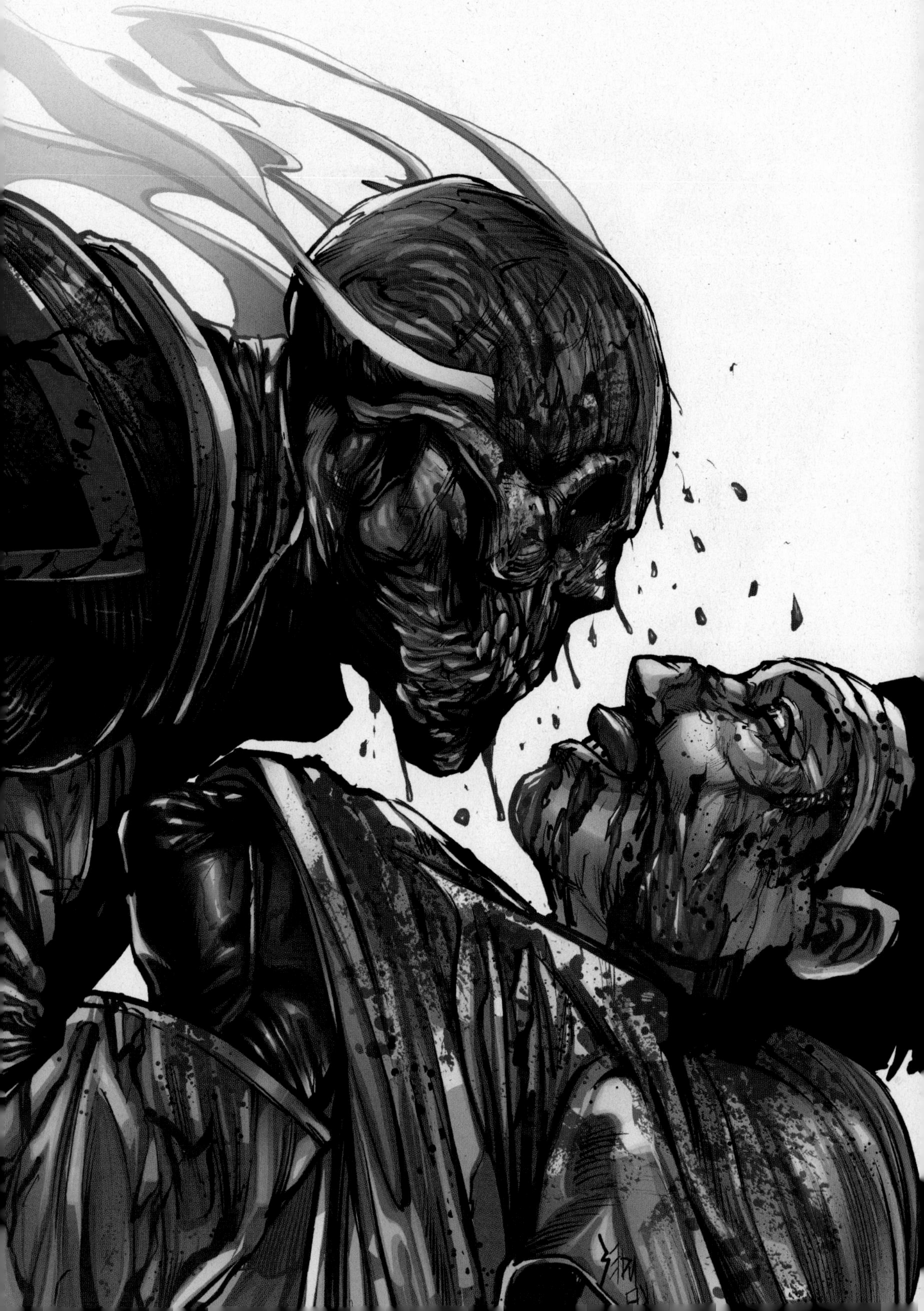

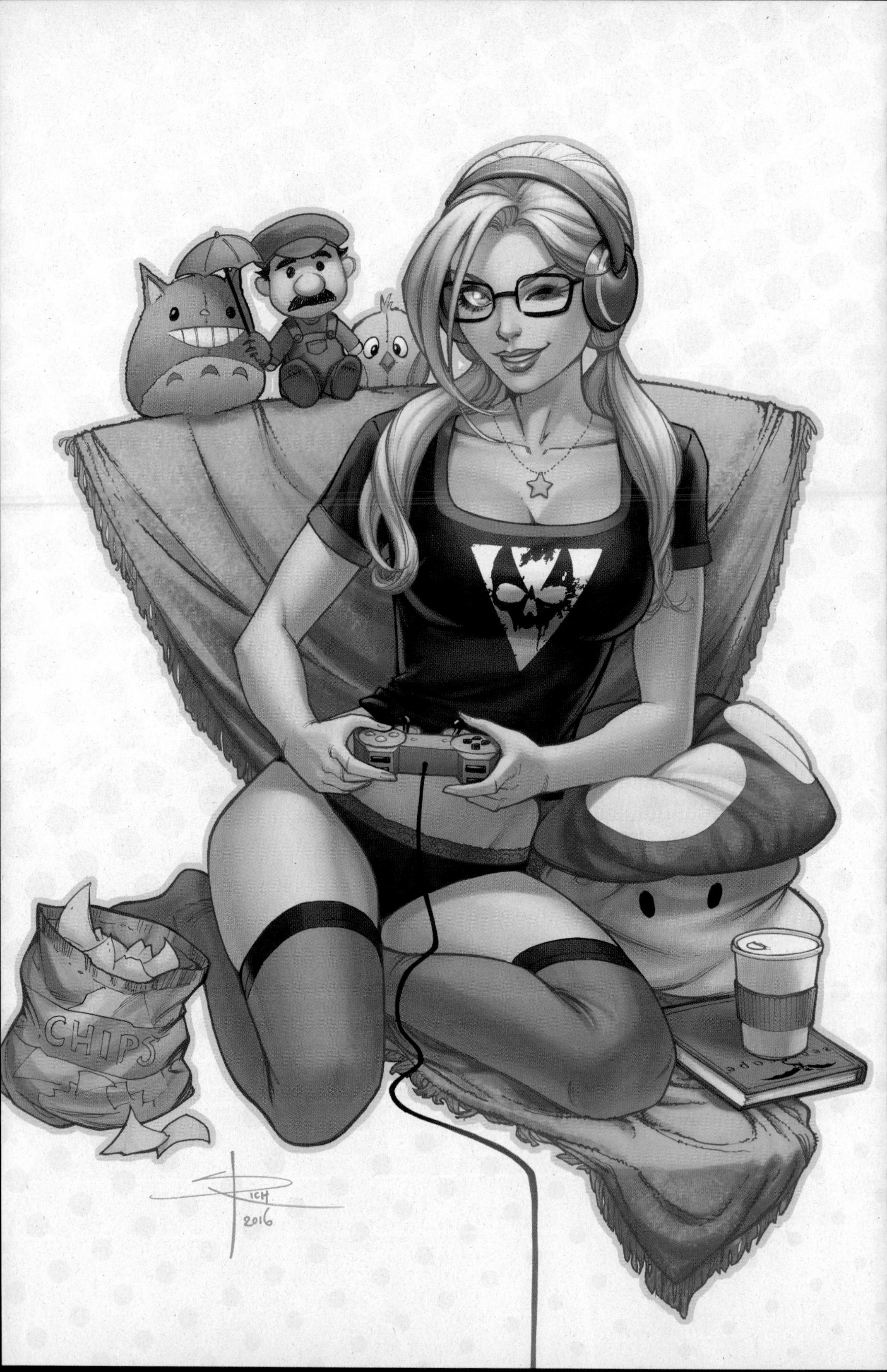
CHIPS

Death Force #3 Cover C

ARTWORK BY SABINE RICH

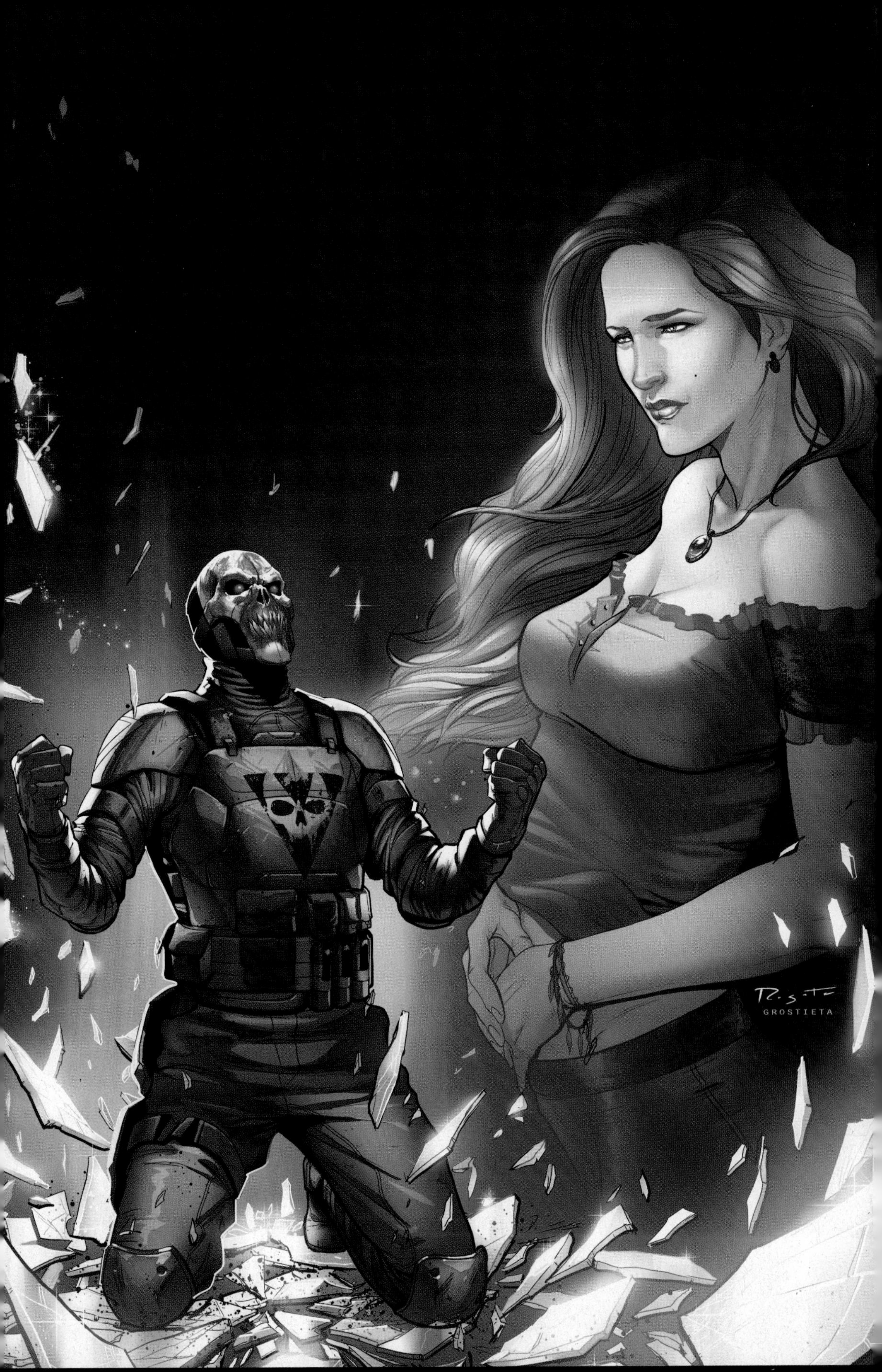
GROSTIETA

Death Force #3 Cover D

ARTWORK BY MARC ROSETE • COLORS BY GROSTIETA

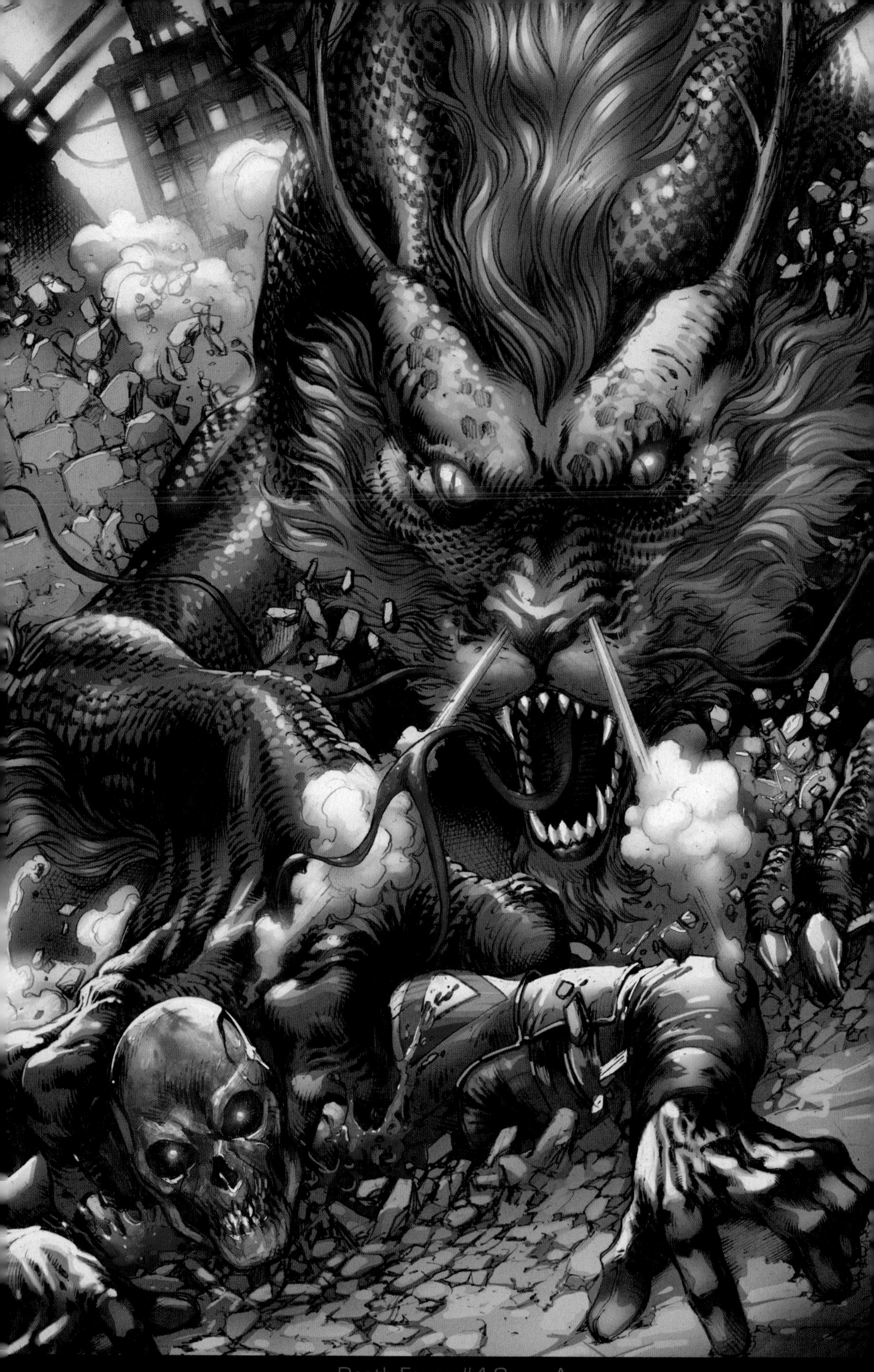

Death Force #4 Cover A

ARTWORK BY JOSE LUIS • COLORS BY GROSTIETA

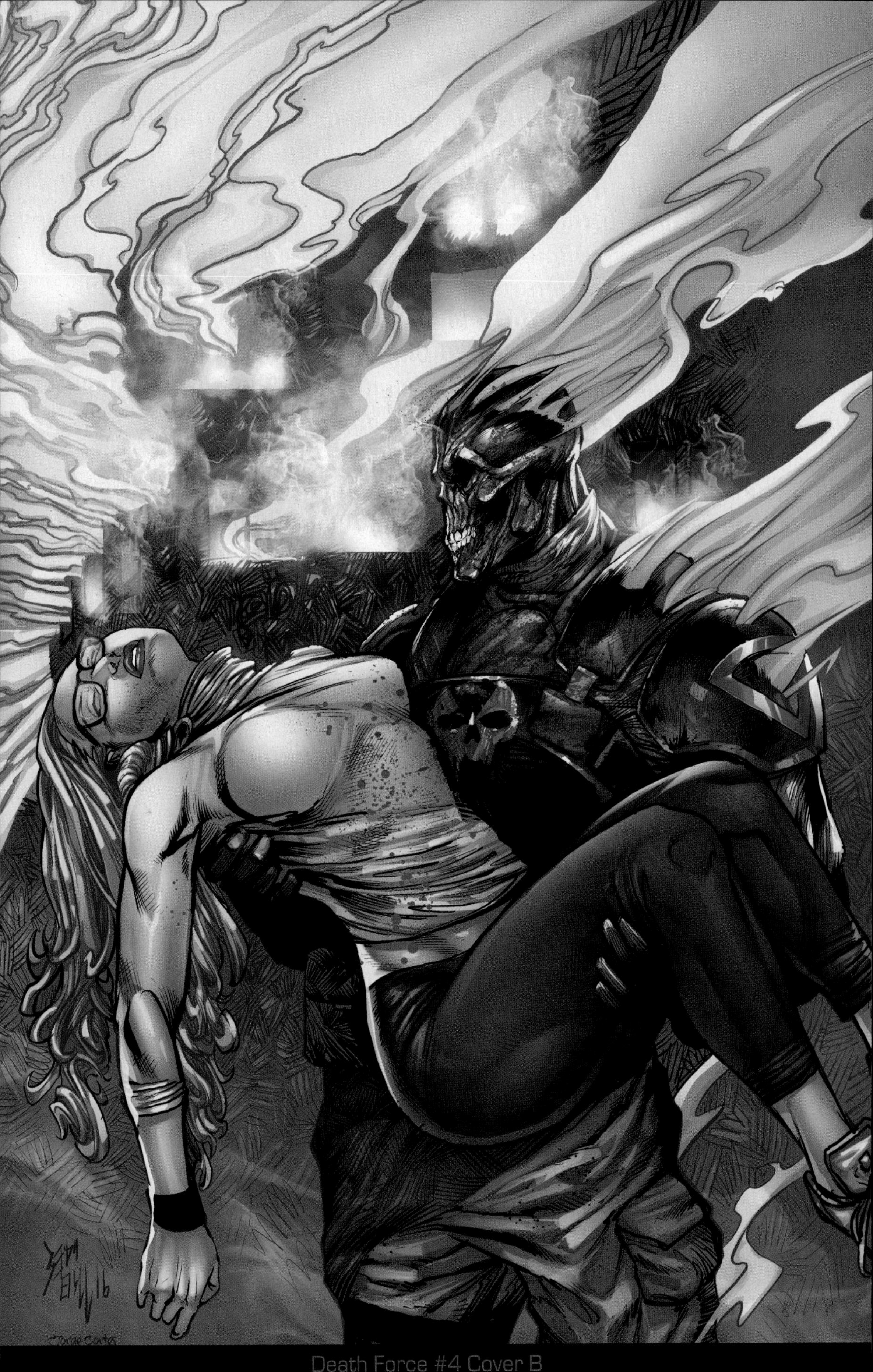

Death Force #4 Cover B

ARTWORK BY SEAN HILL • COLORS BY JORGE CORTES

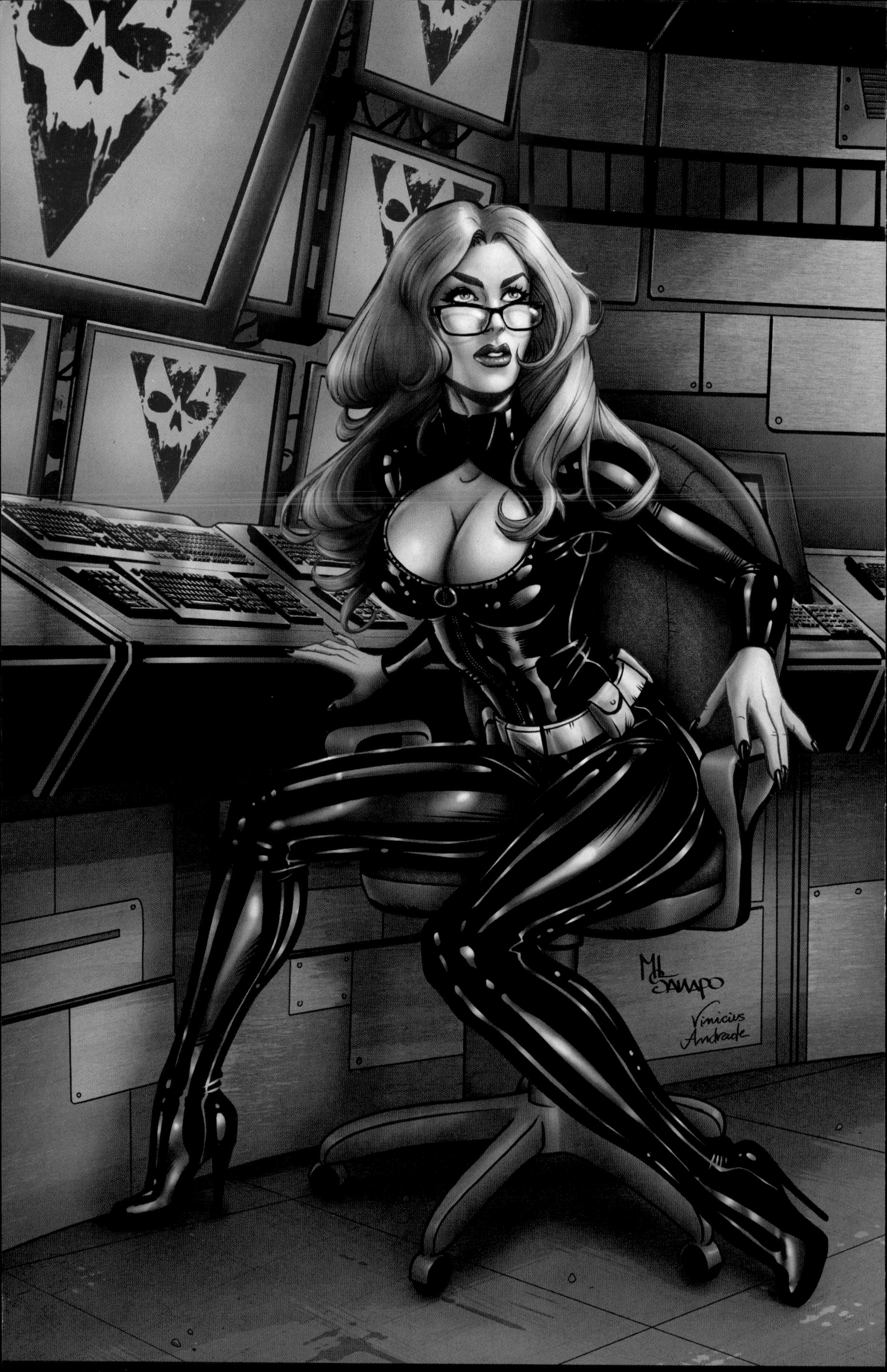
ML SANAPO
Vinicius Andrade

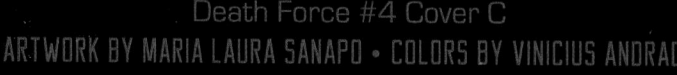

Death Force #4 Cover C

ARTWORK BY MARIA LAURA SANAPO • COLORS BY VINICIUS ANDRADE

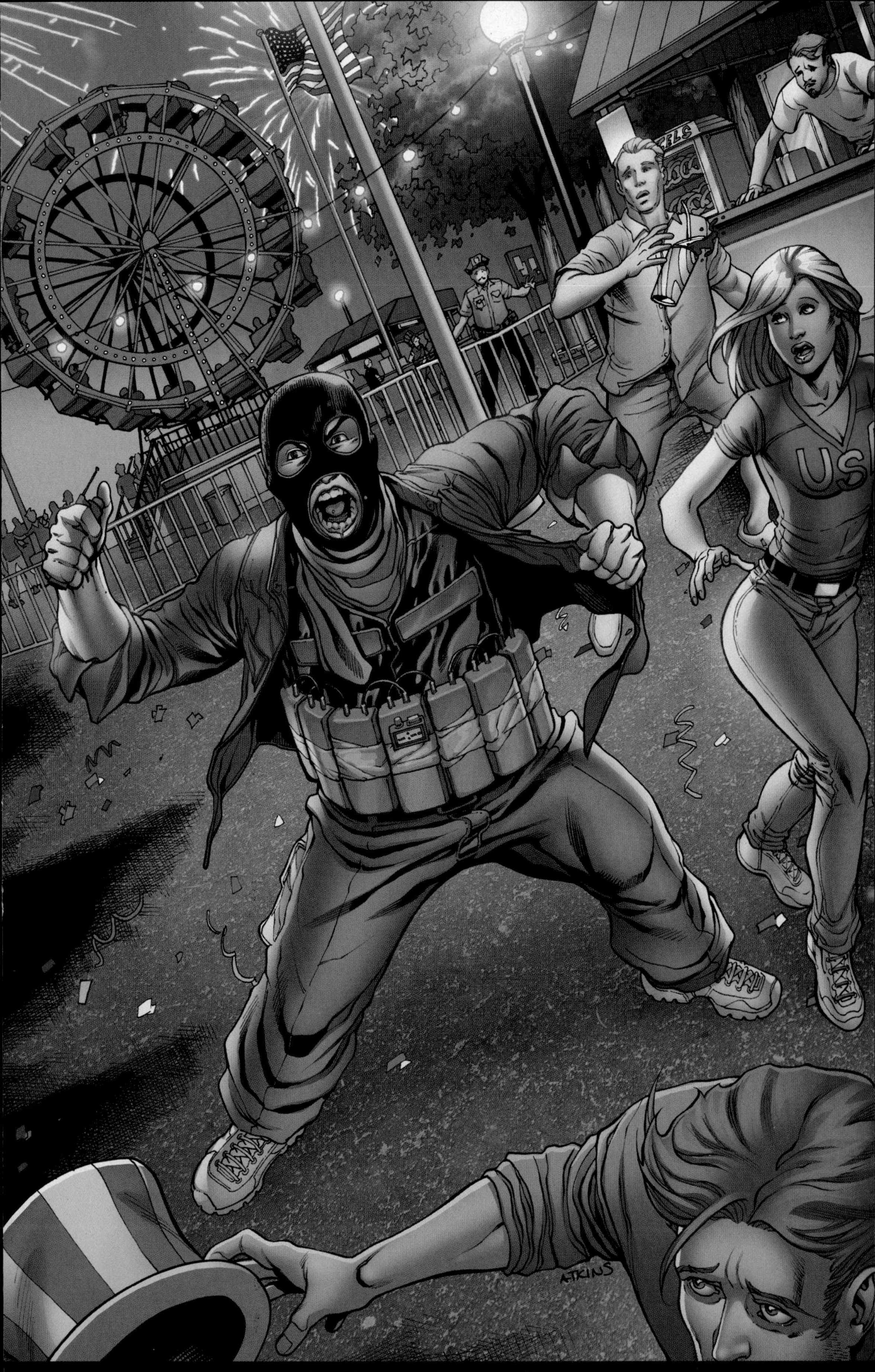
US
ATKINS

Death Force #4 Cover D

ARTWORK BY ROBERT ATKINS • COLORS BY WES HARTMAN

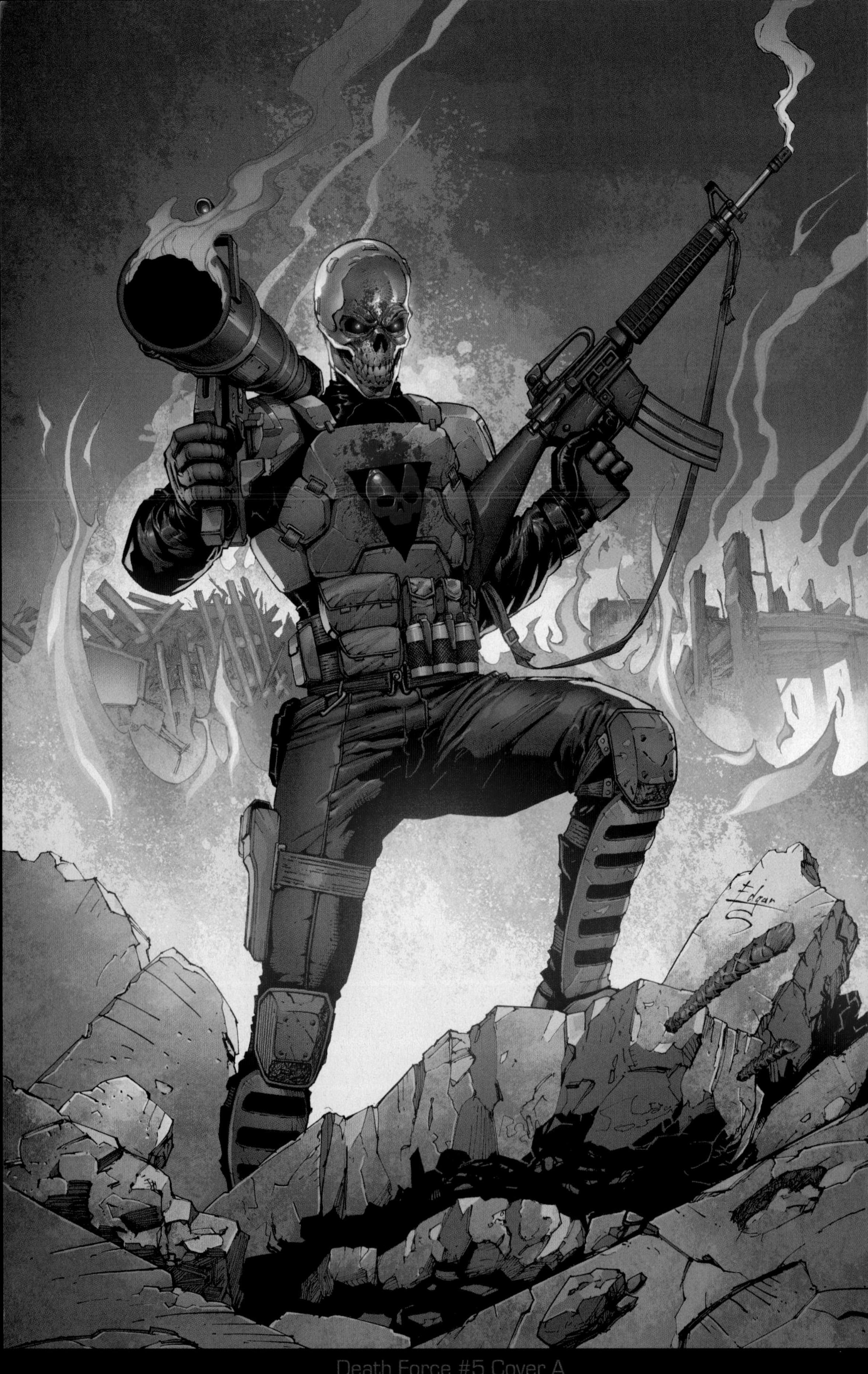
Edgar

Death Force #5 Cover A

ARTWORK BY EDGAR SALAZAR • COLORS BY MICHAEL BARTOLO

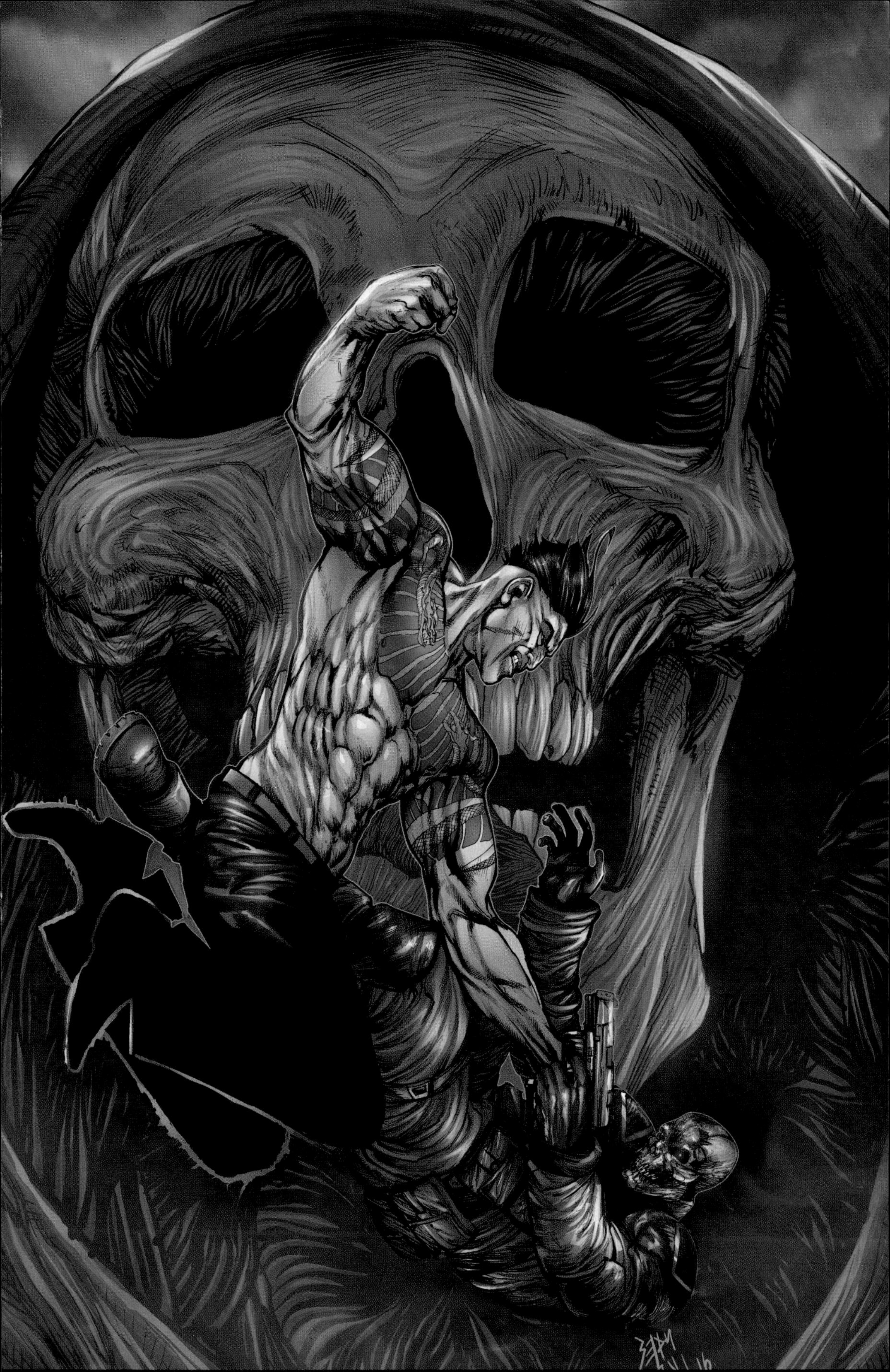

Death Force #5 Cover B

ARTWORK BY SEAN HILL • COLORS BY JORGE CORTES

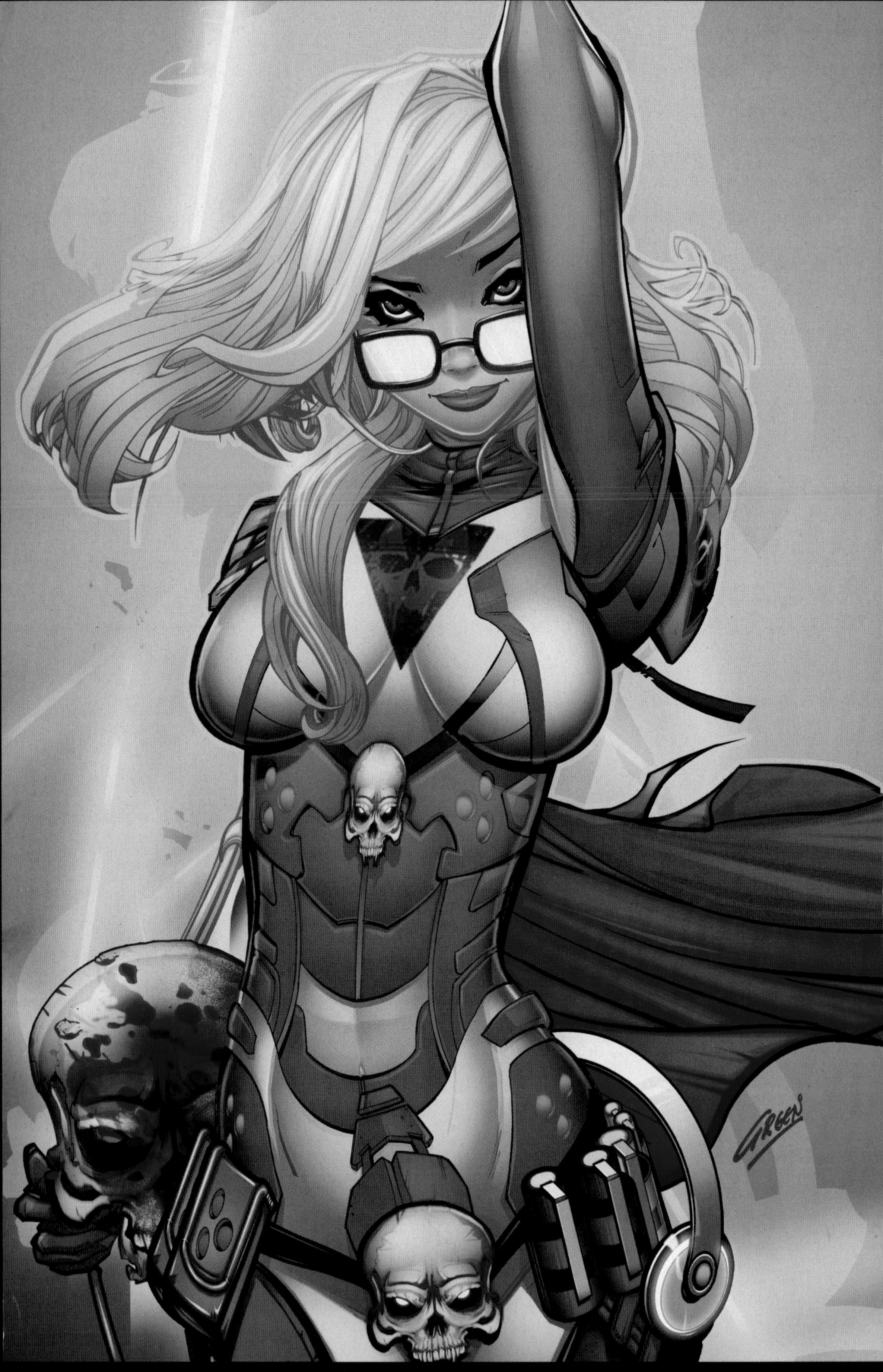
GREEN

Death Force #5 Cover C
ARTWORK BY PAUL GREEN

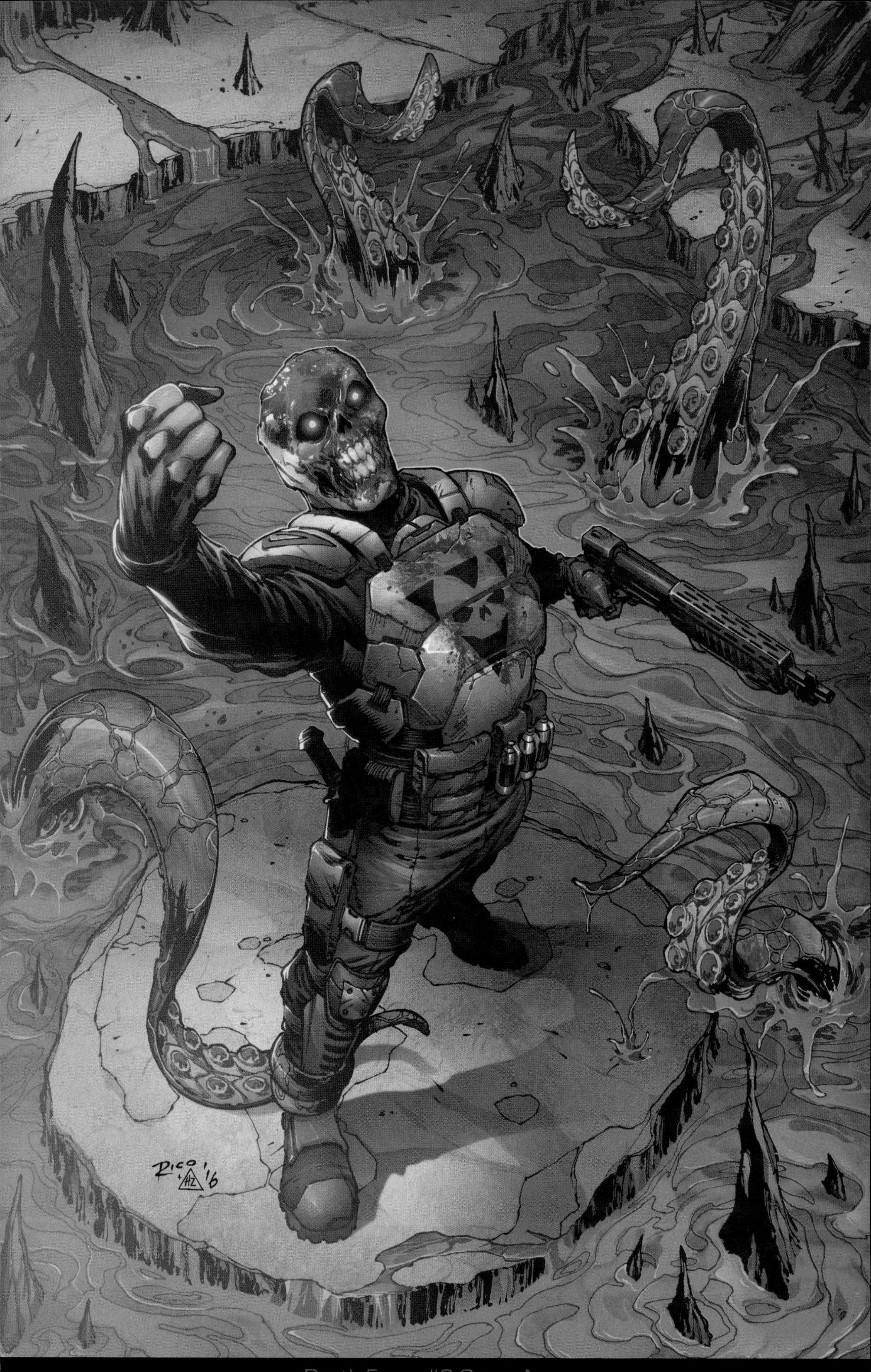

Death Force #6 Cover A

ARTWORK BY IAN RICHARDSON • COLORS BY HEDWIN ZALDIVAR

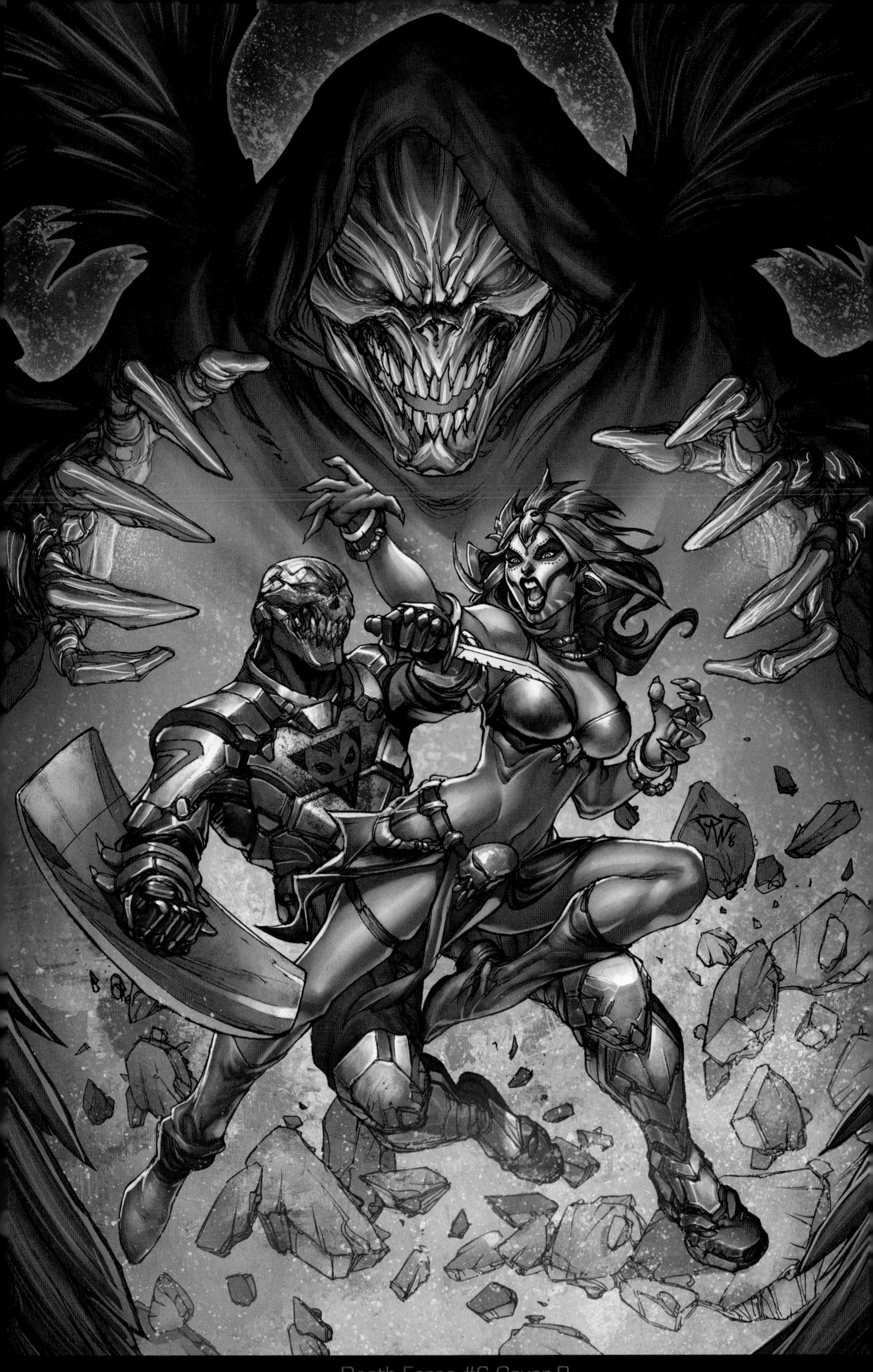

Death Force #6 Cover B

ARTWORK BY PAOLO PANTALENA • COLORS BY ARIF PRIANTO

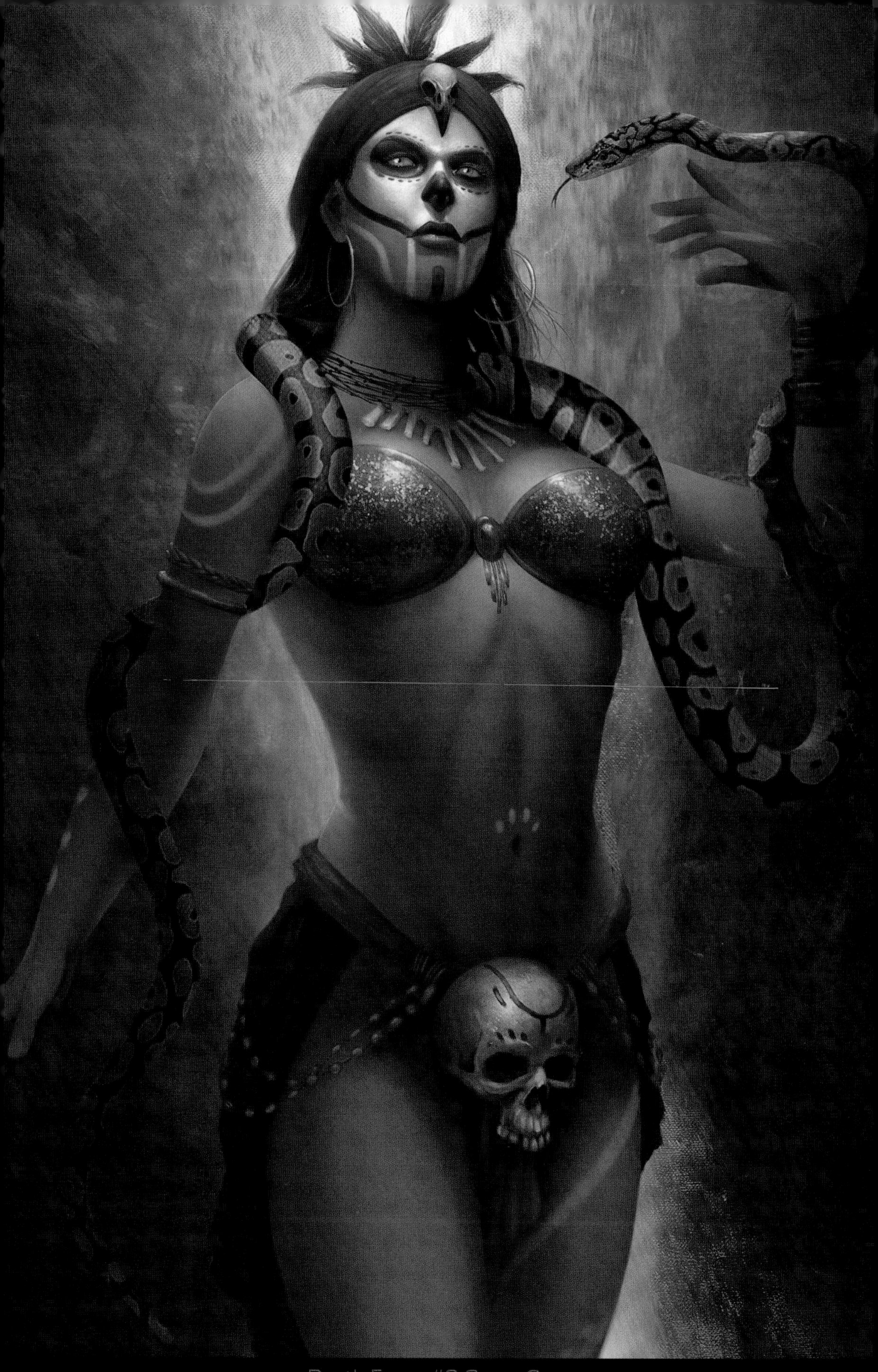

Death Force #6 Cover C
ARTWORK BY MEGURO

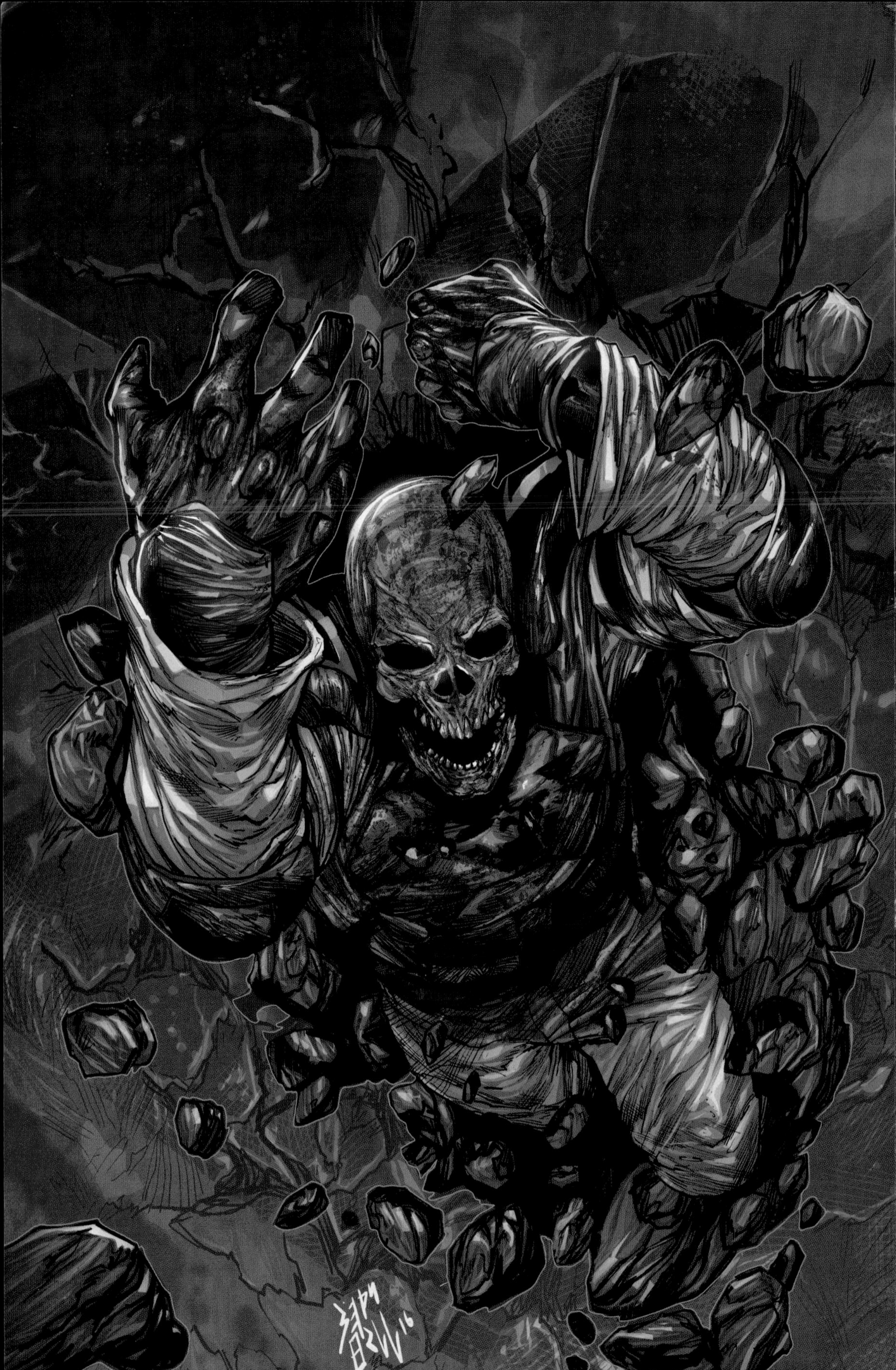

Death Force #6 Cover D

ARTWORK BY SEAN HILL • COLORS BY JORGE CORTES

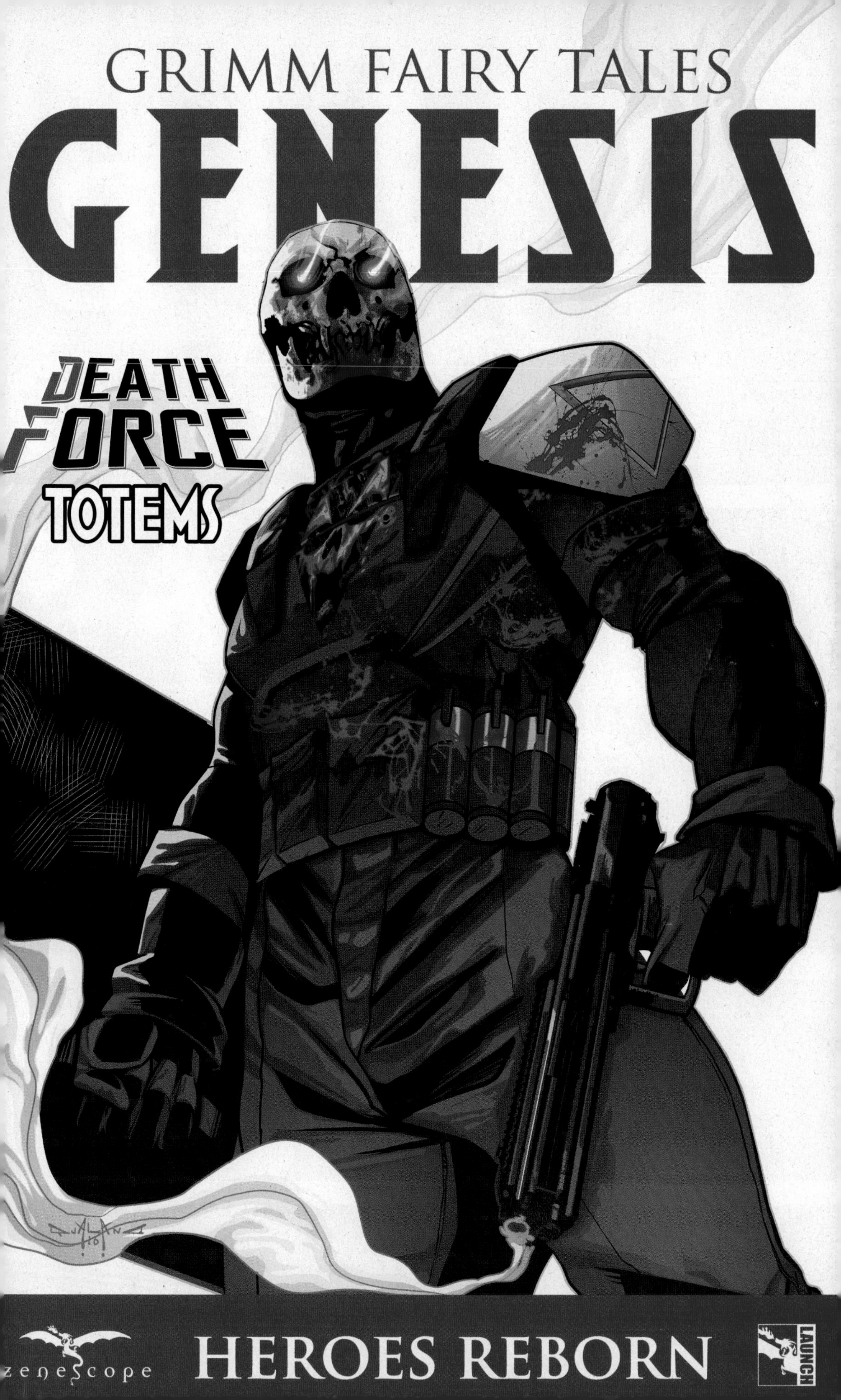
GRIMM FAIRY TALES
GENESIS
DEATH FORCE
TOTEMS
zenescope
HEROES REBORN
LAUNCH

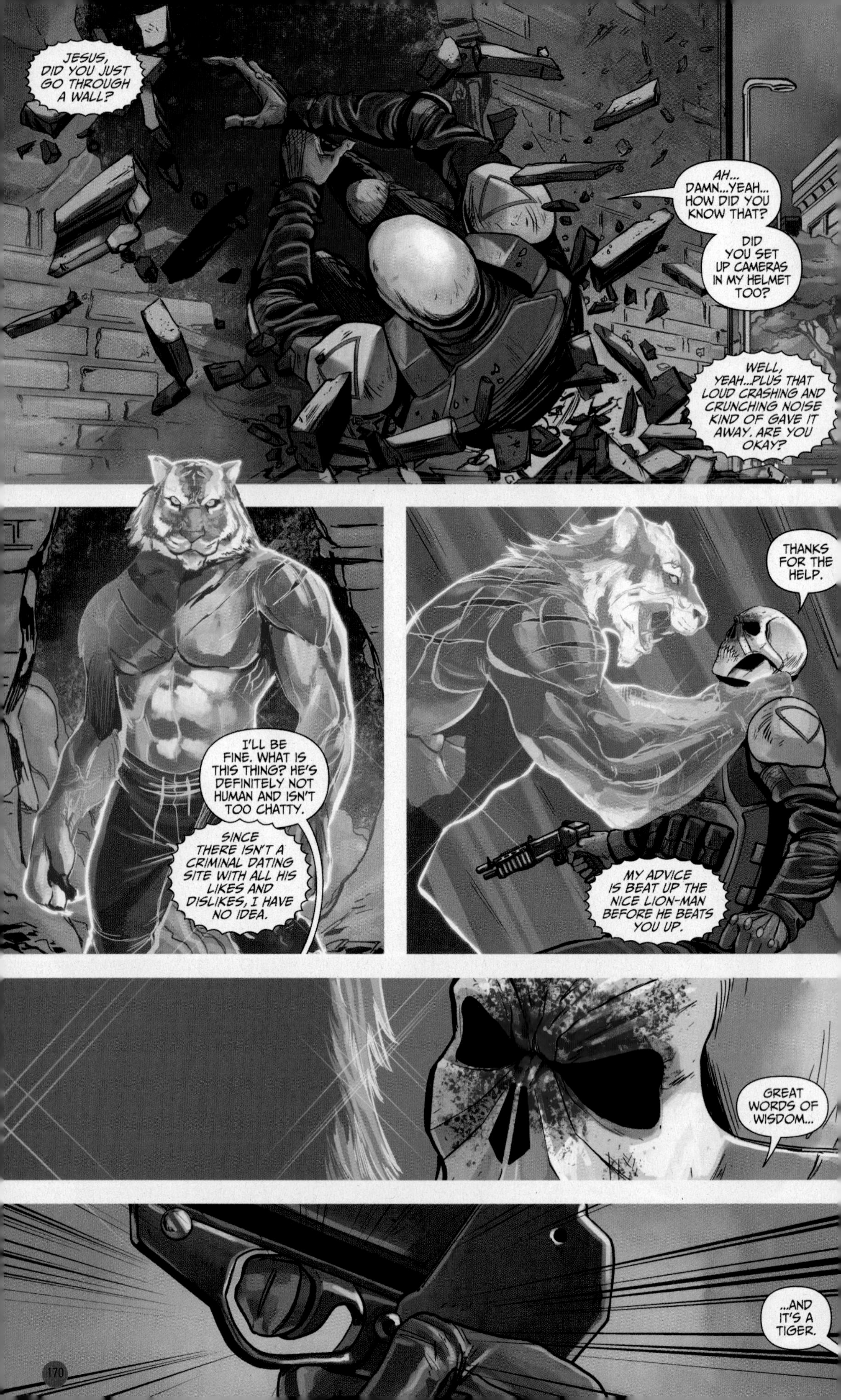
JESUS, DID YOU JUST GO THROUGH A WALL?
AH... DAMN...YEAH... HOW DID YOU KNOW THAT?
DID YOU SET UP CAMERAS IN MY HELMET TOO?
WELL, YEAH...PLUS THAT LOUD CRASHING AND CRUNCHING NOISE KIND OF GAVE IT AWAY. ARE YOU OKAY?
I'LL BE FINE. WHAT IS THIS THING? HE'S DEFINITELY NOT HUMAN AND ISN'T TOO CHATTY.
SINCE THERE ISN'T A CRIMINAL DATING SITE WITH ALL HIS LIKES AND DISLIKES, I HAVE NO IDEA.
THANKS FOR THE HELP.
MY ADVICE IS BEAT UP THE NICE LION-MAN BEFORE HE BEATS YOU UP.
GREAT WORDS OF WISDOM...
...AND IT'S A TIGER.

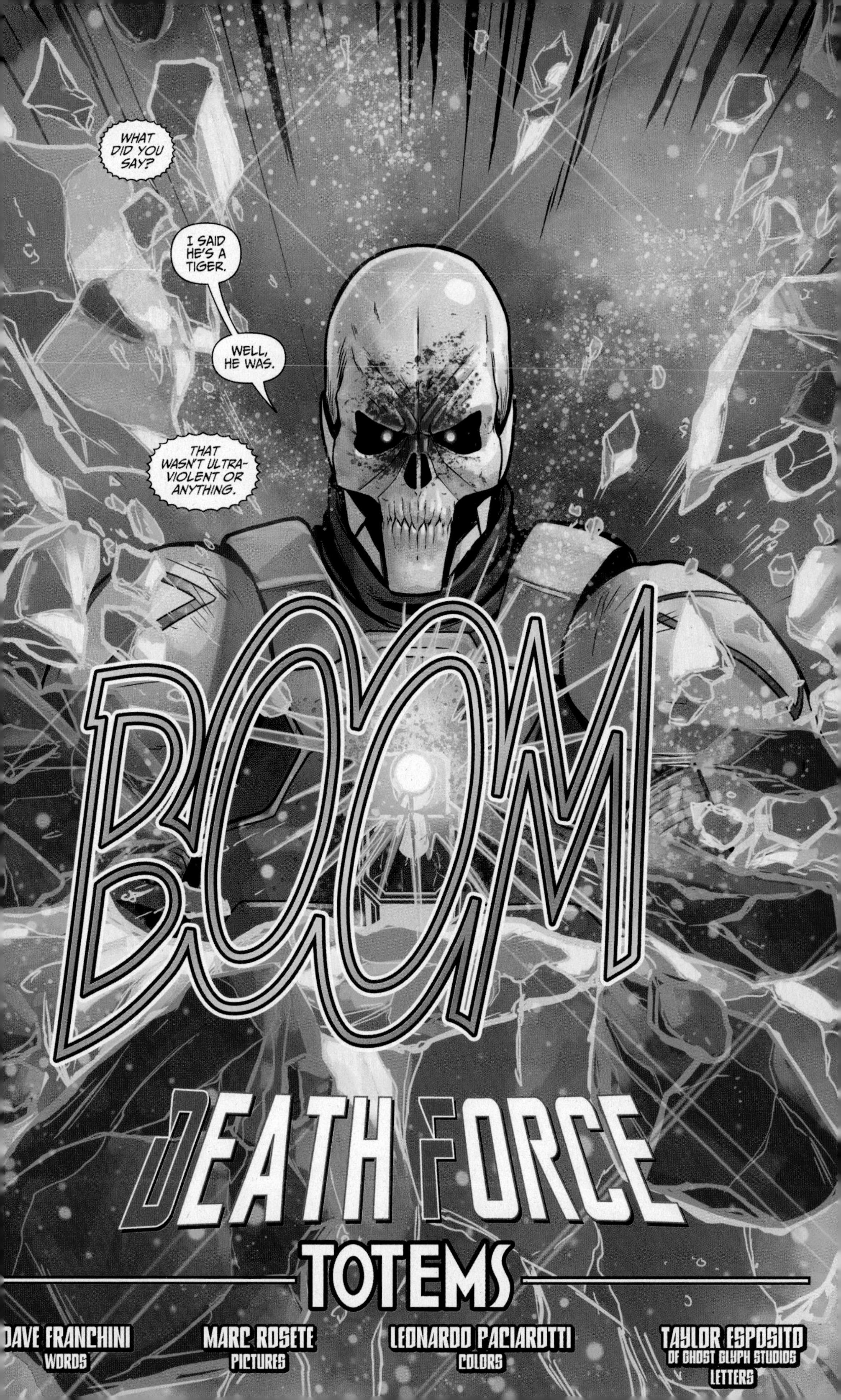

WHAT DID YOU SAY?
I SAID HE'S A TIGER.
WELL, HE WAS.
THAT WASN'T ULTRA-VIOLENT OR ANYTHING.
BOOM
DEATH FORCE
TOTEMS
DAVE FRANCHINI
WORDS
MARC ROSETE
PICTURES
LEONARDO PACIAROTTI
COLORS
TAYLOR ESPOSITO
OF GHOST GLYPH STUDIOS
LETTERS

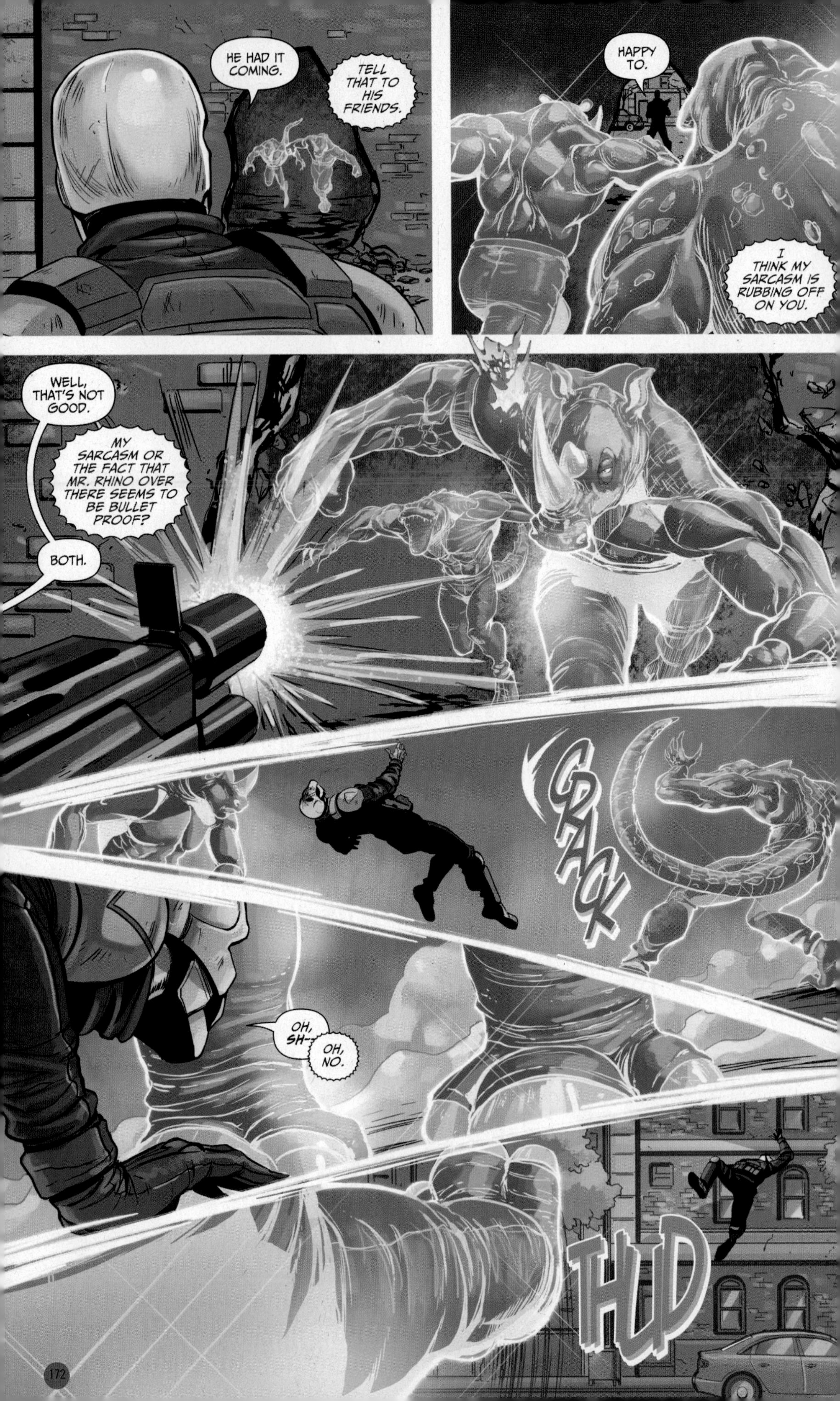
HE HAD IT COMING.
TELL THAT TO HIS FRIENDS.
HAPPY TO.
I THINK MY SARCASM IS RUBBING OFF ON YOU.
WELL, THAT'S NOT GOOD.
MY SARCASM OR THE FACT THAT MR. RHINO OVER THERE SEEMS TO BE BULLET PROOF?
BOTH.
CRACK
OH, SH--
OH, NO.
THUD

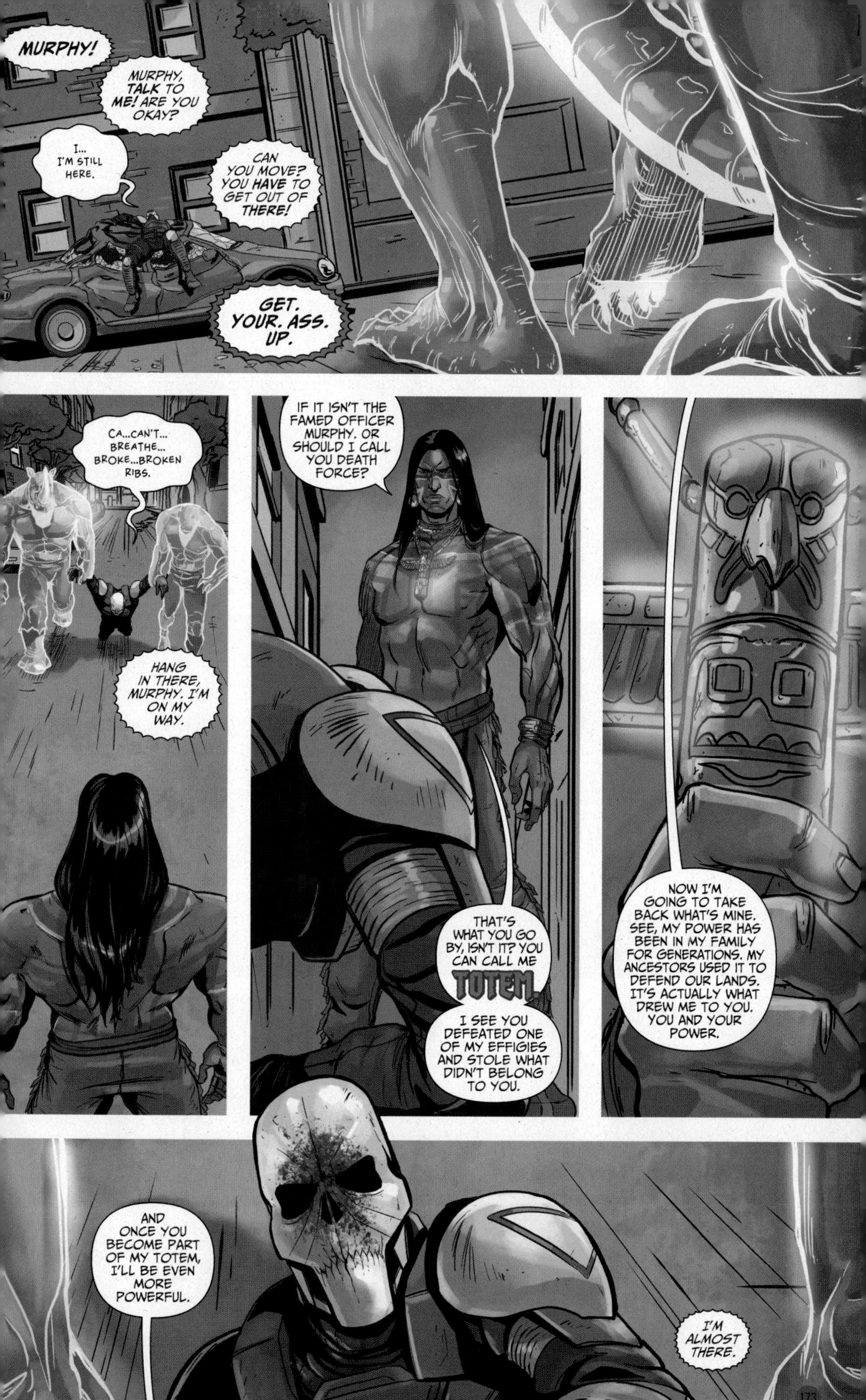
MURPHY!
MURPHY, TALK TO ME! ARE YOU OKAY?
I... I'M STILL HERE.
CAN YOU MOVE? YOU HAVE TO GET OUT OF THERE!
GET. YOUR. ASS. UP.
CA...CAN'T... BREATHE... BROKE...BROKEN RIBS.
HANG IN THERE, MURPHY. I'M ON MY WAY.
IF IT ISN'T THE FAMED OFFICER MURPHY. OR SHOULD I CALL YOU DEATH FORCE?
THAT'S WHAT YOU GO BY, ISN'T IT? YOU CAN CALL ME TOTEM.
I SEE YOU DEFEATED ONE OF MY EFFIGIES AND STOLE WHAT DIDN'T BELONG TO YOU.
NOW I'M GOING TO TAKE BACK WHAT'S MINE. SEE, MY POWER HAS BEEN IN MY FAMILY FOR GENERATIONS. MY ANCESTORS USED IT TO DEFEND OUR LANDS. IT'S ACTUALLY WHAT DREW ME TO YOU. YOU AND YOUR POWER.
AND ONCE YOU BECOME PART OF MY TOTEM, I'LL BE EVEN MORE POWERFUL.
I'M ALMOST THERE.

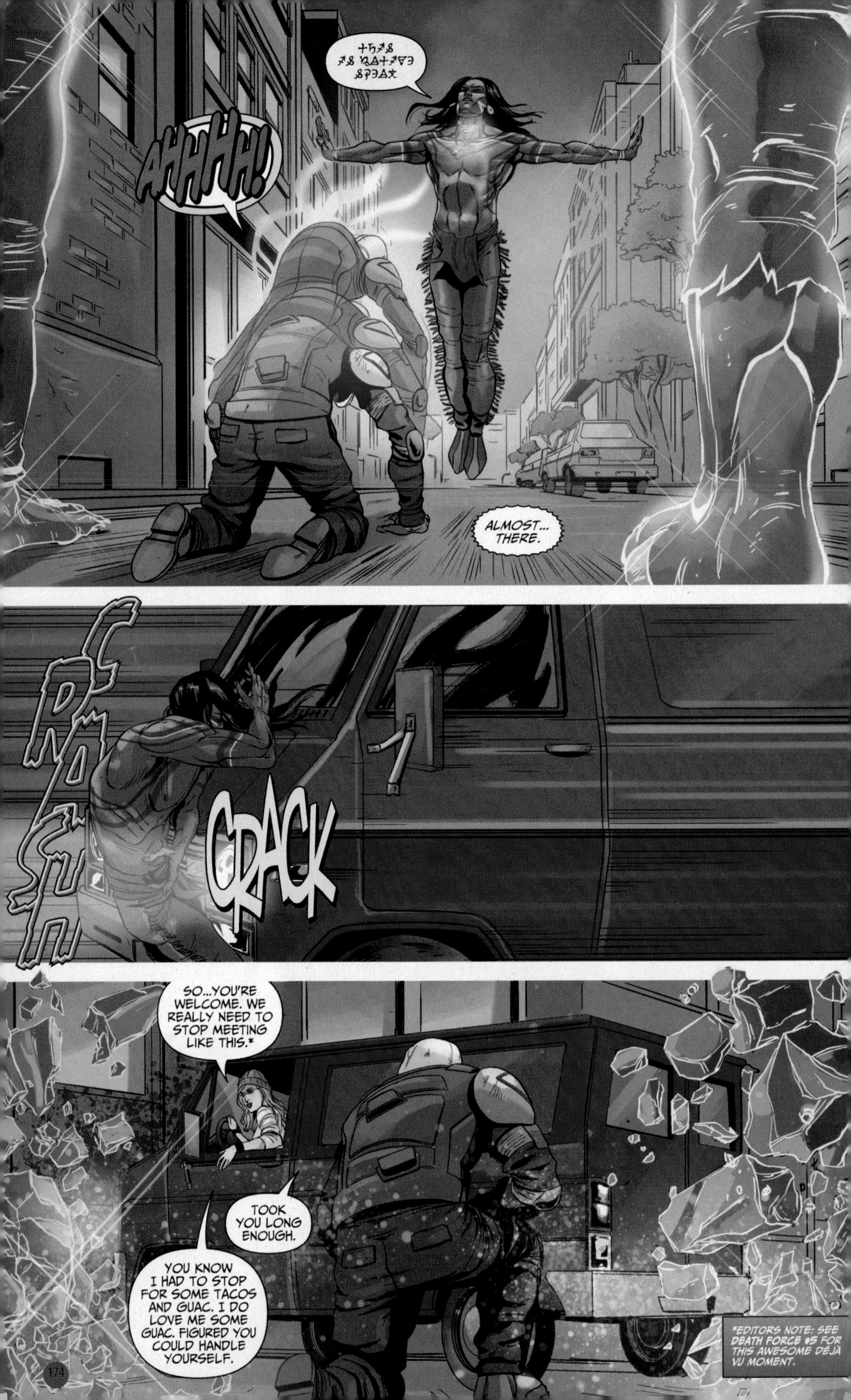
AHHHH!
ALMOST... THERE.
CRASH
CRACK
SO...YOU'RE WELCOME. WE REALLY NEED TO STOP MEETING LIKE THIS.*
TOOK YOU LONG ENOUGH.
YOU KNOW I HAD TO STOP FOR SOME TACOS AND GUAC. I DO LOVE ME SOME GUAC. FIGURED YOU COULD HANDLE YOURSELF.
*EDITORS NOTE: SEE DEATH FORCE #5 FOR THIS AWESOME DÉJÀ VU MOMENT.

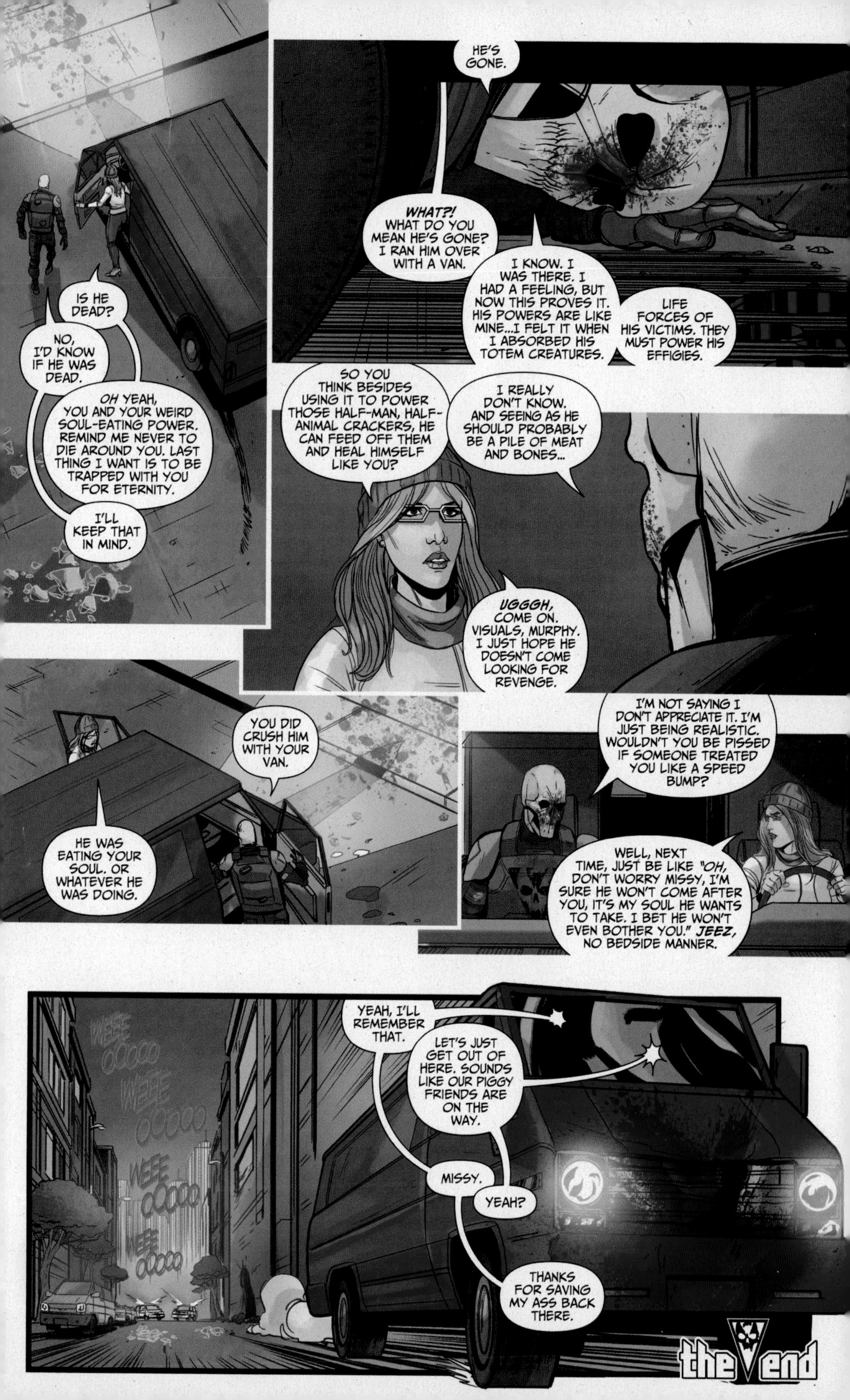
IS HE DEAD?
NO, I'D KNOW IF HE WAS DEAD.
OH YEAH, YOU AND YOUR WEIRD SOUL-EATING POWER. REMIND ME NEVER TO DIE AROUND YOU. LAST THING I WANT IS TO BE TRAPPED WITH YOU FOR ETERNITY.
I'LL KEEP THAT IN MIND.
HE'S GONE.
WHAT?! WHAT DO YOU MEAN HE'S GONE? I RAN HIM OVER WITH A VAN.
I KNOW. I WAS THERE. I HAD A FEELING, BUT NOW THIS PROVES IT. HIS POWERS ARE LIKE MINE...I FELT IT WHEN I ABSORBED HIS TOTEM CREATURES.
LIFE FORCES OF HIS VICTIMS. THEY MUST POWER HIS EFFIGIES.
SO YOU THINK BESIDES USING IT TO POWER THOSE HALF-MAN, HALF-ANIMAL CRACKERS, HE CAN FEED OFF THEM AND HEAL HIMSELF LIKE YOU?
I REALLY DON'T KNOW. AND SEEING AS HE SHOULD PROBABLY BE A PILE OF MEAT AND BONES...
UGGGH, COME ON. VISUALS, MURPHY. I JUST HOPE HE DOESN'T COME LOOKING FOR REVENGE.
YOU DID CRUSH HIM WITH YOUR VAN.
HE WAS EATING YOUR SOUL. OR WHATEVER HE WAS DOING.
I'M NOT SAYING I DON'T APPRECIATE IT. I'M JUST BEING REALISTIC. WOULDN'T YOU BE PISSED IF SOMEONE TREATED YOU LIKE A SPEED BUMP?
WELL, NEXT TIME, JUST BE LIKE "OH, DON'T WORRY MISSY, I'M SURE HE WON'T COME AFTER YOU, IT'S MY SOUL HE WANTS TO TAKE. I BET HE WON'T EVEN BOTHER YOU." JEEZ, NO BEDSIDE MANNER.
YEAH, I'LL REMEMBER THAT.
LET'S JUST GET OUT OF HERE. SOUNDS LIKE OUR PIGGY FRIENDS ARE ON THE WAY.
MISSY.
YEAH?
THANKS FOR SAVING MY ASS BACK THERE.
the end